between the worlds

between the worlds

Readings in Contemporary Neopaganism

Edited by Síân Reid

Canadian Scholars' Press Inc.
Toronto

Between the Worlds: Readings in Contemporary Neopaganism
Edited by Síân Reid

First published in 2006 by
Canadian Scholars' Press Inc.
180 Bloor Street West, Suite 801
Toronto, Ontario
M5S 2V6

www.cspi.org

Canadian Scholars' Press gratefully acknowledges financial support for our publishing activities from the Government of Canada through the Book Publishing Industry Development Program (BPIDP).

Library and Archives Canada Cataloguing in Publication
Between the worlds : readings in contemporary Neopaganism / edited by Síân Reid. -- 1st ed.
Includes bibliographical references.
ISBN 1-55130-314-0
1. Neopaganism. I. Reid, Síân Lee MacDonald, 1966-
BP605.N46B47 2006 299'.94 C2006-904834-7

Cover design, interior design and layout: Aldo Fierro
Front cover photo: "Plain Tree Forest" by Dora Mitsonia / stockXchng. Reprinted by permission of Dora Mitsonia.

Printed and bound in Canada.

Canada

To Naomi Goldenberg, who noticed,
and Charles Gordon, who cared.

table of contents

Acknowledgments • **ix**

Introduction • 1

Part I: The Voices That Inspired

Chapter 1: Charge of the Goddess, *Doreen Valiente* • 17
Chapter 2: Sacred Narratives, *Starhawk* • 21
Chapter 3: I Am a Pagan, *Selena Fox* • 25
Chapter 4: A Religion without Converts, *Margot Adler* • 29
Chapter 5: Why Women Need the Goddess: Phenomenological, Psychological, and Political Reflections, *Carol P. Christ* • 41

Part II: Introduction to Nature or Earth Religions

Chapter 6: We Cast Our Circles Where the Earth Mother Meets the Sky Father, *Sarah Pike* • 67
Chapter 7: Definitions and Expressions of Nature Religion in Shamanic Traditions and Contemporary Paganism, *Barbara Jane Davy* • 79
Chapter 8: Paganism as a World Religion, *Michael York* • 91

Part III: Contemporary Neopaganism and Witchcraft

Chapter 9: Druidry, *Graham Harvey* • 115
Chapter 10: To the Tribe Let There Be Children Born, *Helen A. Berger* • 139
Chapter 11: Wicked Witches of the West: Exploring Court Treatments of Wicca as a Religion, *Lori G. Beaman* • 161
Chapter 12: In Defence of Magic: Philosophical and Theological Rationalization, *Tanya Luhrmann* • 187
Chapter 13: Witch Wars: Factors Contributing to Conflict in Canadian Witchcraft Communities, *Síân Reid* • 219
Chapter 14: Constructing Identity and Divinity: Creating Community in an Elder Religion within a Postmodern World, *Jenny Blain* • 241
Chapter 15: Weaving a Tangled Web? Pagan Ethics and Issues of History, "Race," and Ethnicity in Pagan Identity, *Ann-Marie Gallagher* • 267

Part IV: Feminist Spirituality and Goddess Worship

Chapter 16: Mother and Goddess: The Ideological Force of Symbols, *Lucie Marie-Mai DuFresne* • 297
Chapter 17: The Embodied Goddess: Feminist Witchcraft and Female Divinity, *Wendy Griffin* • 303
Chapter 18: Finding a Goddess, *Ronald Hutton* • 325
Chapter 19: The Roots of Feminist Spirituality, *Cynthia Eller* • 343
Chapter 20: The Colonial Mythology of Feminist Witchcraft, *Chris Klassen* • 361

Copyright Acknowledgments • 385

Acknowledgments

all throughout this book-collating process, the individuals whose work is represented here have been incredibly supportive, making what could have been a tedious process into something I was doing for all of us. I hope I have done their words justice. My daughter Emily has put up with months of stolen evenings and weekends with resignation, if not always grace, and I hope to make it up to her. My husband, David, has lighted my way down this path with love, faith, and coffee. Megan Mueller, my editor, has displayed unflagging enthusiasm, and I wouldn't have made it to the finish line without her. Then there are the many thanks I owe to my cheerleaders, those people who read, critiqued, made suggestions, and steadfastly believed that this was the perfect project for me: Shelley Rabinovitch, Ian Clysdale, Sheryl Elbring, Richard Bott, Kristan Roberge, Candace Pakenham, Nicole Lavigne, and Tim Foster. Keep those pompoms handy!

A NOTE FROM THE PUBLISHER

Thank you for selecting *Between the Worlds: Readings in Contemporary Neopaganism*, edited by Síân Reid. The editor and publisher have devoted considerable time and careful development (including meticulous peer reviews) to this book. We appreciate your recognition of this effort and accomplishment.

TEACHING FEATURES

This volume distinguishes itself on the market in many ways. One key feature is the book's well-written and comprehensive part openers, which help to make the readings all the more accessible to undergraduate students. The part openers add cohesion to the section and to the whole book. The themes of the book are very clearly presented in these section openers.

The general editor, Síân Reid, has also greatly enhanced the book by adding pedagogy to close and complete each section. Each part ends with critical thinking questions pertaining to each reading, detailed annotated suggested reading, and many glossary terms.

Introduction

First, there was nothing, and the womb of the void begat the light.
That light gave form to the void, the form that we call darkness,
and that was the first Goddess.
The darkness gave to the light strength and potency,
and that was the first God.

—Meredydd (1986)

The title of this collection, *Between the Worlds*, is a reference to the modern witchcraft belief that once a magical circle is cast, it exists in a space "between the worlds, and beyond time." It, and all within it, is neither fully part of the material world nor fully part of the spirit world, but hovers, suspended, in a place between them. This collection of readings does much the same—it exists somewhere between the world of embodied pagan practice, and the world of academic intellectual discourse. Readers will find both represented in the voices speaking here.

Pagan studies is an area just beginning to emerge from the study of new religious movements (NRMs) more generally. There have been many scholars, particularly in the field of sociology of religion, engaged in the examination of NRMs for the past 30 years. These innovative or imported religious practices challenged traditional notions about the nature of the religious economy, the relative importance of the dimensions of religiosity, and the ongoing importance of religion for the individual. They raised new moral and ethical questions, especially in the light of the brainwashing/deprogramming controversies of the 1970s, the Jonestown mass suicide in Guyana, the Branch Davidian standoff in Waco, the Solar Temple murders/suicides, and the Heaven's Gate suicides. Most of the research throughout the 1970s and 1980s, however, focused on NRMs that displayed a definite, hierarchical, formal organizational structure, and that actively recruited new members, such as the Unification Church, Scientology, the International Society for Krishna Consciousness, the Jehovah's Witnesses, and the Children of God, all of which have been negatively labelled by the public as "cults." These organizations provided convenient sites for research because they were visible, easily accessible to participant observers, and fairly consistent in their practices from place to place. These features made it possible to study one or two communities and expect that the results obtained would be broadly applicable to other groups of the same type. Modern neopaganism had none of those features.

Until the end of the 1980s, almost no attention was paid to contemporary neopaganism, other than to dismiss it as insignificant. In 1985, Rodney Stark and William Bainbridge, well-known scholars of the religious milieu, commented, "Many current cults, such as the various witchcraft and pagan groups, have reacted to secularization by a headlong plunge back into magic.... In our judgment, these cults are reactionary and have little future" (455).

Early, and influential, pagan author Doreen Valiente agrees that the modern pagan movement is reactionary, not against secularization, but against the elements of modern culture that separate us from the cycles of the earth, and exaggerate our importance as a species. In 1989, she wrote,

> In a sense, the rebirth of witchcraft is a rebellion. It is being carried out by those both young and old who are no longer content to get their religion from the churches or their opinions from the newspapers; who are, moreover, profoundly disillusioned with the scientists who promised us Utopia and gave us the nuclear bomb. (207)

Contemporary paganisms, including indigenous and tribal religions that persist into the modern age, as Michael York will argue in Part II, are "earth religions" or "nature religions." They have in common that they consider the earth itself to be sacred. The earth supports all life. Most practitioners of earth religions do not utterly reject science and the technological innovations that have arisen from it, but they believe strongly that these technologies should be used to affirm life, and not to destroy it—either directly through indiscriminate weapons technologies as Valiente highlights, or indirectly through practices such as monoculture farming.

Today's pagans generally consider themselves to be part of a spiritual movement that, while it may be modern in its immediate, documentable origins, has its roots in the mystical traditions of earlier times. Mysticism is taken to be a sense of direct, unmediated connection with the divine, however conceived. People connect with this mystical and celebratory impulse through a variety of meditative, ritual, devotional, mythological, creative, and magical processes. Scholars, such as those represented in this collection, have started to give these beliefs and practices the same kind of critical attention that they apply to other religious and social phenomena, giving greater insight into both their progressive elements, and, as will become obvious, their not-so-progressive elements. Unlike the participant narratives in Part I, there is no uncritical pompom waving in the later parts of the collection, but instead, serious, thoughtful discussions by scholars from a variety of disciplines, including anthropology, sociology, law, history, religion, and women's studies.

While paganism represents, proportionally, the fastest growing religion in Canada, and possibly in the United States as well, the absolute number of people involved remains very small. The Census of Canada reported 2,295 self-declared pagans in Canada in 1981, 5,530 in 1991, and 21,085 in 2001.[1] This is in a country with a population of over 29 million (2001 census), meaning that one could expect about 70 pagans per 100,000 people. In the United States, information about religious affiliation is not collected by the census, which makes estimating the number of pagan practitioners even more difficult. According to James Lewis, editor of *Magical Religion and Modern Witchcraft* (1996), *The Oxford Handbook of*

New Religious Movements (2004) and co-editor with Shelly Rabinovitch of *The Encyclopedia of Modern Witchcraft and Neo-Paganism* (2002), speculation ranges from a conservative 200,000 to a more robust 750,000 within a population 10 times the size of Canada's (2002:304). Lewis himself believes that even 750,000 is conservative, due the rapid expansion of pagan resources on the Internet (2002:305). However, even if one were to accept that as many as one million Americans might be pagan, that is still only 340 pagans per 100,000 people. On the basis of numbers alone, Stark and Bainbridge might have some justification for dismissing the modern pagan movement as unimportant to the broader social and religious picture.

The cultural significance of neopaganism, however, goes far beyond its proportional presence in the population. With their genesis firmly in the twentieth century, modern paganisms are new religions in an age when secularization theorists have proclaimed that religion is dying. Sociologist Reginald Bibby has documented the declines in both membership and participation in mainstream Canadian religious denominations in three books: *Fragmented Gods* (1987), *Unknown Gods* (1993), and *Restless Gods* (2002). Yet, he argues, interest in the existential and spiritual questions that organized religions have traditionally addressed continues unabated.

> There is good reason to believe that a considerable number of Canadians are failing to associate their interest in mystery and meaning with what religion historically has had to offer.... In other words, Canadians are not in the market for churches. They are, however, very much in the market for the things religion historically has been about. (1993:177)

The questions of truth, morality, meaning, and the relationship between the individual and all that lies outside the individual, with which organized religions have always traditionally dealt, have drifted outside the church walls and been returned to adherents as matters to be decided on a personal basis with reference primarily to their own unique ideas and experience.

Contemporary paganism begins with this principal as a fundamental assumption about spiritual life. The different traditions within paganism all draw from the same pot of inspiration, which includes images, ideas, and symbolic language drawn from the nineteenth- and twentieth-century Romantic movement, the 1960s counterculture, the environmental movement, the feminist movement, ethnic politics, other religious, spiritual and esoteric traditions, psychology, anthropology, fantasy and science fiction, consciousness-raising, encounter and self-help groups. Individual traditions will ladle out a little more or a little less of each of these elements. In general, there is little centralized organization in the pagan movement. While there are umbrella organizations such as the Covenant of the Goddess (CoG), the Pagan Federation, the Troth, and Ár nDraíocht Féin (ADF or A Druid Fellowship), in general, these organizations have no power to impose rules or regulations on groups or individuals, although they may have criteria for membership. The framework provided by any given tradition is expected to be augmented and adjusted in terms of the individual practitioner's own preferences, experiences, and insights.

Yet, despite the strong emphasis on the individual's responsibility for determining the content and form of their own religious practice, a diffuse sense of community exists within and among pagans. Rather than being related by geographical proximity or face-to-face interaction, as has been the case with most pre-modern and early modern forms of community, neopagans constitute an "emotional community"—what Michel Maffesoli calls a "neotribe" (1996). Despite the variations in the specific beliefs and practices of groups and individuals, there are aesthetic, moral, and emotional continuities between them that participants perceive as distinguishing them from other communities. This "collective sensibility" is articulated through the adoption of similar forms of narrative and symbolic expression, which in turn relate people to others in a meaningful way, even if those others are unknown, personally, to the individual. When people are under the impression that what they believe is aberrant and unacceptable, they perceive themselves as separated from others, and alienated from their surroundings. Several scholars (Bloch 1998; Rabinovitch 1992; Reid 2001) have commented on the tendency pagans have of speaking of their pre-pagan selves as being "outsiders," "liminal," or "not belonging." This is not something that a truly radical individualist would find troubling. The collective sentiment that characterizes contemporary paganism is one that is focused around the re-enchantment of the self, of the world, and of social relationships.

The people attracted to modern paganism present a different demographic profile than that of many established religions. Research conducted in the 1990s, before Asatru and druidry contributed substantially to the composition of the pagan community, suggested that pagans were younger than both self-identified members of other religious groups and the population in general. Seventy-five percent of those who participated in Reid's research in 1995 were involved in paganism by the time they were 30 (2001:72). They also have higher than average levels of education: Rabinovitch (1992) and Reid (2001) each report 42 percent of the Canadian pagans they studied had, at minimum, a bachelor's level university degree. American sociologist Helen A. Berger did a survey of pagans to which she received 2,000 responses, 65.4 percent of whom claimed at least a college degree, and 16 percent of whom had completed post-graduate work (1999:8–9). Loretta Orion's study of pagans found that 58.4 percent of her respondents claimed at least a bachelor's degree (1995:67). These are not people who are accepting pagan world views out of ignorance and gullibility, as is claimed by some detractors of paganism.

Secularization theorists present a dark view of the future of religion. Once upon a time, they begin, religious beliefs were inseparable from any other aspect of day-to-day life. This lack of separation often caused early anthropologists to question whether the pre-modern, tribal peoples they studied had a religion at all. As societies became larger and more complex, the political sphere emerged out of the religious sphere as a separate entity. The two were no longer enmeshed in a single, undifferentiated hierarchy, but still had considerable overlap. Secularization theorists argue that the less overlap there is, the more the importance of religion will diminish, until at last, cut off from participation in vital social and political functions, it finally withers away into nothing. Other theorists, such as Anthony Giddens, say that the institutions may vanish, but that as long as people continue to have "spiritual experiences," they will need to render some account of them. He argues that this occurs within the "narrative of the self."

Giddens defines the "narrative of the self" as "the story or stories by means of which self-identity is reflexively understood, both by the individual concerned and by others" (1991:244). The spiritual world view one embraces, in this modern world of many choices, becomes part of what directs and informs the individual's basic understanding of who he or she is. This understanding is expressed through the stories we tell about ourselves and our lives. Listen to Carrie, who first became pagan in her teens, speaking about that experience in her early thirties. She was interviewed as part of Reid's first study on Canadian paganism. Carrie prefaced her commentary by talking about having certain kinds of experiences that were unexplainable within the frameworks she had available before she encountered contemporary witchcraft, which she refers to simply as "the Craft."

> I was really sensitive to how other people were feeling and it was like walking through a laser light show 24 hours a day. I didn't want to be around a lot of other people. I just couldn't cope. I thought I was going crazy—I really did. I thought if I talked to anyone about what was going on, they'd lock me up and throw away the key. I was really frightened.

She describes how paganism helped her to tell her story in a different way, and create the possibility of a different ending.

> It [paganism] told me I wasn't crazy. It told me that people's feelings did radiate a kind of energy, and that there were ways you could tune in on this.... The Craft provided a framework where I wasn't crazy, I just wasn't in control, and it provided me with a way to do something about it. (Reid 2001:215–216)

Carrie's involvement in paganism allowed her not only to transform her vision of herself, but also to transform her relationship to the world around her.

Contemporary paganism can be approached as one reflection of the continuing human struggle for meaning in a time when many traditional forms of meaning have been undermined. That this "meaning" *seems* to contain elements that are at odds with dominant trends in the surrounding society makes it interesting to study. It is magic in an age of science; a nature religion that flourishes in the city. It could be approached as a protest against the rationalization, bureaucratization, and regulation of increasingly large areas of human life. It is certainly one manifestation of the growing trend of reclaiming spirituality from the institutional churches (Bibby 1993). An examination of modern paganism has the potential of giving insight into other non-institutional spiritual movements, even those that, on the basis of theology, might not seem similar. The decentralized character of the movement also suggests new ways to think about "religious community" in this increasingly "wired" age (Cowan 2005). Neopaganism is not a mechanism through which people avoid dealing with reality and modernity, it is a creative expression of their active and engaged response to the particular stresses and conditions that we all face in our late modern world.

NOTE

1. Of course, taking the census as a completely accurate representation of the number of practising pagans in Canada is problematic. The census is completed by the head of household, who may not accurately reflect the chosen religious affiliation of all the other family members. In addition, Reid's 1995 survey asked pagans what they would write as their religion on the census, and fully 25 percent gave responses that would not have been coded as "pagan." Both of these factors would tend to depress the counts. On the other hand, there is no way to determine how many people might have written "pagan" but meant something else like "I don't recognize your right to be asking this question" or "no religion," thus inflating the counts. After all, the 2001 Australian census discovered that approximately one out of every 270 Australians (over 70,000 people!) was a Jedi Knight. (news.bbc.co.uk/2/hi/entertainment/2218456.stm)

REFERENCES

Berger, Helen A. 1999. *A Community of Witches*. Columbia: University of South Carolina Press.

Bibby, Reginald. 1987. *Fragmented Gods.* Toronto: Irwin Publishing.

———. 1993. *Unknown Gods.* Toronto: Stoddart Publishing Company.

———. 2002. *Restless Gods.* Toronto: Stoddart Publishing Company.

Bloch, Jon. 1998. *New Spirituality, Self and Belonging.* Westport: Praeger.

Cowan, Douglas. 2005. *Cyberhenge: Modern Pagans on the Internet.* New York: Routledge.

Giddens, Anthony. 1991. *Modernity and Self-Identity.* Stanford: Stanford University Press.

Lewis, James, ed., 1996. *Magical Religion and Modern Witchcraft.* Albany: State University of New York Press.

———. 2004. *The Oxford Handbook of New Religious Movements.* New York: Oxford University Press.

Maffesoli, Michel. 1996. *The Time of the Tribes.* Translated by Don Smith. Thousand Oaks: Sage Publications.

Meredydd. n.d. *Book of Shadows 1985–1987.* Unpublished. Used by permission of the author.

Orion, Loretta. 1995. *Never Again the Burning Times: Paganism Revived.* Prospect Heights: Waveland Press.

Rabinovitch, Shelley. 1992. "'An' Ye Harm None, Do What Ye Will': Neo-pagans and Witches in Canada." MA thesis, Department of Religion, Carleton University.

———, and James Lewis, eds. 2002. *The Encyclopedia of Modern Witchcraft and Neo-Paganism.* New York: Citadel Press.

Reid, Síân. 2001. "Disorganized Religion: An Exploration of the Neopagan Craft in Canada." PhD dissertation, Department of Sociology and Anthropology, Carleton University.

Stark, Rodney, and William Sims Bainbridge. 1985. *The Future of Religion.* Berkeley: University of California Press.

Valiente, Doreen. 1989. *The Rebirth of Witchcraft.* London: Robert Hale Publishers.

PART I: The Voices That Inspired

witch. Heathen. Pagan. These terms have been demonized by four centuries of religious propaganda. They have been applied to those deemed beyond the reach of conventional morality, conventional life choices, and conventional religion. They designate dangerous outsiders, whose very existence is a threat to all that is good and valued in society. They are also terms that practitioners of a constellation of new religious movements have chosen to describe themselves. Looking to the historical, mythological, literary, symbolic, and folkloric inheritances of Europe, these people have created new religious and spiritual forms that they believe will help link the past to a more sustainable future.

The readings in this section have been chosen to give readers a sense of the mood of pagans and paganism when it first began to be visible in the mainstream in the late 1970s and early 1980s, first in Britain and then in the colonies and former colonies. These practitioner narratives capture rhythm of the movement at that time, which was characterized by a mood of hope and endless possibility, an antidote to the growing conservativism of the Reagan–Thatcher years. The writings of these, their elders, captured the minds and hearts of a young generation that missed the countercultural revolution by a simple accident of birth.

Chapter 1 was written by the grandmother of British witchcraft, Doreen Valiente. Valiente, already a student of the esoteric philosophies of Aleister Crowley and Dion Fortune, met Gerald Gardner in late 1952, after several months of correspondence. She was initiated as a witch in the summer of 1953, just before Midsummer (Valiente 1989:39–40). Valiente worked as Gardner's high priestess (the term for the female leader of a witchcraft group) from 1954 until 1957, when they parted ways. During this time, she substantially rewrote Gardner's *Book of Shadows*, including penning the piece that is now universally known as the *Charge of the Goddess*. Based upon folklorist Charles Godfrey Leland's *Aradia*, and augmented with images drawn from Robert Graves's *The White Goddess*, this piece was spoken by the high-priestess-as-Goddess at every ritual gathering of the coven.

Valiente first wrote the *Charge* in verse, but it is the prose version that is most often used and best remembered. Unlike many proclamations of the central narratives of Judaism and Christianity, such as the Ten Commandments or the Sermon on the Mount, the *Charge of the Goddess* describes and exhorts, but it does not set out prohibitions. The *Charge* paints a haunting picture of a Goddess who is at once powerful and compassionate, loving and stern. She teaches the mysteries to those who would seek them; her worship is celebrated in love, pleasure, and rejoicing. She is the beginning and end of all things, everlasting. The *Charge* was, to Valiente's dismay, published and republished without attribution or permission, as "traditional lore" in dozens of subsequent books. It was not until 1997 that she wrote a companion piece for the male aspects of divinity, the *Charge of the God*, which remains relatively little known.

Chapter 2 is comprised of sacred narratives that appear in Starhawk's first book *The Spiral Dance*. She attributes them to the teachings of the Faery tradition of witchcraft, which she learned in the 1970s from founders Victor and Cora Anderson. The Andersons had obviously had contact with Gardnerian writings at some point because much of the framework is there, even if the content is somewhat different. In addition, Starhawk knew Z. Budapest, whose leading-edge recasting of witchcraft as feminist religion was spreading through the Bay Area counterculture throughout the 1970s. Starhawk, like Valiente, talks about a Goddess, a divine female force that stands at the beginning and end of everything. She talks of the Wheel of the Year, and the spiral of death and rebirth that is so central to witchcraft's beliefs.

The Spiral Dance was enormously influential in North America when it was released in 1979 because British witchcraft books were available only on a limited basis in Canada—in expensive hardcover editions—and almost not at all in the United States. Unlike most of the witchcraft books produced in North America at the time, it was neither a seedy exposé of a morally questionable lifestyle choice, nor was it a spellbook promising power, wealth, and fame. *The Spiral Dance* was an evocative, poetic tribute to the Goddess, the natural world, and to people's capacity to grow and change. It was a how-to book, and at the same time, a why-to book. It combined witchcraft with an exhortation to feminism and activism, and coloured much of the development of witchcraft in North America. In a 1995 survey of Canadian pagans, one question asked what the three most influential books on their pagan practice had been: almost one in five listed *The Spiral Dance* (Reid 2001).

Chapter 3 is a widely circulated piece written by prominent pagan Selena Fox. It has gone through several revisions since she first wrote it; this version dates from the early to mid-1980s, that important breakthrough time for paganism and witchcraft. It is simultaneously a deeply personal statement of faith by Selena Fox herself, and a simple statement of the basic tenets of paganism. Many people, both pagans and the pagan-curious, experienced a deep resonance when they read Fox's words—a profound sense of "Yeah, me too!" "I Am a Pagan" was a statement that could be read and understood by members of other religions as something that reflected a genuine spiritual commitment.

By the 1980s, Fox was already a long-standing pagan practitioner, having established what was then called "Circle Wicca" in the early 1970s. Out of this grew Circle Farm, a rented farmstead in Wisconsin that was its headquarters for festival planning, newsletter production, classes, networking, and other pagan endeavours. In 1980, Circle received tax-exempt status as a religious organization. The publicity and perceived notoriety of Circle

Farm, however, got them evicted by their landlord, and they moved through several other rented sites before they were able to purchase land near Mt. Horeb, Wisconsin, and set up the Circle Sanctuary Nature Preserve. From this haven, Fox and her current husband, Dennis Carpenter, continue to coordinate several newsletters and Web sites, provide a reference library on paganism, and run retreats, festivals, and classes.

Chapter 4 is an excerpt from Margot Adler's groundbreaking *Drawing Down the Moon*, a book that not only documented paganism in the United States, but literally created the concept of "pagan community." Adler wrote: "Individuals may move freely between groups and form their own groups according to their needs, but all the while they remain within a community that defines itself as Pagan. The basic community remains, although the structures may change" (1979:33). Since many pagans became involved in their pagan practice only after reading a substantial amount about it, what Adler described—more optimistic vision than reality when she originally wrote it—eventually because the expectation of new pagans, and eventually an approximation of reality.

Margot Adler was a National Public Radio reporter in the 1970s when she set off on her cross-country search for paganism. With a journalist's keenly honed instincts, she presents the people she meets and the rituals she attends in a balanced manner, rich with description and light on judgment. The chapter reprinted here, "A Religion without Converts," raises an interesting paradox: If, at the time Adler was writing, no one was pagan because they had been "born into" the movement, and there were no converts, then how did these people become involved? What emerges as an answer is a construction of the phenomenon of conversion that is stereotypically drawn from Christian experience—a sudden and dramatic change of world view and behaviour brought on by an influential encounter or mystical experience, such as the apostle Paul experienced on the road to Damascus. Adler describes what she considers to have been an experience of recognition rather than one of conversion. Even though subsequent studies of conversion suggest that, especially in the case of new religious movements, the experience Adler describes is not uncommon (Richardson 1985; Straus 1979; Snow and Machalek 1983; Dawson 1990), most pagans still view the idea of conversion as distasteful, and reject it as a description of their process of affiliation to paganism.

The last essay in this section, "Why Women Need the Goddess," was written by Carol Christ, one of the theologians who, in the 1970s, stopped trying to figure out how women could become equal partners with men in existing religions. She and colleagues such as Mary Daly came to believe women could never be equal partners in religions that denied them equality in the fundamental representations of deity and in the mythic narratives of the religion. In particular, they believed that Judaism and Christianity were not only patriarchal religions, but also religions of the patriarchy, whose latent function was to provide legitimacy and authority to male power figures while denying these to women. Judaism, Christianity, and other established religions were not only reflections of women's subordinate status, but also the causes of it. The patriarchal bias was not a stain that could be repaired or washed away, Christ suggested, it was part of the fundamental cosmology of those religions.

These feminists argued that women did not need an inclusive theology so much as they needed a *thealogy.* "Thealogy" is a term that refers to a spirituality that recognizes the female as divine, and that grows out of, supports, and re-enchants women's lives. It is attributed to Naomi Goldenberg, who, along with Christ, was working with Starhawk in the 1970s. Goldenberg, Christ, and others of that generation saw in feminist witchcraft and Goddess spirituality a potential path away from the inherent difficulties of patriarchal religion. In retrospect, we know that this solution is problematic, as Eller and Klassen will point out in chapters 19 and 20. Christ's words, however, her logical justification for why women needed a different spiritual path, acknowledged the alienation many women were feeling and pointed them toward a brighter alternative.

All of these selections are alike in that they were essentially the right words at the right time. They were words of hope in a disillusioned time—England came to it early after the devastation of World War II. Valiente herself wrote, "In a sense, the rebirth of witchcraft is a rebellion. It is being carried out by those both young and old who are no longer content to get their religion from the churches or their opinions from the newspapers; who are, moreover, profoundly disillusioned with the scientists who promised us Utopia and gave us the nuclear bomb" (1989:207). Valiente's statement suggests exactly the turn back to "nature" from "progress," which was the underpinning to the whole Romantic movement, gone but scarcely forgotten in England. In the United States, the distrust of science and leadership came slightly later, during what some considered a pointless war on foreign soil that swallowed up half a generation of young men. Vietnam, for many, was something that could not be allowed to be repeated, and so they turned away from the authorities, both political and religious, that had permitted it to happen. This section captures the vividness and the rebellious innovation of modern paganism's early years.

REFERENCES

Adler, Margot. 1979. *Drawing Down the Moon.* Boston: Beacon Press.

Dawson, Lorne. 1990. "Self-Affirmation, Freedom and Rationality: Theoretically Elaborating 'Active' Conversions." *Journal for the Scientific Study of Religion* 29, no. 2: 141–163.

Reid, Síân. 2001. "Disorganized Religion: An Exploration of the Neopagan Craft in Canada." PhD dissertation, Department of Sociology and Anthropology, Carleton University.

Richardson, James. 1985. "The Active vs the Passive Convert: Paradigm Conflict in Conversion/Recruitment Research." *Journal for the Scientific Study of Religion* 24, no. 2: 163–179.

Snow, David, and Richard Machalek. 1983. "The Convert as a Social Type." In *Sociological Theory,* edited by Randall Collins, 259–289. San Francisco: Jossey-Bass.

Straus, Roger. 1979. "Religious Conversion as a Personal and Collective Achievement." *Sociological Analysis* 40, no. 2: 158–165.

Valiente, Doreen. 1989. *The Rebirth of Witchcraft.* London: Robert Hale Publishers.

CHAPTER I
Charge of the Goddess

Doreen Valiente

[. . .] The High Priest says:
"Listen to the words of the Great Mother; she who of old was also called among men Artemis, Astarte, Athene, Dione, Melusine, Aphrodite, Cerridwen, Dana, Arianrhod, Isis, Bride,[1] and by many other names."[2]

The High Priestess says:
"Whenever ye have need of any thing, once in the month, and better it be when the moon is full, then shall ye assemble in some secret place and adore the spirit of me, who am Queen of all witches.[3] There shall ye assemble, ye who are fain to learn all sorcery, yet have not won its deepest secrets; to these will I teach things that are yet unknown. And ye shall be free from slavery; and as a sign that ye be really free, ye shall be naked in your rites; and ye shall dance, sing, feast, make music and love, all in my praise. For mine is the ecstasy of the spirit, and mine also is joy on earth; for my law is love unto all beings. Keep pure your highest ideal; strive ever

toward it; let naught stop you or turn you aside. For mine is the secret door that opens upon the Land of Youth, and mine is the cup of the wine of life, and the Cauldron of Cerridwen, which is the Holy Grail of immortality. I am the gracious Goddess, who gives the gift of joy unto the heart of man. Upon earth, I give the knowledge of the spirit eternal; and beyond death, I give peace, and freedom, and reunion with those who have gone before. Nor do I demand sacrifice; for behold, I am the mother of all living, and my love is poured out upon the earth."

The High Priest says:
"Hear ye the words of the Star Goddess; she in the dust of whose feet are the hosts of heaven, and whose body encircles the universe."

The High Priestess says:
"I who am the beauty of the green earth, and the white Moon among the stars, and the mystery of the waters, and the desire of the heart of man, call unto thy soul. Arise, and come unto me. For I am the soul of nature, who gives life to the universe. From me all things proceed, and unto me all things must return; and before my face, beloved of gods and of men, let thine innermost divine self be enfolded in the rapture of the infinite. Let my worship be within the heart that rejoiceth; for behold, all acts of love and pleasure are my rituals. And therefore let there be beauty and strength, power and compassion, honour and humility, mirth and reverence within you. And thou who thinkest to seek for me, know thy seeking and yearning shall avail thee not unless thou knowest the mystery; that if that which thou seekest thou findest not within thee, thou wilt never find it without thee. For behold, I have been with thee from the beginning; and I am that which is attained at the end of desire."

*****

NOTES

1. Pronounced "Breed." If you have a local Goddess-name, by all means add it to the list. While we lived in County Wexford, we used to add Carman, a Wexford Goddess (or heroine or villainess, according to your version) who gave the county and town their Gaelic name of Loch Garman (Loch garman).
2. In the *Book of Shadows*, another sentence follows here: "At her altars the youth of Lacedaemon in Sparta made due sacrifice." The sentence originated from Gardner, not Valiente. Like many covens, we omit it. The Spartan sacrifice, though it has been variously described, was certainly a gruesome business (see for example Robert Graves's *Greek Myths*, para 116.4) and out of keeping with the *Charge*'s later statement "Nor do I demand sacrifice." By the way, the sentence is also inaccurately worded; Sparta was in Lacedaemon, not Lacedaemon in Sparta.
3. "Witcheries" in Doreen Valiente's *Book of Shadows*.

CHAPTER 2

Sacred Narratives

Starhawk

BETWEEN THE WORLDS

Creation[1]

alone, awesome, complete within Herself, the Goddess, She whose name cannot be spoken, floated in the abyss of the outer darkness, before the beginning of all things. And as She looked into the curved mirror of black space, She saw by her own light her radiant reflection, and fell in love with it. She drew it forth by the power that was in Her and made love to Herself, and called Her "Miria, the Wonderful."

Their ecstasy burst forth in the single song of all that is, was, or ever shall be, and with the song came motion, waves that poured outward and became all the spheres and circles of the worlds. The Goddess became filled with love, swollen with love, and She gave birth to a rain of bright spirits that filled the worlds and became all beings.

But in that great movement, Miria was swept away, and as She moved out from the Goddess She became more masculine. First She became the Blue God, the gentle, laughing God of love. Then She became the Green One, vine-covered, rooted in the earth, the spirit of all growing things. At last She became the Horned God, the Hunter whose face is the ruddy sun and yet dark as Death. But always desire draws Him back toward the Goddess, so that He circles Her eternally, seeking to return in love.

All began in love; all seeks to return to love. Love is the law, the teacher of wisdom, and the great revealer of mysteries.

*****

THE WHEEL OF THE YEAR[2]

In love, the Horned God, changing form and changing face, ever seeks the Goddess. In this world, the search and the seeking appear in the Wheel of the Year.

She is the Great Mother who gives birth to Him as the Divine Child Sun at the Winter Solstice. In spring, He is sower and seed who grows with the growing light, green as the new shoots. She is the Initiatrix who teaches Him the mysteries. He is the young bull; She the nymph, seductress. In summer, when light is longest, they meet in union, and the strength of their passion sustains the world. But the God's face darkens as the sun grows weaker, until at last, when the grain is cut for harvest, He too sacrifices Himself to Self that all may be nourished. She is the reaper, the grave of earth to which all must return. Throughout the long nights and darkening days, He sleeps in her womb; in dreams, He is Lord of Death who rules the Land of Youth beyond the gates of night and day. His dark tomb becomes the womb of rebirth, for at Midwinter She again gives birth to Him. The cycle ends and begins again, and the Wheel of the Year turns, on and on.

*****

In a world where the endlessly transforming, erotic dance of God and Goddess weaves radiant through all things, we who step to their rhythm are enraptured with the wonder and mystery of being.

THE GODDESS IN THE KINGDOM OF DEATH[3]

In this world, the Goddess is seen in the moon, the light that shines in darkness, the rain bringer, mover of the tides, Mistress of mysteries. And as the moon waxes and wanes, and walks three nights of its cycle in darkness, so, it is said, the Goddess once spent three nights in the Kingdom of Death.

For in love She ever seeks her other Self, and once, in the winter of the year, when He had disappeared from the green earth, She followed Him and came at last to the gates beyond which the living do not go.

The Guardian of the Gate challenged Her, and She stripped Herself of her clothing and jewels, for nothing may be brought into that land. For love, She was bound as all who enter there must be and brought before Death Himself.

He loved Her, and knelt at her feet, laying before Her his sword and crown, and gave Her the fivefold kiss, and said,

"Do not return to the living world, but stay here with Me, and have peace and rest and comfort."

But She answered, "Why do you cause all things I love and delight in to die and wither away?"

"Lady," He said, "It is the fate of all that lives to die. Everything passes; all fades away. I bring comfort and consolation to those who pass the gates, that they may grow young again. But You are my heart's desire—return not, but stay here with Me."

And She remained with him three days and three nights, and at the end of the third night She took up his crown, and it became a circlet that She placed around her neck, saying:

"Here is the circle of rebirth. Through You all passes out of life, but through Me all may be born again. Everything passes; everything changes. Even death is not eternal. Mine is the mystery of the womb, which is the cauldron of rebirth. Enter into Me and know Me, and You will be free of all fear. For as life is but a journey into death, so death is but a passage back to life, and in Me the circle is ever turning."

In love, He entered into Her, and so was reborn into life. Yet is He known as Lord of Shadows, the comforter and consoler, opener of the gates, King of the Land of Youth, the giver of peace and rest. But She is the gracious mother of all life; from Her all things proceed and to Her they return again. In Her are the mysteries of death and birth; in Her is the fulfillment of all love.

*****

NOTES

1. Oral teaching of the Faery tradition of witchcraft.
2. Oral teaching of the Faery tradition.
3. Oral teaching, Faery tradition.

REFERENCES

Anderson, Victor. *Thorns of the Blood Rose.* San Leandro: Cora Anderson, 1970.

Anima, *An Experimental Journal* 7, no. 2 (1975).

CHAPTER 3
I Am a Pagan

Selena Fox

I am a Pagan. I am a part of the whole of nature. The rocks, the animals, the plants, the elements are my relatives. Other humans are my sisters and brothers, whatever their races, colours, ages, nationalities, creeds, or sexual preferences. The earth is my mother and the sky is my father. The sun and moon are my grandparents, and the stars my ancestors. I am part of this large family of nature, not the master of it. I have my own special part to play and I seek to play that part to the best of my ability. I seek to live in harmony with others in the family of nature, treating others with respect, not abuse.

I am a Pagan. I celebrate the changing seasons, the turning of the Wheel of the Year with music, feasting, rituals, and celebrations. Halloween is a time for paying homage to my ancestors and friends who have passed into the spirit world and a time to gaze into the future. Yule, the winter solstice, is a festival of peace, light, and celebration of the new sun, and my home is filled with the sacred holly, mistletoe, and evergreen. Candlemas, Imbolg, or groundhog day at the beginning of February is a festival of purification. A time for clearing away blockages to prepare for the coming of spring and new growth. Ostara, the spring equinox, I celebrate the greening of the earth by sharing coloured eggs with friends. May Eve is a festival of fertility and creativity, and I decorate myself with bright colours and flowers and dance the maypole to bless gardens and projects. Summer solstice, Leitha, is a grand gathering time when I meet old friends and greet new ones, and celebrate the change of the sun by burning the Yule wreath made six months before. Lughnassad, Lammas, is a celebration of summer and I give thanks for the first fruits of the harvest, and energize harvests to come. Fall equinox, Mabon, is the time of thanksgiving for the harvests I've gathered. And at Samhain, the year starts again.

I am a Pagan. I pay attention to the seasons within myself—of beginnings, growth, fruition, harvest, endings, rest, and beginnings again. Life is a circle with many cycles.

I am a Pagan. I work magic by the moon to help and to heal myself and others. I activate beginnings in the waxing, energize manifestations at the full, clear away obstructions at the waning, and experience the wisdom of transformation at the dark. I take part in circles at the new and full moons, and I know that my circles are part of the whole web of circles that meet at these times around the planet.

I am a Pagan. With every death there is a rebirth. For every problem there is a solution and an opportunity for growth. I create my own reality with my thoughts, feelings, and actions. Whatever I send out always returns. I seek to abide by the Rede: An ye harm none, do what ye will. When I work magic, before I raise and direct energy, I seek always to look at the larger picture, of which my needs are only a part. When problems come my way, I seek to understand their cause and messages as part of my finding a solution. In doing healing work, I seek to correct the underlying cause, rather than just treat symptoms.

I am a Pagan. I acknowledge that the divine is everywhere, in the energy of life. I am animistic. I sense the life force in the oak tree, on the hill, in the herbs in the garden, in the birds singing at the window, in the boulders on the hill, in myself, and yes, even in "things" such as my car and computer. I understand that everything has its physical and non-physical aspect. The physical and spiritual are deeply intertwined, not separate, and one is not better than the other.

I am a Pagan. I know that divine force has many facets and I acknowledge a variety of Goddesses and Gods. I also understand the underlying unity of all. My encounters with Pagan Goddesses and Gods have transformed and enriched my life. Hecate appeared at a death to teach me of release and rebirth. As a young child, Artemis flowed through me to scare off a rapist. Selene of the bright moon brings me visions and my name. I have heard Pan play his pipes in the glade, and Cernunnos has appeared to me in the forest as a young stag. I've experienced the union of the Goddess and God while making love to my mate in the fields on Beltane Eve. Bast has helped me find lost cats for others. Isis has spoken to me in bursts of radiance in the deep of the night and in flows of energy through my hands while doing healings.

I am a Pagan. My worship is one of communion, not grovelling. I shape my views with others when I sense it is right, but I do not proselytize—there are many ways, not one way, of spiritual growth. My holy places are under the open sky ... in the stone circle in the oak grove on the top of the mound ... on the vision rock on the high cliff ... in the ring in the open meadow ... in the sweatlodge by the stream ... by the clear pool of the sacred spring. Yet my worship can be anywhere ... my magic circle is portable. I can call to the four quarters, to the earth and the sky, and to the central spirit point wherever I may be.

I am a Pagan. I journey to the Otherworld in my dreams, my meditations, my rituals. I use magical tools to aid me in my journeys and my magics—incense, cauldron, candles, chalices of water, pentacles of salt, crystals, feathers, bells, rattle and drum, wand and staff, athame, mirror. I fly with my consciousness through time and space. I return with insights. I go between the worlds for healing, growth, and transformation. Psychic perception is a natural, not a supernatural, part of living.

I am a Pagan. I attune myself to the four elements of nature—earth, air, fire, water, and to the fifth element, spirit, which is a force that connects all. I see these elements as parts of myself—my physical body is my earth, my intellect my air, my emotions my water, my will my fire, and my inner self my spirit. I endeavour to keep myself healthy and in balance in all these parts of self.

I am a Pagan. I hear the cries of Mother Earth. I see the pollution of the air, the soil, the waters. I see the games being played by nations with the fire of nuclear weapons. I see spiritual pollution too—selfishness, hatred, greed for money and for power, despair. I sense these things, but I sense too a cleansing, healing energy manifesting on the planet. I know that I can help bring the planet into greater balance by seeking balance in my own life. I know that my attitudes, my way of living can make a difference. I endeavour to be a channel for healing and balance.

I am a Pagan.

CHAPTER 4
A Religion without Converts

Margot Adler

how do people become neopagans? This question assumes great importance when we consider that neopagan groups rarely proselytize and certain of them are quite selective. There are few converts. In most cases, word of mouth, a discussion between friends, a lecture, a book, or an article provides the entry point. But these events merely confirm some original, private experience, so that the most common feeling of those who have named themselves Pagans is something like "I finally found a group that has the same religious perceptions I always had." A common phrase you hear is "I've come home," or, as one woman told me excitedly after a lecture, "I always knew I had a religion, I just never knew it had a name."

Alison Harlow, a systems analyst at a large medical research centre in California, described her first experience this way:

> It was Christmas Eve and I was singing in the choir of a lovely church at the edge of a lake, and the church was filled with beautiful decorations.

> It was full moon, and the moon was shining right through the glass windows of the church. I looked out and felt something very special happening, but it didn't seem to be happening inside the church.
>
> After the Midnight Mass was over and everyone adjourned to the parish house for coffee, I knew I needed to be alone for a minute, so I left my husband and climbed up the hill behind the church. I sat on this hill looking at the full moon, and I could hear the sound of coffee cups clinking and the murmur of conversation from the parish house.
>
> I was looking down on all this, when suddenly I felt a "presence." It seemed very ancient and wise and definitely female. I can't describe it any closer than that, but I felt that this presence, this being, was looking down on me, on this church and these people and saying, "The poor little ones! They mean so well and they understand so little."
>
> I felt that whoever "she" was, she was incredibly old and patient; she was exasperated with the way things were going on the planet, but she hadn't given up hope that we would start making some sense of the world. So, after that, I knew I had to find out more about her.

Harlow is now a priestess in the Craft, working in a self-created tradition that deals mostly, but not exclusively, with women. As a result of her experience, she began a complex journey to find out about the history and experience of goddess worship. This search led her, through various readings, into contact with a number of Craft traditions, until she ended up writing a column on feminism and witchcraft for the neopagan magazine *Nemeton* (now defunct). It is perhaps only fair, at this point, to describe my own entry into this same world.

When I was a small child, I had the good fortune to enter an unusual New York City grammar school (City and Country) that allowed its students to immerse themselves in historical periods to such an extent that we often seemed to live in them. At the age of 12, a traditional time for rites of passage, that historical period was ancient Greece. I remember entering into the Greek myths as if I had returned to my true homeland.

My friends and I lived through the battles of the *Iliad*; we read the historical novels of Mary Renault and Caroline Dale Snedeker[1] and took the parts of ancient heroes and heroines in plays and fantasy. I wrote hymns to gods and goddesses and poured libations (of water) onto the grass of neighbouring parks. In my deepest and most secret moments I daydreamed that I had become these beings, feeling what it would be like to be Artemis or Athena. I acted out the old myths and created new ones, in fantasy and private play. It was a great and deep secret that found its way into brief diary entries and unskilled drawings. But like many inner things, it was not unique to me.

I have since discovered that these experiences are common. The pantheons may differ according to circumstances, class, ethnic and cultural background, opportunity, and even chance. There are children in the United States whose pantheons come from "Star Trek,"[2] while their parents remember the days of Buck Rogers. The archetypal images seem to wander in and out of the fantasies of millions of children, disguised in contemporary forms. That I and most of my friends had the opportunity to take our archetypes from the rich pantheon of ancient Greece was a result of class and opportunity, nothing more.

What were these fantasies of gods and goddesses? What was their use, their purpose? I see them now as daydreams used in the struggle toward my own becoming. They were hardly idle, though, since they focused on stronger and healthier "role models" than the images of women projected in the late 1950s. The fantasies enabled me to contact stronger parts of myself, to embolden my vision of myself. Besides, these experiences were filled with power, intensity, and even ecstasy that, on reflection, seem religious or spiritual.

As I grew up, I forced myself to deny these experiences of childhood. At first I missed them; then I did not quite remember what I missed. They became a strange discarded part of youthful fantasy. No one told me directly, "People don't worship the Greek gods anymore, much less attempt to become them through ritual and fantasy," but the messages around me were clear enough. Such daydreams did not fit into the society I lived in, and even to talk about them was impossible. It became easier to discuss the most intimate personal, emotional, or sexual experiences than to talk of these earlier experiences. To reveal them was a kind of magical violation.

Religion had no official place in my childhood world. I was brought up in a family of agnostics and atheists. Still, feeling that there was some dimension lacking in their lives, I embarked on a quasi-religious search as a teenager. I felt ecstatic power in the Catholic mass (as long as it was in Latin); I went to Quaker meetings and visited synagogues and churches. Today it seems to me I thirsted for the power and richness of those original experiences, though I found only beliefs and dogmas that seemed irrelevant or even contradictory to them. I wanted permission for those experiences, but not if it would poison my integrity or my commitment to living and acting in the world.

I remember coming across the famous words of Marx on religion: "Religion is the sigh of the hard-pressed, the heart of a heartless world, the soul of soulless conditions, the opium of the people...."[3] And having no place to put this experience of Goddess nor freedom enough to continue the ancient practice I had stumbled on, I gradually left it behind, and set my sights on the soulless conditions. It was 1964, I was in Berkeley, and there were many soulless conditions with which to concern myself.

In 1971, while working as a political reporter for Pacifica Radio in Washington, D.C., I became involved in various environmentalist and ecological concerns. During that year John McPhee wrote a series of articles for *The New Yorker* called "Encounters with the Archdruid," later published as a book. The articles narrated three wilderness journeys made by David Brower (president of Friends of the Earth and former head of the Sierra Club) in the company of three of his enemies on environmental issues. Two passages from this book come to mind as emotional springboards to the events that followed. The first was Brower's statement that the ecology movement was really a spiritual movement. "We are in a kind of religion," he said, "an ethic with regard to terrain, and this religion is closest to the Buddhist, I suppose." The second quote that comes to mind is much stranger; one of Brower's enemies, a developer, spoke against the practices of conservationists and called Brower "a druid." "Ancient druids used to sacrifice human beings under oak trees," the developer said. "Modern druids worship trees and sacrifice human beings to those trees."[4]

The two quotes struck me deeply and I began to search for a religious framework that might be appropriate to ecological principles. I started by searching for druids.

Around that time two noted historians, Arnold Toynbee and Lynn White, wrote essays in which they claimed that there was, in fact, a religious dimension to the environmental crisis.

Toynbee's article appeared in 1972, in the *International Journal of Environmental Studies.* Its main point was that worldwide ecological problems were due in part to a religious cause, "the rise of monotheism," and that the verse in Genesis (1:28), "Be fruitful and multiply and replenish the Earth and subdue it," had become biblical sanction for human beings to assert their rights over all nature. Toynbee felt that his education in pre-Christian Greek and Latin literature had had "a deeper and more enduring effect on my *Weltanschauung*" than his Christian upbringing:

> In popular pre-Christian Greek religion, divinity was inherent in all natural phenomena, including those that man had tamed and domesticated. Divinity was present in springs and rivers and the sea; in trees, both the wild oak and the cultivated olive-tree; in corn and vines; in mountains; in earthquakes and lightning and thunder. The godhead was diffused throughout the phenomena. It was plural, not singular; a pantheon, not a unique almighty super-human person. When the Graeco-Roman World was converted to Christianity, the divinity was drained out of nature and was concentrated in one unique transcendent God. "Pan is dead." "The oracles are dumb." Bronsgrove is no longer a wood that is sacrosanct because it is animated by the god Bron....

The Judeo-Christian tradition gave licence for exploitation. Toynbee advised "reverting from the *Weltanschauung* of monotheism to the *Weltanschauung* of pantheism, which is older and was once universal."

> The plight in which post-Industrial-Revolution man has now landed himself is one more demonstration that man is not the master of his environment—not even when supposedly armed with a warrant, issued by a supposedly unique and omnipotent God with a human-like personality, delegating to man plenipotentiary powers. Nature is now demonstrating to us that she does not recognize the validity of this

> alleged warrant, and she is warning us that, if man insists on trying to execute it, he will commit this outrage on nature at his peril.[5]

While Toynbee stopped short of advocating a return to polytheism, and implied that many of the pre-Christian deities were too crude for our age, his basic perception was strikingly similar to the impulse that led to the creation of many neopagan groups.

The article by Lynn White had appeared several years earlier in *Science* and had begun quite a controversy. While much of White's article, "The Historical Roots of Our Ecologic Crisis," dealt with changes in methods of farming and agriculture over the centuries, a few of its points were strikingly similar to Toynbee's. White observed that "the victory of Christianity over paganism was the greatest psychic revolution in the history of our culture."

> Christianity in absolute contrast to ancient paganism ... not only established a dualism of man and nature but also insisted that it is God's will that man exploit nature for his proper ends.... In antiquity every tree, every spring, every stream, every hill had its own *genius loci*, its guardian spirit.... By destroying pagan animism, Christianity made it possible to exploit nature in a mood of indifference to the feeling of natural objects.[6]

In the following years I searched in books and articles for an ecological-religious framework compatible with my own politics and commitment to the world. I soon entered into a lengthy correspondence with a coven of witches in Essex, England. Being no less a victim of stereotypes than most, I pictured the couple who led this group as in their thirties and middle class. But Doris and Vic Stuart turned out to be in their late forties and fifties. He was an old unionist and socialist and she was a factory worker.[7] At this period, I also contacted a pagan group in Wales. Frankly, at the time I thought that corresponding with witches was bizarre and even amusing. I certainly had no thought that there might be any link between these groups and my own experience of Goddess, which still came to me, unbidden, at odd moments.

One day the coven in Essex sent me a tape recording of some rituals. The first one on the tape was called "The Drawing Down of the Moon." I did not know it then, but in this ritual, one of the most serious and beautiful in the modern Craft, the priest *invokes* into the priestess (or, depending on your point of view, she *evokes* from within herself) the goddess or triple goddess, symbolized by the phases of the moon. She is known by a thousand names, and among them were those I had used as a child. In some Craft rituals the priestess goes into a trance and speaks; in other traditions the ritual is a more formal dramatic dialogue, often of intense beauty, in which, again, the priestess speaks, taking the role of the goddess. In both instances the priestess functions as the goddess incarnate, within the circle.

I found a quiet place and played the tape. The music in the background was perhaps by Brahms. A man and woman spoke with English accents. When it came time for the invocation, the words came clearly:

> Listen to the words of the Great Mother, who was of old also called Artemis, Astarte, Melusine, Aphrodite, Diana, Brigit, and many other names....[8]

A feeling of power and emotion came over me. For, after all, how different was that ritual from the magical rituals of my childhood? The contents of the tape had simply given me *permission* to accept a part of my own psyche that I had denied for years—and then extend it.

Like most neopagans, I never converted in the accepted sense—I never adopted any new beliefs. I simply accepted, reaffirmed, and extended a very old experience. I allowed certain kinds of feelings and ways of being back into my life.

I tell these stories in a book that contains little personal history in order to respond to the statement I frequently hear: I don't *believe* in *that*! This is the standard response to many of the ideas and people with which this book is concerned. But *belief* has never seemed very relevant to the experiences and processes of the groups that call themselves, collectively, the neopagan movement.[9]

In my seven years of contact with these groups I was never asked to *believe* in anything. I was told a few dogmas by people who hadn't ridded themselves of the tendency to dogmatize, but I rejected those. In the next chapters you will encounter priests and priestesses who say that they are philosophical agnostics and that this has never inhibited their participation in or leadership of neopagan and Craft groups. Others will tell you that the gods and goddesses are "ethereal beings." Still others have called them symbols, powers, archetypes, or "something deep and strong within the self to be contacted," or even "something akin to the force of poetry and art."

As one scholar has noted, it is a religion "of atmosphere instead of faith; a cosmos, in a word, constructed by the imagination...."[10]

My own role has been that of observer-participant. I began by trying to find reasons for my involvement and then travelled across the country to visit hundreds of people in order to contrast my own experiences with theirs. By the end of my travels I found that many of my early assumptions were incorrect.

For example, I found that neopagan groups were very diverse in class and ethnic background. My first experiences brought me in touch with a much broader spectrum of people than I had known in the student movements of the 1960s. The first three covens I encountered in New York and England were composed largely of working-class and lower-middle-class people. Later, I met covens and groups composed predominantly of upper-middle-class intellectuals. Then I met groups whose members worked as insurance salesmen, bus drivers, police, and secretaries. All my class stereotypes began to fall by the wayside.

Another assumption, and one I was slow to drop, was that the neopagan resurgence was, fundamentally, a reaction against science, technology, progress. My own involvement had come through a kind of Luddite reaction, so I assumed it was typical. But in many interviews neopagans and witches supported high technologies, scientific inquiry, and space exploration. It is true that most neopagans feel that we abuse technology; they often support "alternative" technologies—solar, wind, etc.—and hold a biological rather than a mechanistic world view.

In general, I have tried to be aware of my own biases and to make them clear so that, if you wish, you can steer between the shoals.

Lastly, a few words about the reasons for this neopagan resurgence.

One standard psychological explanation is that people join these groups to gain power over others or to banish feelings of inadequacy and insecurity. Obviously (some of the studies referred to later show this) some people do join magical and religious groups in order to gain self-mastery, in the sense of practical knowledge of psychology and the workings of the psyche, so they can function better in the world. But this reason was not among the six primary reasons that pagans and witches gave me in answer to the questions "Why is this phenomenon occurring? Why are you involved?"

Many of their reasons are novel, and completely at odds with common assumptions.

Beauty, Vision, Imagination. A number of neopagans told me that their religious views were part of a general visionary quest that included involvement with poetry, art, drama, music, science fiction, and fantasy. At least four witches in different parts of the country spoke of religion as a human need for beauty.

Intellectual Satisfaction. Many told me that reading and collecting odd books had been the prime influence in their religious decision. This came as a surprise to me. In particular, most of the midwesterners said flatly that the wide dissemination of strange and fascinating books had been the main factor in creating a neopagan resurgence. And while class and profession vary widely among neopagans, almost all are avid readers. This does not seem to depend on their educational level; it holds true for high-school dropouts as well as PhDs.

Growth. A more predictable answer, this ambiguous word was given frequently. Most pagans see their lives not as straight roads to specific goals, but as processes—evolution, change, or an increase in understanding. Neopagans often see themselves as pursuing the quests of the mystery traditions: initiations into the workings of life, death, and rebirth.

Feminism. For many women, this was the main reason for involvement. Large numbers of women have been seeking a spiritual framework outside the patriarchal religions that have dominated the Western world for the last several thousand years. Many who wanted to find a spiritual side to their feminism entered the Craft because of its emphasis on goddess worship. Neopagan witchcraft groups range from those with a mixture of female and male deities to those that focus on the monotheistic worship of the Mother Goddess. The latter, the feminist witches, are among the newest and most outspoken members of the neopagan revival.

Environmental Response. Many of those interviewed said that neopaganism was a response to a planet in crisis. Almost all the pagan traditions emphasize reverence for nature. Many witches consider the Craft a repository of survival skills, both psychic and physical (like the things one might be taught in an Outward Bound camp). Other pagans told me that a revival of animism was needed to counter the forces destroying the natural world.[11]

Freedom. Another unexpected answer. The Frosts, who run one of the largest witchcraft correspondence courses in the country, described the Craft as "religion without the middleman." Many people said that they had become pagans because they could be themselves and act as they chose, without what they felt were medieval notions of sin and guilt. Others wanted to participate in rituals rather than observe them. The leader of the Georgian tradition, a Craft tradition with a dozen covens in the United States, told me that freedom was his prime reason for making an independent religious decision.

This last reason seemed most remarkable. The freedom that is characteristic of the neopagan resurgence sets the movement far apart from most of the new religions of the 1960s and 1970s. How is this freedom possible? Why have these groups refused to succumb to rigid hierarchies and institutionalization? And how is it possible for them to exist in relative harmony, in spite of their different rituals and deities? These groups can exist this way because the neopagan religious framework is based on a polytheistic outlook—a view that allows differing perspectives and ideas to coexist.

NOTES

1. Among those books influencing my childhood were: Caroline Dale Snedeker, *The Spartan* (or *The Coward of Thermopylae*) (New York: Doubleday, 1911) and *The Perilous Seat* (New York: Doubleday, 1923); Mary Renault, *The King Must Die* (New York: Pantheon, 1958).
2. For an understanding of Star Trek literature, see J. Lichtenberg, S. Marshak, and J. Winston, *Star Trek Lives* (New York: Bantam, 1975); see also spin-off Star Trek myths written by fans in Jacquelin Lichtenberg, *Kraith Collected*, vol. I, and issues of Babel, a "Trekie" fan magazine.
3. The famous "opium of the people" quote is almost never given in full. My favourite translation is in Christopher Caudwell, *Further Studies in a Dying Culture* (London: The Bodley Head, 1949), 75–76: "Religious misery is at once the expression of real misery and a protest against that misery. Religion is the sigh of the hard pressed creature, the heart of a heartless world, the spirit of unspiritual conditions. It is the opium of the people." For a more accessible version, see Karl Marx, *Selected Writings in Sociology and Social Philosophy*, translated by T.B. Bottomore (New York: McGraw-Hill, 1964), 27.
4. John McPhee, *Encounters with the Archdruid* (New York: Farrar, Straus and Giroux, 1971), 84, 95.
5. Arnold Toynbee, "The Religious Background of the Present Environmental Crisis," *International journal of Environmental Studies* III (1972). Also published under the title "The Genesis of Pollution," in *Horizon* XV, no. 3 (Summer 1973): 4–9.
6. Lynn White, Jr., "The Historical Roots of Our Ecologic Crisis," *Science* 155 (March 10, 1967): 1203–1207. Also in *The Environmental Handbook*, edited by Garrett de Bell (New York: Ballantine, 1970), 12–26. Quotations on 19 and 20.
7. See "An Interview with Doris and Sylvester [Vic] Stuart," *Earth Religion News* 1, no. 4 (1974): 23–25.
8. Published versions of this ritual—often called *The Charge of the Goddess*—can be found in *The Grimoire of Lady Sheba* (St. Paul: Llewellyn, 1972), 145–147, and in Stewart Farrar, *What Witches Do* (New York: Coward, McCann & Geoghegan, 1971), 193–194. The version on the Stuarts' tape that I heard was written by neopagan writer Ed Fitch.

9. This attitude toward *belief* is actually not uncommon among writers who treat "occult" subjects. For example, D. Arthur Kelly writes in "Theories of Knowledge and the I Ching," "I cannot say that I 'believe' in the I Ching; rather, I would say that I have learnt a great deal about life and the universe from a contemplation of its 'teachings'" (*Gnostica* IV, no. 5 [January 1975]: 33).
10. Robert S. Ellwood, Jr., *Religious and Spiritual Groups in Modern America* (Englewood Cliffs: Prentice-Hall, 1973), 189.

11. In "An Interview with Doris and Sylvester Stuart," 24, Sylvester Stuart observes, "I see Wicca as the only hope of the survivors of mankind after there has been a complete breakdown in our present type of society, a breakdown which I see coming in the forseeable future." Stuart said he saw the Craft as a repository for survival skills.

CHAPTER 5

Why Women Need the Goddess: Phenomenological, Psychological, and Political Reflections

Carol P. Christ

At the close of Ntosake Shange's stupendously successful Broadway play *For Colored Girls Who Have Considered Suicide When the Rainbow Is Enuf*, a tall, beautiful Black woman rises from despair to cry out, "I found God in myself and I loved her fiercely."[1] Her discovery is echoed by women around the country who meet spontaneously in small groups on full moons, solstices, and equinoxes to celebrate the Goddess as symbol of life and death powers and waxing and waning energies in the universe and in themselves.[2]

> It is the night of the full moon. Nine women stand in a circle, on a rocky hill above the city. The western sky is rosy with the setting sun; in the east the moon's face begins to peer above the horizon.... The woman pours out a cup of wine onto the earth, refills it and

> raises it high. "Hail, Tana, Mother of mothers!" she cries. "Awaken from your long sleep, and return to your children again!"[3]

What are the political and psychological effects of this fierce new love of the divine in themselves for women whose spiritual experience has been focused by the male God of Judaism and Christianity? Is the spiritual dimension of feminism a passing diversion, an escape from difficult but necessary political work? Or does the emergence of the symbol of Goddess among women have significant political and psychological ramifications for the feminist movement?

To answer this question, we must first understand the importance of religious symbols and rituals in human life and consider the effect of male symbolism of God on women. According to anthropologist Clifford Geertz, religious symbols shape a cultural ethos, defining the deepest values of a society and the persons in it. "Religion," Geertz writes "is a system of symbols which act to produce powerful, pervasive, and long-lasting moods and motivations"[4] in the people of a given culture. A "mood" for Geertz is a psychological attitude such as awe, trust, and respect, while a "motivation" is the *social* and *political* trajectory created by a mood that transforms mythos into ethos, symbol system into social and political reality. Symbols have both psychological and political effects because they create the inner conditions (deep-seated attitudes and feelings) that lead people to feel comfortable with or to accept social and political arrangements that correspond to the symbol system.

Because religion has such a compelling hold on the deep psyches of so many people, feminists cannot afford to leave it in the hands of the fathers. Even people who no longer "believe in God" or participate in the institutional structure of patriarchal religion still may not be free of the power of the symbolism of God the Father. A symbol's effect does not depend on rational assent, for a symbol also functions on levels of the psyche other than the rational. Religion fulfills deep psychic needs by providing symbols and rituals that enable people to cope with limit situations[5] in human life (death, evil, suffering) and to pass through life's important transitions (birth, sexuality, death). Even people who consider themselves completely secularized will often find themselves sitting in a church or synagogue when a friend or relative gets married, or when a parent or friend has died. The symbols associated with these important rituals cannot fail to affect the deep or unconscious structures of the mind of even a person who has rejected these symbolisms on a conscious level—especially if the person is under stress. The reason for the continuing effect of religious symbols is that the mind abhors a vacuum. Symbol systems cannot simply be rejected, they must be replaced. Where there is not any replacement, the mind will revert to familiar structures at times of crisis, bafflement, or defeat.

Religions centred on the worship of a male God create "moods" and "motivations" that keep women in a state of psychological dependence on men and male authority, while at the same legitimating the *political* and *social* authority of fathers and sons in the institutions of society.

Religious symbol systems focused around exclusively male images of divinity create the impression that female power can never be fully legitimate or wholly beneficent. This message need never be explicitly stated (as, for example, it is in the story of Eve) for its effect to be felt. A woman completely ignorant of the myths of female evil in biblical religion nonetheless acknowledges the anomaly of female power when she prays exclusively to a male God. She may see herself as like God (created in the image of God) only by denying her own sexual identity and affirming God's transcendence of sexual identity. But she can never have the experience that is freely available to every man and boy in her culture, of having her full sexual identity affirmed as being in the image and likeness of God. In Geertz's terms, her "mood" is one of trust in male power as salvific and distrust of female power in herself and other women as inferior or dangerous. Such a powerful, pervasive, and long-lasting "mood" cannot fail to become a "motivation" that translates into social and political reality.

In *Beyond God the Father*, feminist theologian Mary Daly detailed the psychological and political ramifications of father religion for women. "If God in 'his' heaven is a father ruling his people," she wrote, "then it is the 'nature' of things and according to divine plan and the order of the universe that society be male dominated. Within this context, a *mystification of roles* takes place: The husband dominating his wife represents God 'himself.' The images and values of a given society have been projected into the realm of dogmas and 'Articles of Faith,' and these in turn justify the social structures which have given rise to them and which sustain their plausibility."[6]

Philosopher Simone de Beauvoir was well aware of the function of patriarchal religion as legitimater of male power. As she wrote, "Man enjoys the great advantage of having a god endorse the code he writes; and since man exercises a sovereign authority over women it is especially fortunate that this authority has been vested in him by the Supreme Being. For the Jew, Mohammedans, and Christians, among others, man is Master by divine right; the fear of God will therefore repress any impulse to revolt in the downtrodden female."[7]

This brief discussion of the psychological and political effects of God religion puts us in an excellent position to begin to understand the significance of the symbol of Goddess for women. In discussing the meaning of the Goddess, my method will first be phenomenological. I will isolate a meaning of the symbol of the Goddess as it has emerged in the lives of contemporary women. I will then discuss its psychological and political significance by contrasting the "moods" and "motivations" engendered by Goddess symbols with those engendered by Christian symbolism. I will also correlate Goddess symbolism with themes that have emerged in the women's movement in order to show how Goddess symbolism undergirds and legitimates the concerns of the women's movement, much as God symbolism in Christianity undergirded the interests of men in patriarchy. I will discuss four aspects of Goddess symbolism here: the Goddess as affirmation of female power, the female body, the female will, and women's bonds and heritage. There are, of course, many other meanings of the Goddess that I will not discuss here.

The sources for the symbol of the Goddess in contemporary spirituality are traditions of Goddess worship and modern women's experience. The ancient Mediterranean, pre-Christian European, Native American, Mesoamerican, Hindu, African, and other traditions are rich sources for Goddess symbolism. But these traditions are filtered through modern women's experiences. Traditions of Goddesses, subordination to gods, for example, are ignored. Ancient traditions are tapped selectively and eclectically, but they are not considered authoritative for modern consciousness. The Goddess symbol has emerged spontaneously in the dreams, fantasies, and thoughts of many women around the country in the past several years. Kirsten Grimstad and Susan Rennie reported that they were surprised to discover widespread interest in spirituality, including the Goddess, among feminists around the country in the summer of 1974.[8] *WomanSpirit* magazine, which published its first issue in 1974 and has contributors from across the United States, has expressed the grassroots nature of the women's spirituality movement. In 1976, a journal, *Lady Unique*, devoted to the Goddess emerged. In 1975, the first women's spirituality conference was held in Boston and attended by 1,800 women. In 1978, a University of Santa Cruz course on the Goddess drew over 500 people. Sources for this essay are these manifestations of the Goddess in modern women's experiences as reported in *WomanSpirit*, *Lady Unique*, and elsewhere, and as expressed in conversations I have had with women who have been thinking about the Goddess and women's spirituality.

The simplest and most basic meaning of the symbol of Goddess is the acknowledgment of the legitimacy of female power as a beneficient and independent power. A woman who echoes Ntosake Shange's dramatic statement, "I found God in myself and I loved her fiercely," is saying "Female power is strong and creative." She is saying that the divine principle, the saving and sustaining power, is in herself, that she will no longer look to men or male figures as saviours. The strength and independence of female power can be intuited by contemplating ancient and modern images of the Goddess. This meaning of the symbol of Goddess is simple and obvious, and yet it is difficult for many to comprehend. It stands in sharp contrast to the paradigms of female dependence on males that have been predominant in Western religion and culture. The internationally acclaimed novelist Monique Wittig captured the novelty and flavour of the affirmation of female power when she wrote, in her mythic work *Les Guerilleres*,

> There was a time when you were not a slave, remember that. You walked alone, full of laughter, you bathed bare-bellied. You say you have lost all recollection of it, remember ... you say there are no words to describe it, you say it does not exist. But remember. Make an effort to remember. Or, failing that, invent.[9]

While Wittig does not speak directly of the Goddess here, she captures the "mood" of joyous celebration of female freedom and independence that is created in women who define their identities through the symbol of Goddess. Artist Mary Beth Edelson expressed the political "motivations" inspired by the Goddess when she wrote,

> The ascending archetypal symbols of the feminine unfold today in the psyche of modern Every woman. They encompass the multiple forms of the Great Goddess. Reaching across the centuries we take the hands of our Ancient Sisters. The Great Goddess alive and well is rising to announce to the patriarchs that their 5,000 years are up—Hallelujah! Here we come.[10]

The affirmation of female power contained in the Goddess symbol has both psychological and political consequences. Psychologically, it means the defeat of the view engendered by patriarchy that women's power is inferior and dangerous. This new "mood" of affirmation of female power also leads to new "motivations"; it supports and undergirds women's trust in their own power and the power of other women in family and society.

If the simplest meaning of the Goddess symbol is an affirmation of the legitimacy and beneficience of female power, then a question immediately arises, "Is the Goddess simply female power writ large, and if so, why bother with the symbol of Goddess at all? Or does the symbol refer to a Goddess 'out there' who is not reducible to a human potential?" The many women who have rediscovered the power of Goddess would give three answers to this question: (1) The Goddess is divine female, a personification who can be invoked in prayer and ritual; (2) the Goddess is symbol of the life, death, and rebirth energy in nature and culture, in personal and communal life, and (3) the Goddess is symbol of the affirmation of the legitimacy and beauty of female power (made possible by the new becoming of women in the women's liberation movement). If one were to ask these women which answer is the "correct" one, different responses would be given. Some would assert that the Goddess definitely is not "out there," that the symbol of a divinity "out there" is part of the legacy of patriarchal oppression, which brings with it the authoritarianism, hierarchicalism, and dogmatic rigidity associated with biblical monotheistic religions. They might assert that the Goddess symbol reflects the sacred power within women and nature, suggesting the connectedness between women's cycles of menstruation, birth, and menopause, and the life and death cycles of the universe. Others seem quite comfortable with the notion of Goddess as a divine female protector and creator and would find their experience of Goddess limited by the assertion that she is not also out there as well as within themselves and in all natural processes. When asked what the symbol of Goddess means, feminist priestess Starhawk replied, "It all depends on how I feel. When I feel weak, she is someone who can help and protect me. When I feel strong, she is the symbol of my own power. At other times I feel her as the natural energy in my body and the world."[11] How are we to evaluate such a statement? Theologians might call these the words of a sloppy thinker. But my deepest intuition tells me they contain a wisdom that Western theological thought has lost.

To theologians, these differing views of the "meaning" of the symbol of Goddess might seem to threaten a replay of the trinitarian controversies. Is there, perhaps, a way of doing theology that would not lead immediately into dogmatic controversy, which would not require theologians to say definitively that one understanding is true and the others are false? Could people's relation to a common symbol be made primary and varying interpretations be acknowledged? The diversity of explications of the meaning of the Goddess symbol suggests that symbols have a richer significance than any explications of their meaning can express, a point literary critics have long insisted on. This phenomenological fact suggests that theologians may need to give more than lip service to a theory of symbol in which the symbol is viewed as the primary fact and the meanings are viewed as secondary. It also suggests that a *thea*logy[12] of the Goddess would be very different from the *theo*logy we have known in the West. But to spell out this notion of the primacy of *symbol* in thealogy in contrast to the primacy of the *explanation* in theology would be the topic of another paper. Let me simply state that women, who have been deprived of a female religious symbol system for centuries, are therefore in an excellent position to recognize the power and primacy of symbols. I believe women must develop a theory of symbol and thealogy congruent with their experience at the same time as they "remember and invent" new symbol systems.

A second important implication of the Goddess symbol for women is the affirmation of the female body and the life cycle expressed in it. Because of women's unique position as menstruants, birthgivers, and those who have traditionally cared for the young and the dying, women's connection to the body, nature, and this world has been obvious. Women were denigrated because they seemed more carnal, fleshy, and earthy than the culture-creating males.[13] The misogynist antibody tradition in Western thought is symbolized in the myth of Eve who is traditionally viewed as a sexual temptress, the epitome of women's carnal nature. This tradition reaches its nadir in the *Malleus Maleficarum* (*The Hammer of Evil-Doing Women*), which states, "All witchcraft stems from carnal lust, which in women is insatiable."[14] The Virgin Mary, the positive female image in Christianity, does not contradict Christian denigration of the female body and its powers. The Virgin Mary is revered because she, in her perpetual virginity, transcends the carnal sexuality attributed to most women.

The denigration of the female body is expressed in cultural and religious taboos surrounding menstruation, childbirth, and menopause in women. While menstruation taboos may have originated in a perception of the awesome powers of the female body,[15] they degenerated into a simple perception that there is something "wrong" with female bodily functions. Menstruating women were forbidden to enter the sanctuary in ancient Hebrew and pre-modern Christian communities. Although only Orthodox Jews still enforce religious taboos against menstruant women, few women in our culture grow up affirming their menstruation as a connection to sacred power. Most women learn that menstruation is a curse and grow up believing that the bloody facts of menstruation are best hidden away. Feminists challenge this attitude to the female body. Judy Chicago's art piece "Menstruation Bathroom" broke these menstrual taboos. In a sterile white bathroom, she exhibited boxes of Tampax and Kotex on an open shelf, and the wastepaper basket was overflowing with bloody tampons and sanitary napkins.[16] Many women who viewed the piece felt relieved to have their "dirty secret" out in the open.

The denigration of the female body and its powers is further expressed in Western culture's attitudes toward childbirth.[17] Religious iconography does not celebrate the birthgiver, and there is no theology or ritual that enables a woman to celebrate the process of birth as a spiritual experience. Indeed, Jewish and Christian traditions also had blood taboos concerning the woman who had recently given birth. While these religious taboos are rarely enforced today (again, only by Orthodox Jews), they have secular equivalents. Giving birth is treated as a disease requiring hospitalization, and the woman is viewed as a passive object, anesthetized to ensure her acquiescence to the will of the doctor. The women's liberation movement has challenged these cultural attitudes, and many feminists have joined with advocates of natural childbirth and home birth in emphasizing the need for women to control and take pride in their bodies, including the birth process.

Western culture also gives little dignity to the post-menopausal or aging woman. It is no secret that our culture is based on a denial of aging and death, and that women suffer more severely from this denial than men. Women are placed on a pedestal and considered powerful when they are young and beautiful, but they are said to lose this power as they age. As feminists have pointed out, the "power" of the young woman is illusory, since beauty standards are defined by men, and since few women are considered (or consider themselves) beautiful for more than a few years of their lives. Some men are viewed as wise and authoritative in age, but old women are pitied and shunned. Religious iconography supports this cultural attitude toward aging women. The purity and virginity of Mary and the female saints is often expressed in the iconographic convention of perpetual youth. Moreover, religious mythology associates aging women with evil in the symbol of the wicked old witch. Feminists have challenged cultural myths of aging women and have urged women to reject patriarchal beauty standards and to celebrate the distinctive beauty of women of all ages.

The symbol of Goddess aids the process of naming and reclaiming the female body and its cycles and processes. In the ancient world and among modern women, the Goddess symbol represents the birth, death, and rebirth processes of the natural and human worlds. The female body is viewed as the direct incarnation of waxing and waning, life and death, cycles in the universe. This is sometimes expressed through the symbolic connection between the 28-day cycles of menstruation and the 28-day cycles of the moon. Moreover, the Goddess is celebrated in the triple aspect of youth, maturity, and age, or maiden, mother, and crone. The potentiality of the young girl is celebrated in the nymph or maiden aspect of the Goddess. The Goddess as mother is sometimes depicted giving birth, and giving birth is viewed as a symbol for all the creative, life-giving powers of the universe.[18] The life-giving powers of the Goddess in her creative aspect are not limited to physical birth, for the Goddess is also seen as the creator of all the arts of civilization, including healing, writing, and the giving of just law. Women in the middle of life who are not physical mothers may give birth to poems, songs, and books, or nurture other women, men, and children. They too are incarnations of the Goddess in her creative, life-giving aspect. At the end of life, women incarnate the crone aspect of the Goddess. The wise old woman, the woman who knows from experience what life is about, the woman whose closeness to her own death gives her a distance and perspective on the problems of life, is celebrated as the third aspect of the Goddess. Thus, women learn to value youth, creativity, and wisdom in themselves and other women.

The possibilities of reclaiming the female body and its cycles have been expressed in a number of Goddess-centred rituals. Hallie Mountainwing and Barby My Own created a summer solstice ritual to celebrate menstruation and birth. The women simulated a birth canal and birthed each other into their circle. They raised power by placing their hands on each other's bellies and chanting together. Finally they marked each other's faces with rich, dark menstrual blood saying, "This is the blood that promises renewal. This is the blood that promises sustenance. This is the blood that promises life."[19] From hidden dirty secret to symbol of the life power of the Goddess, women's blood has come full circle. Other women have created rituals that celebrate the crone aspect of the Goddess. Z. Budapest believes that the crone aspect of the Goddess is predominant in the fall, especially at Halloween, an ancient holiday. On this day, the wisdom of the old woman is celebrated, and it is also recognized that the old must die so that the new can be born.

The "mood" created by the symbol of the Goddess in triple aspect is one of positive, joyful affirmation of the female body and its cycles and acceptance of aging and death as well as life. The "motivations" are to overcome menstrual taboos, to return the birth process to the hands of women, and to change cultural attitudes about age and death. Changing cultural attitudes toward the female body could go a long way toward overcoming the spirit-flesh, mind-body dualisms of Western culture, since, as Ruether has pointed out, the denigration of the female body is at the heart of these dualisms. The Goddess as symbol of the revaluation of the body and nature thus also undergirds the human potential and ecology movements. The "mood" is one of affirmation, awe, and respect for the body and nature, and the "motivation" is to respect the teachings of the body and the rights of all living beings.

A third important implication of the Goddess symbol for women is the positive valuation of will in a Goddess-centred ritual, especially in Goddess-centred ritual magic and spell-casting in womanspirit and feminist witchcraft circles. The basic notion behind ritual magic and spell-casting is energy as power. Here the Goddess is a centre or focus of power and energy; she is the personification of the energy that flows between beings in the natural and human worlds. In Goddess circles, energy is raised by chanting or dancing. According to Starhawk, "Witches conceive of psychic energy as having form and substance that can be perceived and directed by those with a trained awareness. The power generated within the circle is built into a cone form, and at its peak is released—to the Goddess, to reenergize the members of the coven, or to do a specific work such as healing."[20] In ritual magic, the energy raised is directed by willpower. Women who celebrate in Goddess circles believe they can achieve their wills in the world.

The emphasis on the will is important for women because women traditionally have been taught to devalue their wills, to believe that they cannot achieve their will through their own power, and even to suspect that the assertion of will is evil. Faith Wildung's poem "Waiting," from which I will quote only a short segment, sums up women's sense that their lives are defined not by their own will, but by waiting for others to take the initiative.

Waiting for my breasts to develop
Waiting to wear a bra
Waiting to menstruate

Waiting for life to begin, Waiting—
Waiting to be somebody

Waiting to get married
Waiting for my wedding day
Waiting for my wedding night

Waiting for the end of the day
Waiting for sleep.
Waiting ...[21]

Patriarchal religion has enforced the view that female initiative and will are evil through the juxtaposition of Eve and Mary. Eve caused the fall by asserting her will against the command of God, while Mary began the new age with her response to God's initiative, "Let it be done to me according to thy word" (Luke 1:38). Even for men, patriarchal religion values the passive will subordinate to divine initiative. The classical doctrines of sin and grace view sin as the prideful assertion of will and grace as the obedient subordination of the human will to the divine initiative or order. While this view of will might be questioned from a human perspective, Valerie Saiving has argued that it has particularly deleterious consequences for women in Western culture. According to Saiving, Western culture encourages males in the assertion of will, and thus it may make some sense to view the male form of sin as an excess of will. But since culture discourages females in the assertion of will, the traditional doctrines of sin and grace encourage women to remain in their form of sin, which is self-negation or insufficient assertion of will.[22] One possible reason the will is denigrated in a patriarchal religious framework is that both human and divine will are often pictured as arbitrary, self-initiated, and exercised without regard for other wills.

In a Goddess-centred context, in contrast, the will is valued. *A woman is encouraged to know her will, to believe that her will is valid, and to believe that her will can be achieved in the world*, three powers traditionally denied to her in patriarchy. In a Goddess-centred framework, a woman's will is not subordinated to the Lord God as king and ruler, nor to men as his representatives. Thus a woman is not reduced to waiting and acquiescing in the wills of others as she is in patriarchy. But neither does she adopt the egocentric form of will that pursues self-interest without regard for the interests of others.

The Goddess-centred context provides a different understanding of the will than that available in the traditional patriarchal religious framework. In the Goddess framework, will can be achieved only when it is exercised in harmony with the energies and wills of other beings. Wise women, for example, raise a cone of healing energy at the full moon or solstice when the lunar or solar energies are at their high points with respect to the earth. This discipline encourages them to recognize that not all times are propitious for the achieving of every will. Similarly, they know that spring is a time for new beginnings in work and love, summer a time for producing external manifestations of inner potentialities, and fall or winter times for stripping down to the inner core and extending roots. Such awareness of waxing and waning processes in the universe discourages arbitrary egocentred assertion of will, while at the same time encouraging the assertion of individual will in co-operation with natural energies and the energies created by the wills of others. Wise women also have a tradition that whatever is sent out will be returned and this reminds them to assert their wills in co-operative and healing rather than egocentric and destructive ways. This view of will allows women to begin to recognize, claim, and assert their wills without adopting the worst characteristics of the patriarchal understanding and use of will. In the Goddess-centred framework, the "mood" is one of positive affirmation of personal will in the context of the energies of other wills or beings. The "motivation" is for women to know and assert their wills in co-operation with other wills and energies. This of course does not mean that women always assert their wills in positive and life-affirming ways. Women's capacity for evil is, of course, as great as men's. My purpose is simply to contrast the differing attitudes toward the exercise of will per se, and the female will in particular, in Goddess-centred religion and in the Christian God-centred religion.

The fourth and final aspect of Goddess symbolism that I will discuss here is the significance of the Goddess for a revaluation of woman's bonds and heritage. As Virginia Woolf has said, "Chloe liked Olivia"; a statement about a woman's relation to another woman is a sentence that rarely occurs in fiction. Men have written the stories, and they have written about women almost exclusively in their relations to men.[23] The celebrations of women's bonds to each other, as mothers and daughters, as colleagues and coworkers, as sisters, friends, and lovers, is beginning to occur in the new literature and culture created by women in the women's movement. While I believe that the revaluing of each of these bonds is important, I will focus on the mother-daughter bond, in part because I believe it may be the key to the others.

Adrienne Rich has pointed out that the mother-daughter bond, perhaps the most important of woman's bonds, "resonant with charges ... the flow of energy between two biologically alike bodies, one of which has lain in amniotic bliss inside the other, one of which has labored to give birth to the other,"[24] is rarely celebrated in patriarchal religion and culture. Christianity celebrates the father's relation to the son and the mother's relation to the son, but the story of mother and daughter is missing. So, too, in patriarchal literature and psychology the mothers and the daughters rarely exist. Volumes have been written about the Oedipal complex, but little has been written about the girl's relation to her mother. Moreover, as de Beauvoir has noted, the mother-daughter relation is distorted in patriarchy because the mother must give her daughter over to men in a male-defined culture in which women are viewed as inferior. The mother must socialize her daughter to become subordinate to men, and if her daughter challenges patriarchal norms, the mother is likely to defend the patriarchal structures against her own daughter.[25]

These patterns are changing in the new culture created by women in which the bonds of women to women are beginning to be celebrated. Holly Near has written several songs that celebrate women's bonds and women's heritage. In one of her finest songs she writes of an "old-time woman" who is "waiting to die." A young woman feels for the life that has passed the old woman by and begins to cry, but the old woman looks her in the eye and says, "If I had not suffered, you wouldn't be wearing those jeans / Being an old-time woman ain't as bad as it seems."[26] This song, which Near has said was inspired by her grandmother, expresses and celebrates a bond and a heritage passed down from one woman to another. In another of Near's songs, she sings of "a hiking-boot mother who's seeing the world / For the first time with her own little girl." In this song, the mother tells the drifter who has been travelling with her to pack up and travel alone if he thinks "traveling three is a drag" because "I've got a little one who loves me as much as you need me / And darling, that's loving enough."[27] This song is significant because the mother places her relationship to her daughter above her relationship to a man, something women rarely do in patriarchy.[28]

Almost the only story of mothers and daughters that has been transmitted in Western culture is the myth of Demeter and Persephone, which was the basis of religious rites celebrated by women only, the Thesmophoria, and later formed the basis of the Eleusian mysteries, which were open to all who spoke Greek. In this story, the daughter, Persephone, is raped away from her mother, Demeter, by the god of the underworld. Unwilling to accept this state of affairs, Demeter rages and withholds fertility from the earth until her daughter is returned to her. What is important for women in this story is that a mother fights for her daughter and for her relation to her daughter. This is completely different from the mother's relation to her daughter in patriarchy. The "mood" created by the story of Demeter and Persephone is one of celebration of the mother-daughter bond, and the "motivation" is for mothers and daughters to affirm the heritage passed on from mother to daughter and to reject the patriarchal pattern where the primary loyalties of mother and daughter must be to men.

The symbol of Goddess has much to offer women who are struggling to be rid of the "powerful, pervasive, and long-lasting moods and motivations" of devaluation of female power, denigration of the female body, distrust of female will, and denial of the women's bonds and heritage that have been engendered by patriarchal religion. As women struggle to create a new culture in which women's power, bodies, will, and bonds are celebrated, it seems natural that the Goddess would re-emerge as symbol of the newfound beauty, strength, and power of women.

NOTES

1. From the original cast album, Buddah Records, 1976.
2. See Susan Rennie and Kristen Grimstad, "Spiritual Explorations Cross-Country," *Quest* I, no. 4 (1975): 49–51; and *WomanSpirit* magazine.
3. See Starhawk, "Witchcraft and Women's Culture," [...].
4. Geertz, "Religion as a Cultural System," in William L. Lessa and Evon V. Vogt, eds., *Reader in Comparative Religion*, 2nd ed. (New York: Harper & Row, 1972), 206.
5. Geertz, p. 210.
6. Mary Daly, *Beyond God the Father* (Boston: Beacon Press, 1974), 13; italics added.
7. Simone de Beauvoir, *The Second Sex*, translated by H.M. Parshleys (New York: Alfred A. Knopf, 1953).
8. See Rennie and Grimstad.
9. *Les Guerilleres*, translated by David LeVay (New York: Avon Books, 1971), 89. Also quoted in Morgan MacFarland, "Witchcraft: The Art of Remembering," *Quest* 7, no. 4 (1975): 41.
10. "Speaking for Myself," *Lady Unique* I (1976): 56.
11. Personal communication.
12. A term coined by Naomi Goldenberg to refer to reflection on the meaning of the symbol of Goddess.
13. This theory of the origins of the Western dualism is stated by Rosemary Ruether in *New Woman: New Earth* (New York: Seabury Press, 1975), and elsewhere.
14. Heinrich Kramer and Jacob Sprenger, *Malleus Maleficarum* (New York: Dover, 1971), 47.
15. See Rita M. Gross, "Menstruation and Childbirth as Ritual and Religious Experience in the Religion of the Australian Aborigines," *The Journal of the American Academy of Religion* 45, no. 4, Supplement (1977): 1147–1181.
16. Judy Chicago, *Through the Flower* (New York: Doubleday & Company, 1975), plate 4, 106–107.
17. See Adrienne Rich, *Of Woman Born* (New York: Bantam Books, 1977), chapters 6 and 7.

18. See James Mellaart, *Earliest Civilizations of the Near East* (New York: McGraw-Hill, 1965), 92.
19. Barbry My Own, "Ursa Maior: Menstrual Moon Celebration," in *Moon, Moon*, edited by Anne Kent Rush (Berkeley and New York: Moon Books and Random House, 1976), 374–387.
20. Starhawk, *The Spiral Dance: The Rebirth of the Ancient Religion of the Great Goddess* (San Francisco: Harper & Row Publishers, 1979).
21. In Chicago, *Through the Flower*, 213–217.
22. Valerie Saiving, "The Human Situation: A Feminine View," *Journal of Religion* 40 (1960): 100–112, [...].
23. Virgina Woolf, *A Room of One's Own* (New York: Harcourt Brace Jovanovich, 1928), 86.
24. Rich, *Of Woman Born*, 226.
25. De Beauvoir, 448–449.
26. "Old Time Woman," lyrics by Jeffrey Langley and Holly Near, from *Holly Near: A Live Album*, Redwood Records, 1974.
27. "Started Out Fine" by Holly Near from *Holly Near: A Live Album.*
28. Rich, *Of Woman Born*, 223.

QUESTIONS FOR CRITICAL THOUGHT

Chapter 1: Valiente

1. What does the Goddess, as presented here by Valiente, enjoin people to do? Are these activities that are customarily singled out in other religions?
2. What sorts of words and phrases are applied to the Goddess in this piece? How do these compare with the descriptions applied to other deities with whom you are familiar?
3. Witchcraft has come, over time, to be identified by some as a "women's religion." Is there any sense in Valiente's *Charge* that the Goddess is speaking only to women, or especially to women?

Chapter 2: Starhawk

1. Compare Starhawk's creation story to the account of creation in Genesis. How do the images and the language used differ?
2. In what ways does Starhawk's creation narrative challenge the foundation of patriarchy?
3. How does Starhawk characterize the relationship between the God and the Goddess? What might this imply about relationships between men and women?
4. In the narrative "The Goddess in the Kingdom of Death," there are strong echoes of Valiente's *The Charge of the Goddess*, a piece known to have been written in the twentieth century. Yet, she calls it "traditional." What does this imply about the meaning of tradition in neopaganism?
5. What answer does "The Goddess in the Kingdom of Death" offer to the question "What happens to us after we die?"

Chapter 3: Fox

1. Fox presents her description of her own spirituality as a counterpoint to her perception of mainstream religion. What characteristics does she implicitly attribute to mainstream religions?
2. Fox wrote this piece in the early 1980s. Are there statements here that you believe are more widely acknowledged in mainstream discourse now than they would have been then? Are there elements that are no longer as relevant as they might once have been?

3. Statements of belief, such as Fox's, must be acted upon in order to create the desired changes in the world. What sorts of activities might support the values Fox articulates?

Chapter 4: Adler

1. Adler presents neopaganism as non-dogmatic, a religion that does not require a uniform set of beliefs of its adherents. If not beliefs, then what else is there around which this religion could coalesce?
2. How does Adler link the environmental movement and the neopagan movement?
3. If Adler and Harlow's experiences are not conversion, what are they? What does this denial imply about what Adler thinks conversion is like?

Chapter 5: Christ

1. Christ explicitly discusses four types of affirmations that Goddess symbolism offers to women, while acknowledging that there are other meanings of the Goddess that she does not discuss. What might these be?
2. This essay discusses why women, in particular, need the Goddess. Do men need the Goddess? Why or why not?
3. Christ emphasizes that women need to develop a positive and affirming relationship to their bodies as a counter to the anti-body theologies of Christianity and Judaism. While this may create a psychological benefit for women, it still leaves them more identified with physicality than men are. Is this an adequate antidote to patriarchal narratives of the body? Why or why not?
4. Is it sufficient for individual women to embrace the Goddess in order to produce the reorientation of values that Christ suggests is possible, or would it require some kind of institutional legitimation by the broader society? If so, how might that be achieved?

SUGGESTED READING

Cunningham, Scott. 1988. *Wicca: A Guide for the Solitary Practitioner.* St. Paul: Llewellyn.

From the late 1980s to the late 1990s, this was the handbook of North American eclectic witchcraft, especially among solitaries. Cunningham takes a bottom-up approach to constructing your own witchcraft practice, rather than following the apprenticeship pattern that characterizes British witchcraft. A less stridently feminist, less activist, discovery-based witchcraft than Starhawk's.

Farrar, Janet, and Stewart Farrar. 1984. *The Witches' Way: Principals, Rituals and Beliefs of Modern Witchcraft*. London: Robert Hale.

Sometimes packaged with the Farrar's 1981 book *Eight Sabbats for Witches* as *A Witches' Bible Complete*, this book gives a practical and theoretical elaboration of many of witchcraft's key tenets, including magic and reincarnation. It also provides the text of the initiation rituals at each of the three degrees, and rituals to celebrate rites of passages, such as menarche, handfasting, and the birth of a child.

Matthews, Caitlín, ed. 1990. *Voices of the Goddess*. Wellingborough: The Aquarian Press.

A collection of essays, written by practitioners of a variety of pagan paths, that express the multiple meanings and diverse interpretations of what it is to worship the Goddess in a modern world.

Stone, Merlin. 1976. *When God Was a Woman*. New York: Dorset.

This feminist reinterpretation of Paleolithic and Neolithic archaeological finds inspired second wave feminists to re-embrace the idea of the great Goddess, first popularized in the Romantic period by folklorists. The great Goddess, and her allegedly peaceful matriarchal societies, gave women the sense that if they had once been powerful, they could be so again.

Valiente, Doreen. 1989. *The Rebirth of Witchcraft*. London: Robert Hale.

This is Valiente's own account of the early years of modern British witchcraft, including her opinions about the origins of some of Gerald Gardner's materials. Interesting for those with a historical curiosity, especially if read alongside of Aidan Kelly's *Crafting the Art of Magic*, and Ronald Hutton's *The Triumph of the Moon*.

GLOSSARY

Animism: The belief that natural objects and phenomena have indwelling spirits, souls, or consciousness.

Archetype: A term derived from Jungian psychology meaning the primal patterns that are embedded in the collective unconscious and emerge in cultural symbolism and representations to characterize experience. Culturally significant images or themes. An archetype is what is left of a given representation when you have stripped all of the culturally specific elements from it. For example, a story similar to Cinderella exists in many cultures, but the specifics of the narrative differ.

Misogyny: Hatred of women. Social structures and ideologies that construct women as intrinsically inferior to men are considered by feminist theorists to be misogynist.

Phenomenology: A form of study that takes phenomena as they appear in our conscious experience, and tries to extract from it the essential characteristics of that experience. Phenomenology tends to move from the specific to the universal.

Weltanschauug: German. Used in English to mean world view. The basic framework through which all experience is interpreted.

PART II
Introduction to Nature or Earth Religions

What are the characteristics that set paganism apart from Western mainstream religions? Most people will immediately seize upon the belief in the possibility of "magic," although the importance of magic varies both within and between pagan traditions. Far more fundamental is the orientation to locating "the spiritual" within the world (immanently), rather than outside of it (transcendently). Pagans orient their mythologies and celebrations toward the cycles of the living world, even when most of them live in urban environments far removed from the agricultural symbolism that informs their sacred narratives and from the actual geographies in which they are rooted.

This section opens with Sara Pike's descriptive account of arriving at a festival. Festivals are significant in modern paganism because they provide a temporary venue in which one can immerse oneself in a wholly pagan environment. As a minority spirituality, and a poorly understood one at that, there are many aspects of practitioners' pagan identities and practices that are concealed or spoken of only in hushed tones in their daily lives. Most festivals are also ecumenical; they welcome adherents of all pagan paths, and even the pagan-curious, so long as they abide by the festival's rules and are not disruptive. Festivals can provide a place to meet new friends, renew old acquaintances, network, share knowledge, swap songs and chants, and to re-energize oneself spiritually.

Why is this narrative placed at the beginning of the "nature religion" section of this book? Because it provides a vivid contrast between the pagan discourse around nature—which tends to be wild, pristine nature in North America, and pastoral countryside in Britain—and the reality of most pagans' personal encounters with nature. Paganism, in the twenty-first century, is a primarily urban phenomenon. While many festivals require attendees to camp, there is a sizable contingent of regular festival goers who interpret that term very broadly, driving to their campsites and unloading elaborate camp kitchens, enormous tents, and inflatable furniture. The picture presented by Pike is not one that easily fits with the ideas evoked by the concept of "nature religion." It is offered as a backdrop and a counterpoint to the other two readings in this section.

In Chapter 7, Barbara Davy links contemporary paganism and both traditional and neo-shamanism through examining the extent to which they can be considered expressions of "nature religion." It is important to note that she is not trying to conflate paganism and shamanism. While both tend toward a mystical engagement with the "other-than-human world" and may have similarities in some rites of divination and prophesy (Asatru *seídhr* is a good example), shamanism is a practice within a broader religious and spiritual framework, while paganism is a religious framework that can, but does not necessarily, incorporate shamanic elements.

For Davy, one of the important similarities between these is that they are both performed in a non-institutionalized setting. There is no building that says "Church of Shamanism"—shamans operate as particular kinds of religious specialists whose role is defined as an integral part of the culture from which they come. Similarly, there is not a comprehensive "Church of Paganism." Although there is an increasing level of institutionalization across the movement, it is neither consistent nor monolithic. Mystical traditions tend to privilege experience over belief, and the incorporation of individual mystical experiences, in this case, the sense of mutual relationship between individuals and "other than human persons" in the "more than human world." Not only is "nature" the symbolic centre of these spiritual practices, it is also something worthy of the same moral consideration one would extend to another person. This arises out of the fact that both these systems are rooted in animism (see the Glossary in Part I). She concludes that while both paganism and shamanism are expressive of nature religion, they are not exhaustively defined by it, and there are important differences between the two groups. This article is an excellent source of references for further reading on shamanism and shamanic traditions.

Chapter 8 is the introduction to Michael York's book *Pagan Theology.* In this piece, York presents two main arguments. The first is a conceptualization of religion that allows the practices and spiritualities that will be discussed in Part III to clearly qualify. This is important because many of the ways in which religions have been studied in the past marginalize both neopaganism and indigenous tribal spiritualities as lesser forms of religion, or even as false or misguided religion—thus devaluing both the practices and the practitioners. York argues that, in our modern world, all forms of authority and authoritative pronouncements are being questioned. The authority of individuals to choose their own perspective on the world is thereby strengthened. York states that all religions are maps, guidelines for moving through a world characterized by particular features. Just as what is noted on a topographical map will be different from what is noted on a city ordinance map, York says, so the features emphasized in different religions will be different. He notes that all religions, nature religions included, specify a relationship between human beings and the material and non-material realms of experience, and all are legitimate to their adherents. York believes that religions specify a cosmology—a view of the world. Not all cosmologies are religious, but all religions embody cosmology.

York's second argument in this introduction is the one that is somewhat controversial among contemporary pagan practitioners and scholars, especially in North America. He suggests that it is less useful to study contemporary paganism as a subset of "Western religions," where this is taken to mean European Christianity and Judaism and their North American derivatives, than it would be to study these paganisms in a group with other indigenous paganisms. He notes that Christian missionaries, as one example, lumped all of the indigenous traditions they encountered together as "paganism," and he considers this an insight about the quality of these practices that scholars of contemporary paganism would do well to adopt. This makes some contemporary pagans uncomfortable because they have gone to some lengths to be viewed as different from other indigenous spiritualities, in part to prevent such as identification from being taken as a licence to appropriate practices from groups that have already suffered enormous damage from centuries of colonialism. Some pagans would argue that contemporary paganism is not an indigenous European tradition as much as it is trying to recapture the spirit of what indigenous European paganism might have been, had it survived aggressive Christianization. These tensions are seen particularly in the dialogue between Wiccans and reconstructionists. York's reply to the assertion that reconstructions are not authentically indigenous is that many spiritualities widely accepted as indigenous, such as many North American practices, are also reconstructions, and for the same reason—aggressive Christianization. The usefulness of York's idea here is one that will only be demonstrated through research undertaken from this premise, to see if it produces useful insights.

The essays included in this section introduce interesting comparisons, concepts, and arguments that form some of the theoretical backdrop of discussion about contemporary paganisms. They frame important questions such as: What does it mean to practitioners to be pagan? What is the relationship between contemporary paganism and other world religions? How does the focus on immanent sacrality shape paganism? And, in what ways, if any, can contemporary paganism be seen as "nature religion"? These are questions to which studies of contemporary paganism must be held accountable, and to which they must respond.

CHAPTER 6
We Cast Our Circles Where the Earth Mother Meets the Sky Father

Sarah Pike

The carved sign on the driveway reads "Lothlorien." This nature sanctuary amid the wooded hills and valleys of southern Indiana, a site for many neopagan festivals, takes its name from J.R.R. Tolkien's *Lord of the Rings*, a popular book among neopagans.[1] In his fantasy masterpiece, Tolkien named the enchanted land of the wise and ancient elves Lothlorien. On first encountering a Lothlorien festival in full swing, it seemed that neopagan festivals were a feast for the senses.

My first foray into the world of festivals was in May 1991, when I attended ELFest, an annual spring festival sponsored by the Elf Lore Family (ELF) at Lothlorien. The site was a convenient 45-minute drive from Bloomington, Indiana, where I was a graduate student at the time. Soft drum beats and notes from a flute mingled discordantly with the sounds of "flying saucer rock" as I walked through "Avalon," the main festival field. Clusters of colourful tents were set up under the canopy of trees.

Small campers and vans lined the circular gravel driveway. Festival goers were roaming informally around campsites, gathering at tables covered with books on witchcraft and long, hooded robes for sale or talking with and greeting friends. A woman who smelled of incense and roses and whose naked body was more than half covered with tattoos of flowers and dragons, smiled broadly at me. Two men wearing black leather boots and dark cloaks walked by, deep in conversation. Farther along the road, a young man with bronzed skin juggled balls as he talked to another man wrapped at the waist in a tie-dye cloth and carrying a rainbow-coloured parasol. The festival field was alive with music, quiet conversation, naked skin, and bodies adorned with costumes and elaborate jewellery. I passed an aura reader and merchants selling jewellery and crystals as I followed signs to Thunder Shrine, the dome-covered ritual circle where a group of drummers had gathered and a woman dressed in chain mail was dancing around the fire to an African beat. How does a place like this come to be, I wondered, and that is what I began asking my new festival acquaintances.

Of the festival sponsors that I am familiar with, ELF is typical in that it centres around two or three experienced spiritual leaders and relies on a core group of people to organize festivals and coordinate festival volunteers. These men and women are the ones who put in the long hours necessary to bring the festival into being, and in doing so are centrally important in creating the mood of a festival.[2] The Elf Lore Family, which organizes ELFest and Wild Magick, has fluctuated in structure over the years that I have been acquainted with it (1991–1996) but has generally functioned as a volunteer organization directed by a group of elders. ELF was founded by Terry Whitefeather and a small group of friends, who organized their first small festivals at state parks in southern Indiana. Because of ELF's growth and the difficulties involved with using state-owned public lands, Terry and his friends began looking for wooded land to purchase and in 1987 bought the land that would be named Lothlorien. During the years I attended ELF festivals, ELF was organized in hierarchical levels. The "elders" were the most powerful decision makers and generally had been active in the community for the longest time. They oversaw land use, festival planning, publicity, registration, publication of rules and guidelines, and festival security. They also dealt with conflicts that arose during festivals, such as a charge of sexual harassment that I will discuss later. ELF "clan" worked as "apprentices" to elders and helped with the various kinds of work necessary to run the festival, such as cleanup and security. Elders, clan, and other volunteers planned the festival program in advance by corresponding with men and women who wanted to conduct workshops and rituals. They also organized work crews that prepared the festival site in the weeks preceding festivals. During festivals, "parking trolls" directed off-loading and parking while other ELF clan members organized volunteers and registered incoming festival goers.

Festival planning begins months in advance when announcements are sent out and posted on neopagan organizations' Web sites, then circulated via e-mail by members of listservs and newsgroups. Calls are sent out seeking workshop presenters to submit their proposals; well-known neopagans are invited to be guests and sometimes offered a small stipend for their participation (most workshop presenters are not paid, although they receive free or discounted admission). Most festivals require that all participants contribute to the community in some way, from presenting workshops to emptying recycling containers. These jobs typically include registration, kitchen staff (when there is a kitchen), fire building, recycling crew, and first-aid assistance. Festival goers may barter longer work shifts in exchange for free admittance or discounted festival fees. Volunteer work crews clear and mark trails through the woods, set up recycling containers and toilets, rope off and mark ritual and workshop space, and collect firewood.

There is no neopagan governing body or central organization to set festival guidelines, and the variations between festival locations, workshop topics, and religious commitment can be striking. Nevertheless, most festivals follow an ordered pattern of activities, which include the following: opening ceremony; workshops scheduled in the mornings and afternoons; evening rituals and performances; late-night drumming and dancing, fire circles and coffeehouses; a community feast; and a closing ritual.

Festival goers often travel long distances, usually by car in order to carry camping supplies and costumes. Welcome centres and gateways are set up near festival entrances. On arrival, all participants go through a formal check-in procedure during which they pay festival fees, sign up for work shifts (four hours of "work sharing" at Pagan Spirit Gathering [PSG] is typical), pick up festival programs, and receive some kind of identification. At PSG 1994, all participants were given a "spirit bag," a necklace composed of a piece of yarn tied around a tiny cloth bag that held herbs, a stone, and a tiny crystal. The festival guide explained that "this special amulet is a symbol of the PSG community spirit.... It was assembled and blessed at the Earth Keeper's gathering held at Circle Sanctuary just prior to this year's PSG." These necklaces were to be worn at all times to identify festival goers and prevent outsiders from sneaking in, but they also served as a symbol of the festival that participants could take home with them. After checking in at the festival entrance, participants were directed to find a campsite. Campsites are occasionally set aside for groups of people with common interests or concerns, such as "family camping" or "12-step support camp," but usually festival goers camp with friends. Some people prefer to camp on the outskirts of the festival community, while others choose to pitch their tents near the late-night fire circle, where they can be sure to hear drumming all night long. Soon after arrival, festival goers change into their festival clothes and their neopagan jewellery or remove their clothes, and walk through the festival grounds looking for old friends.

Almost all neopagan festivals include an opening ceremony during which spirits and deities are called and requested to be present at the festival and to protect the festival space. The language of "community" is also invoked to remind festival participants that they are part of "the web of life," to borrow a metaphor from Rites of Spring 1997, where a web was woven by festival participants in the central festival field. Pantheacon 1997 started off with an opening ritual to "call in blessings upon this gathering of the tribes," according to the Pantheacon program.

Rituals of many kinds are included in a festival, ranging from small private ceremonies at campsites to large public rituals.[3] Rituals also take place within the festival workshops that are scheduled throughout the days of a festival. The Women's Healing Circle and the Grief Ritual were two of the workshop rituals at Rites of Spring 1997. Night is reserved for concerts, performances, dances, and large rituals. Although contests are rarely part of neopagan festivals, perhaps because they conflict with the egalitarian focus of festivals, festivals usually include a variety of performances that are planned in advance.

Festival participants spend their days attending workshops, talking to friends, receiving massage therapy, getting their bodies painted, shopping for new ritual wear, and browsing through the merchants' area. At large festivals, several workshops run simultaneously throughout the mornings and afternoons. Anyone with a certain amount of experience in the community and a good idea for a discussion topic or skill to share with a group can run a workshop. The Starwood 1998 program listed 78 presenters and 200 workshops, performances, and rituals scheduled over five and a half days. Workshop topics included healing ("The Healing Drum for Everyone" and "Alchemical Healing"), ritual skills ("Sacred Theatre" and "Abortion Ritual Design"), education about neopagan and other cultural traditions ("Druidry Ancient and Modern," "Goddess of Hebrews, Goddess of Jews," and "Buddhist Mandalas and the Cosmic Symbolism of the Tibetan Stupa"), crafts or tool making ("Amulet-Making Workshop" and "Batik Prayer Flags and Banners"), and alternative lifestyles ("A Bouquet of Lovers: Open Relationships in a Pagan Tribal Context" and "Living in Community as an Act of Revolution").

Meal arrangements at festivals range from food grilled over individual campfires to a YMCA summer camp dining hall filled with hundreds of neopagans. Festivals generally require participants to take their own food and cook at their campsites. At the large festivals like Starwood and ELFest, free food or food vending was available, and Rites of Spring offered cafeteria-style dining. Most festivals also include a communal feast of some kind. ELFest 1992 featured a community potluck and Pagan Spirit Gathering 1992 included an astrological feast/potluck. Rites of Spring organizers invited all festival goers to their medieval feast, which was cooked in the camp kitchen and served as a sit-down meal with multiple courses. Neopagan meals tend to include more vegetarian options than other American collective events, but the feasts I attended were diverse, offering hamburgers, gourmet vegetarian dishes, and ethnic food—Middle Eastern falafel or Indian curries. Unlike festivals that celebrate regional or ethnic identity, there is no pattern to the foods or any attempt to make them symbolic of group identity.

Neopagan identity is primarily expressed at festivals through music and dance. Drums and percussion instruments are common at many workshops and chanting often occurs at the beginning and end of workshop sessions. There are hundreds of neopagan chants, some newly invented and others makeovers of older songs. Chants originate with one community then spread throughout the North American neopagan community to the extent that often no one knows who started the chant in the first place. For example, I had heard "Air I am, Fire I am, Water, Earth, and Spirit I am" at several midwestern festivals before hearing it at Rites of Spring in Massachusetts and learning that it is attributed to Rites of Spring organizer Andras Corban Arthen. Formal concerts and informal drumming sessions take place at most of the larger festivals. Starwood featured Jeff "Magnus" McBride's magic show before the procession and lighting of the Saturday night bonfire. (McBride, who was named Hollywood's Magic Castle Magician of the Year and NBC's World's Greatest Magician, according to the Starwood program, has appeared at several neopagan festivals.) Pagan Spirit Gathering 1993 featured a talent show, and Rites of Spring 1997 included a neopagan soap opera called "All My Avatars" and an indoor concert by percussionists Circle, Skin, and Bone. Starwood XV presented seven musical acts, ranging from Behavior, a "free-form Rock instrumental combo," to Djoliba, featuring "Lansana Kouyate from Guinea, West Africa, where his family have carried on the tradition of their Malinke tribe through music as Griots: sacred storytellers."[4] Dances can be planned, as was the Guiser's Ball, a costumed dance at Rites of Spring 1997, or they can be impromptu.

Major festival rituals usually take place on Friday and Saturday nights and are open to all festival goers. These rituals involve much planning because they include hundreds of people from a wide range of neopagan traditions and ritual experiences—complete beginners who have never before participated in a ritual and seasoned ritual leaders. Major rituals may be planned by a small group usually led by someone who is well known among the local or national neopagan community as an effective ritual facilitator. Ritual planners often ask for volunteers and plan the ritual through workshops or meetings with volunteers before the ritual takes place, though the main theme is established in advance. Preparations include writing scripts for invocations of deities and spirits into the ritual circle and making costumes and masks. Ritual organizers must balance the importance of participation—everyone wants to experience the ritual, not simply watch—with a carefully structured ritual that powerfully affects all participants, is beautiful to witness, and communicates something meaningful. These formal rituals can be complex, theatrical performances with a stated focus or theme like "The Descent of Persephone" at ELFest 1991 or "Remembering Salem" at Pagan Spirit Gathering 1992. These rituals are more like performances or ritual theater conducted by a coven—Children of the Laughing Greenwood coven organized the Remembering Salem ritual at Pagan Spirit Gathering in 1992—or a small ritual group that is accustomed to working together and spends a considerable amount of time planning and preparing in advance of the festival. Many main rituals include two phases: a carefully planned performance by a small group of ritualists and a participatory activity that involves everyone.

The Web Ritual at Rites of Spring 1997 was a successful example of this kind of ritual. It began with a performance during which various powers were called into the ritual circle by core members of the Earth-Spirit Community. During the second part of the ritual, everyone present contributed in some way to the "web of community." In preparation for the participants' contributions, festival programs were sent out with maps to festival goers after they preregistered (most, though not all of, the larger festivals require preregistration). "The Official Program Oracle of Rites of Spring XIX" described the ritual as follows: "Our web takes root this year as Pagan land-based communities manifest around the country and we bring our spirituality concretely into our everyday lives. We will listen to the rhythm of the earth and affirm these changes and the awareness that they bring of our deep connection to the land. We will fill the web with our passion to nourish and sustain these bonds. Come with your own strands of yarn to weave into the web and with any objects you have brought to add to it." As with most neopagan rituals, participants in the web ritual entered ritual space through a marked entrance—in this case a wooden bridge with branches arched over it. Often participants are smudged with sage or sprinkled with water as they enter—a form of purification and a signal to them that they have entered ritual space. Drumming and other kinds of percussion usually take place as participants gather at a ritual site. When several hundred people had formed into a circle around the Rites of Spring ritual field and were chanting softly to the drumming, Andras Arthen, EarthSpirit's founder, strode into our circle carrying a long, carved staff with a deer's skull on the top. His body was draped with animal skins, his face was painted, and he wore a long, flowing skirt and leather boots. Andras silently "cast" a circle, marking the ritual space by walking around the assembled circle of people and raising his staff to the four directions.

Casting a circle is the standard opening for most rituals and is performed in many ways, depending on the preferences of the ritual's organizers. The circle bounds ritual space to create a safe and sacred area in which participants can focus on the ritual performance and their own experience of the ritual. After the circle has been cast, deities and elements of earth, air, water, fire, and spirit are usually called into the circle to lend their powers to the ritual. In the web ritual this was done by performers who were dressed as particular elements. Andras's wife, Deirdre Arthen, next entered the circle and walked around it a few times passing in front of the participants, singing as she went. She had covered herself with earthy things: bark, moss, and leaves. Representatives of elemental spirits soon followed her dressed in black leotards and wearing large masks that symbolized the four elements. The first wore a tree mask made from large pieces of bark; a fire mask followed, then a water mask with blue and green streamers; finally a participant wearing a white air mask danced into the circle. Each elemental spirit moved around the circle several times, performing its own unique steps and gestures, followed by percussionists playing different beats. Deirdre, the priestess, then initiated the weaving. People from the circle began to move forward to pick up the ropes that extended from the maypole to stakes in the ground. They stood holding the stakes as other participants wove yarn and string in and out of the ropes. The drumming continued throughout this process while everyone repeated a weaving chant: "Weavers, weavers, we are weaving the web of life." Some people danced as they wove and tied small feathers, beads, and other decorative objects to the string. Others traded yarn and twine with each other or threw them up over the ends of the ropes near the top of the maypole, catching them on the other side of the rope. This process continued until everyone's twine and yarn were woven and a colourful web had been created (see Photo 6.1).

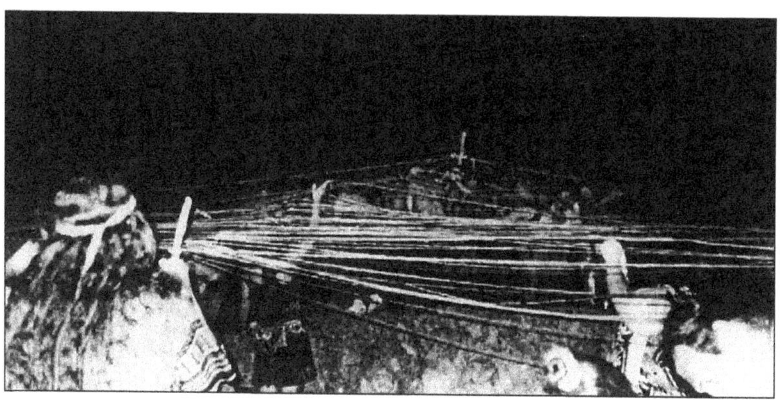

Photo 6.1: Community webweaving was a part of the blessing of the sacred mound created at 1999 Pagan Spirit Gathering. Courtesy Circle Sanctuary archives. Photo by Selena Fox.

All ritual events are optional and some festival goers prefer to sit around their small campfires visiting with friends and discussing magical techniques for hours. Festival evenings may be simply social or may combine serious and focused ritual work. At night the campground resembles a medieval village with candles and fires burning, populated by men and women in long, hooded cloaks. Some festival goers gather late at night in coffeehouses for storytelling and socializing, while others join the drumming around the festival fire. Late-night festival fires usually occur after formal rituals and sometimes extend through the night. They tend to be loosely organized, without a stated goal. Rites of Spring's fire, however, is more tightly organized; it is billed in the festival program as "the place to go for impromptu tribal drumming and dancing especially between dawn and dusk.... Please don't use this fire for casual socializing." As the drumming gathers momentum and dancers bare their skin at late-night fires, a circle of festival goers gathers around the fire to watch, and, if they feel so moved, to join the circle of drummers and dancers.

Most festivals include a closing event of some sort. At Rites of Spring's closing ritual, everyone formed a large circle around the maypole, where the community web was still suspended over the field. We collapsed the web by pulling up the stakes that held the string and yarn. Participants were told that after the ritual they could cut off pieces of the collapsed web to take home with them. The festival organizers called some of the people who had made significant contributions to the festival community to the centre of the circle, where they were thanked: the drummers, the "next generation," and the staff. Then everyone participated in a Spiral Dance that wound around the field while chanting "Carry it on to the children, carry it out on the street, carry it to the ones you know and to the ones you meet. Carry it light on your shoulders, carry it deep in your soul, for we have been blessed with magic, and the magic will make us whole." This closing chant was an attempt to bridge festival events with the outside world. As the spiral of festival goers holding hands wound its way to the edge of the field and it was time to depart from the ritual grounds, each person stopped by the pile of dirt that was formed during the opening ritual by the handfuls of dirt that each festival participant was asked to bring from home. A hollow had been dug in the mound and within it were colourful stones for each person to carry home with them. After participants picked up their stones, they walked to the top of the hill and passed through the same gateway where they had been greeted when they first arrived.

NOTES

1. Neopagans create images of festivals as magical worlds out of the mythological stories, fantasy, and science fiction that many of them have loved since childhood. In her ethnography of neopagans in contemporary England, T.M. Luhrman argues that neopagan rituals recreate the experience of reading childhood fantasies such as C.S. Lewis's Narnia stories, J.R.R. Tolkien's *Lord of the Rings*, Ursula LeGuin's *Earthsea Trilogy*, Marion Zimmer Bradley's *Mists of Avalon*, Dion Fortune's *Sea Priestess* and *Moon Magic*, and Dennis Wheatley's *The Devil Rides Out*. "These are probably the novels most magicians would choose as the most important fictional works about magic.... Most of them say that they loved these books or that these novels were what excited them about the idea of practicing magic" (T.M. Luhrman, *Persuasions of the Witch's Craft: Ritual Magic in Contemporary England* [Cambridge: Harvard University

Press, 1989], 87). Most of Luhrman's findings can be applied to American neopagans. Festivals, however, seem to be much more central to the neopagan movement in the United States; one exception is the huge yearly festival that takes place near Stonehenge.

2. Circle Sanctuary, which sponsors PSG, revolves around Selena Fox, Dennis Carpenter, and other paid staff members who live or work at Circle Sanctuary in Mt. Horeb, Wisconsin (http://www.circlesanctuary.org/page2.html). Rites of Spring and Twilight Covening are sponsored by the EarthSpirit Community: Deirdre Pulgram Arthen, Andras Corban Arthen, and a close group of Arthen friends and family, originally based in the Boston area, but now living in western Massachusetts (http://www.earthspirit.com/). Starwood is organized by the Association for Consciousness Exploration (ACE) and is primarily held together by Jeff Rosenbaum (home base in Cleveland, Ohio) and other members of the Chameleon Club (http://www.rosencomet.com/LINKS/index.html). Ancient Ways and Pantheacon are organized by the Ancient Ways store in Berkeley, California, whose owner Glenn Turner is the main organizer (http://www.conjure.com/AW/). These important people are usually acknowledged in festival programs, as are other staff. The Rites of Spring XIX program lists the following staff positions: coordinators, program coordinators, operations, registration, Healers Hall coordinator, Late Nite at Rites, volunteer coordinators, family programming, performances, feast coordinators, EarthSpirit store, merchants coordinator, fire circle guardian, broadsheet, sound and light technicians, chefs, fair coordinator, ground central, newcomer coordinator, Guiser's Ball, rides coordinator, Web site, mask making and ritual installations, and program book production.
3. For an excellent discussion of neopagan rituals as an art form, see Sabina Magliocco, "Ritual Is My Chosen Art Form: The Creation of Ritual as Folk Art among Contemporary Pagans," in *Magical Religion and Modern Witchcraft*, edited by James R. Lewis (Albany: State University of New York Press, 1996), 93–119.
4. Starwood XV festival program.

REFERENCES

Bradley, Marion Zimmer. 1982. *The Mists of Avalon*. London: Sphere.

Fortune, Dion. [1956] 1985. *Moon Magic*. York Beach: Samuel Weiser.

———. [1959] 1985. *The Sea Priestess*. York Beach: Samuel Weiser.

LeGuin, Ursula. 1968. *A Wizard of Earth Sea*. Emeryville: Parnassus Press.

Lewis, C.S. 1950. *The Lion, the Witch and the Wardrobe*. New York: Macmillan.

Luhrman, T.M. 1989. *Persuasions of the Witch's Craft: Ritual Magic in Contemporary England*. Cambridge: Harvard University Press.

Magliocco, Sabina. 1996. "Ritual Is My Chosen Art Form: The Creation of Ritual as Folk Art among Contemporary Pagans." In *Magical Religion and Modern Witchcraft*, edited by James R. Lewis. New York: State University of New York Press.

Pike, Sarah. 2000. "Desert Gods, Apocalyptic Art and the Making of Sacred Space at the Burning Man Festival." In *God and the Details: Popular Religon and Everyday Life*, edited by Kate McCarthy and Eric Mazur. New York: Routledge.

Tolkien, J.R.R. 1965. *The Lord of the Rings*, 3 vols. New York: Houghton Mifflin.

Wheatley, Dennis. 1954. *The Devil Rides Out*. New York: Arrow Books.

CHAPTER 7
Definitions and Expressions of Nature Religion in Shamanic Traditions and Contemporary Paganism

Barbara Jane Davy

"nature religion" is a useful term for discussing religion beyond institutional contexts, such as some contemporary pagan and shamanic traditions. Despite problems inherent with lumping together traditions seen as the "others" of mainstream religious groups, "nature religion" is a useful category because it makes visible a way of being religious that is often obscured in the study of institutionalized religions, a way that does not recognize a supernatural realm, that does not understand transcendence as transcendence of nature.

I understand "nature religion" to refer to religious traditions in which nature is the milieu of the sacred, and within which the idea of transcendence of nature is unimportant or irrelevant to religious practice. By this definition, contemporary paganism and shamanic traditions are both expressive of nature religion, but not exhaustively defined by nature religion.[1] People who practise nature religion venerate the natural world, not in the sense of worship, but in terms of feeling deep respect for the power of "other-than-human persons" within the "more-than-human world."

The concept "more-than-human world" comes from David Abram's *The Spell of the Sensuous* (1996). It refers to the natural world inclusive of all living entities, including others generally not understood to be alive, such as rocks, or part of the natural (as opposed to supernatural) world, such as spirits. It is more-than-human also in the sense that the term indicates that there is more to the world than is experienced by humans, and more to it than fits into human categories. The concept "other-than-human person" comes from A. Irving Hallowell's essay "Ojibwa Ontology, Behavior and World View" (Hallowell 1969). It indicates an understanding of "person" that includes entities not generally considered to be persons in Euro-Canadian and Euro-American discourses. Rocks and spirits as well as plants and animals can thus be understood to be participants in the more-than-human world.

The term "nature religion" entered the discourse of religious studies through Catherine Albanese's pioneering study, *Nature Religion in America: From the Algonkian Indians to the New Age* (1990).[2] Albanese defines nature religion as a contemporary social construct for traditions in which nature is the symbolic centre, with associated beliefs, practices, and values. Her definition does not limit nature religion to those groups who consciously take nature as their symbolic centre, which allows her to include Native American traditions. [...]

Nature religion bears some resemblance to Robert Redfield's (1969) concept of "little traditions" as opposed to the "great traditions" associated with the world religions. The great traditions are the traditions that are preserved in texts and institutions, whereas the little traditions are the traditions of the common people, which tend to be similarly focused, cross-culturally, on the concerns of daily life. Albanese's concept of nature religion highlights the importance of nature in such non-institutionalized traditions, whether or not they occur within the world religions and have corresponding "great traditions."

*****

There are at least two ambiguities in my contention that nature religion is religion in which the idea of a transcendent reality is unimportant or irrelevant to religious practice. Even if it can be agreed that in nature religion transcendence of nature is irrelevant, there is little consensus about what "transcendence" and "nature" mean within religious practice. Practitioners of nature religion do tend to express belief in some form of "otherland" or non-ordinary reality. However, this need not be construed as a transcendence of the natural world. One can experience the fact that there is more to the world than the commonly accepted version of reality, while maintaining that the more-than-human world is part of the natural world. The otherland, in my experience, is not transcendent to the physical world, nor is it more real than everyday reality. It is continuous if not contiguous with this land of ordinary reality. This is all there is, but nature is far more complex than human ideas of it. Transcendence is in recognizing that there is more to know about the world, not in escaping the world.

Admittedly, the issue of transcendence of, or in, nature remains an "unresolved dialectic" to borrow a phrase from Michael York (York 1994:16 cited by Sutcliffe in Pearson et al. 1998:34). Whether or not one includes transcendence in paganism, for example, depends on what one includes as pagan. This makes it impossible to describe paganism as being exclusively a nature religion, but not all pagan traditions are expressive of nature religion, by my definition.

I intentionally leave "nature" undefined in my definition of nature religion. "Nature" can mean many different things, but most of those meanings can be inserted into my definition without compromising its meaning. In saying that in nature religion, nature is the milieu of the sacred, "nature" can mean the land, the earth, or the cosmos, depending on the specific religious tradition being described in terms of nature religion. It does not require the tradition to express an understanding of nature as a concept.[3]

Albanese classifies Native American traditions and contemporary pagan traditions as nature religion. She discusses the Goddess religion of Charlene Spretnak and the witchcraft of Starhawk, two prominent American practitioners of contemporary paganism. Contemporary paganism is often called "neopaganism" in American academic discourse. "Contemporary paganism" is the term more consistently employed in Britain. Both are used in Canada, but practitioners, both in Britain and throughout North America, tend to refer to themselves simply as "Pagans."[4] The addition of "contemporary" is necessary in the discourse of the study of religion, to distinguish this group from the use of "pagan" to refer to non-Christian/Jewish/Muslim people, and the ancient religions of Greece and Rome. The prefix *neo-* does not specify a time period, and practitioners tend to see it as pejorative, indicating that academics have judged the movement to be inauthentic.

Definitions of contemporary paganism usually specifically include reference to it as a nature religion. Margot Adler defines paganism as a polytheistic nature religion, including ancient Egyptian, Greek, and Roman traditions, as well as indigenous and folk religions worldwide (Adler 1979) "Contemporary paganism" then would include contemporary expressions of these religious traditions. Graham Harvey, describing contemporary British paganism, also defines contemporary paganism as a polytheistic nature religion (Harvey 1997). [...]

In subsequent scholarly refinements of Albanese's concept of nature religion, the association with both Native tradition and contemporary paganism has been preserved, and developed more than any other aspect of the trends in American culture that she identified as nature religion. In *Nature Religion Today: Paganism in the Modern World* (Pearson et al. 1998), terminology seems to slip easily between shamanism, indigenous tradition, paganism, and the New Age.

It is relatively unproblematic to characterize contemporary paganism as nature religion. Adler's work suggests that it was associated with the idea of "nature religions" as early as the 1960s. The Church of All Worlds, a contemporary pagan group partially inspired by Robert Heinlein's novel *Stranger in a Strange Land*, was, she says, key in popularizing a sense of common purpose as neopagans, and as practitioners of nature religion.

The fact that contemporary pagans self-identify both as contemporary pagans and as practitioners of nature religion makes the identification of their traditions as nature religion reasonably straightforward.

It is less clear if shamanic traditions can be meaningfully described as nature religion. Specifically, the shamanism familiar to historians of religion may bear little resemblance to my definition of nature religion. Åke Hultkrantz, in his essay "A Definition of Shamanism," published in *Temenos* (1973), for example, defines shamanism as a religious complex (of beliefs, rites, and traditions), clustered around the shaman, characterized by ecstasy or soul flight, and contact with the supernatural world on behalf of individuals in their community. Hultkrantz aims to give a functional and "phenomenological" description of shamanism, taking Siberian shamans as his prototype, rather than basing his view on the etymology of the word "shaman." However, he argues for continuity with how the term has been used in the "old sources," and the "meaning of the word as a technical term" (Hultkrantz 1973:27). He does not justify this discourse, but merely recapitulates what the definition of "shamanism" is in the discourse of the history of religions, following the trail set by Mircea Eliade in *Shamanism: Archaic Techniques of Ecstasy* (1972).

Hultkrantz attempts to outline a "phenomenological" basis of shamanism through identifying a "basic pattern," which can be taken as "a concrete religious and social institution" (Hultkrantz 1973:27). He finds this necessary because if such a pattern cannot be identified, the term cannot be applied cross-culturally. He acknowledges that not all characteristics of Tungus shamans are found elsewhere, while insisting that certain other traits may be called shamanic, returning to the existing discourse on what a shaman is as a basis for saying that these other traits should be called "shamanic." Shamanism, at this point, has already become a cultural construct with a pronounced tendency to define rather than describe.

Mihály Hoppál, in an essay titled "Shamanism: An Archaic and/or Recent System of Beliefs" (1987), redefines shamanism as a "*belief system*" in hopes of avoiding the social scientific tendency to "constitute rather than describe" what is studied (Hoppál 1987:76).

Hoppál acknowledges Siberia is the "*locus classicus*" of shamanism, and defines the shaman as a symbolic mediator of liminal spheres, and one who balances power within his/her community, a social role found in North and South America as well.

Hoppál recognizes that "shamanism" is a problematic term because it is applied to widely different cultures, and suggests that I.M. Lewis's definition of "shaman" as a charismatic religious role, involving control of spirits, provides a useful analytic tool because this concept can more easily be applied cross-culturally (Hoppál 1987:93). Hoppál agrees with Hultkrantz that shamanism is a "complex of beliefs, rites, and traditions clustered around the shaman and his activities," and should be thought of as a configuration within a religion rather than itself a religion (Hoppál 1987:94). Hoppál's understanding of shamanism does not indicate whether or not it could be classified as nature religion.

Shamanism is more easily identified as nature religion in Michael Harner's writing (*The Way of the Shaman*, 1980), but his work is less easily identified as "genuinely" shamanic. Harner suggests that in shamanism, "our," meaning Euro-American, connections to nature are renewed. A two-way communication is reopened between humans and plants, animals, rocks, and air, in which these others are met as persons, perceived as "family" rather than "environment" (Harner 1980:xiii). This looks like nature religion. However, Harner follows Eliade's tradition in describing shamanism as a set of techniques, "a methodology" for reaching ecstasy, characterized by Harner as the "shamanic state of consciousness." He presents these techniques as a cross-culturally uniform set of methods, conveying little sense of the community situatedness of shamanic traditions. The shaman is here presented as a mediator between ordinary and shamanic states of consciousness, rebalancing power to help people.

Gordon MacLellan, in his essay "Dancing on the Edge: Shamanism in Modern Britain" (1996) presents a view of shamanism that is congruent with my understanding of nature religion. The key to a shaman's reality, in his view, is that "all that exists lives." Because we eat living souls, these spirits have to be "reckoned with" (MacLellan 1996:138). That is, mediation with these others is necessary. Generally, in MacLellan's understanding, shamans work with spirits and trance, mediating relations with all the others in the local area. This mediation may take place in what he calls "the Otherworld," but it would be misleading to think of this as a transcendent, in the sense of suprasensory, reality. MacLellan describes the Otherworld not as supernatural, but as the dream that the land is dreaming, and notes that it is not the same in Britain as in other places (MacLellan 1996:141). MacLellan lives in a more-than-human world, and practises nature religion.

MacLellan argues that there is no one "shamanism," but rather, it is expressed differently depending on cultural context. Shamanism is, he says, "rooted in people, land, and spirit," and changes through time (MacLellan 1996:145). He understands himself as a "modern shaman," engaged with mediating between the Otherworld and the modern world, for example, by both explaining to spirits why a road is being built, and demonstrating against the building of the road.

As with Harner, MacLellan's shamanism is more easily identified as nature religion, while being somewhat distanced from shamanism as it has been constructed in the discourse of the history of religion.[5] The shamanic tradition of MacLellan is expressive of nature religion. That of Harner is less so. Hoppál's definition allows room for specific shamanic traditions to be considered as expressive of nature religion or not. Hultkrantz's definition of shamanism is presented in terms incompatible with nature religion, since he follows Eliade in positing that a marker of shamanism is that the shaman goes into ecstasy to contact the supernatural. A tradition that includes a notion of the supernatural as standing outside the natural world is incompatible with my understanding of nature religion.

When shamanism is constructed as a cross-cultural category, as in Hoppál, and more pronouncedly in Hultkrantz and Eliade, tendencies toward nature religion are obscured. This is particularly evident in the insistence of the latter two that shamans are shamans because they access the supernatural. The evidence presented by contemporary ethnographies of Native American traditions, such as those of Jean-Guy Goulet (1998), and Marie-Françoise Guédon (1994, 1999), among others, suggests that nature religion might be a useful category of inquiry for shamanic traditions. Increasingly, ethnographers of indigenous traditions are rejecting the idea of the supernatural as irrelevant to the people and cultures they study. It seems possible that the "shamanism" identified in the history of religions is more fiction than reality, and that more shamanic traditions may be expressive of nature religion than sources like Hultkrantz would indicate.

However, the inclusion of shamanic and or shamanistic traditions remains more problematic than the characterization of contemporary pagan traditions as nature religion. Both "shamanism" and "nature religion" are constructs, and there is a temptation in using constructs to construct what is studied to demonstrate what one wants to be present. Speaking as a pagan, it is tempting to describe shamanism as that which pagan religion aspires to, the more it is nature religion. Many pagans admire Native traditions, and some are more wary of issues of appropriation than others. There is a longing in some pagans to be indigenous, less problematically expressed as a desire to become embedded in the place they live, as described in Chas Clifton's essay "Nature Religion for Real" (1998). The inclusion of shamanic traditions under the same umbrella as contemporary paganism feeds the desire of some contemporary pagans to see themselves as being in continuity with Native traditions. [...]

The inclusion of shamanic traditions and contemporary paganism under the rubric "nature religion" should not be allowed to disguise real differences between these groups of traditions. There are similarities, and overlap between the two, but there are also differences. Contemporary pagans, for example, tend to be urbanites, and to get more inspiration from books than local nature, no matter how much Adler, Clifton, and myself might wish this were not the case. Furthermore, it should not be supposed that nature religion exhaustively defines either contemporary paganism or shamanic traditions. There are strains of contemporary paganism that do not identify with nature religion, and shamanic traditions that posit a transcendent reality.

NOTES

1. There are, of course, a variety of expressions of nature religion not addressed in this paper. See, for example, Bron Taylor's discussion of nature religion in environmental movements in "Earth and Nature-Based Spirituality: From Deep Ecology to Scientific Paganism (a Study in Two Parts" *Religion* 31 (April, June 2001).

2. There are earlier uses of the term "nature religion" that Albanese does not address in this work. Hegel used the term in a similar manner, and distinguishes his usage from his contemporaries (see Hegel, *Lectures on the Philosophy of Religion*, vol. II, especially p. 522).
3. This is problematic in the study of Native American traditions. Upon hearing an oral presentation of this paper, one scholar remarked that the elders he knows would not recognize themselves in a description of "nature religion" because their language does not have words for the Western concepts of "nature" and "religion." While this is probably true, it does not negate the value of the term "nature religion" as a tool of study. Many pagans also object that they do not practise "religion" but "spirituality," and understand "religion" to refer exclusively to organized church religion. The introduction of terms like implicit religion, invisible religion, and nature religion are intended to broaden the Western understanding of what religion is. The term "nature religion" is intended to indicate that the idea of "supernatural" is nonsensical to practitioners of this type of religion, so having a concept of "nature" understood as opposed to "culture" or "supernatural" should not be grounds for rejecting the term but embracing it.
4. Increasingly, contemporary pagans in Canada and the United Stares are calling themselves "Wiccan," and their religion/spirituality "Wicca." These terms were previously associated more exclusively with British initiatory traditions derived from Gerald Gardner.
5. MacLellan distinguishes between "shamanistic" using the methods of shamanism, and "shamanic" belonging to the principles of shamanism (MacLellan 1996:146), which suggests that he might not view Harner's shamanism as genuinely "shamanic." Basically, MacLellan implies, one cannot learn to be a shaman at a weekend seminar, such the type Harner offers.

REFERENCES

Abram, David. 1996. *The Spell of the Sensuous: Perception and Language in a More-Than-Human-World.* New York: Vintage (Random House).

Adler, Margot, 1979. *Drawing Down the Moon: Witches, Druids, Goddess-Worshippers, and Other Pagans in America Today.* Boston: Beacon Press.

Adler, Margot. 1986. *Drawing down the Moon: Witches, Druids, Goddess-Worshippers, and Other Pagans in America Today*, rev. and expanded ed. Boston: Beacon Press.

Albanese, Catherine. 1990. *Nature Religion in America: From the Algonkian Indians to the New Age.* Chicago: University of Chicago Press.

Clifton, Chas S. 1998. "Nature Religion for Real." *Gnosis: A Journal of the Western Inner Traditions* 46: 16–20.

D'Apremont, Anne-Laure Ferlat, et al. 2001. "The Nature of the Divine: Transcendence and Immanence in Contemporary Pagan Theology." *The Pomegranate: The Journal of Pagan Studies* 16: 4–16.

Eliade, Mircea. 1972. *Shamanism: Archaic Techniques of Ecstasy.* Bollingen Series LXXVI. Princeton.

Goulet, Jean-Guy. 1998. *Ways of Knowing: Experience, Knowledge, and Power among the Dene Tha.* Vancouver: UBC Press.

Guédon, Marie-Françoise. 1994. "Dene Ways and the Ethnographer's Culture." In *Being Changed by Cross-Cultural Encounters: The Anthropology of Extraordinary Experience*, edited by David E. Young and Jean-Guy Goulet, 39–70. Peterborough: Broadview Press.

———. 1999. "Of Big Animals, Women and Shamans in Nabesna Country, a Tale of Assumed Identities." Unpublished manuscript.

Hallowell, A. Irving. 1969. "Ojibwa Ontology, Behaviour and World View." In *Primitive Views of the World*, edited by Stanley Diamond, 49–82. New York: Columbia University Press.

Harner, Michael. 1980. *The Way of the Shaman: A Guide to Power and Healing.* New York: Bantam.

Harvey, Graham. 1997. *Contemporary Paganism: Listening People, Speaking Earth.* New York: New York University Press.

Hegel, Georg Wilhelm Friedrich. 1987. *Lectures on the Philosophy of Religion*, vol. II, edited by Peter C. Hodgson and translated by R.F. Brown et al. Berkeley: University of California Press.

Hoppál, Mihály. 1987. "Shamanism: An Archaic and/or Recent System of Beliefs." In *Shamanism: An Expanded View of Reality*, edited by Shirley Nicholson, 76–99. Wheaton: Theosophical Publishing House.

Hultkrantz, Åke. 1973. "A Definition of Shamanism." *Temenos: Studies in Comparative Religion* 9: 25–37.

MacLellan, Gordon. 1996. "Dancing on the Edge: Shamanism in Modern Britain." In *Paganism Today: Wiccans, Druids, the Goddess and Ancient Earth Traditions for the Twenty-First Century*, edited by Graham Harvey and Charlotte Hardman, 138–148. London: Thorsons (HarperCollins).

Pearson, Joanne, Richard H. Roberts, and Geoffrey Samuel, eds. 1998. *Nature Religion Today: Paganism in the Modern World*. Edinburgh: Edinburgh University Press.

Redfield, Robert. 1969. *The Little Community and Peasant Society and Culture.* Chicago: Phoenix Books (University of Chicago).

CHAPTER 8
Paganism as a World Religion

Michael York

I believe in the supernatural, but I cannot demonstrate its existence. It is, by definition, beyond the empirical dimension of factual truths. Thomas Aquinas coined the term to refer to what is thought to be privileged above the agency and laws of nature, but I prefer the term "preternatural" as encompassing whatever is other than the ordinary, explicable, and natural. If we accept the preternatural as simply what is miraculously other than the natural or empirical, it carries the general understanding of what we mean by the supernatural but without connotations of hierarchy, that is, as something "better" than the natural. It is in this sense that I use the term "supernatural," as a non-hierarchical preternatural reality.

The path between the supernatural and humanity is one way. We cannot approach it or interact with the supernatural as we can with the world itself; at best we can only prepare ourselves for its possible intrusion. The supernatural reveals itself to us, but we are unable to measure it and appraise it with our laboratory methods of science. It is "beyond" them and "beyond" our reliable means of control.

Religion, however we wish to define it, is a compilation of suggestions and techniques by which we might become receptive to the supernatural and encourage or discourage its operation within our lives. Some religions might dismiss it altogether; others, like Theravada Buddhism, devalue the supernatural without denying its reality. But other religions incorporate various understandings of the supernatural into their formulations of what is meaningful or valuable in the human enterprise, either individually or collectively.

My own understanding of religion is as a shared apprehension of the world, humanity, and the supernatural and their interrelation. Each religion formulates a comprehension of what these three poles of existence are in ways that provide significance and the location of value for its respective adherents. Some dismiss or devalue the supernatural; some dismiss or devalue the world—but they all have a position on empirical and superempirical realities and their relationships to humanity. Those things that are accepted as valuable and meaningful within any given religious framework become its foci. This includes delineating the scope of possibility.

Perhaps an advantageous approach to understanding religion is to think of each individual religion as functioning like a map. There are many different ways of constructing a map, different features to be emphasized or ignored, different areas to be covered, and different ways of using the map. Maps can be complex or simple, out-of-date or useful for the given place and time at hand, accurate or misleading. But each map is recognized by its focus and range of emphases.

The use of a map depends in part on the authority that has constructed it. One might be drawn by an explorer into a new territory. Another might be compiled by the National Geographic Society. If we do not respect the map drawer, however, as presenting either an accurate or useful likeness, the map at best becomes something of idiosyncratic and antiquarian interest and not something to be used to find our local supermarket or the direction to Kathmandu.

A religion, like a map, depends on the authority we invest in it. If we have little or no respect for whoever has formulated the religion, its mapmaker so to speak, we will have little occasion to consult its schematization from the vantage point of a user. Christians respect the authority of Jesus

Christ, his disciples, the church fathers, and the clergy. Muslims respect Muhammad, the Qur'an, and perhaps the imams or jurists. Confucians accept Confucius and Mencius as authorities who drew and legitimated the Confucian map. Scientologists turn to L. Ron Hubbard; Sannyasins to Osho; The Family to Moses David Berg, the Bible, and institutional directives; the Church Universal and Triumphant to Elizabeth Claire Prophet and her conveyance of messages from the "ascended masters"; and so forth. Each identifiable religion has a tradition or canon that it accepts as its prevailing authority.

In our modern world, however, with its growing questioning of all authority and its ever emerging cosmopolitan encounter with other traditions and different maps, there is a growing tendency for the individual to draw from within as well as from a range of available external resources to construct his or her own map. In this process, much of the individual's spiritual journey is achieved through a trial-and-error methodology of experimentation and innovation. But the individual is emerging as his or her own authority, perhaps one that is then invested in some other authority, such as the Buddha, a Tibetan lama, a rabbi, a charismatic healer, or channeller, or perhaps one that is left with the self alone. Part of our contemporary intellectual and emotional ferment springs from the plethora of spiritual maps now available as well as the growing confidence for a do-it-yourself undertaking in cartographic construction of one's personal world view.

The most obvious aspect of religion and maps is that they are representations and are not the territory itself. The map is not Banaras or Bath or Aix-en-Provence but a tool for finding one's way within those particular places. They are drawings and not the Ganges River or the thermal spring of Sulis Minerva.

The same thing applies to religions. They are formulations meant to help the individual navigate the intricacies of the world, non-empirical influence, and human life. They are not these things in themselves.

In the development of cartography, modern improvements have refined our mapmaking propensities with newer methods of data collecting, information analysis, and construction. To keep up with contemporary socio-cultural changes, religious maps must evolve as well. The increasing disquiet and internal dialogue within the world's major religions as well as the continual emergence of new religious movements may be reflections of the current need for revised blueprints in the development of more suitably commensurate spiritual frameworks for our complicated times.

If religions are to be seen as unfolding maps of greater degrees of complexity, they can still be only as valid as the authority that is invested in them. The atheist and agnostic disinvest credible authority concerning spiritual validity, but for the world majority, traditional ecclesiastical institutions—church, synagogue, mosque, or temple, and their established clergies and prophets—still retain legitimacy. Nevertheless, as mainstream religion continues to lose its former public role vis-à-vis society as a whole, many in today's pluralistic and consumeristic social milieu have felt comfortable investing their trust in a guru or charismatic leader. In these cases, authority has been transferred from the traditional institution to an innovative particularity.

This growth in sectarianism is perhaps balanced by one in individual exegesis. In the great turn-of-the-millennium proliferation of spiritual authority, the locus of religious mapping credibility now extends from the established church to include, for followings of varying sizes, the self-proclaimed saint or revered prophet as well as, in many cases, simply the individual consumer herself or himself with little or no socio-religious connections to others or allegiance to any exterior figure or institution. In this way, religions are simply the different plans that different people find accurate or at least useful in determining their relationships with one another, the world in which they live, and the non-empirical as a possibly additional factor.

The point I wish to stress here is that each religious orientation has a right to legitimacy to the degree that its respective adherents so choose. Mind control or brainwashing by sinister manipulators is another matter, but what may look to be unfair coercion, intimidation, or duping from the outside can often be seen from an entirely different perspective from inside. Every religion has means for indoctrinating or acculturating its members, and some are more successful than others. But in every case, at some point the individual invests in the perceived legitimacy of the respective faith. As the Dalai Lama put it, we all are different, and therefore we need different kinds of religions. At the bottom line, a map is only as good as its user considers it to be, and just as many of us employ different kinds of maps for different reasons, so too many of us subscribe to different religions for various reasons—reasons that vary from having been born into a particular religion to those shaped by our developmental history and events in our life. Religious choice becomes something we judge for ourselves and in general refrain from judging for others.

As both a pagan practitioner and a religious studies academic, I am interested in paganism both personally and objectively. Since the advent of Christianity, paganism has generally been dismissed as a travesty of religion. This dismissal is, of course, a historical development that has little foundation beyond the built-in prejudices of a rival perspective. The attitude I take in this book is that paganism is a religion. It is not a parody but a legitimate, albeit different and distinctive, form of belief. The crux of the problem is how we define religion, any religion. From the layperson's perspective, there are doubtless many answers to this question. But scholars themselves are no more in agreement over what constitutes it. Indeed, academics provide not only an enormous range of conflicting understandings but also various breakdowns concerning the various kinds of religion. In order to understand paganism as a world religion, therefore, we must tease apart our understandings of religion itself as a broad category of human experience. If we can discern the nature and types of religion, we can then understand paganism as simply a particular form of religion.

The phenomenologist of religion Ninian Smart (1996) argued that there are two primary kinds of religion: that of *bhakti* and that of *dhyana*. The former involves worshiping the personhood of its focus. It tends to be theistic and involves a numinous or awe-inspiring experience. *Dhyana*, by contrast, is usually less theistic, concentrates on contemplation, and involves experiencing a mystical consciousness. The reality of religions, however, is that these two forms do not exist as completely separate categories but as two poles of a continuum along which different religions can be located—from non-theistic through idealistic and realistic forms of quasi monism and idealistic, theistic, and realistic forms of monism, to personalistic theism. While Smart regards both polytheism and secular atheism as additional systems beyond the scope of this continuum, he considers shamanism as possibly the ancestor of both the *bhakti* and *dhyana* religious experiences. He also assesses the *panenhenic* experience (Zaehner 1957) as yet another type whose emphasis is on the dramatic experience of the individual's oneness with the cosmos. Unlike the necessary duality and numinousness of *bhakti* and the non-theistic contemplation of Theravada and Mahayana Buddhism, the panenhenic is centred on union with an ultimate.

Smart (1996) has little or nothing to say about paganism per se, and the word "pagan" is completely absent from John Hinnells's *A Handbook of Living Religions* (1984). Paganism gets only a mention in *The World's Religions* (1988), edited by Stewart Sutherland and others, in connection with William Frend's history, "Christianity in the First Five Centuries," and with Hugh Wybrew's exposition of Russian Orthodox Christianity. In both cases, the term refers to non-Christian targets to be converted. The designations "pagan" and "paganism" also find no place in Keith Crim's *Abingdon Dictionary of Living Religions* (1981) and Hendrik Kraemer's *World Cultures and World Religions* (1960). In John Bowker's *The Oxford Dictionary of World Religions* (1997) we find three brief entries, "Neo-Paganism," the "Pagan Pathfinders," and "Witchcraft." While Smart discusses the earliest religions; the Indian South Asia, China, Japan, Polynesian and Melanesian religions; the ancient Near Eastern religions; and the classical African religions in his *The World's Religions* (1989), paganism is mentioned only in his discussion "The Greek and Roman World" and then only infrequently.

Part of this problem is one of terminology. There is a reluctance to consider various indigenous religions as pagan despite the ostensible similarities they often have with the pre-Christian practices of Europe. A brief exception to this general tendency is found in William Young's *The World's Religions* (1995), in which he recognizes Christian missionaries' use of the term "paganism" to refer to the indigenous religion of American Indians. In fact, Young claims that this pejorative term came to be applied to any indigenous population untouched by the Christian gospel, and he sees neopaganism as a deliberate attempt to revive the earlier beliefs and practices. Young also continues the traditional understanding of the term "pagan" as a Roman reference to the "countryside," explaining the rural populace as the last to be converted to the new religion that first took root in the urban centres of the Roman Empire. Ronald Hutton, however, disputes this etymology and claims instead that the term derives from *paganus*, or "civilian," in contrast to early Christians who considered themselves as "soldiers of Christ." But Pierre Chuvin claims that this understanding fell into disuse before *paganus* entered the vernacular in the sense of pagan. He argues instead that *pagani* were simply "people of the place" who preserved their local traditions.[1]

While Ninian Smart's analytic is helpful for the study of religions, no religion is presented as non-theistic liberationism, quasi monism, realistic monism, personalistic theism, and so forth but instead as Christianity, Judaism, Hinduism, Buddhism, and the like or some form thereof. Among the broad sweep of world religions, a designation is required for the competing perspective encompassing or delineated by animism, polytheism, pantheism, and shamanism. One objection to using the term "pagan" is that it represents a Eurocentric imperialism that denies indigenous peoples their separate identities. Some would have the term "pagan" used solely for the pre-Christian European traditions.

There are two objections to using the term in this narrower sense. The first is a boundary-drawing question: What inherently distinguishes the European traditions from the Indo-European complex from which they descend other than the accident of geographic location? If the ancient European civilizations were pagan, why would not the related Indian and Iranian civilizations in their earliest expression be pagan also? If the line is arbitrary in the first place, it can just as easily be drawn elsewhere and more inclusively if need be. Second, I maintain that subsuming primal religiosities under a Eurocentric label is not "politically incorrect" but an ethnocentric blinder that prevents us from being able to appreciate the natural kinship between indigenous tribal religion and European paganism. Although Christian missionaries used the term "pagan" pejoratively, they at least recognized the similarities among the faiths to which they were opposed. My argument is essentially that if they can do it, we can do it too. In other words, as a general designation in today's more cosmopolitan world, it is time to rescue paganism from its historically negative connotations to be a useful and more affirmative endorsement of a neglected practice and marginalized world view.

NOTE

1. Chuvin (1990:8ff). See also Jones and Pennick (1995:1).

REFERENCES

Bowker, John. 1997. *The Oxford Dictionary of World Religions*. Oxford: Oxford University Press.

Chuvin, Pierre. 1990. *A Chronicle of the Last Pagans*, translated by B.A. Archer. Cambridge: Harvard University Press.

Crim, Keith, ed. 1981. *Abingdon Dictionary of Living Religions*. Nashville: Abingdon.

Hinnells, John R., ed. 1984. *A Handbook of Living Religions*. Harmondsworth: Viking.

Hutton, Ronald. 1991. *The Pagan Religions of the Ancient British Isles: Their Nature and Legacy*. Oxford: Blackwell.

———. 1999. *Triumph of the Moon: A History of Modern Witchcraft*. Oxford: Oxford University Press.

Jones, Prudence, and Nigel Pennick. 1995. *A History of Pagan Europe*. London: Routledge.

Kraemer, Hendrik. 1960. *World Cultures and World Religions: The Coming Dialogue*. London: Lutterworth.

Smart, Ninian. 1989. *The World's Religions: Old Traditions and Modern Transformations*. Cambridge: Cambridge University Press.

———. 1996. *Dimensions of the Sacred: An Anatomy of the World's Beliefs*.
Berkeley and Los Angeles: University of California Press.

Sutherland, Stewart, Leslie Holden, Peter Clarke, and Friedhelm Hardy, eds. 1988. *The World's Religions*. London: Routledge.

Young, William A. 1995. *The World's Religions: Worldviews and Contemporary Issues*. Englewood Cliffs: Prentice-Hall.

Zaehner, Robert Charles. 1957. *Mysticism, Sacred and Profane*. Oxford: Oxford University Press.

QUESTIONS FOR CRITICAL THOUGHT

Chapter 6: Pike

1. Are there other events you can think of that are similar to what Pike describes? What characteristics are the same? What is different?
2. Many "outsiders," looking at pagan festivals, assume that this is what day-to-day life is like for neopagans. Why is this unlikely to be the case?
3. What is the significance of having an opening and a closing ritual? What might these contribute to the experience of the festival participants?
4. Much of the research that has been conducted about pagans has used festivals as a key data-gathering site. Given Pike's description of festivals, how might this data be biased?

Chapter 7: Davy

1. Davy says that "nature religions" are those that do not "understand transcendence as the transcendence of nature." In what ways are "religions of the Book" oriented toward the transcendence of nature?
2. Given the definitions of shamanism presented by Hoppál and Hultkrantz, are there shamanic practices or roles in mainstream Western religions?
3. According to Davy, must nature religion contain shamanic practices?
4. How might shamanic practice be "useful" for a group of people? What might motivate them to engage in it?

Chapter 8: York

1. York compares religious systems to maps, in that maps help us to locate ourselves and orient our actions with reference to meaning, values, and ontology. In York's framework, is it possible to work without a map?
2. York argues that all indigenous traditions have similarities in world view that justify treating them under the umbrella category of "pagan." However, most social theorists of religion consider that religion consists of both beliefs and associated practices. Is York privileging belief over behaviour in his characterization of "pagan" religion?

3. Neopaganism is not an indigenous religion. What arguments do you think York might use to include it in the "pagan" category?

SUGGESTED READING

Albanese, Catherine. 1990. *Nature Religion in America: From the Algonkian Indians to the New Age*. Chicago: Chicago University Press.

This is the book to which most other references to paganism as "nature religion" refer. While not confining itself to the modern pagan scene, it elaborates those features that she sees as common among those religions and spiritualities for which the natural world is a central metaphor.

Lovelock, James. 1995. *The Ages of Gaia*. London: Oxford University Press.

James Lovelock's Gaia theory, the idea that it is useful to conceptualize the planet as a single living organism, has been enormously influential among both environmentalists and pagans (not that these are mutually exclusive groups!). In this book, Lovelock traces the development of the planet's ecosystems, and hints at what we can expect if changes are not made to humans' interference in it.

Pearson, Jo, et al., eds. 1998. *Nature Religion Today: Paganism in the Modern World*. Edinburgh: Edinburgh University Press.

A collection of academic essays focusing on contemporary paganism as nature religion from a variety of disciplinary perspectives. This book is the proceedings of a conference on "Alternative Spiritualities and the New Age," held in England, and contains essays by several of the authors who are also represented in this collection.

Taylor, Bron, ed. 2005. *Encyclopedia of Religion and Nature*. New York: Continuum Press.

A comprehensive collection on the relationships with the natural world embedded in both traditional and alternative religions, as well as material on the religious aspects of the modern environmental movement. Taylor's own research is in the area of deep ecology, and his other books are rich resources on militant environmentalism.

Taylor, Charles. 1989. *Sources of the Self: The Making of Modern Identity*. Cambridge: Harvard University Press.

Sources of the Self is a philosophical exploration of how societies have conceptualized the nature of "self" and the relationship between "self" and "other." In this book, Taylor tracks the way in which the natural world was shifted out of the realm of moral consideration by the Renaissance focus on the empirical, and the eventual rise of science.

GLOSSARY

Ethnocentric: Belief in the superiority of one's own ethnic group, religion, or race. The tendency to look at the world only from the perspective of one's own culture.

Ethnography: The qualitative study of a cultural group, produced through months or years of immersion as a participant observer within that group.

Numinous: The mystical experience of spiritual or divine presence, a sense of awe-inspiring wonder that one is in contact with a force that exceeds the boundaries of the individual.

Pantheism: The belief that all things contain spirit/divinity, that there is no distinction between "the divine" and "the world." The idea that all things are simultaneously a revelation of the divine and a part of the divine.

Preternatural: Those phenomena that cannot be explained solely with reference to empirical reality.

PART III
Contemporary Neopaganism and Witchcraft

twenty-five years ago, it was fairly safe to assume that when someone said "paganism" he or she meant "witchcraft." The majority of the books that had been published, and the majority of pagan groups and organizations that were at all visible to those outside the pagan sphere were, explicitly or implicitly, witchcraft groups. This is no longer the case. Other paganisms have been gaining in strength over the past 20 years, and are quite adamant that they have different orientations to the spiritual world than does witchcraft. If you read the literature produced by these branches of paganism, this is obvious; however, in day-to-day practice, the distinctions are more blurred. First of all, contemporary paganisms tend to be syncretic and borrow ideas and practices from one another, and from mainstream religions as well. Second, in many cases, pagan practitioners often move between different traditions, perhaps starting in witchcraft and later moving to Asatru, or being a druidic practitioner who also circles with an all-female coven.

Druidry, like witchcraft, has its symbolic roots in the British Isles. Asatru is oriented to the world of pre-Christian Scandinavia and Iceland. Asatruar (practitioners of Asatru) draw a strong distinction between themselves and those who choose to use the Norse gods and goddesses in a Wiccan circle. In fact, Asatruar generally reject the labels "pagan" and "paganism" in favour of "heathen" and "heathenry." Asatru is oriented to reconstruction of documented past practices in a manner that renders them plausible in modern circumstances. They rely heavily on the archaeological and literary evidence of those cultures to provide the framework and justification for their practices. Wicca, they argue, is inventing new practices, and projecting them into the future through the lens of an imagined past.

Druidry does a little of both. Druids are inspired by a religious class whose existence is documented, but about which little information exists. To complicate matters, most of the information that is available about druids and their practices two millennia ago was recorded by their enemies, the Romans. So, like witchcraft practitioners, druids are trying to reconnect to the pre-Christian spirituality and values of the ancient British Isles; however, unlike many expressions of witchcraft, druidic practice is generally tied to the physical and spiritual landscape in which these practices take place. It is, in a sense, not as portable—druids must always address and acknowledge the spirits of that particular land, not of some metaphorical abstraction of "the land."

Both Asatru and Druidry tend to have a less lopsided male to female ratio than is found in witchcraft, at least anecdotally. Little systematic research about these groups has been conducted, and thus one is forced to rely on the very few ethnographies that exist, supplemented by books that are produced by practitioners primarily for other practitioners. With witchcraft, one is more fortunate. Since the 1989 publication of Tanya Luhrmann's *Persuasions of the Witch's Craft*, widely acknowledged to be the first good academic treatment of witchcraft, more scholars have taken up the study of the phenomenon of witchcraft from ethnographic, anthropological, sociological, historical, and literary perspectives, providing a broad and thoughtful range of resources from which others can draw. This section aims to give readers an introduction to Druidry and Asatru, as well as to highlight some of the significant and ongoing work that is being done on contemporary witchcraft.

Graham Harvey begins this section with an excellent overview of druidry, tracing both its symbolic and its documentable history. This distinction is important, because while the pre-Christian druids were undoubtably pagan, the label "druid" was specifically appropriated by a group of philanthropic Christians before it was reclaimed by contemporary pagans. Harvey emphasizes the convergence of purposes among both pagan and non-pagan druids, rather than highlighting their differences. Both are concerned with improving lives, preserving nature, and nurturing both appreciation of and participation in cultural life. The picture Harvey paints of druidry and druids is striking in its activity and engagement. While study and knowledge are admirable, more worthy of respect is the outcome of study in terms of the application of knowledge in the world. Unlike the critique sometimes made of witchcraft practitioners, that they are more concerned with their own spiritual progress than about the world around them, druidry would appear to have no purpose were there not a broader world with which to engage. A druid does not endeavour to live well in an effort to improve their karma or their personal relationship with the earth or the deity, a druid lives well in order that she or he can teach others to live well, so as to improve the world we all inhabit, or so Harvey implies.

While there is certainly a ritual component to druidry, Harvey downplays its importance relative to the other activities in which druids are expected to engage. Significantly, particularly in contrast with witchcraft, Harvey makes no mention of magic or spellcraft. While some druids may choose to engage in these, they are by no means as central to druidry as they are to many witchcraft traditions. Harvey does mention the use of divination, but he links it to study. Divination is one of many ways to get information. It is not linked with magic, spellwork, or other ways of manipulating the energy of the universe. In comparison with both witchcraft and Asatru, there seems to be an important commitment in druidry to engage with the non-pagan community. This is a prudent and pragmatic orientation, since after all, the modern developed world consists primarily of people who would not self-identify as any sort of pagan whatsoever.

The growth of previously less well-known forms of paganism is not the only change that time has wrought, however. Helen Berger's article focuses on the changes that are occurring in contemporary witchcraft as its longevity changes the demographic profile of its adherents. She notes that witchcraft began as a religion of adults who made a free and informed choice to become involved. In another book, *Voices from the Pagan Census* (Berger, Leach, and Shaffer 2003:27–28) Berger notes that in 1993, most pagans she surveyed were between the ages of 20 and 49, with the single largest band being between 30 and 39. This range is consistent with Reid's 1996 survey data on Canadian pagans, although her largest single band is between 20 and 29. The most important implication of this, for Berger, is that the majority of pagans are now in their peak child-bearing years, which in turn leads to a younger generation who, unlike their elders, are being raised pagan. This is significant not only because the original structures and practices of paganism were not designed to accommodate children, but also because religious groups comprised primarily of "converts" have been observed to have different characteristics than those that gain their membership primarily through reproduction.

One of the issues that plagues many religious groups, mainstream or not, is what is known as the "free-rider" problem. Free-riders are those who partake of the benefits of group membership without making much of a contribution to the production of those benefits (Iannacone 1997:35–36). This can be seen throughout paganism, where most "collective" activities from festivals to public circles and classes, are organized, directed, and staged by a very small number of the people who actually attend. This puts enormous strain on the time and energy of the people who do the work, and can mean high levels of burnout and turnover among the groups' most committed members.

Levels of free-riding tend to be higher in groups that gain the majority of their membership through reproduction (since membership costs in these religions tend to be low), and in groups that permit membership in multiple groups (since the same energy will be spread over multiple groups, rather than being devoted to a single one). One way that groups can address this is by demanding exclusivity, or by being sufficiently stigmatized that participation in other competing activities is limited (Finke 1997:54–56). This challenge to long-term group viability is present in all voluntary organizations, but it is has the potential to be particularly acute in paganism, since it is experiencing a decrease in stigma (Reid 2005), does not demand exclusivity, and is increasing the proportion of its membership gained through reproduction. Therefore, Berger's article is especially apt, as how paganism integrates its children into its structures and activities is going to become an increasingly important element of its long-term viability.

The longer paganism exists, and the larger it becomes, the more it will come into contact with other social structures and institutions. Lori Beaman's article explores the interaction of contemporary witches with the Canadian legal system. While she notes that the number of cases that exist is very small, she also observes patterns that should cause pagans of all traditions some concern. She argues that the support for freedom of religion as outlined in the Canadian Charter of Rights and Freedoms, as well as in human rights code and common law, is really support for a particular kind of religious organization. Minority religions that have different structures and radically different beliefs, she suggests, are less likely to receive the same level of legal protection of their religious freedoms.

Beaman notes that the main legal arena in which witchcraft and its practice are a matter of contention and examination by the courts is in family law, particularly child custody. The practice of witchcraft becomes part of what goes into considering a parent "fit" or "unfit." What is most disturbing about these cases is the pervasive ignorance about witchcraft practices. In addition, the expert witnesses called to explain and defend Wicca as a valid religious practice are uniformly those outside of the religion itself. Either academics researching paganism or Christian clerics are called upon to give evidence as to the threat witchcraft might potentially pose to society or members thereof. Beaman argues that this is not a phenomenon unique to Wicca, but that it is widespread with respect to minority religions. Only through the approval of mainstream religious organizations can minority religions receive validation.

After a careful examination of case law, bureaucratic, and legal structures as they impact Wicca in Canada, Beaman concludes that the misconceptions about Wicca that are present in Canadian society more generally are equally present in the court system. Evidence about Wicca put forth by "expert witnesses" outside of the religion does not always reflect the understandings the religion has of itself. Because of the decentralized and minimally hierarchical organization of Wicca, it is difficult for these groups to gain the same access to the benefits of recognition as a religion as mainstream groups enjoy. All of this, she suggests, points to a normative construction of religion in Canada that effectively excludes or marginalizes not only Wicca, but other minority religions as well.

Tanya Luhrmann focuses on another characteristic of many paganisms that can act to marginalize adherents: the belief in and practice of magic. Magic is the central theme of her 1989 monograph *Persuasions of the Witch's Craft*. In her introduction to that book, she states her research interest quite bluntly: "Magicians are ordinary, well-educated, usually middle-class people. They are not psychotically deluded, and they are not driven to practice by socioeconomic desperation. By some process, when they get involved with magic—whatever the reasons that sparked their interest—they learn to find it eminently sensible" (1989:7) Luhrmann is interested in how that occurs.

The chapter that is included here falls near the end of her book. In it, she analyzes the discursive strategies used by magical practitioners to defend their practices from outside criticism. She refers to these as "rationalizations" and notes that while there are four types employed, they are not mutually exclusive. Depending on the context in which the defence is being made, an individual practitioner may use one or more of these discursive strategies. In a different context, the same practitioner might respond with a different defence. She argues that all of these strategies involve treating the truth-claims of magic differently than those of the mundane world. She illustrates each of the four rationalization strategies with concrete examples drawn from discussions she had with people during the course of her intensive fieldwork. She notes that magicians and theologians, while seemingly quite different, have a central difficulty in common—the challenge of making credible assertions about a metaphysical reality. She argues that magicians' persistence in offering these rationalizations arises out of the important place in their self-narratives that magic has come to occupy, and concludes that it is this symbolic and narrative centrality that makes it so difficult to dissuade practitioners as to the efficacy of magic.

Reid's article focuses on the dynamics between contemporary pagan groups that exist in proximity to one another. While conducting interview research in 1998, she noticed that when she asked witchcraft practitioners what they disliked most about the Craft, the phenomenon of "witch wars" came up again and again. In this chapter, Reid focuses on the structural and interpersonal dynamics that make witchcraft communities both sensitive and prone to discord. She argues that almost all of these conflicts erupt around issues of legitimacy and authority, both things that are much more easily settled within groups than between them, since there is no overarching hierarchy to make those determinations. Issues of authority and legitimacy must be settled entirely in the sphere of interaction. Because of this, younger, smaller communities are more prone to these conflicts than larger, more established communities. When a community reaches a certain size, it can support more functions, and there is less need for groups to compete for membership and attendance. Also, established communities are more likely to have had their conflicts in the past, and learned better strategies for coping with discord than those they started with. A larger proportion of the membership of a relatively established community will also have a more realistic view of what a "pagan community" actually entails, as opposed to the harmonious, idealized vision of community that is presented in many books directed toward new pagans. As the Internet gains in importance as a networking tool among pagans—which was not the case when Reid did her original research—it will be interesting to see how the nature of these conflicts around authority and legitimacy change form.

Jenny Blain's piece explores the tensions within the constructions of religion, identity, and community within Asatru (Scandinavian and Germanic reconstructionist paganism). She begins by outlining how reconstructionist pagans of all varieties are different from those in the more general, eclectic witchcraft and paganism stream. She argues that reconstructionists are more sensitive to the cultural specificity of their practices and would not, for example, do a ritual where the god figure was Thor and the Goddess figure was Isis. They are also less likely to universalize their concept of deity, rejecting the "all the gods are one god and all the Goddesses one Goddess and together they are one" construction commonly found in witchcraft. Both sacred narrative and cosmology are more consistent among reconstructionists than other pagans, since they are being constructed with reference to the same mythological and poetic sources.

So, having outlined the features of reconstructionists more generally, Blain moves on to the characteristics of Asatru in particular. She focuses on the centrality of "the lore"—literary material about the Germanic cultures in question that has survived at least from the Middle Ages, some of it older. While practitioners all make reference to the same pool of material, however, individuals are the ones who interpret that material, and enact those interpretations within their religious life. For Asatruar, Blain suggests, there is no clearly demarcated distinction between religious and secular life. In fact, this is not unique to Asatru, or even to pagan religions more generally. Many Christian denominations believe that only through living your faith in your everyday life are you authentically doing God's work.

Blain also addresses the tension within Asatru over what can be called Asatru. While witches suffer under Renaissance and Reformation stereotypes left over from the witch persecutions and fight against the label "Satanist," heathens labour against a more recent and more menacing stereotype—that of the White supremacist neo-Nazi. Some White supremacist groups have adopted the designation Odinist for their beliefs and practices, leading to confusion between these groups and mainstream Asatru when, as Blain points out, they are no more like reconstructionist Asatru than Christian Identity is like your local, mainstream Protestant denomination.

Finally, Blain addresses the tension between individualism and community within Asatru. It is often said that getting pagans to agree on something is like herding cats. Reid discussed this problem in relation to witchcraft, and Blain revisits it here with Asatru as a focus. She notes that community was obviously an important feature of the world view that the Asatruar are trying to recreate, but since Asatru is still actively constructing itself, newcomers cannot simply be shown what is required and how things are done. Not only is it desirable to have practices be consonant with the lore, but it is also important that they be individually meaningful. This leads to a tension around authority between those whose personally meaningful practices differ in ways that cannot be reconciled. Blain cites William Bainbridge arguing that a sense of community, and more importantly, the experience of a tangible sense of community, is necessary if Asatru is to survive and thrive as a contemporary religion. Blain seems more confident that this can occur in Britain than she does that it will happen in North America.

Anne-Marie Gallagher picks up on the tensions around discourses of race, ethnicity, history, and nation that are raised by Blain and takes the analysis further. She argues that most popular pagan texts play somewhat fast and loose with history, and fail to adequately contextualize the "ancient times" or the "pre-Christian era" to which they refer in terms of actual dates, sometimes lacking even a geographical location in which to situate the narratives. She notes especially the appropriation of the term "Celtic" to refer en masse to the Gaelic-speaking cultures of Scotland, Ireland, Wales, Cornwall, and Brittany. While it is true that the languages that existed in these places before English and French became dominant all belong to the same group, throughout most of the periods that pagan texts attempt to evoke, there was no sense of shared ethnicity. An Irishman was just as much of a foreigner as an Englishman to the people of Scotland or Wales.

The consequence of romanticizing and distorting cultures, Gallagher suggests, is to overlook the real, concrete material and ideological struggles of those within the culture. It is to turn them into happy cardboard cutouts embodying those qualities we have chosen to ascribe to them. This serves to perpetuate the oppression under which they struggle. The restriction of British cultural antecedents to those whose White European heritage predates the arrival of non-White immigrants also marginalizes the cultures of these people, in effect by saying "the history that has made this country great is not your history." Will Indian or African origin Britons never come to be authentically British, she asks? Gallagher also puts under scrutiny the often-lauded emphasis on personal responsibility for the conditions of one's own life. She notes that this can create a culture of victim blaming, in which people are held individually accountable for the effects of things over which they have little control, such as poverty, disease, or natural disasters. There is a tendency to ignore structural inequalities, and the fact that people in other places do not necessarily enjoy the same economic and political freedoms as White Westerners do.

Gallagher expands upon her analysis of race by looking at the extent to which the discourse of paganism can be appropriated by Aryan neo-fascist initiatives. These groups appeal to those on the extreme right, and are generally White supremacist, sexist, and homophobic. They are able to piggyback on pagan discourse where that discourse uncritically venerates past cultures, particularly inasmuch as those past cultures are believed to be "White" cultures. These organizations can also use the pagan doctrine of personal responsibility to actively discourage attempts to assist immigrant minorities or oppressed people worldwide, since their difficulties are, after all, either of their own making, or a result of their negative karma.

To counteract these appropriations of paganism by the New Right, and to mitigate the thoughtlessness and insensitivity that sometimes sees pagans appropriating elements of other spiritualities and trivializing or distorting them, Gallagher argues that pagans must recognize that spirituality and politics are not distinct and separate things. Like her feminist sisters before her, Gallagher is making a statement that the personal is political, and she is emphasizing the importance of an engaged politics that recognizes and celebrates diversity.

In conclusion, it may be said that scholarship on contemporary paganism has broadened and deepened since Luhrmann's work in 1989. More traditions are represented within it, and on the whole, it has been able to move from issues of description (What do pagans do?) to issues of analysis (What are the implications of what pagans do, and how they do it?) The widely observed tendency of most pagans to be voracious readers (Luhrmann 1989; Berger 1999; Reid 2001) has created an interesting dialectic in some areas of paganism, where participants read the scholarly observations and analyses of their practices and discourses, and then incorporate the issues these scholars have raised in their discussions among themselves, thus potentially leading to more considered and theorized practices. While some will argue that contemporary paganism is no longer a "new religious movement," an existence of less than 150 years is still new in the sphere of world religions. Paganism can be expected to undergo substantial change as time passes, since it is likely to be more responsive to changes in material and ideological conditions than religions that have a more defined sense of normative tradition. Contemporary pagan groups will remain of lasting interests to scholars because of the unique insights they offer about spiritual and religious adaptations to a world in which radical individualism, constructed realities, and elective affinities have become the new buzzwords.

REFERENCES

Berger, Helen A. 1999. *A Community of Witches.* Columbia: University of South Carolina Press.

Berger, Helen A., Evan A. Leach, and Leigh S. Shaffer. 2003. *Voices from the Pagan Census.* Columbia: University of South Carolina Press.

Finke, Roger. 1997. "The Consequences of Religious Competition: Supply-Side Explanations for Religious Change." In *Rational Choice Theory and Religion: Summary and Assessment*, edited by Lawrence Young, 45–61. New York: Routledge.

Iannaccone, Laurence. 1997. "Rational Choice: Framework for the Scientific Study of Religion." In *Rational Choice Theory and Religion: Summary and Assessment*, edited by Lawrence Young, 25–45. New York: Routledge.

Luhrmann, Tanya. 1989. *Persuasions of the Witch's Craft.* London: Oxford University Press.

Reid, Síân. 2001. "Disorganized Religion: An Exploration of the Neopagan Craft in Canada." PhD dissertation, Department of Sociology and Anthropology, Carleton University.

———. 2005. "Renovating the Broom Closet: Factors Contributing to the Growth of Contemporary Paganism in Canada." *The Pomegranate: The International Journal of Pagan Studies* 7, no. 2 (November): 128–140.

CHAPTER 9
Druidry

Graham Harvey

> Like Druids everywhere they believed in the essential unity of all life, the healing power of plants, the natural rhythm of the seasons and the burning alive of anyone who didn't approach all this in the right frame of mind....[1]

Druids have been part of the religious, cultural and charitable life of western Europe at least since the eighteenth century. There are now druids in most European countries, and most countries where people of European ancestry live.[2] Not all of them are pagan, not all of them have Celtic ancestors, not all of them speak Celtic languages, and not all of them agree on what "druid" means. Perhaps the only thing that they all agree on is that human sacrifice is not part of druidry! Some say it never was and that this was just Roman propaganda to justify the slaughter of a previously respected class of wise and religious people.

This chapter is devoted to the pagan druids of the contemporary world. Mention will be made of various groups of druids, which are referred to as "orders" or "groves." The discussion begins, albeit briefly, with some mention of historical druids of both ancient and modern times. This redresses the balance of skepticism frequently voiced by academics.

LOOKING BACK, LOOKING DOWN

Archaeologists often think that they alone have the right to determine the validity of other people's claims to be druids. They insist that they know what druids really did and believed, and what they did not do and did not believe. Only Iron Age druids are authentic. Druids can only be seen as figures of the remote past. An eighteenth-, nineteenth-, or twentieth-century "druid" cannot be considered authentic.

It is claimed that the ancient druids were a Celtic priestly caste, political leaders entrusted with memorizing lengthy genealogies, and had nothing whatever to do with Stonehenge or any other pre-Celtic stone circle. Furthermore, only those to whom this description applies can call themselves druids. Applying the same approach to Christianity would lead to the rejection of all church-going, hierarchical, creed-believing—and non-Jewish—people who dared claim that name. This is clearly nonsense.

Druidry may well have ceased to exist as a living tradition during the Roman period, perhaps surviving slightly longer in Ireland. There was no room for their political skills under Roman administration and their religious services may have been replaced by other functionaries. With the rise to power of Christianity any surviving druids, as in Ireland, rapidly lost their primary functions. There is little doubt that archaeologists and historians have clarified our understanding of ancient druids and ancient Celtic religions in general, but there is no reason for the blanket dismissal of all other users of the name "druid." Being wrong does not negate being religious, just as much as being sincere is no guarantee of correctness. People who named themselves druids in the eighteenth century had their own reasons for doing so. Some were rejecting the *forms* of Christianity available at the time and developing new social forms that they chose to associate with an ancient, ancestral and archetypal name. In the nineteenth century the name "druid" was also associated with close-knit, caring communities of cultured and peaceful people, which made it an apt symbol for charitable groups. Druids remained powerfully emotive figures for cultural and linguistic traditions, especially those threatened by dominant and hostile foreign powers. They were recruited into movements aimed at strengthening cultural and national identities, particularly in Brittany and Wales. For some, druids inspired revolutionary zeal against English or French cultural, administrative, and religious control. In England the Ancient Order of Druids was formed and continues as a charitable peaceable fraternity that does not involve itself—as a group—in religion or politics. A considerable number of druids can legitimately be described as belonging to a distinct type of Freemasonry, one in which antiquarian interests, fraternal clubs, and charity combine.

Welsh, Cornish, Breton, and other Celtic cultural druidries could stress the bardic arts without compromising the predominant Christianity of their members. Most druids until recently have in fact been good Catholics, Anglicans, Methodists, or whatever form of Christianity was most culturally vibrant in any particular area. In some areas, especially the Celtic ones, druidry is still largely cultural and not usually religious, let alone pagan. The first explicit signal of the rebirth of pagan druidry was the publication of a Breton journal, *Kad*, in 1936 which

> announced the formation of a Breuriez Spered Adnevezi, a "Fraternity of Regenerating Belief," inviting the Bretons to renounce the authority of the (French) State and of the Christian Church simultaneously in order to encourage a return to Celtic roots.[3]

In the 1960s and 1970s increasing numbers of pagans began to consider themselves to be druids and either joined existing druid orders or formed new ones. It is these pagan druids who are the subject of our discussion here.

TYPES AND STEREOTYPES

The archetypal druid is a bearded man in a white robe greeting the rising sun at Stonehenge or talking on equal terms with a venerable oak tree. They are not seen as sinister, unlike witches in folk and fairy tales and in trial records who haunt graveyards at midnight and conjure evil from simmering cauldrons.[4] While the witch stereotype is not applicable to those who name themselves "witches" today, except in that many are female and they do often meet after sunset, many druids fit their stereotype more closely. The majority do wear white robes for ceremonies, which are often conducted in daylight in public places, though not often at Stonehenge at the moment; many are male, though not all are bearded and many converse with trees. However, while these things are suggestive they are not of the essence.

Ancient druidry was divided into three types or classes: Bards, Ovates, and Druids.[5] If Bards were essentially poets and Druids were essentially priestly politicians, the Ovates were prophetic seers. In fact these are not entirely adequate descriptions, but they are suggestive of aspects of druidry that have been significant both in antiquity, in the period of the Romantic revival, and in the contemporary world. Druidry is no longer a profession in the sense of a career, but is a profession of faith or commitment to a nature-centred spirituality. It lost political control with Roman and Christian dominance, and lost prophetic authority when the Otherworld became suspect as a source of inspiration. Poets, however, maintained a strong position in many places by reciting lengthy genealogies for the wealthy and entertaining people with traditional stories, epics, and songs. Maintenance of the bardic arts, perhaps in a lesser form, permitted the renaissance of druidry in various ages, beginning with cultural, linguistic, and artistic forms. While druids today may not do or believe the same things as their ancestors, it is possible that the druidry of the future will be closer to that of antiquity than that of the recent past. The following sections explore contemporary druidry as the latest incarnation of an abiding obsession with archetypal characters that is reaching toward a potential future. Various druid orders are mentioned, but none is taken as an ideal or a pattern.

Bards

Many druid activities take place "in the eye of the sun," that is in daylight, out of doors, and in public. Of course, druids do many important things privately, indoors and at night too, and not all of these are merely preparatory for the "open" events. As well as celebrating the midsummer or midwinter solstice sunrises, many druids spend a night in vigil and some hold a ceremony at midnight. Druidry may no longer require the 20 years of training that ancient writers refer to, but many druid orders do encourage study, practise, and meditation. Several orders have guided systems of learning based on correspondence courses and/or recommended reading material. Full participation in ceremonies may require understanding of a considerable body of information, e.g., the associations of the cardinal directions and ceremonial etiquette. All this is dealt with apart from the "in the eye of the sun" celebrations. In local groups or individually, druids study and prepare. Then they bring their understandings, their crafted poetry, songs, art, experiences, and passions, to shared events.

According to one contemporary bard, "to be a bard is to learn to listen."[6] The whole druidic tradition is said by the Chosen Chief of the Order of Bards, Ovates, and Druids to be aural, not oral.[7] Not only do trainee bards need to listen and memorize stories, songs, poems, and other carriers of wisdom, they also need to listen to themselves, to other people, and to all the voices of the speaking earth. They have to hear what is needed and then, drawing on inner resources or tradition, hear the appropriate words or music for the occasion. Bards are distinguishable from entertainers, poets, or babblers by the aptness of their contribution. Bards are not meant to be just poets, but inspired poets, not just musicians, but inspired musicians. In practice, anyone who recites a poem, of whatever quality, may be called a bard by fellow druids. The title, however, may merely be politely used during the occasion of their recitation. To be spoken of as a bard between ceremonies, or to be thought of as a real bard, is a recognition of both talent and inspiration.

In druidry, inspiration is named Awen and is envisaged as more than motivation or stimulus. It is experienced as descending on people or as rising up through them from the ground. Awen is a "flowing spirit" given by the goddess. Both the goddess and Awen can be invoked, invited, called to, and called upon to manifest themselves, make themselves known, or express themselves through the bard. To be possessed by the muse is perhaps only a weak metaphor for most people today, but it is certainly part of what earlier writers saw in the activities of Awen. Giraldus Cambrensis described people in twelfth-century Wales "called Awenyddion who behave as if they are possessed."[8] They were not only gifted poets but visionaries totally controlled physically, emotionally, intellectually, and in every other way by Awen. Today few bards experience this overwhelming prophetic or shamanic state. According to Andy Letcher, however,

> Stories are precious things and have a life of their own. Open yourself to stories and you open yourself to a depth of understanding that far surpasses the paltry efforts of the intellect. There is an old storytelling tradition that when you tell a story, you imagine the person who told it to you is stood behind you. The person who told them is stood behind them and so on. A whole chain of ghosts connecting the tradition and giving it its momentum. You don't need to tell a story, you just need to open your mouth and it will happily tell itself, propelled by the life it has been given by the weight of all those ancestors.[9]

Perhaps these storytelling ancestors include goddesses—ancestors and deities are frequently indistinguishable from each other in pagan and polytheistic traditions. Andy Letcher is a talented storyteller and musician—perhaps troubadour is the correct word—who strives to practise and improve his skills, repertoire, and delivery. These gifts are, however, reinforced by the clear, palpable sense of inspiration (inspiriting) when the introductions are over and the story begins or the music emerges from the tuning up.

The invocation of Awen is not only or even primarily an individual activity or experience. Most druidic ceremonies include some form of chant both invoking and expressing Awen. The assembled group together still themselves, gently take a deep breath, and chant "Awen" or "A-I-O" in one long unbroken breath. This is usually repeated three times. Such chanting shifts the consciousness of participants. Before the chant it is possible to feel like an observer of the select few who establish the circular space in which the ceremony takes place and that there is a division between participants and observers or, worse, clergy and laity. The chant makes everyone a participant, which is what they are meant to be from the beginning. Those who greet the four directions and mark the circle are supposed to be giving voice to what the entire company is thinking, feeling, doing, envisaging. Participating in the chant changes this from imagination or intention into experienced reality. The chant enchants; it is not only a symbol or an expression of hope that Awen will descend or rise, but an experience of inspiration. Awen flows not only into the bard but through the bard, around the circle and outwards, changing the world, which witnesses the story or the song.

The following sections return to activities in the circle, which might be seen as the preserve of ovates or druids. As a central part of many druid rituals is a specifically bardic event, often named an *Eisteddfod*. These are usually performances by musicians or poets, either prepared beforehand or offered spontaneously, but in both cases intended to complement the theme or mood of the festival or occasion. Performances occur not only during rituals, but also as organized contests or competitions that are central to the Welsh term *Eisteddfod*. The term might also be translated by "session," evocative of events in Irish pubs and clubs the world over in which musicians sit and play together, sharing their tunes, and enjoying each other's brief solo performances. Besides the bardic episodes in their ceremonies and the organized contests, druidic bards also participate in sessions. These might take place as entertainments during a summer camp, or a pub get-together, while spending a night in the woods, or as an inspiring part of anti-road or quarry protests.

Just as druids prefer to conduct their public ceremonies in white robes rather than in jeans, many prefer their bards to play harps— especially the clarsach—rather than electric guitars. However, there are many druidic bards who prefer more contemporary means of expression. Equally, some consider the recitation of high medieval epics such as the branches of the *Mabinogio*[10] to be more bardic than contemporary poetry. Others refuse the traditional insistence that bardic poetry must be in particular metres or languages (Welsh or Breton, for example). They are happy to write and recite poems on contemporary themes in their own style.

Such variations derive from differences between the druid orders as well as individual preferences of bards and their audiences. In ceremonies and *Eisteddfodau,* acoustic stringed instruments are more common than any others. Some pagans share with New Agers an affection for the clarsach, sometimes accompanied by the human voice. Other popular instruments are drums, especially Irish bodhrans, didgeridoos, guitars, rattles, flutes, and whistles. Bagpipes of various sorts (Scottish, Irish, Northumbrian, and Cantabrian) are not unknown in rituals, but are more common in less formal situations. Part of the appeal of such instruments might be the feeling of other times and other places (Otherworldliness?) they evoke. More specifically, the harps and bodhrans provide a Celtic flavour, evoking the Celtic Iron Age: a popular form of the Golden Age myth.[11] If this can be a symptom of twentieth-century consumerism and, at the same time, dissatisfaction with such "market-led" lifestyles, it is also true that such instruments affect an alteration of consciousness. The complex harmonies of the harp and the powerful rhythms of the drum demand a refocusing of attention on things other than the noise of traffic, the bustle and hassle of everyday life, and the call to the pursuit of wealth. The poet and the singer provide additional enchantments, seducing or provoking the listener to seek access to and expression of increased intimacy with the earth.

Some druid orders are involved in the revival of folk traditions like the Abbot of Misrule, May Day, and other seasonal festivities. The Secular Order of Druids refuses the trivialization of these traditions in their polite Victorian forms, in which they are subverted for the education of children or improvement of adults. They include a boisterous, humorous, and blatantly sexual cucumber dance in the Morris tradition in their very public May Day celebrations. They also encourage adults to dance round the maypole, have created a new hobby horse like Cornwall's Padstow horse, and include a fool or jester among the chief officers in their ceremonies. All these have a serious intention: to cause a much wider response than a preciously "spiritual" event might attract. Even in their serious involvement in protests against quarrying and restricted access to sacred sites, the Order attempts to use colourful drama and humour to gain a sympathetic hearing. Sometimes this has been misunderstood by more "serious-minded" pagans, but is frequently effective in enticing people to celebrate the seasons and participate in festivities and protests.

Druid bards are not strangers to technology, though they might object to some of its uses and indeed to some technologies. Their involvement in music is not just for the entertainment and enlightenment of fellow druids, but is often well known outside druidry. Although they do not advertise their druidry there are druidic bards in all corners of the music industry: from traditional Irish to rave. As with many other pagan paths, druidry does not seek converts or attempt to persuade everyone to join their group, agree with their beliefs, or participate in their activities. Much of the "message" of druidry is concerned with the affirmation of life—that of the individual and that of the earth. The bardic arts of music, storytelling, poetry, literature, painting, photography, and so on, are excellent vehicles for encouraging people to live more ecologically responsible or more just lives, for example. To this end druid bards participate with like-minded and similarly concerned people in all manner of artistic activities.

Awen is therefore evoked not only by harpists wearing "Celtic" jewellery but also by the DJs and other musicians in (Acid) House clubs. In such events everyone is encouraged and enabled to participate and not merely to observe. According to Terence McKenna, rave music, lights, and dance replicate rhythms intended to

> actually change neurological states, and large groups of people getting together in the presence of this kind of music are creating a telepathic community, a bonding ...

In such communal experiences people experiment with shamanic techniques and recontextualize shamanic world views. These technological shamans

> act as exemplars by making this cosmic journey to the domain of the Gaian ideas, and then bringing them back in the form of art, to the struggle to save the world.[12]

One British club, Megatripolis, opened with a druid ritual. At another the organizer was initiated as "the first Bard of the dance of the modern age"—the latest expression of a tradition of druid involvement in the arts. This is motivated partly by a desire to encourage and celebrate popular participation in the arts, partly by an affirmation of recreation or re-creation and creativity and partly by a recognition that the arts manifest the spirit of the age. The dialogue between the spirit of the age and the flowing spirit of Awen might be difficult in some circumstances, but not, for some druids at least, in the case of raves that articulate Gaian awareness. Rave techno-shamans and druid bards celebrate their dwelling within the interconnected ecosystem of a living earth, their relationships with "all our relations." They are also involved in "the struggle to save the world" and participate responsibly in the "ecology of souls."[13]

Returning from the rave to the grove, it is worth noting that much of the ceremony of druidry is bardic. Druids process into the circle, carrying signs and symbols of the natural or ancestral worlds, chanting or playing instruments. They greet the cardinal directions or invite Celtic deities to participate. Within the circle, apart from the *Eisteddfodau*, there is movement and drama, for example, the enactment of the John Barleycorn folksong at harvest. Much of this certainly depends on a depth of understanding that must be acquired by study and experience, but it is typically expressed in poetic or dramatic form. Druids do not interrupt their ceremonies to preach evangelistic or educative sermons. They celebrate. Observers may witness drama and hear poetry and music, but they will not be offered creeds to assent to or "meanings" to understand. This may be baffling to those who desire information, but celebration is not the way druidry imparts information; it prefers to celebrate the seasons and nature, honour life, and affirm the various relationships of participants and others. The private learning sessions and the public celebrations balance one another, but the most typically druid events are the celebrations that re-enchant life. Lengthy explanations prevent such enchantment taking place, much as they destroy the impact of a joke. There are, however, books and correspondence courses that impart information. Production of these teaching materials is part of the function of the Druids, who are discussed after the following section on Ovates.

Ovates

If the task of the Bard is to bring the wisdom of the past to bear on the present, then the task of the Ovate is to discover the wisdom of the future. If Bards are those who listen to ancestral voices, Ovates are those who listen to the voices of the Otherworld or other-than-human people. Both listen to nature and respond to Awen, but their typical methods of expression vary. Bardic poetry and music aim to encourage the flow of Awen, so that listeners can respond and themselves be inspired. Ovates are facilitators, healers, changers of situations. They interpret signs, blend remedies, and ask questions. Few druid orders have specific groups labelled "bards" or "ovates" distinguishable from their "druids," but most recognize the usefulness of such terms if applied broadly or loosely. Orders might also differ on exactly where the province of the bard ends and that of the ovate begins.

One of the most common techniques of gaining understanding in druidry is through a complex system of tree lore. Each tree is associated with a particular mood, action, phase of life, deity, or ancestor. Stories gather round the trees, along with other, more "natural" inhabitants such as birds, insects, fungi, and animals. All these, singly or together, can tell the observant Ovate much. Certainly much of this system is of recent origin, an inspired response to the needs of the contemporary world. It draws, however, on aspects of folk tradition, story, and legend, combined with a knowledge of natural history and traditional human use of particular trees. For example, the alder tree naturally grows by water, and its wood was used for bridge piles, and its bark for tanning leather; a decoction of its bark, buds, or twigs can be used to relieve sore throats, and it is linked to the character Brân the Blessed in *Branwen Daughter of Llyr.*[14] Contemplation of these and other properties of the alder will reveal it to be an apt symbol for companionship and support.

A series of symbols for each tree can be carved on sticks or drawn on cards, perhaps with a picture of the tree, to form portable divinatory systems akin to the better-known runes. Iolo Morganwg and Robert Graves—themselves inspired bards—are the two people most responsible for these complex but elegant and evocative systems.[15] The most commonly used symbols are those of the Irish ogham (pronounced *oam*) alphabet, of which the earliest examples seem to have been carved on stones in the fourth century CE. By an "imaginative play with the initials of the letters of the alphabet"[16] a medieval scholar associated the ogham characters with tree names and placed them in what is now regarded as a traditional order, beginning "Beithe Luis Nin."[17] Robert Graves made this the centre of his "historical grammar of poetic myth," *The White Goddess*.[18] He is said to have written to a stranger in 1955:

> Some day scholars will sort out the White Goddess grain from the chaff. It's a crazy book and I didn't mean to write it.[19]

In fact scholars (especially classicists, historians, and folklorists) have not received the book well. Poets, playwrights, and pagans, however, have mined it for materials to use both as foundations and adornments in their own works.

Another set of symbols, carved on wood and bearing similar associations, is called coelbren. This system was possibly invented by Iolo Morganwg, collector and creator of druidic traditions, about 160 years before Graves was inspired to write his book. Its greatest exposition so far is in the works of Kaledon Naddair who, like Graves with whom he often disagrees, associates the symbols with characters, creatures, and episodes in an array of "Keltic Folk and Faerie Tales."[20]

Just as others might cast a series of runes, so Ovates cast ogham or coelbren sticks or lay out cards. These might guide a meditation, develop a story, give insight into a problem, or foretell future possibilities. The authors of the many books, pamphlets, and sets of cards related to ogham or coelbren also intend their users to increase their understanding of trees and not merely to parrot the books they read. It is surprising but not uncommon, however, to find considerable ignorance about trees: some druids seem unable to tell an oak from an ash, or may from blackthorn.

Apart from divination, Ovates also engage in healing therapies. These too might be related to tree and plant lore: herbalism and homeopathy are both popular. The entire range of conventional and alternative therapies is used by and practised by contemporary Ovates.

If many of these therapies deal with the body, some also focus on more "spiritual" adjustments, treating disease and dis-ease.

Sweat lodges have become increasingly popular in European and American druidry in the last decade—perhaps an expression of the popularity of shamanism. These are temporary domed structures from which all light is excluded and in which rocks heated in a fire outside the lodge are sprinkled with water, which becomes steam. Their role among contemporary druids, as learned directly from Lakota, other Native Americans, or through ethnographic descriptions, is communal personal rededication to honouring the Earth. The intense experience undergone both in preparation for the sweat lodge—including fasting, building the lodge, collecting firewood, rocks, and water—and within its dark, steamy confines is a purification. The body sweats out impurities, but the sweat lodge is far more than a sauna taken for hygiene or pleasure. Jordan Paper describes the traditional ceremony as

> a potent, communal ritual of confession, catharsis, decision-making, and direct communication with sacred beings.[21]

If "those Oglalas who still keep the traditions" are the "Earth People,"[22] this too is an apt description of druids who participate in such ceremonies. Unlike New Agers, who seem to do it for the "spiritual fix" or individual self-affirmation, which it seems to provide, Druids treat sweat lodge as an initiation. They are refined through affirming neighbourliness and facing weaknesses. Everything about the sweat lodge—its structure, materials, experience, atmosphere, and effects—reinforces a message about relating respectfully to the Earth and to "all our relations," including those with whom one shares this creative womb. The Ovate facilitating the ceremony, for example, introduces participants to the etiquette involved in relating to stones. Participants—initiates—take time to consider their motivations, aims, desires, abilities, weaknesses, and relationships. They emerge as new people, taking their first steps toward different or more dedicated ways of walking the earth. As such, perhaps Ovates are initiators of personal ecological responsibility and of justice in all human dealings with wider nature.

Ovates function as therapists healing individual illnesses and rifts between humanity and those we share Earth with. They introduce people to other-than-human people such as trees and rocks and guide them in considering ways of expressing their inclinations toward ecological living. Whether using ogham or sweat lodges they teach that the world is not all that it seems, and that there is more than is seen. Bards listen to the voice of the ancestors and repeat what they have heard in stories, poems, and songs. Ovates look at the world and show it to others in signs, symbols, and models.

To traditional Christians the world is a temporary dwelling, a departure lounge where people determine their eternal destination: heaven or hell. In druidry and other nature religions earth is home and there is no other destination to which to aspire. However, the world recognized by secular science is only a part of the whole according to druid tradition, there are other places and other dimensions. In Celtic mythology the Otherworld, its regions, seasons, and inhabitants, frequently erupt into this "ordinary" world. In birth, death, and lesser crises people can be affected by the Otherworld, not always in ways that they welcome. At seasonal festivals the Otherworld and this world stand open to one another. Much of this mythology is accepted by contemporary druids, but it does not eclipse participation in the everyday world of "mundane" reality. Another way of looking at the world (the clarification of which might also be the work of Iolo Morganwg) is as a series of concentric circles. Our current lives take place within the Circles of Abred, which are formed both by the multiple relationships of living beings—the "web of life"—and by the process of rebirth.

Classical sources say that the Celtic druids believed in the "transmigration of souls," or metempsychosis. Some today see this as the equivalent of reincarnation, though not as a vicious circle from which to seek liberation. Others understand it to mean that some essential part of each individual can join with others within new physical forms when their present body dies. Whether people have "progressed" from being animals or plants, or whether all physical forms are equal but different within these circles, the idea expresses the kinship and mutuality of living beings. The Circles of Abred emerge from the Circle of Annwn (pronounced *anoon*): a chaotic simmering cauldron containing all potential forms and manifestations. Annwn and Abred are more complex than merely "past" and "present." They exist simultaneously, and there is a temporal progression within the Circles of Abred as the manifest forms, which have emerged from Annwn, are born, grow, die, and are reborn. Contemporary druids disagree on whether there is a purpose or goal to life in the Circles of Abred. Are people intended to improve and progress to "higher" forms, or is it enough to experience the rich diversities of life? Beyond Abred is the Circle of Gwynvid, a state of perfection for each and every form. Beyond that but pervading everything is Ceugant, the causative and perhaps divine realm. Not all druids are convinced by this model of the universe, some seeing it as too heavily influenced by Christianity, especially in its eighteenth-century deist form, but it is evocative for others.

Whether drawing on classical sources, medieval poetry, the creative writings of the "druid renaissance," or more recent facts and fictions, contemporary Ovates offer guidance in relating to the world. By leading people to various "points of view," which reveal the possibilities open to them, Ovates help them to find their place in the world.

Druids

Ancient druids were powerful political and spiritual leaders. Today's druids are leaders of groups whose central spiritual concerns have political ramifications. Whatever druidry was in the past, it is now a variety of paganism, an honouring of nature and of ancestral sacred sites. Although not all druid orders divide their members into the three groups, bards, ovates, and druids, it is still useful to consider the activities of some members of such groups as druidic. That is, just as there are Druidic Bards and Druidic Ovates, there are Druidic Druids. Conversely, while it is possible to speak of druids as people who perform particular functions, roles, or activities, *most* members of druid groups call themselves druids, whatever they do. There is no suggestion here that only leaders can legitimately name themselves druids any more than only bishops can call themselves Christians. That said, this section discusses the role of Druids within contemporary druidry.

The primary activity of a Druid is organization. Local groups (groves) and national organizations (orders) are centred on Druids. Their leadership is based on natural or learned abilities, on their understanding of the tradition, their inspired vision of potentially fruitful activities. Most contemporary orders expect their leadership to be capable as Bards and Ovates but also to be able to act decisively and facilitate group activities. They are expected to respond to the inspiration of Awen and to be in touch with the ancestors and the spirit of the age. Druidry, in common with other varieties of paganism, is not a rejection of the world, a retreat into Utopian dreaming, or a revolutionary overturning of the existing order. It might sometimes express similar aspirations or engage in similar activities to Utopian or revolutionary groups, e.g., in its celebration of nature or its opposition to motorway building, but Druids are engaged with the world. Druids are expected to provide opportunities for Bards and Ovates to fulfill their roles and improve their skills. They arrange gatherings in which celebration combines with recreation and planning. The Order of Bards, Ovates, and Druids arranges summer camps at which people who might know each other only through a newsletter or correspondence can meet to work and celebrate. There are workshops, sharing sessions, *Eisteddfodau*, ceremonies, sweat lodges, walks in the woods, socializing, and the opportunity for initiations. People make contacts that are fruitful or continuing contacts—e.g., they might discover a common interest in working with environmental groups or in regular visits to a particular ancient sacred site.

In addition to arranging such gatherings, Druids act as ritual leaders during ceremonies. They might lead processions into and around circular ritual areas, initiate the conversion of these spaces into sacred places, call upon others to participate, guide ceremonies through their stages, and finally declare their endings. Druids do not usually act alone in such ceremonies; they are communal affairs with a number of actors or speakers, in which all are encouraged to participate. Druids introduce the chanting of the Awen and the declaration of "the Druid's prayer." In its original eighteenth century form this addressed God, but in its more contemporary pagan form it is addressed most often to goddess, but sometimes to God and Goddess, God alone, God/dess, or to spirit.

Grant O Goddess, thy protection
and in protection, strength
and in strength, understanding
and in understanding, knowledge
and in knowledge, the knowledge of justice
and in the knowledge of justice, the love of it
and in the love of it, the love of all existences
and in the love of all existences, the love of Goddess and all
goodness.

For most people who recite this "prayer," three things seem to be central: firstly, acceptance of a place within a tradition; secondly, the desire for greater understanding with its concomitant responsibility; and thirdly, the affirmation of justice and love. To say these words with others "in the eye of the sun" *is* to be a druid, to be linked to all other speakers of the words, and all druids, including those from before the prayer was written (again by Iolo Morganwg). People who join druid groups want to understand the way the world works, how it came to be as it is, how it might be possible to prevent ecological disaster, how to relate more intimately or more justly with trees and other living beings. The druids of the orders facilitate their initiatory path and exploration of these areas and encourage the expression of knowledge, not only in intellectual form but in responsible living. This necessarily involves teaching. Druids provide instruction to other members of their group, they write books or correspondence course material, and they give lectures or participate in discussions. Druidic teaching is not dogmatic or doctrinal but exploratory of different ways of responding to ancestral, visionary, and contemporary inspiration and to the spirits of place and the age. While the different druid orders draw on the same traditional material (including mythology, history, poetry, imagination, and places), they express their understandings in different ways. They might be more bardic, more public, more politically involved, more esoteric, more interested in Stonehenge, Glastonbury, or another sacred site, more ceremonial, and so on.

Druids also act as the public representatives of their groups. Contact between one order and another, or between the orders and other religious groups, the media, police, and other interested parties, is largely the responsibility of Druids. For example, the Council of British Druid Orders is an umbrella organization for many, though not all, of the British orders. Observers from other organizations (e.g., the Pagan Federation and Breton Druids) also attend. The council is not a controlling organization but a forum for debate and for arranging potential mutual activities, such as seasonal celebrations or representations to organizations affecting druid interests. It also produces a journal, *The Druids' Voice*, which contains features, debate, news, reviews, and matters of interest to all sorts of druid groups.

Druids have also initiated the Gorsedd of the Bards of Caer Abiri, a celebratory network of people who celebrate at Avebury stone circle. This is open to anyone who has an affection for Avebury, not only druids and not only pagans. It is not in competition with other groups and focuses on bardic celebrations rather than teaching or activism. On the other hand, the existence of many different druid orders, who may co-operate in some ventures, indicates a diversity which on occasions is far from harmonious. The orders remain distinct and offer their members different styles, activities, and attitudes.

Druids lead the more public presentation of druidry, engaging in interfaith dialogue with other religionists or in media events. Isaac Bonewits's vision for the future of druidry includes far more public events, some mediated by TV stations and others led by a professionally trained clergy. His "A Druid Fellowship" (ADF) is one of the many American pagan organizations establishing a clergy training program and wishing to offer its services in ways similar to those of other religious communities.[23] Aside from any problems with Christian fundamentalist opposition, he is aware that this would radically change the current inclusive and non-hierarchical social structures of paganism.[24]

Given that paganism is rooted in a deep concern with ecology and is in part a response to intimations of disaster threatening earth's life, druidry is necessarily involved in eco-drama. In many pagan traditions knowledge brings with it responsibility to act. Ovates cannot treat trees merely as symbols in arcane divinatory systems. Their discovery of the natural history of trees will, sooner or later, reveal the extent of the destruction of trees, woodlands, forests, and the rich habitats they provided. In druidry this cannot remain simply an idea or awareness, it must be translated into some sort of action. Just as the Welsh and Breton druid renaissance was conceived as a response to cultural and political oppression, so the pagan druid renaissance frequently involves itself in contemporary demonstrations of affection for nature. The Roman accusation that the druids were bloodthirsty slaughterers has rarely been evoked and the druid as peace-loving, wise, and just nature venerator has insinuated itself deep into the modern consciousness. The sight of druids non-violently opposing the destruction of an oak wood by motorway builders might provoke reconsideration of the values of a society willing to cover the land with tarmac.

Druids function within druidic orders as leaders, facilitators, organizers, initiators. They are not priests controlling congregations, nor are they administrators continuously demanding increasing commitment of workers. Their role is closely allied to the ideal set by representative democracy: a few are chosen to speak for the majority, but they are expected to be completely accountable to those they represent. Druids are expected to continue to use the bardic and ovate senses: hearing and seeing. They are not expected to be exclusively vocal.

GRADES, HIERARCHIES, AND DRUID TIME

The three functions discussed above—Bards, Ovates, and Druids—once labelled jobs done by druids. Now they can be treated as initiatory grades: newcomers, even ones who may be neither musical nor poetic, are Bards. They progress, if they can, to being Ovates and thence become Druids. They might tell their friends that they are druids, which functions both as a goal and as the name of their spirituality. Many druid orders are trying to alter the perception that a bard is merely a trainee druid. Since the druid tradition is primarily bardic and survived only because of bards, this is a positive move. Progression within druid groups can easily be marked in other ways, just as improvement as a bard can be marked best by greater recognition as a bard, rather than applying the label ovate.

Most druid orders are led by a chosen chief, whom outsiders, especially the media, frequently call the "arch druid." Arch druid is traditionally an honorific, suggesting significant contributions to the order. Chosen Chief better expresses the degree to which leaders of groups maintain their positions by the continuing choice of the group and their own acceptance of that position. Most druid orders are currently led by male chosen Chiefs, but this is not obligatory. Some chosen chiefs have an equal female partner who shares the role and title of chief.

There are other roles within the different orders: e.g., scribe, sword-bearer, secretary, jester. These have significant functions to play in the running of the order and in ceremonies. One Chosen Chief regularly refers to the "conscience" of his order whose unofficial burden is to remind the Chief that noon has long since past, the ceremony should be in full swing, and it is time to leave the pub. Despite the offices and efforts of the "conscience," druid ceremonies run according to druid time, which rarely coincides with any mechanical or electrical method of time keeping. Though this title may be unique, the relaxed attitude to time and the humour with which it is treated are widespread in paganism and other nature-respecting religions.

*****

LOOKING FORWARD

Druids are not the only pagans who speak with Celtic deities or are concerned with Celtic and pre-Celtic sacred sites. Many other pagans draw inspiration from their understanding of Celtic religion. Developments in druidry run parallel to the growth of such pagan understandings. At the end of the nineteenth century druidry was thought of as a monotheistic philosophical tradition. Now it has more in common with the rich and varied polytheism archaeologists have reconstructed from Celtic Iron Age finds. Druids and other pagans now refer to a host of deities and traditions that earlier, more Christian druids would have considered irrelevant and ungodly. This is not to argue that contemporary druids are necessarily practising exactly the same religion as the Iron Age ancestors, but only that they are trying to do so. Druidry is not a thing of the past, it is a present reality that shows every sign of growing significantly, both in the number of its adherents and in coherence, in the future. It is one of the most vibrant ways in which people in the West are seeking to find ways to relate more justly, more harmoniously, and more pleasurably with the earth and all her inhabitants. Druidry encourages the use of all the senses in responding to the speaking, living earth.

NOTES

1. Pratchett, *The Light Fantastic*, 56–57.
2. Carr-Gomm, *The Druid Renaissance*, contains valuable regional discussions.
3. Raoult, "The Druid Revival in Brittany, France and Europe," 115.
4. For the antiquity and origins of this stereotype, see Harvey, "The Suffering of Witches and Children."
5. Descriptions of Gaul's druidry speak of *bardos*, *vātis*, and *druid*; compare the similar Irish *bard*, *fáith*, and *drui*.
6. Letcher, "So You Wanna Be a Bard?"
7. Carr-Gomm, *The Druid Renaissance*, 6.
8. Thorpe, *Gerald of Wales*, 246.
9. Letcher, "So You Wanna Be a Bard?" 39.
10. Gantz, *The Mabinogion*.
11. Bowman, "The Commodification of the Celt" and "Cardiac Celts."
12. The Shamen with McKenna, *Re: Evolution*.
13. McKenna with Zuvuya, *Dream Matrix Telemetry*.
14. Gantz, *The Mabinogion*, 66–82.
15. There are more uncharitable designations for their work in this context.
16. Personal correspondence from Dáithí Ó hÓgáin, University College, Dublin.
17. See Calder, *Auraicept na n-Éces: The Scholars Primer*, a seventeenth-century transcription of medieval texts.
18. Graves, *The White Goddess*.
19. Seymour-Smith, *Robert Graves: His Life and Work*, 405.
20. See especially Naddair, *Ogham, Koelbren and Runic* and *Keltic Folk and Faerie Tales*.

21. Paper, "Cosmological Implications of Pan-Indian Sacred Pipe Ritual," 302.
22. Wallace Black Elk, quoted in Detwiler, "'All My Relatives': Persons in Oglala Religion," 243.
23. Also see Kelly, *Crafting the Art of Magic*, 142–143.
24. Bonewits, "The Druid Revival in Modern America."

REFERENCES

Bonewits, Philip E.I. 1996. "The Druid Revival in Modern America." In *The Druid Renaissance*, edited by Philip Carr-Gomm, 73–88. London: Thorsons.

Bowman, Marion. 1994. "The Commodification of the Celt: New Age/ Neo-Pagan Consumerism." *Folklore in Use* 2: 143–152.

———. 1996. "Cardiac Celts: Images of the Celts in Contemporary Paganism." In *Paganism Today*, edited by Graham Harvey and Charlotte Hardman, 242–251. London: Thorsons.

Calder, George, ed. 1917. *Auraicept na n-Éces: The Scholars Primer.* Edinburgh: John Grant.

Carr-Gomm, Philip, ed. 1996a. *The Druid Renaissance.* London: Thorsons.

———. 1996b. "Returning to the Source." In *A Druid Source Book*, edited by John Matthews, 5–6. London: Cassell.

Detwiler, Fritz. 1992. "'All My Relatives': Persons in Oglala Religion." *Religion* 22: 235–246.

Gantz, Jeffrey, trans. 1976. *The Mabinogion.* Harmondsworth: Penguin.

Graves, Robert. 1948. *The White Goddess.* London: Faber and Faber.

Greenwood, Susan. 1996. "The Magical Will, Gender and Power in Magical Practices." In *Paganism Today*, edited by Graham Harvey and Charlotte Hardman, 191–203. London: Thorsons.

Grey, Mary. 1991. "Claiming Power-in-Relation: Exploring the Ethics of Connection." *Journal of Feminist Studies in Religion* 7, no. 1: 7–18.

———. 1992. "The Dark Knowing of Morgan Le Fay: Women, Evil and Theodicy." In *Women's Voices: Essays in Contemporary Feminist Theology*, edited by Teresa Elwes, 111–130. London: Marshall Pickering.

Griffin, Susan. 1984. *Woman and Nature: The Roaring inside Her.* London: Women's Press.

Grigg, Richard. 1995. *When God Becomes Goddess.* New York: Continuum.

Grundy, Stephan. 1994. "Interface with Stephan Grundy." *Pagan Voice* 32: 11.

Gundarsson, KveldúlfR H., ed. 1993. *Our Troth.* Tempe: Ring of Troth.

Hackett, Jo Ann. 1989. "Can a Sexist Model Liberate Us? Ancient Near Eastern 'Fertility' Goddesses." *Journal of Feminist Studies in Religion* 5, no. 1: 65–76.

Halifax, Joan. 1991. *Shaman Voices: A Survey of Visionary Narratives.* London: Arkana.

Hallowell, A. Irving. 1960. "Objibwa Ontology, Behavior and World View." In *Culture in History: Essays in Honour of Paul Radin*, edited by Stanley Diamond, 19–52. New York: Columbia University Press.

Hampson, Daphne. 1990. *Theology and Feminism.* Oxford: Blackwell.

Harding, M. Esther. 1971. *Woman's Mysteries Ancient and Modern.* New York: Harper & Row.

Harner, Michael. 1972. *The Jivaro: People of the Sacred Waterfalls.* Berkeley: University of California Press.

———. 1990. *The Way of the Shaman.* San Francisco: Harper & Row.

Harris, Adrian. 1996. "Sacred Ecology." In *Paganism Today*, edited by Graham Harvey and Charlotte Hardman, 149–156. London: Thorsons.

Harvey, Graham. 1995. "The Suffering of Witches and Children: Uses of the Witchcraft Passages in the Bible." In *Words Remembered, Texts Renewed: Festschrift for Prof. John F.A. Sawyer*, edited by Jon Davies, Graham Harvey, and Wilfred Watson, 113–134. Sheffield: Sheffield Academic Press.

———, and Charlotte Hardman, eds. 1996. *Paganism Today.* London: Thorsons.

Kelly, Aidan. 1991. *Crafting the Art of Magic. Book 1: A History of Modern Witchcraft, 1939–1964.* St. Paul: Llewellyn.

Letcher, Andy. 1996. "So You Wanna Be a Bard?" In *Druidry: Native Spirituality in Britain*, edited by Philip Shallcrass, 38–41. St. Leonards-on-Sea: The British Druid Order.

McKenna, Terence, with Zuvuya. 1993. *Dream Matrix Telemetry.* Delec CD 2012. Gerrards Cross: Delerium.

Naddair, Kaledon. 1986. *Ogham, Koelbren and Runic.* Edinburgh: Keltia.

———. 1987. *Keltic Folk and Faerie Tales.* London: Century.

Paper, Jordan. 1988. "Cosmological Implications of Pan-Indian Sacred Pipe Ritual." *Amerindian Cosmology: Special Joint Issue of the Canadian Journal of Native Studies* 7, no. 2 and *Cosmos* 4: 297–306.

Pratchett, Terry. 1986. *The Light Fantastic.* Gerrards Cross: Smythe. *1988. New York: Signet.

Raoult, Michel. 1996. "The Druid Revival in Brittany, France and Europe." In *The Druid Renaissance*, edited by Philip Carr-Gomm, 100–122. London: Thorsons.

Seymour-Smith, Martin. 1982. *Robert Graves: His Life and Work.* London: Hutchinson.

Shamen with Terence McKenna. 1993. *Re: Evolution.* 118TP7CD. London: One Little Indian.

Thorpe, Lewis. 1978. *Gerald of Wales.* Harmondsworth: Penguin.

CHAPTER 10
To the Tribe Let There Be Children Born

Helen A. Berger

A group of about 20 witches has gathered at the end of August to wiccan, that is, to initiate into the faith, the newborn child of two of the leaders of the New England witchcraft community. The group has gathered in a suburban state park, near the child's home, where it has held a number of outdoor rituals. True to Augusts in New England, the day is hot and sunny. The sunlight filters through the trees, which provide some shade and project an abstract pattern on the ground and the surrounding people. Where there is no cover the sun burns down. The child, who is a little over a month old, is kept in the shade of a tree. As the ritual is about to begin, his mother dresses him in her family's baptismal robes. The child begins to cry as his mother puts the white silk robe and pink embroidered outer-robe on him. Pictures are taken of the child with his mother, his father, and all three together. Members of the congregation joke about the child's objecting to these pictures when he turns 14.

As is traditional in this religion, the participants in the ritual form into a circle, in this case around a 3-foot-deep hole that has been dug in preparation. Four people are asked to volunteer to call forth the four quarters (east, west, south, and north) and to explain these to the child who is entering his first "circle of power." The child's father, holding a large sword, addresses the crying child, who is held in his mother's arms near the centre of the circle. The child is told that this is the first time he will walk this path, but it will not be the last. With the sword the father, while he chants a magical incantation, traces in the air a replica of the circle we have formed. The symbolic circle is formed to hold the positive energy created by the participants and to keep out all harm and evil.

The child's mother carries him around the circle clockwise, stopping first in front of the person who is calling in the powers of the east and who explains to the child that the east, whose element is air, holds the power of intellect. The spirits of the east are then called into the circle. In turn the child is introduced to the south, whose element is fire and who is the power of passion; the west, whose element is water and who is the power of emotion and intuition; and finally the north, earth, the power of life, of growth and regeneration. In turn the spirits of each of these directions, or quarters, are invited to bring their power into the circle.

After the circle has been consecrated, the father removes the child's afterbirth from a plastic bag and places it in the hole in the centre of the circle. The afterbirth has been stored in the family's freezer since the child's birth. The blood from the afterbirth runs down the father's hand and into the hole. The air is permeated with the sweet smells of blood and sweat. Addressing the child, the father tells him that this umbilical cord sustained him for the nine months he was attached to his mother; now there is a new rope, a white one that will spiritually attach him to the mother of us all, Mother Earth. A white silken rope is dipped in the child's birth blood, which has also been kept in the family freezer awaiting this ritual. The child is anointed with his own blood, some of which splashes on his silk gowns. The remainder of his birth blood is poured into the hole, which is subsequently filled with dirt.

Throughout the ritual the participants stand, maintaining the form of the circle. They are there to witness the rite and to contribute their "energy." Each person is believed to have personal powers, whether he or she is aware of them or not, that can be used for magical or spiritual workings. Those who are cognizant of their powers have the ability to direct them and lend them to the work at hand. To further contribute their will to this wiccaning all the participants are asked to pick a piece of ribbon upon which they will make a wish for the child's future. The colour of the ribbon corresponds to a particular direction and the spirits associated with it. Yellow is chosen for wishes associated with the east, or intellect; red for the south, or passion; blue for the west, or intuition; green for the north, the Mother Earth; and white for spirit. The child's mother requests that each person's wish be some aspect of his or her own personality that he or she wants the child to possess. For example, a green ribbon would be chosen if you wished the child a love of nature. I pick red and wish the child passion for people and for life. Most people have chosen blue, the colour associated with emotions and intuition, although all the colours and hence all the elements are represented. The disproportionate representation of blue is not surprising, because within this group there is an emphasis on intuitive knowledge and inspirations. People come forward randomly to present their wishes and tie ribbons on a branch that is held by the mother. The last two people to tie a ribbon on the branch are the child's parents, both of whom pick white, the colour associated with the spirit. After everyone has tied a ribbon to the branch, the circle is declared open. A light picnic lunch is served while the participants admire the baby, and his mother opens the gifts that people have brought for him—baby blankets, clothing, and toys. Several people note how much the child looks like his father, who has said that he felt his wife was giving birth to him as he saw his son emerge from the womb. I overhear a discussion of the child's good fortune in being born into such a magical family. There are hopes that with this good pedigree he will grow into a man of spiritual and magical power. As the event comes to a close and we begin to walk toward our cars, the high priestess of a local coven comments on the growing number of children being born in the community. Quoting from the Bible that she read as a youth in a traditional Christian church, she remarks: "To the tribe let there be children born that it might be mighty."

*****

THE NEXT GENERATION

The main ritual at Rites of Spring was as usual delayed by the need to create intricate props and coordinate the efforts of an amateur crew. The organizers had put up makeshift dividers to block off the main field as they prepared the area for the ritual. Accustomed to operating on "Pagan Standard Time," people wandered into the woods, went for a walk to the lake, or milled around chatting until we were invited into the circle. A bell was rung and drumming begun to call everyone who wished to participate into the field. About 200 people formed into an uneven, amoeba-like circle around a lilac-covered mound constructed to mimic the shape of a pregnant woman's swollen abdomen. It was a warm sunny day at the end of May and the aroma of the lilacs filled the air.

The drumming came to a halt as one of the organizers walked into the centre of the group and welcomed us. She said that prior to the casting of the circle the children of the community would bless the circle in their own manner. Eleven children ranging in age from about 3 to 10 years came into the field singing and ringing bells. The children were sandwiched between a man who was drumming to keep the beat and a woman following to look after all the stragglers. Everyone smiled as the children's thin voices were heard singing of mother earth, father sky, and the flowers in the garden. The children and their two adult attendants danced around the circle singing and then left for another area of the camp to play games as the ritual continued.

The ritual focused on fertility in nature and in the participants' lives. As the ritual was about to end, the womb-like structure broke open, and out of it stepped a woman—naked, in her last trimester of pregnancy, wearing a garland of lilacs. A gasp could be heard around the circle as she ascended from the earth. She looked beautiful, full of life and expectancy. She was the symbol of the second face of the goddess—the mother—and of fecundity in life and nature. She and the children who graced the circle prior to its being cast also represent the changes that are occurring within the neopagan community as the next generation is born.

As the religion and its participants age, more and more children are being born to neopagan parents. In "The Pagan Census" 41.3 percent of our respondents stated that they have children, and only .02 percent did not answer this question (Berger et al. n.d.). I would estimate conservatively that more than 82,600 children are being raised in neopagan families throughout the United States.[1]

A bright 12-year-old girl, commenting on growing up in a neopagan family, confided, "Well, in school it [being a neopagan] sort of does [affect me] 'cause it's dangerous—you can't say what you are—like if someone asks you your religion, then you are in a tight spot" (Shara Mayfire interview 1995). To protect Shara and their other two children, her parents have joined a local Unitarian Universalist church. Shara's mother, Bonnie, told me that the Unitarians are open enough to permit her and her husband to feel comfortable, while providing a religious affiliation for their children that is recognized by their conservative neighbours. Bonnie's children can openly speak about their participation in the Unitarian Universalist church, although they are careful not to mention the neopagan rituals that are practised in their home or the festival the family attends each year.

When I asked Shara if she knew any other neopagan youngsters, she said she suspected that there may be others in the area, "but you know you can't ask them because if they're not [neopagan] you're in deep deep trouble" (Shara Mayfire interview 1995). Her nine-year-old brother interjected, "You can ask them their religion, but they are likely to do the same thing as you" (A. Mayfire interview 1995). Some parents, like Shara's, are joining the Unitarian Universalist church so they and their children will have a socially acceptable religious affiliation.[2] Others have excluded their children from their religious practice, while still others are attempting to raise their children as practising neopagans.

The Place of Children

The debate over the integration of children into the religion is occurring in the same venues as those used by neopagans to exchange ideas on how to run a coven or create a ritual—that is, in books, journal articles, and discussions on the Internet. Although no consensus has been reached, both the terms and language of the debate are defined within this literature. The debate goes to the heart of how the religion will be defined. A tension exists between the conception of the religion as a spiritual path or paths that each person can choose to join, and the "old religion" that unifies a community. The contradiction between the two conceptions of Wicca became apparent only as children were brought into the religion.

Neopagans have expressed concerns about both the method and appropriateness of bringing children into this new religion. Writing in a neopagan journal, Michael Sontag voices his apprehension that the religion will become diluted if children are raised as neopagans and witches. "By bringing people on to the magickal path, as opposed to them finding the path themselves, we run the risk of finding ourselves dealing with an increasingly apathetic magickal community" (Sontag 1994:13). Sontag worries that the neopagan community could eventually suffer from the same problems he perceives among organized religions—a preponderance of participants who are only nominally involved. He asserts that the community would be better served by focusing on the personal growth and initiation of spiritual seekers than by expending time training children. Although Sontag's misgivings about the effect of children on the religion are shared by others, these concerns are more often voiced by people who are childless. Most parents are more concerned about their children than the effect their children may have on the religion.

Neopagan parents are anxious about their offspring having the same negative experiences they themselves endured as children when their parents forced them to attend religious services that bored them. They want their children to be free to develop their own spiritual interests. As one neopagan mother wrote, "When I think of the next generation, I do not think of it in terms of Pagan or Magick, but in terms of individuals each finding their own unique path through the world—no matter what that might be" (Stanford-Blake 1994:21). On the whole, neopagan parents support the notion of their children's following their own spiritual interests. Their child-rearing techniques reflect the ideology of openness and anti-authoritarianism that permeates this religion. However, like most parents, neopagans hope their children will develop in healthy and productive ways and have interests the parents can respect.

Holly Teague (1994), a neopagan mother who advocates that children be free to find their own spiritual path, described her experience with her daughter. Teague had initially taken her young daughter out into the woods to create a sacred circle. As children are believed to be more spiritually open, Teague presumed that her daughter would intuit the four directions (east, north, west, and south) and the elements (air, earth, water, and fire) that correspond to them. She discovered that while her daughter did begin by equating north with the earth, she did not correctly identify the elements that correspond to the other three directions. Although initially the mother was disappointed, she came to see that it was more important to permit her child to enjoy working in a magical circle than to ensure that she did it in the *correct* way. Instead of telling the child what to do, Teague waited to be asked before instructing her daughter. Since the child was uncertain of the procedures, she frequently turned to her mother for help and was gently guided in the art of casting a circle. Teague wrote about this incident as a primer for other parents on techniques they could use to foster their children's self-development.

Another parent, Jaq Hawkins, also wants his children to freely choose their own spiritual paths, yet he modifies that wish by asserting, "I've asked myself what I would do if my child fell in with the 'wrong' crowd at the delicate age of fifteen and joined a cult of Jesus freaks. It's a frightening thought, and one I have no answer for as yet" (1994:2). Although parents may hope that their path is followed by their children, most neopagan parents are willing, at least in principle, to accept that their children will grow to adulthood and choose either another religion or secularism. O'Gaea, author of *The Family Wicca Book* (1993:24), discloses, "I fantasize that Explorer [her son] will marry a nice Wiccan girl and raise bouncing Wiccan babies—but he might not."

Parents also worry about involving their children in a non-traditional religion. Sue Curewitz, one of the leaders of EarthSpirit Community, was surprised when she learned from a group of teenagers that their parents, who had been active within the neopagan community, had chosen not to raise their children as pagans. She believes the parents were afraid their children would suffer repercussions in school or in the larger society if it were known that they were witches or neopagans (Curewitz 1989:26). One respondent to "The Pagan Census" stated, "I'd like to raise my son in the craft ... but I don't want the town bullies to crap on my son for being different" (Berger and Arthen, n.d.:2433). Jenet, the editor of *The Labryinth,* which describes itself as a newsletter for pagan families, reiterates this concern by suggesting that parents should be careful using the word "witch," or speaking of gods and goddesses, particularly if they live in the Bible Belt or in areas with many fundamentalist Christians. She worries that children, in describing their religious beliefs, will endanger the family in hostile communities (Jenet 1994d:9). However, even if children are not consciously raised in this new religion, they will be influenced by their parents' beliefs and practices. As Ashleen O'Gaea maintains, "Unless you never speak to your kids and never do anything religiously different from your Christian family or neighbors, unless Wicca has not changed your life at all, you are raising your children to the craft" (1993:39).

More pertinent than either parents' ambivalence about giving their children complete freedom or their fear of involving them in their unorthodox lifestyle is the issue of how children are forcing this religion to confront its own process of maturation. Ceisiwr Serith (1994:ix) contends: "As the young Pagan movement starts to leave its adolescent years behind and its members raise children, the problem becomes more acute. Are we to remain a religion of converts, or will we be able to develop an organic form of Paganism for our children?" Creating an *organic form* of neopaganism will result in a less individualized religion that can be taught to and includes children. It will also increase the probability of the religion's continuing to exist. Religions such as the Shakers declined, at least in part, because they were completely dependent on converts (Kephart 1982). The inclusion of children in new religions transforms the organization and practices of the group (Balch 1988; Richardson 1985). With the birth of "witchlings," as the witches jokingly call their own children, this new religion could become firmly entrenched in the United States, albeit in an altered form.

Teaching the religion to children involves creating traditions. As Jenet asserts, "In order to leave a Pagan legacy for our children, we need traditions to pass on. In order to have meaningful traditions we will have to make them ourselves" (1995b:14). The creation of traditions is part of the process of routinization. Because children enjoy repetition, the rituals are likely to become systematized. I have already seen elements of this as groups that at one time created new rituals for every Sabbat have begun to repeat the rituals. One witch justified the reuse of old rituals: "They become more magically powerful with repetition." They also become less spontaneous and less unique.

Children and Rituals

Wicca is an experiential religion that focuses on ritual participation. Because few children have been involved in the movement until recently, both rituals and training have been formulated for adults. Neopagan adults have been trained in ritual practices as well as a variety of skills—such as raising energy, astral projection, performing magic, and using medicinal herbs—through classes, workshops, books, and magazines. Adult witches read widely about Wicca, neopaganism, and ancient and contemporary pagan cultures. Teaching children about paganism requires a different form of training than that used for adults. Jenet cautions against subjecting children to "Paganism 101 at a lower reading level" (1994c:13).[3] Two journals for neopagan children are being published, *How about Magic (HAM)* and *Witches and Witchlings*.[4] There are also a growing number of children's books with neopagan themes. Parents purchase these books and journals to help their children understand elements of neopagan practice and also feel part of a community. The readings, however, are secondary to involving children in ritual practice.

Neopagan rituals appear welcoming to children, who can actively participate instead of being required to sit still and listen to a sermon. Children are believed to more easily access the divine, as they have not yet fully developed a rational, talking self. But as one neopagan noted: "How much more do we forget the needs of children attending our magickal rites? More often than not, if they are not shuttled off to a different room to be supervised by the unfortunate of the month, they shuffle and murmur their way through the mechanics of a ceremony in which they have little interest or understanding" (Manor 1994:15). Rituals, which are designed to access the younger self, are created for adults who are capable of concentrating on guided meditation and understanding dialogue phrased partially in Elizabethan English.

Children can also break the concentration of the adults. I recently attended an initiation ritual for two women into MoonTide coven, whose members have three children under the age of two.[5] Gordon, a large and active eight-month-old, was in attendance with his mother, as was the youngest child, Lisa, who had turned one month old that day. Lisa's mother, Abby, was the high priestess for the ritual. As the ritual began, Abby gave Lisa to her father, who put her in a carrier, which he hung around his chest. Throughout the ritual Abby became distracted as her baby cried. As soon as the essential part of the ritual was completed, she reached for her newborn and began breast-feeding. Gordon, in the meantime, was being passed from woman to woman to stop him from reaching for the candles on the altar. The moment the ritual ended, the candles were blown out and then moved to prevent Gordon from hurting himself. This coven is committed to creating a family-oriented religion, in which the participation of children is welcomed. However, other groups, particularly those in which only one couple or member has a child, are less tolerant of the distraction of children.

Ceisiwr Serith, a strong advocate of the integration of children into the religion, suggests that they not be included in rituals geared for adults. "A mistake often made by Pagan parents is to bring the children into Wiccan rituals or, at the least, to compose rituals based closely on what is done by a coven. This arises from a misunderstanding of the role of Mystery Religions in culture" (Serith 1994:8). According to Serith, covens are the modern equivalent of a mystery religion. He contends that in traditional pagan societies mystery groups were always reserved for adults because children not only would disrupt rituals, but also would not benefit from them. He asserts that in these societies children would be included in some community rituals and all family rituals. Serith argues that neopagans should similarly integrate their children into the religion through both family rituals and daily life practices.

Within Wicca all adult initiates are trained to be priests and priestesses who can create and ultimately lead a ritual. The goal for young children is different; parents want their children to become comfortable with rituals and with basic principles of paganism. As Northage-Orr (1994:6) contends, "A love of, and affinity for ritual, like the ability to read, is best cultivated early on."

In family celebrations children are often invited to cast the circle or invoke one of the directions. If the child is old enough, she or he is solicited to read a part of the ritual. The rituals created with the inclusion of children in mind are shorter and worded in language that children can read or at least easily understand. Music, dance, and pageantry, elements that appear in all neopagan rituals, are easily adapted for children. Children's rituals are less formal than those for adults only, but to help develop a sense of tradition, they are more consistent.

Children are taught to put their lives in tune with the cycle of the year through the celebration of the Sabbats. Many of these neopagan celebrations correspond to Christian or secular holidays. As neopagans frequently note, this is not an accident; many Christian celebrations were devised to coincide with older pagan holidays. For instance, Christmas and Easter fall close to the more ancient celebrations of Yule and the spring equinox respectively. Bringing evergreens into one's home in the middle of the winter, a German pre-Christian practice, is common in Christian countries. Spring fertility symbols of chicks, eggs, and rabbits have been incorporated into the celebration of Easter. Similarly, the integration of some pagan celebrations, such as dancing around the maypole for Beltane (May 1), have been absorbed into popular culture. These convergences help to facilitate the normalization of some neopagan practices. However, many of the basic differences between neopaganism and more mainstream American religions have also become evident.

In describing his daughter's response to death, Jaq Hawkins notes: "She now accepts reincarnation so naturally that the recent death of one of her human playmates in a house fire was accepted as stoically as such news would be accepted by a Buddhist monk. Her only regret was that she wouldn't see him again in this life, because he would come back as a baby in a different family and not live near her anymore" (Hawkins 1994:2). Neopagans view death as part of the cycle of life. Most neopagans believe in reincarnation—death is seen as both necessary for renewal and a period of rest. The notion of death as a time of renewal is presented in Deirdre Pulgram Arthen's book for children, *Walking with Mother Earth*. In this simple tale, Mother Earth is met by Lord Death, who is portrayed as a handsome and kindly man. He convinces Mother Earth that she needs a rest. But Mother Earth asks: "'What of my children if I go with you?

They cannot survive without my love. I cannot destroy them.' The Lord of Death replied, 'They will not be destroyed. When you leave, their spirits will go deep within to rest as well. When you return, so too will they, refreshed with new life'" (Arthen 1992:25).

Death is celebrated at the Sabbat of Samhain (Halloween). Because of the emphasis on rebirth and renewal the holiday is not morbid. It provides an avenue for children to mourn pets, relatives, and friends who have died. Although this holiday shares elements with the Halloween celebrations common in the United States on October 31, its focus is different. Neopagan children make jack-o'-lanterns, dress up in costumes, and go trick-or-treating. However, they also participate in family rituals related to death and mourning.

To involve children in the Sabbats, parents engage offspring in activities that evoke the spirit of the season and the upcoming holiday. The activities recommended for neopagan children are similar to arts and crafts projects that all children do, with this difference: For neopagans, these projects are devised to help align children with nature and to make them aware of the spiritual significance of the season. For example, at Imbolc (February 1), which celebrates the growing strength of the sun and the approach of spring, parents may teach their children to make candles that can be used in ritual (McArthur 1994). Imbolc is celebrated by lighting a large number of candles to symbolize the increase in the amount of sunlight each day. One Wiccan mother told me that, instead of a formal Imbolc ritual, she and her husband participate in an informal celebration of the holiday with their children. The electric lights are turned off, the house is illuminated with candles, and the parents tell their children stories, such as the myth of the quickening of the sun king in the great mother. The children in turn are invited to tell stories and to reflect on the ending of winter and coming of spring. Making candles is part of the fun and the symbolism of the holiday for the children.

Rites of Passage

Rites of passage, such as the wiccaning described earlier and ceremonies marking the transition from childhood to adulthood, are being created by neopagans. The welcoming rite—referred to as a wiccaning, a saining, or a paganing—serves a threefold purpose: to introduce the child to the deities and ask for their help and protection as the child grows; to give the community an opportunity to meet and bless the child; and to bring the child into his or her first sacred circle. Welcoming rituals do not commit the child to pagan goddesses and gods or to a particular spiritual path. At Alex's wiccaning in September 1996, the high priest of his parents' coven addressed the three-month-old: "I, as High Priest can open the [spiritual] door for you. But neither I, nor your parents, nor anyone else can make you walk through that door. When you grow older you must decide whether you will enter this door or choose another—but remember, all walk in spirit and whatever path you pick must therefore be with spirit."[6] As is usual with families in Wicca, the parents are ambivalent about the child's ultimately leaving the religion.

The most varied of the Wiccan rituals that I have attended are sainings. In all instances the child is introduced to the four directions, given good wishes and words of wisdom by the participants, and awarded goddess parents.[7] Other aspects of the ritual, however, vary widely. The wiccaning described in the prologue is the only birth ritual I have attended in which the child's birth blood was used, although I have read about others (Curewitz 1990; Campanelli 1994; McArthur 1994). Other welcoming rituals I have attended have taken place in either the parents' or the high priestess's home, where the use of blood may have been deemed inappropriate. For instance, Alex's parents did not use his birth blood or placenta in his wiccaning, which took place in their dining room, but they do have his placenta in their freezer and plan to bury it in a private ritual before the first frost. Some parents may not be allowed to appropriate the afterbirth at the hospital or birthing centre. And some covens or parents may be uncomfortable handling the afterbirth.

MoonTide coven's saining ritual for Lisa anticipated her next rite of passage. All the participants were asked to write words of wisdom on a card that was collected during the ritual by Abby, who promised to keep them unread until Lisa reached puberty. By creating rituals to celebrate their children's sexual maturity, neopagans hope to address a lack that they feel exists in American culture. As Jenet asserts, "When there is no longer a common extracurricular rite of passage for early adolescents, less savory common experiences have an open field for entry. Parents can hope that today's students have decided not to join in popular culture's rite of passage in gangs, drugs or guns" (1994a:3). Because of the long period that offspring remain dependent in contemporary society, some neopagans are developing two separate rituals to denote different stages of maturity. The first ritual occurs around the time of puberty and the second when the child graduates from high school or is preparing to leave home. These rituals mark the transition from childhood to adolescence or adulthood for both the parents and their progeny.

Puberty rites are gender specific, unisex rituals. As Serith asserts: "Only a man can make a man, and only a woman can acknowledge a woman" (1994:10). The distinction between the acknowledgment of womanhood and the "making" of manhood is reflected in the puberty rites of neopagans. Probably more than any others, these rituals highlight the essentialism of gender roles, even though in a latent form, within Wicca.

The girl's ritual underscores her metamorphosis into womanhood. In one rendition of this ritual, a woman who represents the east, the element of air and of intellect, says to the young woman:

> Know that as a woman
> Once in the month when your blood flows
> Or the Moon is full, your mind will be
> Open and receptive to things unseen.
> Learn to see with the mind's eye,
> And listen to the wind
> Heed your inner voice,
> To be a woman is to gain Wisdom. (Campanelli 1994:43)

The rituals for boys, like those for girls, focus on the spiritual as well as physical changes the boy experiences.[8] Boys are expected to endure an ordeal prior to being recognized as men. The notion of men's proving themselves through an ordeal is common among indigenous groups. Although symbolically Wiccan boys are expected to face their mortality, in reality they are never placed in any danger.

The lack of real risk may mitigate against the boys' experiencing a psychological transformation into manhood. Zack, the founder of *HAM*, comments about his puberty rite: "I felt that the rite of passage let me into the men's circle and the whole male aspect of magic. But I never really felt I was a man until the truck fell on me. My rite of passage didn't do that" (quoted in Judith 1993:85). The experience that Zack felt resulted in his passage to manhood was one in which he almost died.

Similarly, the girls' rites of passage may or may not result in their feeling like women. The rituals do celebrate and affirm the changes that are occurring in their bodies. However, within the larger society there is little validation of the new status of either females or males. The children remain in middle school, economically dependent on their parents and socially unprepared to begin a family. Furthermore, the dispersion of neopagans throughout the country means there is no stable face-to-face community to acknowledge the new adult on a daily basis and ensure that the parents change their behaviour toward their minor offspring.

These rites of passage nonetheless remain important, as they help to create a community of interest [...]. Even if the rituals do not ultimately help to define a passage from youth to adulthood, they provide a shared set of rites in which Wiccan children participate. The inclusion in the sacred circles of extended kin and friends—many from outside Wicca—to celebrate the family's life passages also affirms Wiccans in their practices.

*****

Magical Children

Neopagan children are taught to view the world through the magical and mystical lenses. As Ashleen O'Gaea contends, "Nearly everything we do at home can be done with Wicca in mind. From rearranging a room to brushing hair, everything can be a spell.... And if we share mundane blessings with our children it will become second nature to them" (1993:25). Within Wicca, all of life and its activities become imbued with spirituality. Joan, who had been raised in a Wiccan family and was pregnant with her first child when I interviewed her, noted that although the child would grow up knowing about all religions and would have the option of choosing a religion, the child would be raised "understanding the healing aspect and communicating with the animals and nature and taking on the [magical] responsibility—the child will be raised with that every day of its life and that will be very natural; and the child will know that is from the Craft" (Joan interview 1989).

Susan, the high priestess of the MoonTide coven, is starting a nursery school for pagan children that she hopes to expand into a day school. She told me that the goddess had guided her in this decision. Initially, she had not wanted to become involved with educating young children, having already raised a family of her own, but "the goddess hit me on the side of the head with the proverbial two-by-four and I knew this was something I had to do." She came to believe the creation of a school was necessary to protect neopagan children from becoming psychically and magically crippled.

Susan contends that she and other neopagan adults were harmed as children in "nominally" secular schools. Imps, spirit guides, and god forces that the child spoke to were reinterpreted in the schools as imaginary friends. Susan argues that we were all trained to ignore and reinterpret psychic experiences as either coincidences, imagination, or psychological displacement. She asserts that pagan adults must now spend their time and energy trying to revitalize their psychic and magical abilities, which they were naturally attuned to as children. Susan feels that the next generation must be saved from being thwarted as their parents have been.

According to Susan, the public schools, which claim to be secular, actually incorporate Judeo-Christian ideals and celebrations. For example, children make Christmas cards and sing Christmas carols in school. Halloween is a time to decorate the classroom with pictures of disfigured women, who are referred to as witches, dressed in black, and flying on broomsticks. Susan feels that, on the whole, public schools are harmful to neopagan children. Every neopagan parent to whom I have spoken has expressed similar sentiments. One pagan on the Internet notes, "I didn't like seeing my stepdaughter coming home parroting the cowan [secular], no blatantly Xian [Christian] ... stuff she was exposed to at school.... Think what our childhoods might have been like if we'd been brought up by people that didn't force us to disbelieve the guidance of the spirits" (Magical Rat 1994).

Although children are believed to be born in synchrony with the spiritual world, their natural ability can be either developed or impeded. Parents use a number of techniques to help their children develop their magical abilities, including meditation, rituals, and other forms of raising energy. To overcome the larger society's skepticism about magic, parents use concrete examples to demonstrate to their children that magic does work. For instance, O'Gaea (1993) points out to her son his successful use of his psychic powers when he was thinking or talking about a friend and that person then telephoned.

Some aspects of the mystical and magical beliefs and practices of neopagans have resonance in more mainstream religions. Catholics light candles to ask saints to intercede on their behalf. Fundamentalist Christians speak of Christ's guiding them or being part of their everyday life. However, even with these similarities there remains a fundamental difference between espousing witchcraft and participating in Christianity. Danzger (1989) notes that being a Christian, even a fundamentalist or a devout one, is a form of "hyperconformism" in the United States. In comparison, witchcraft and magic are treated with either disdain or fear. Although the disdain and fear of magical practices affect all neopagans, these attitudes especially complicate for parents the involvement of their children in Wiccan practices.

Because neopagans live in the secular world, their children are required to bifurcate their lives into the magical, enchanted world of Wicca and the secular society. Most neopagan adults compartmentalize their lives successfully. Magic and mysticism do not become directly or openly incorporated into their professional or mundane lives. Many remain in the "broom closet" in the larger society. Even those who are open about their religion do not normally conduct rituals or enter trances at work. Children, particularly younger children, who are trained to participate in meditation and working magic may have a more difficult time compartmentalizing. Jenet contends that "as parents who are Pagan and Wiccan we need to teach our children a series of 'know-hows' in order to know how to live in two worlds" (1995a:10). Eluba, the mother of two pagan children, similarly notes, "if you have them [children] in normal schools they have to lead a double life." However, she goes on to suggest that, while this creates some difficulty for the children, "the skills that being part of a Pagan community are imparting to them will be invaluable to them as they grow up—when they are grown up—they will be nourished and encouraged" (Eluba interview 1990).

In an interview before her first pregnancy, the mother of the boy whose wiccaning I described in the prologue, now a mother of two neopagan children, defined paganism as "the [celebration of the] cycle of the seasons and the full moon rituals and working with symbol and ritual and those sorts of things—and it is wonderful" (Jane interview 1987). Neopagan children are born into a community that celebrates nature, through both rituals and ecological practices. The children are encouraged to recycle, create gardens, and pick up trash.

Many aspects of neopagan children's upbringing are the same as that of other middle-class children in the United States. Neopagan parents try to teach their children self-respect, respect for others, and respect for the ecosystem. However, neopagan children are also encouraged by both their parents and the neopagan community to develop their magical personas and psychic abilities, through rituals and other mystical practices.

Almost every witch I have spoken to has raised concerns about the negative stereotypes that surround the term "witch." This is intensified for children. Joan, an adult raised in a Wiccan family, remarks about her childhood: "Kids at that age—still in grammar school, are nasty anyway, looking for someone to be the scapegoat, like the fat kid or the one with braces and for us it was the witches" (Joan interview 1989). A generation later, things have not changed significantly. Eluba notes, "In some ways it's been incredibly difficult for them [her children]. Children are nothing if not little animals of peer pressure and being different is difficult no matter who you are" (Eluba interview 1990). Because they worry that their children may suffer discrimination, parents, more than other participants, are eager for their religious practice to be seen as legitimate. The growth in the number of children being born to adherents is forcing a decentralized community to start to rethink and redefine itself. Witchcraft and neopaganism, which grew out of the counterculture, are becoming more conservative. Tradition, continuity, and restrained sexuality become more important as children enter the circle.

NOTES

1. This figure is based on the [...]estimate of 200,000 neopagans living in the United States. The estimate of the number of children is probably low because some neopagans have more than one child. However, since mothers and fathers may each have completed a survey, both claiming the same children, I have for the purpose of this estimate assumed each of the respondents had only one child.
2. Enough neopagans have joined the Unitarian Universalist Association for a group, the Covenant of Unitarian Universalist Pagans (CUUPs), to have formed. [...]
3. Pagans jokingly refer to introductory courses on the Craft offered at occult bookstores or adult education centres as Wicca or Witchcraft 101.
4. *HAM* was developed as a journal for pagan children by an adolescent neopagan whose father is the editor of *Green Egg*, one of the oldest pagan journals in the United States. *HAM* was initially distributed by *Green Egg*. The acronym *HAM* was chosen as a play on Dr. Seuss's children's book *Green Eggs and Ham*.
5. [...] In this chapter I have used pseudonyms for their mundane names.
6. This quote is from my fieldnotes written after the ritual. I have tried as much as possible to reproduce the speech as it was presented.
7. The terms "godparents" and "guardians" are also used.
8. I am dependent on written accounts and descriptions by my male informants of boys' puberty rites.

REFERENCES

Arthen, Deirdre Pulgram. 1992. *Walking with Mother Earth*. West Boxford: D & J Publications.

Balch, Robert. 1988. "Money and Power in Utopia: An Economic History of the Love Family." In *Money and Power in New Religions*, edited by James T. Richardson, 185–222. Lewiston: The Edwin Mellen Press.

Berger, Helen A., and Andras Corbin Arthen. n.d. "The Pagan Census—Qualitative Data."

———, Andras Corbin Arthen, Evan Leach, and Leigh S. Shaffer. n.d. "The Pagan Census—The Statistical Analysis."

Campanelli, Pauline. 1994. *Rites of Passage: The Pagan Wheel of Life.* St. Paul: Llewellyn Publications.

Curewitz, Sue. 1989. "Pagan Rites of Passages: Puberty." *FireHeart* (Spring/Summer): 24–26, 56.

———. 1990. "Pagan Rites of Passages: A Celebration of Birth." *FireHeart* 5: 8–10, 54.

Danzger, M. Herbert. 1989. *Returning to Tradition.* New Haven: Yale University Press.

Hawkins, Jaq. 1994. "What Do We Teach Our Children?" *Mezlim: Practical Magick for Today* 5, no. 4: 1–3.

Jenet. 1994a. "Becoming Men and Women." *The Labryinth* 2 (Imbolc): 2–3.

———. 1994b. "Track 1." *The Labryinth* 2 (Beltane): 4–5.

———. 1994c. "Track 5." *The Labryinth* 2 (Beltane): 11–13.

———. 1994d. "Track 3." *The Labryinth* 3 (Lammas): 8–9.

———. 1995a. "Track 3." *The Labyrinth* 3 (Imbolc): 10–11.

———. 1995b. "Track 5." *The Labyrinth* 3 (Imbolc): 14.

Judith, Anodea. 1993. "Between the Worlds: Late Adolescence and Early Adulthood in Modern Paganism." In *Modern Rites of Passage: Witchcraft Today Book Two*, edited by Chas S. Clifton, 75–92. St. Paul: Llewellyn Publications.

Kephart, William. 1982. *Extraordinary Groups: The Sociology of Unconventional Lifestyles*, 2nd ed. New York: St. Martin's Press.

Magical Rat. 1994. Internet communication on newsgroup Alt.Pagan, December 14.

Manor, Lisa Dugan. 1994. "Welcome to the Hundred Acre Wood." *Mezlim: Practical Magick for Today* 5, no. 4: 15–16.

McArthur, Margie. 1994. *WiccaCraft for Families.* Langley: Phoenix Publishing.

Northage-Orr, Althea. 1994. "Working with Children." *Mezlim: Practical Magick for Today* 5, no. 4: 6–9.

O'Gaea, Ashleen. 1993. *The Family Wicca Book.* St. Paul: Llewellyn Publications.

Richardson, James T. 1985. "The Deformation of New Religions: Impacts of Societal and Organizational Factors." In *Cults, Culture and the Law,* edited by T. Robbins, W. Shepard, and J. McBride. Chico: Scholars Press.

Serith, Ceisiwr. 1994. *The Pagan Family: Handing the Old Ways Down.* St. Paul: Llewellyn Publications.

Sontag, Michael. 1994. "Children, Magick and Realism." *Mezlim: Practical Magick for Today* 5, no. 4: 12–13

Stanford-Blake, Donna. 1994. "Pagan Parenting: My Perspective." *Mezlim: Practical Magick for Today* 5, no. 4: 21.

Teague, Holly. 1994. "Children: The Next Generation." *Mezlim: Practical Magick for Today* 5, no. 4: 19–20.

CHAPTER 11

Wicked Witches of the West: Exploring Court Treatments of Wicca as a Religion[1]

Lori G. Beaman

The popular "Harry Potter" children's series by J.K. Rowling has brought about a contemporary discussion of witches and magic in popular media. Some of the discussion focuses on the "problem" of the occult, witches and evil, and their potential threat to social order. A variety of authorities pronounce on the potentially negative effects of children dabbling in the occult. A faculty member of an evangelical university recently assessed the books in this way: "The stories use magic and witchcraft in the same way as the fairytales of old. It's not used in a realistic way, that witchcraft really exists."[2] Such a challenge to the "reality" of witchcraft also emerges in Canada's Criminal Code, through the criminalization of witchcraft, sorcery, enchantment or conjuration, and fortune-telling as a way to negate the existence of any expression of spirituality that might take magic and miracles out of the hands of the proper male deity/ies.

The reaction to witches, and now to Wicca, in the course of human history reflects the social construction of the boundaries of what constitutes "normal" behaviour, beliefs, and spirituality. Most often, spirituality in the West is properly expressed through the exclusive worship of a male deity, despite the fact that it is women who are primarily responsible for the transmission of religious values and beliefs through their role in childhood socialization. It has been in the context of the patriarchal and hierarchical organization of existing religion that Wicca has developed as a means of empowerment for men, and perhaps especially for women, that stands in marked contrast to many other expressions of human spirituality. Thus, the reaction to Wicca can give us clues to the social construction of "normal" religious expression in Canadian society.

In this paper, I argue that support for freedom of religion as set out in the Canadian Charter of Rights and Freedoms and as articulated in human rights codes and the common law is really support for a particular kind of religious expression and organization. Those religions that do not conform to "traditional" models of religious practice are less likely to receive expansive protection for their spiritual goals. As a normalizing discourse, the law incorporates narrow definitions of what counts as religion worthy of constitutional protection. Especially vulnerable are those religions on the margins, more specifically those that fall outside of the traditional Protestant/Catholic split in Canadian religious participation. Although religious groups outside of these traditions constitute the minority of religious participants in Canada, it is for this very reason that they pose a unique challenge to the boundaries of the religious "normal" constructed by law. As a religion that is on the margins, the Craft, or Wicca, is part of the religious minority.[3] While the focus of this paper is on Canada, similar arguments can be made for many other countries as well (see York 2003; Hume 1995). In essence, the protection of freedom of religion plays out according to the specific religious terrain of each culture.

Those who call themselves, or have been called, witches have a long history of persecution in Western history (see Noonan 2002; Faith 1993), and although they are no longer sanctioned by being burned or hanged, contemporary witches remain a marginalized group, often confused with Satan worshippers and practitioners of black magic.

The suspicion surrounding contemporary witches has been incorporated in law, which preserves the status quo by prioritizing and protecting mainstream traditional religious groups. As a "non-conforming" religious group, Wicca is excluded from the privileges law accords to other, more mainstream, religions. In part, the exclusion of Wicca can be attributed to the fact that the majority of its adherents are women.[4] Thus, as in many other areas of social life, the lives and needs of women become denigrated in the perpetuation of patriarchy through the law. Wicca challenges the male metaphors so prevalent in most mainstream religions, especially the Christian notion of God the father (Scarboro and Luck 1997).[5]

Religious and legal discourses collude[6] to exclude Wicca from mainstream definitions of religion. As a religion that rejects the notion of the practitioner as needy or inadequate, Wicca threatens the order of mainstream religion by eliminating or reducing hierarchy (Scarboro and Luck 1997, see also Griffin 1995 and 2000). Empowerment, rather than submission, is emphasized through Wiccan practice and belief.[7] Luff identifies nine values, beliefs, or themes that are central to the Craft: independence, passion and emotion, love, the cycle of life, psychic powers, rejection of hierarchical social structures, no separation of politics and spirituality, the celebration of the physical aspects of life, and healing (1990:97–98). It is easy to see why the tenets of Wicca are perceived as a threat to the established order, and to the hierarchical basis of religion.

It should not be surprising that law colludes in the normalization process that preserves a dichotomy in which some religions are constructed as "normal" and others are labelled as dangerous cults. Harold Berman notes the similarities of law and religion, identifying tradition, rituals, authority, and moral universality as the underpinnings of the sanctity of law, which he identifies as its religious dimension (Berman 1991). Both institutions preserve a status quo that reifies patriarchal relations. That Wicca is on the boundaries is therefore predictable in that it rejects the hierarchical underpinnings that are central to both law and religion.

The power of law is its ability to set the boundaries of normal while maintaining that its fact-finding abilities produce a truth that is arrived at objectively and in a value-neutral way. Thus, in the case of witches and the Craft, the law sets up normal religion as those traditions that fall within the experience of the majority of Canadians. In earlier times the finding that one was a witch often resulted in torture and/or death. Today there are more subtle forms of punishment for transgressions from the norm, through the use of labels like "crazy" or "unfit mothers" or "unsuitable fathers" (see Frigon 1994).[8] Such labels are not outside of the law, but rather are reinforced by it as boundaries of the normal. Nonetheless, Canadian law claims to offer protection of religious expression.

The protection of religious expression is constitutionally mandated in a number of ways, but primarily through section 2(a), which states that "Everyone has the following fundamental freedoms: (a) freedom of conscience and religion." Section 15 also protects religious expression in relation to the issue of equality: "Every individual is equal before and under the law and has the right to the equal protection and equal benefit of the law without discrimination, in particular, without discrimination based on race, national or ethnic origin, colour, religion...." It is, however, a bit of a contradiction that while religious expression is protected in section 2, the preamble of the Charter of Rights and Freedoms acknowledges the supremacy of God, giving the Charter a suspiciously and specifically Christian tone and leaving the Goddess outside of the contemplation of the Charter.

WICCA IN CANADIAN SOCIETY

In contrast to the information available on their United States counterparts, there is a paucity of research on Canadian Wiccans. However, the Wiccan movement shares similar characteristics on both sides of the border.[9] Generally speaking, the Goddess is a powerful and central symbol for Wiccans,[10] who emphasize the achievement of ecstasy through ritual. This extends beyond individual ecstasy: "through symbols in ritual and interaction Pagan Witches construct forms of extraordinary magical consciousness which is a challenge to the one-dimensional secular bureaucratized reality which we assume in everyday life and conventional religion" (Kirkpatrick et al. 1986:37). Wicca is both non-hierarchical and non-dogmatic, giving it a fluidity and diversity that other religions often lack.[11] Wiccans share a respect and concern for nature, and frame many of their rituals with natural cycles, such as the seasons, the moon, and menstruation (see Neitz 1990 for a detailed discussion; also Griffin 2000). Wicca offers an opportunity to express spirituality both individually and in the context of a small group without the oppressive hierarchy imposed by other organized religions.[12] It also politicizes the oppression of women while at the same time emphasizing healing (see Greenwood 1996). Needless to say, Wicca has held special appeal for women, who sometimes feel out of place in the patriarchal structure of much organized religion (see Beaman 2001).

Wiccan beliefs are dominated by a central moral principle: Do what you will, but harm no one.[13] Wiccans believe that when harm is done, it will return to the sender magnified. Although not all Wiccan groups are feminist or woman-centred, many covens, as well as solo practitioners, in North America are. In Canada, the number of witches is unknown,[14] but we do know that adherents of new religious movements make up less than 1 percent of Canadians (Bibby 1987). Certainly there can be no argument that Wicca falls within the "religious minority" category, which is the central focus in this paper.

WICCA AND CANADIAN LEGAL HISTORY

The legal history of the persecution of witches in Canada is an interesting one and, like so much of Canadian law, has its origins in Britain. While England abolished the widespread witch-hunting of the sixteenth and seventeenth centuries, it preserved this past time in more subtle ways in the Witchcraft Act. Early cases conflate all manner of practices under the general heading of "witchcraft," a tendency that still exists today. The statutory trajectory in Canada begins with the Witchcraft Act, 1735 9 Geo 2c5. It essentially criminalized pretending to "exercise or use any kind of witchcraft, sorcery, enchantment, or conjuration." This eventually became codified in the Vagrancy Act, 1824, and then section 443 of the Criminal Code of Canada, which prior to 1954 read:

> Every one is guilty of an indictable offence and liable to one year's imprisonment who pretends to exercise or use any kind of witchcraft, sorcery, enchantment or conjuration, or undertakes to tell fortunes, or pretend from his skill or knowledge in any occult or crafty science, to discover where or in what manner any goods or chattels supposed to have been stolen or lost may be found.

Regina v. Stanley confirmed that the method of fortune-telling did not matter. A 1955 amendment to the Criminal Code added the word "fraudulently," thus introducing the possibility that some supernatural communing is possible and that such activities are not always fraudulent. However, case law seems to have quashed that possibility and while *Dazenbrook* held that evidence of fraudulent intention became necessary with the amendment, subsequent cases have eroded such an interpretation, perhaps the most important being *Labrosse v. The Queen*. In that 1987 decision, the Supreme Court of Canada upheld the conviction of the accused, accepting the finding of the trial judge that whether or not the accused believed she had special powers to predict the future was irrelevant. The trial judge stated: "The accused knows full well that she has no basis for her claim to be able to predict what will happen in people's futures." On this basis, the requirement of fraudulence under the Criminal Code was met (see also *Regina v. Corbeil*).

Presently, the Criminal Code section covers witchcraft under "Pretending to Practise Witchcraft, etc.," section 365, which reads very similarly to its predecessors:

> Every one who fraudulently
> (a) pretends to exercise or to use any kind of witchcraft, sorcery, enchantment or conjuration,
> (b) undertakes, for a consideration, to tell fortunes, or
> (c) pretends from his skill in or knowledge of an occult or crafty science to discover where or in what manner anything that is supposed to have been stolen or lost may be found,
> is guilty of an offence punishable on summary conviction.

The constitutionality of this section in relation to sections 2(a) and 15 has actually been considered by the Ontario District Court in *R. v. Duarte.*[15] In that case, the accused prescribed special tea for an emotionally upset woman. No specific mention of Wicca is made, but the accused makes the argument that the practices outlined in section 365 should be considered to fall under the category of "religion." The Court states that the purpose of the protection of religious freedom is to "protect true freedom of religion by trying to curb the charlatans." After examining the nature of religion as set out in *Big M. Drug Mart*[16] and *Edwards Books*[17] the Court concluded that the practices of the accused were religious. However, although the Court held that there is no obligation on the accused to present evidence as to whether there was honesty in his belief that he possessed healing powers, the evidence of the Crown as to his dishonesty was accepted. All that was required to prove dishonesty, it seemed, was evidence that the accused accepted payment for his prescription. The Court refused to overturn the guilty finding of the trial judge. The decisions turns on the lower Court's assessment of the accused's credibility. Freedom of religion seems to get lost as an issue in this case as a result of the need to balance freedom of religion with protection from charlatans.[18]

The Criminal Code section continues the conflation of witchcraft with a wide variety of other practices, and clearly does not consider Wicca as a religion. Lynne Hume points out, in her analysis of the nearly identical provision of the Australian Criminal Code, that there is a presumption underlying the law that people simply cannot do these sorts of things (work magic). Therefore, any claim to be able to do them is automatically fraudulent. In other words, the baseline approach of the law is that many of the practices associated with modern witchcraft are impossible. Note that this same presumption does not apply to Christian faith healers, who can publicly perform their miracles and simultaneously request financial support. Although there is admittedly some skepticism in relation to such acts, even within Christian circles, they are not criminalized per se.

How, then, is the law able to support a distinction between conjuring and prayer? Scientific discourse and the discourse of mainstream religion set the boundaries of the possible within law. While it is possible for mainstream Christians to pray to God and to be heard, it is not possible for those outside of Christian religions to commune with the dead for advice, particularly if it relates to lost objects. In *Rex v. Pollock*, the Court states outright that Parliament believed that lost objects cannot be found using "crafty science." This of course stands in interesting contrast to the use of psychics by police to locate bodies, which could presumably fall into the category of "lost objects" (see Lyons and Truzzi 1991 for a discussion of the use of psychics or "sensitives" by law enforcement agencies).

LEGAL BOUNDARIES AND WICCA

In this section, I will explore the legal parameters of religious expression and how it limits, rather than protects, the everyday actions of Wiccans. Firstly, the constitutional and human rights protection of freedom of religion should offer Wiccans some reassurance that, particularly as participants in a minority religion, they are guaranteed some protection for their beliefs and practices. Given its relatively recent enactment, it is premature to determine the applicability of the Canadian Charter of Rights and Freedoms; however, the pattern of case law related to other religious minorities should not engender optimism among Wiccans. Secondly, cases in which the courts have had to think about Wicca have arisen primarily in the areas of custody, and in relation to one particular section of the Criminal Code.[19] From these cases, and those cases in which Wicca is casually mentioned, we can conclude that there is a general ignorance about the beliefs of practices of Wiccans, reflecting the misconceptions about Wicca that are pervasive in our society. Finally, "administrative" laws and policies like the authority to solemnize marriages and the attainment of tax-exempt status as a religious organization are *indicia* of a group's legal status as a religious organization, as well as their social recognition as a religion. I will discuss each of these three areas in turn.

a. Religious Freedom in Canada

Constitutionally, the interpretation of the meaning of freedom of religion under section 2(a) of the Charter has been broad. The courts have expressed a reluctance to place "internal" limits on the freedom of religion guaranteed in the Charter.[20] Unlike the United States' jurisprudence, the distinction between belief and practice has received little attention from Canadian courts.[21] Freedom of religion is interpreted to include both belief and practice. However, one of the ways in which the courts have been able to skirt the issue of what constitutes a religion is to use a section 1 analysis to limit the breadth of religious freedom. Section 1 of the Charter of Rights and Freedoms states: "The Canadian Charter of Rights and Freedoms guarantees the rights and freedoms set out in it subject only to such reasonable limits prescribed by law as can be demonstrably justified in a free and democratic society." An early Charter decision in which the court uses section 1 as a limit to religious freedom is *Edwards Books.* In that case, the Court found a violation of 2(a) rights in that the Sunday closing laws compromised the religious freedom of non-Christian groups. A section 1 analysis "saved" the Sunday closing laws as being a reasonable limit in a free and democratic society. Similarly, in *Re Sheena B*[22] the 2(a) rights of Jehovah's Witness parents were found to have been violated by the state's intervention in their daughter's medical care, but such intervention was justified under section 1. Both cases involved religious minorities. In essence, although there appears to be a sweeping and inclusive protection of religious freedom in Canada, the section 1 limitation is a powerful tool in the establishment and maintenance of religious normalcy.

We might speculate that the potentially more fruitful pursuit of religious protection for Wiccans (or any religious minority) might be under section 15.[23] Section 15 states that "every individual is equal before and under the law and has the right to the equal protection and equal benefit of the law without discrimination and, in particular, without discrimination based on race, national or ethnic origin, colour, religion, sex, age, or mental or physical disability." Under section 15, an argument could be made that an individual is being discriminated against on the basis of her religious beliefs, or that Wiccans are being discriminated against as a group. However, in general, those who fall within the gamut of traditional religious beliefs and practices are protected by the law, and those whose beliefs fall outside of the "normal" are not protected. The discourse surrounding such discrimination is subtle and relies on the social construction of the boundaries of religious normalcy. For example, the religious mainstream mediates law and society in this instance through participation in the legal construction of the sphere of religious expression eligible for protection. The establishment of "the normal" has a long history of mainstream religious groups contributing to boundary construction. In *Rex v. Pollock* the Court cites "the Very Reverend" Dean Harris, described as "the well-known Canadian ecclesiastic," for guidance on the meaning of particular words in the Court's interpretation of the Witchcraft Act, 1736. We rarely see Wiccan authorities relied upon for information in legal processes. The "expert" is located outside of minority religious groups. It is only through validation of the mainstream religious expert that law accepts "questionable" beliefs and practices.

b. Wicca in Case Law

Beyond the constitutional and human rights provisions, it is important to examine the way in which the courts talk about Wicca specifically. There are several challenges involved in the process of analyzing case law dealing with witches. First, there simply are not that many cases. Another challenge is the questionable relationship between some practices and witchcraft—specifically fortune-telling. Since we rarely hear the voices of the accused in case reports, it is difficult to tell whether they see themselves as Wiccan. The tendency of the courts to lump together witchcraft and any practice that is seen as remotely related to the occult further complicates matters. This is, in part, ignorance about Wicca, but also can be attributed to the fluid nature of Wicca itself, and to the diversity of its participants (see Griffin 2000).

Custody cases provide an interesting example of the potential vulnerability of Wiccans when they come before the courts, and indeed, when they enter the realm of legal discourse at the mundane, behind closed doors level of the law office. Unfortunately, most of those cases remain "private," so we must rely on case law for our examples.[24] Two interesting cases involve Wiccan fathers. In *Ryan v. Ryan* the Court held that the father should not be denied access based on his interests in the Rosicrucian Order and "witchcraft and the occult and a belief in the paranormal." The Court stated that "it would only be where it would create unhealthy ideas in a young mind and disturb the influence of the mother as custodian over the child that such interests would serve to diminish or eliminate the right of access between the father and child." However, the Court was careful to prohibit the father from interfering with the Catholic mother's right to raise the child in her religious tradition, barring him from talking to the child about his religious beliefs. Specifically, the Court ordered that "the Applicant not introduce the child to nor encourage a belief on the part of the child in any religious or philosophical influences whatsoever other than those of Roman Catholicism unless the Respondent agrees." Given the respondent mother's objection to religious beliefs other than her own, it is highly unlikely that the access father would have the opportunity to talk to the child about his beliefs in the near future.[25] The Court was concerned that the father might introduce the child to beliefs that might frighten him, without consideration for the fact that many children find references to the body and blood of Christ, and to burning in Hell for all eternity, frightening.

In *Gay v. Kingston* an Alberta court examined the Wiccan father's beliefs in some detail. In that case the custodial mother objected to the father having access because of his involvement in Wicca. The Court stated: "To some, the very name conjures visions of a satanic cult performing bloody rituals with scorpions, cauldrons and magic wands." Interestingly, the Court went on to consider the father's evidence on his religion:

> GDG admits that the members of his faith are called witches but denies that he has seen or been involved in any activity which could be described as abhorrent or even controversial. He has described certain "spells" which he has used, but when questioned by the court, his answers led me to the conclusion that these so-called "spells" could readily be compared to certain rituals and prayers used in more conventional religious services. He describes his faith as being "nature based"; he believes in the "duality of gods"; he sees the divine with many faces; he worships more than one god. Is this so very different from the beliefs of the millions of adherents to the Hindu faith? Or the beliefs of the various North American aboriginal peoples?[26]

The father agreed to abstain from discussing his religion with his son until he was at least 12. In examining the content of the father's beliefs the Court came to the conclusion that access would not be contrary to the best interests of the child, the ultimate test in any contest surrounding children.[27]

The degree to which the courts should examine the content of religious beliefs is an ongoing debate that has perhaps seen more heated discussion in the United States than in Canada. One of the advantages of excluding the content of religion from examination is that, at least on the surface, courts are prevented from making value judgments and creating hierarchies of religious beliefs. The danger of subjecting the content of particular religious doctrines/practices/beliefs to court scrutiny is illustrated in *Re Church of Scientology and the Queen* (No. 6),[28] in which we see the Ontario Court of Appeal taking a skeptical view of the artifacts, beliefs, and practices of Scientology. But that case also illustrates the danger of leaving religious beliefs outside of or on the periphery of court consideration. The Court seems to distance itself from any examination of the content of Scientology, while at the same time making cursory and disparaging comments about the practices of Scientologists. Yet the allegations of fraud made against the Church of Scientology could be made against most any other group were their practices to be subjected to similar scrutiny. More importantly, in mainstream religious groups such activities are constructed as both normal and legal.

Similar concerns arise in relation to Wicca. The legal discussion of Wicca has been less than well informed, with the possible exceptions of the custody cases discussed above.[29] In those, the Court seemed to have no qualms about exploring the content of the father's religious beliefs, and did so with reasonable accuracy. Whether the courts had expert evidence on Wiccan practices remains unclear, but from a reading of the cases we can tentatively conclude that they did not. Unfortunately, the Criminal Code treatment of "witchcraft, etc.," and the casual mention of Wicca in other cases would suggest that there is a general ignorance about Wiccan practices that permeates the courts and the legal system.

For example, in *R. v. Koehn*, the Court mentions the fact that the accused, who is convicted of killing a three-and-a-half-year-old boy, is a witch. The court does say that "Wiccan"[30] does not play a role in the death of the child, but the very raising of the issue of Mr. Koehn's involvement implicates Wicca in the murder. Another such damaging mention of Wicca is found in *R. v. KG*, a case involving a sexual assault of an "adopted" daughter. In that case, the accused's former wife is mentioned as potentially being a witch, and thus invoking fear in the victim. In *R. v. Reddick*, the alleged involvement of the accused in witchcraft and pedophilia (mentioned in the same sentence) are noted as appropriate (negative) evidence respecting the character of the accused. His link to Wicca is described as his being "a member of an unusual occult group." In *R. v. Dixon* the mother-in-law of the accused is mentioned as practising witchcraft and therefore she is assessed as being a malign influence. Although the Court does not accept this line of defence, it describes witchcraft as a "cult." While these reference are minor, they represent the perception of Wicca as being outside of the normal, and the general lumping together of Wicca with vaguely negative practices and beliefs outside of more mainstream religious traditions. Indeed, it is clear that in most cases the courts do not consider the religious nature of Wicca at all, or the content of Wiccan beliefs. Such casual incorrect references to Wicca serve to reinforce the popular tendency to confuse Wicca with Satan worship, or other vaguely sinister "occult" practices.

Equally as troubling, however, is the case of *R. v. Appleby*, in which the Court does explore the truth of a statement by the accused, charged with carrying a concealed weapon. The accused claimed that he was a "witch and follower of the cult of Wicca and the use of drugs and the carrying of the knife were part of his religion." The expert evidence accepted by the Court is disturbing. The expert described Wicca as being "a man who practices magic." The word "Wicca" is now used primarily to describe a particular belief system and its attendant practices (Griffin 2000). The expert also testified that "the use in Wicca of drugs is common but not universal." Drug use is not encouraged among Wiccans and it is certainly not a prescribed component of ritual (Griffin 2000). On the topic of Wicca as a religion, the expert stated: "It is not a religion in the common sense and is not universally acknowledged—but to those who practice it—yes—it is a religion." What is "common sense" religion? And what is the empirical evidence of the common use of drugs in Wicca? The Court rejected the symbolic nature of the knife carried by the (male) accused,[31] holding that "I find it totally ludicrous and simply untenable that the accused, a self-confessed witch and a deliberate drug user and substance abuser who takes drugs and conceals a dangerous weapon for the purposes of, or under veil or guise, of his beliefs, religious or otherwise, in the occult, magic, mystery and the craft of Wicca should for those reasons and under such circumstances, have a right or privilege to do so." Here the substance abuse of the accused becomes transposed from a personal practice and addiction to a component of his religious belief system, yet drug use and abuse is no more a part of Wiccan practice and ritual than it is of Roman Catholic or Protestant ritual.

While the general pattern of legal decision making is one of misunderstanding and arguably discrimination, there are occasionally decisions that incorporate an incredible sensitivity to the assessment of minority religions. One such case involving Wicca is *Re Humber College and O.P.S.E.U.*, a 1987 decision of a labour arbitration board. That case involved an employee grievance alleging that he had been improperly denied a leave of absence to celebrate the Wiccan holidays, Samhain and Beltane. The collective agreement provided for paid leave for religious reasons. The board allowed the grievance after carefully examining the content of the employee's religious beliefs. Both the employee and an expert witness provided details about Wicca. The board noted:

> There is always an inherent danger in a description of a religion by a non-adherent, and we embark on a description of Wica with some caution. To whatever extent our description proves inaccurate, we hope that it will be understood that no disrespect is intended. (268)

Later, the board reformulated the question at hand to avoid having to determine "whether Wicca constitutes a religion."

> It is surely very presumptuous for a board of arbitration to purport to decide what is and what is not religion; indeed, that is a dangerous question for any secular authority to attempt to answer. (271)

The board goes on to consider the testimony of the expert, who is an ordained minister of the United Church of Canada:

> Professor Evans made a strong plea not to judge other religions from an essentially Christian perspective, a perspective which, he testified, has led in the past to persecution and suppression of a number of pagan religions, including the aboriginal spirituality of North America.... It was Professor Evans' expert opinion that Wicca is a religion, in both the ordinary and the technical sense of the word. (272)

While this case is evidence of the potential of law to be sensitive to minority religions, it does have several limitations that are worth noting. Firstly, while the board decides in the employee's favour, it does limit the damages based on the employee's "secrecy." Admittedly this is a difficult position—the employer must have enough information to make an informed decision. However, like the temple rituals of Mormons, Wiccan rituals and practices are somewhat secret. Secondly, although the expert involved was clearly sympathetic to the Wiccan faith and seems to have played a role in the board's sensitive approach, it is a bit troubling that a mainstream religious authority was required to validate the position of Wicca as a religion. Finally, and with no disrespect intended, the deciding body is an administrative tribunal, not a court. Thus while we may be encouraged that there is a careful consideration of Wicca within a legal decision-making process, it is not representative of the approach of all courts, or the law generally.

c. The Bureaucratic Realm

Certainly, in realms of law other than those that are specifically constitutional, Wicca has not been recognized as deserving of the same legal privileges as "mainstream" religions. Of specific interest are the administrative decisions made by bureaucratic gatekeepers. Unlike case law and legislation, these processes and decisions remain largely obscured and particularly difficult to document in any systematic manner. They reinforce the dominant religious order, while remaining sheltered by bureaucratic "neutrality."

In Canada, Síân Reid focuses on two specific examples of bureaucratic exclusion in her work—the ability to solemnize marriage and the achievement of tax-exempt status as a religious group—to support her argument that Wicca is not taken seriously by the state as a religion. The essence of Reid's argument is that the lack of hierarchical structure in Wicca poses a serious barrier to access to the legal privileges and protections available to other religions. Further, she argues, the fact that it is the individual, and not the group or congregation, that is the "fundamental working unit" of Wicca also poses challenges. In addition, the lack of a formal priesthood or trained clergy means that Wicca may be excluded from the legal status that includes the ability to perform basic rites like marriage:

> In the case of marriages, all of the existing provincial marriage legislation incorporates provisions that require that those registered to perform legal marriages as clergy: 1) have an application for registration submitted on their behalf by the religious body to which they belong; 2) be duly ordained or appointed according to the rites and usages of the religious body to which they belong; 3) be duly recognized by the religious body to which they belong as authorized to solemnize marriage. These requirements presume a centralized administrative structure, and a comprehensive and consistent set of practices around the differentiation between "clergy" and "laity." (1994:9)

Similar difficulties arise when Wiccans try to "fit" into Revenue Canada guidelines for charities. There is a bias in these provisions that privileges a particular kind of organizational structure and indeed forces a specific form of organization if a group wishes to be included. As Reid points out, "most covens and small groups are unlikely to prepare bylaws, a statement of purpose, a constitution or a trust document" (1994:14), thus excluding them by virtue of their organizational structure from privileges accorded other religions. This, of course, may have its advantages in that it protects, to some measure, Wiccans from state control and regulation.

At a broader level, if we think about how religion is conceptualized in law, it is apparent that not only organizationally, but in terms of beliefs, Wicca falls outside of the legally and socially constructed boundaries of normal religious dogma. When the courts do attempt to support minority religions, immigration, rather than non-conventional forms of religious belief and expression, is seen as the source of religious difference in Canada.

CONCLUSIONS

With such a small percentage of people engaged in new religious movements in Canada, it might be argued that how the courts perceive them is inconsequential. However, it is small group protection that exemplifies a state's sincerity in the protection of religious freedom. Wicca is a particularly compelling example because it challenges the religious hegemony that is, in Canada, largely Christian. The ways in which Wicca is described in most case law, and the fact that some of its practices are still criminalized, would indicate that Wicca continues to be a site for the demonization of its practitioners.

Shupe and Bromley (1978) argue that when marginal religious groups are perceived as a "clear and present danger to cherished values," they become socially constructed as evil. As a secretive and relatively unknown religion, Wicca is especially susceptible to being constructed as "evil." By conflating Wicca with Satanism, it is easy to portray it as embodying evil. Even when it is separated from Satanism, Wicca is still presented as a threat to "Christian society." While this may not evoke the same reactions as it did in the sixteenth and seventeenth centuries, it does, nonetheless, constitute a threat to some sort of perceived social order. As Shupe and Bromley point out, "In Colonial America women were considered to be more likely to become possessed or be seduced into pacts with the Devil. In modern America youthful instability and idealism are perceived as qualities that render young persons prey to unscrupulous exploitation" (1978:75). We are not so far removed from the age of hysteria. Women, particularly young women, are still treated as being easily influenced and vulnerable, and therefore, of course, in need of protection. As a religion that attracts young women, Wicca is easily targeted as a malign influence on the vulnerable. What could be more dangerous than a religion that emphasizes women's bodies (in non-objectifying ways), women's empowerment, and the value of women?

The identification process also connects to a larger social malaise recently identified in North American society. A general lack of morals, values, Christian commitment, family connectedness (especially to a "traditional" nuclear family), and a longing for a return to the "good old days" has left marginal groups particularly vulnerable to accusations of being part of the cause of the evil in our society. Through its woman-centred beliefs and practices Wicca does threaten the social order, which is built on the foundation of continued patriarchal relations and established institutions. Majority religions are also threatened by Wicca. Women have formed the backbone of church support—what if they found a religion in which they were the focus? What if they became the priests instead of the polishers of silver? But male Wiccans are also vulnerable, for they are perceived as being complicit in the destruction of the nuclear family. By worshipping a goddess alongside of a god, they are not behaving as "real" men.

The processes of identification and neutralization identified by Shupe and Bromley are revealed at the point at which women are identified as "witches" and punished. The criminalization of practices associated with witchcraft is just one small part of this process. Generally speaking, those who identify as witches are cast outside of the "normal." We move then, drawing on the words of Michel Foucault, from the spectacle to the gaze, in which women are socially controlled through the social construction of the normal woman, the normal mother, and the normal religion. It is important to recognize that these controls impact on different women and groups of women differently. For example, lesbian women are already relegated to the margins for their sexuality (see Lahey 1999); and more so if they choose to become mothers (see Waccholz 2000). So too, male witches challenge established gender roles in that they participate in a religion that undermines patriarchal order. Freely expressing one's religious commitment as a witch renders one especially vulnerable in this case.

Legal tradition, including legislative protection of freedom of religion, would suggest that religious freedom is an important component of Canadian culture. However, an examination of case law, which is an important site of interpretation, reveals that religion is conceptualized within very narrow boundaries. Wiccans are not the only marginalized and vulnerable group—Aboriginals, new religious movements, and immigrants whose spirituality is practised outside of the Christian tradition are all relegated to the margins of legal protection. This paper is a call for an exploration of the boundaries of the religious "normal" as they are constructed within law.

NOTES

1. I am grateful for the financial support of the Social Sciences and Humanities Research Council for this research. Thank you to Rebecca Johnson for her suggestions on an earlier draft. Deanna Taylor and Cameron Gleadow are also owed thanks for their invaluable research assistance. A draft of this paper was presented at the annual meetings of the Society for the Scientific Study of Religion, Houston, Texas, 2000.
2. Reported in the June 24, 2000, issue of the *Telegraph-Journal.*
3. For a careful working through of the complexities of the religious minority/majority dichotomy, see Wright (2000).
4. Berger estimates that approximately 65–75 percent of Wiccans are women (1999).
5. Some forms of Wicca challenge male metaphors more explicitly than do others. Dianic witches, for example, are separatist and politically active. See Lozano and Foltz (1990); also Finley (1991).
6. For a detailed discussion of the collusion of discourses, see Smart (1989).
7. Interestingly, although women see their involvement in Wicca as a source of empowerment, it has historically been seen as a sign of women's "spiritual inferiority which rendered them especially susceptible to the allures of malevolent forces" (Anderson and Gordon 1978:173). See Christ (1982) for a more detailed discussion of the implications of goddess worship and the specifics of empowerment. See also Goldenberg (1979) for an overview of feminist witchcraft.
8. The social construction of the normal involves arguments similar to those that would identify the legitimation of political authority as an explanation for the early witch persecutions. See Migliore (1983).

9. Catharine Cookson summarizes the legal obstacles faced by Wiccans in the United States. They are: child custody, zoning disputes, challenges under the Establishment Clause, and tax-exempt status challenges. Establishment clause cases form a uniquely U.S. jurisprudence because Canada does not have a constitutional anti-establishment clause. For a discussion of establishment challenges related to Wicca, see DeMitchell (1994).
10. "Even in groups in which both the female and male deities are venerated, the goddess is seen as more important than the gods" (Berger et al. 2003:5).
11. This does not mean, however, that there is no routinization within Wicca. Helen Berger (1999) argues that this has occurred both in the sharing of information about rituals as well as through the "celebrity status" of some individuals.
12. For an examination of women's strategies for coping with the patriarchal structure of organized religion, see Winter et al. (1994).
13. "The magical concern about morality seems to serve two purposes. On the one hand, it suggests that the elusive forces are real, powerful and significant by emphasizing the increased responsibility of the magician: if black magic is prohibited, it must be because it has an effect" (Luhrmann 1989:81).
14. Berger estimates that there are 150,000–300,000 Wiccans in the United States; Griffin, citing Smoley, estimates the Goddess community at 500,000. Sîân Reid reports that Statistics Canada indicates 21,085 people self-identified as pagans on the 2001 Census of Canada.
15. 1990 O.J. no. 690, May 1990.
16. 18 C.C.C. (3rd) 385.
17. 30 C.C.C. (3rd) 385.
18. See also *R. v. Turgeon* [1993] A.Q. no. 523.
19. In the United States, parents have brought lawsuits against several school districts for "promoting" Wicca in violation of the anti-establishment clause of the U.S. constitution. For a discussion see DeMitchell (1994).
20. This does not mean that no limits have been considered. Indeed in some cases it is not clear whether the court is imposing internal limits or using section 1 to place limits on the interpretation of freedom of religion.

21. The most recent Supreme Court of Canada decision on religion, *Trinity Western* (decided in May 2001), qualifies this statement somewhat. There, the Court makes a clear distinction between belief and practice.
22. *Re Sheena B.* 176 N.R. SCC.
23. Section 15 has not yet been used as fully as it might be. In *Adler* 140 DLR 4th, 385 it is raised as a possible way to support an argument for state support for denominational schools. In her dissent, L'Heureux-Dube J found that the failure of the Ontario government to provide funding for denominational schools constituted a violation of section 15.
24. For a general discussion of religion and custody, see Van Praagh (1997). A casual mention of Wicca is made in *Athanasopoulos v. Nitz* [1993] BCJ 2151. In that case the access mother is reputed to have "been involved in witchcraft, attended black masses and may have an interest in the occult." The mother admitted that she had attended black masses and had dabbled in the occult. Her commitment to the Wiccan faith is not mentioned, despite the inclusion of witchcraft in the list of accusations that were seen to potentially impact on the ability of the mother as an access parent.
25. This case is in sharp contrast to the subsequently decided SCC decision in *Young v. Young*, which might have had an impact on the access father's right to talk about his beliefs, although *P(D) v. SC*, handed down on the same day, suggests that marginal religions may still be treated as breeding grounds for fanaticism.
26. 1992 AJ 1171.
27. An interesting contrast to this sensitive discussion is found in *Johnson v. Johnson*, 83 Sask. R. 315, in which the Court states: "If the father were an adherent to satanism or any form of witchcraft the anxiety of the mother would be well founded."
28. 31 CCC (3rd) 449 Ont CA.
29. *Dettmer v. London* 799 F 2nd Fourth Circuit Federal Appeals Court 1986 decision affirmed that Wicca is a religion for 1st Amendment purposes. In deciding this, the district court did examine the content of Wiccan beliefs and practices. The Australian courts have left open the possibility of Wicca being included as a religion through their definition of religion in

The Church of the New Faith. See Lynn Hume (1995) for a development of this analysis.

30. The Court misuses Wicca and Wiccan in its brief discussion of this issue.
31. The Court stated, "A weapon does not cease to be a weapon because it is a religious symbol."

REFERENCES

Anderson, Alan, and Raymond Gordon. 1978. "Witchcraft and the Status of Women—the case of England." *British Journal of Sociology* 29, no. 2: 171–184.

Barker, Eileen. 1987. "New Religions and Cults in Europe." In *The Encyclopedia of Religion*, edited by Mircea Elide, 405–410. New York: Free Press.

Beaman, Lori G. 2001. "Introduction to Gender and Religion." In *Sociology of Religion: A Reader*, edited by M. Emerson, William Mirola, Susanne Monahan, 115–143. Englewood Hills: Prentice Hall.

Berger, Helen A. 1999. *A Community of Witches: Contemporary Neo-Paganism and Witchcraft in the United States*. Columbia: University of South Carolina Press.

Berger, Helen A. et al. 2003. *Voices from the Pagan Census: A National Survey of Witches & Neopagans in the United States*. Columbia: University of South Carolina Press.

Berman, Harold J. 1991. "Law and Religion in the Development of a World Order." *Sociological Analysis* 52, no. 1: 36.

Bibby, Reginald. 1987. *Fragmented Gods: The Poverty and Potential of Religion in Canada*. Toronto: Irwin.

Christ, Carol P. 1982. "Why Women Need the Goddess: Phenomenological, Psychological, and Political Reflections." In *The Politics of Women's Spirituality: Essays on the Rise of Spiritual Power within the Feminist Movement*, edited by Charlene Spretnak, 71–85. Garden City: Anchor Books.

Cookson, Catharine. 1997. "Reports from the Trenches: A Case Study of Religious Freedom Issues Faced by Wiccans Practicing in the United States." *Journal of Church and State* 39, no. 2: 723–748.

DeMitchell, Todd A. 1994. "Witches, Cauldrons, and 'Wicca' in the Public School Curriculum: Is Government Establishing a Religion? The Courts Think Not." *International Journal of Educational Reform* 3, no. 4: 474–480.

Faith, Karlene. 1993. *Unruly Women: The Politics of Confinement and Resistance.* Vancouver: Press Gang Publishers.

Finley, Nancy J. 1991. "Political Activism and Feminist Spirituality." *Sociological Analysis* 2, no. 4: 349–362.

Foucault, Michel. 1979. *Discipline and Punish: The Birth of the Prison.* Translated by Alan Sheridan. New York: Vintage.

Frigon, Sylvie. 1994. "Femmes, Heresies et Controle Social: Des Sorcieres aux Sages-Femmes et au-Dela." *Canadian Journal of Women and the Law* 7: 133.

Garrett, Clarke. 1977. "Women and Witches: Patterns of Analysis." *Signs: Journal of Women in Culture and Society* 3, no. 21: 461–470.

Goldenberg, Naomi R. 1979. *Changing of the Gods: Feminism and the End of Traditional Religion.* Boston: Beacon Press.

Greenwood, Susan. 1996. "Feminist Witchcraft: A Transformatory Politics." In *Practising Feminism: Identity, Difference, Power,* edited by Nickie Charles and Felicia Hughes-Freeland, 109–134. London: Routledge.

Griffin, Wendy. 1995. "The Embodied Goddess: Feminist Witchcraft and Female Divinity." *Sociology of Religion* 56, no. 1: 35–48.

———, ed. 2000. *Daughters of the Goddess: Studies of Healing, Identity, and Empowerment.* New York: AltaMira Press.

hooks, bell. 1994. *Outlaw Culture: Resisting Representations.* New York: Routledge.

Hume, Lynne. 1995. "Witchcraft and the Law in Australia." *Journal of Church and State* 37: 135–150.

Kamir, Orit. 2000. *Every Breath You Take: Stalking Narratives and the Law.* Ann Arbor: University of Michigan Press.

Kirkpatrick, R. George, Rich Rainey, and Kathryn Ruby. 1986. "An Empirical Study of Wiccan Religion in Postindustrial Society." *Free Inquiry in Creative Sociology* 14, no. 1: 33–37.

Lahey, Kathleen A. 1999. *Are We "Persons" Yet? Law and Sexuality in Canada.* Toronto: University of Toronto Press.

Lozano, Wendy G., and Tanice G. Foltz. 1990. "Into the Darkness: An Ethnographic Study of Witchcraft and Death." *Qualitative Sociology* 13, no. 3: 211–234.

Luhrmann, Tanya. 1989. *Persuasions of the Witch's Craft.* Oxford: Oxford University Press.

Lyons, Arthur, and Marcello Truzzi. 1991. *The Blue Sense: Psychic Detectives and Crime.* New York: Warner Books.

Luff, Tracy L. 1990. "Wicce: Adding a Spiritual Dimension to Feminism." *Berkeley Journal of Sociology* 35: 91–105.

Migliore, Sam. 1983. "The Doctor, the Lawyer and the Melancholy Witch." *Anthropologica* 25, no. 2: 163–192.

Neitz, Mary Jo. 1990. "In Goddess We Trust." In *In Gods We Trust: New Patterns of Religious Pluralism in America*, edited by Thomas Robbins and Dick Anthony, 353–372. New Brunswick: Transaction Publishers.

Noonan, Sheila. 2002. "Of Death, Desire and Knowledge: Law and Social Control of Witches in Renaissance Europe." *Social Context and Social Location in the Sociology of Law*, edited by Gayle MacDonald, 91–129. Toronto: Broadview Press.

Reid, Síân. 1994. "Illegitimate Religion: Neopagan Witchcraft and the Institutional Sanction of Religion in Canada." Paper presented at the Learneds in Calgary.

———. 1999. "Witch Wars: The Tensions between Ideology and Practice in Canadian Neopagan Communities." Paper presented at the Qualitative Analysis Conference in Fredericton.

Scarboro, Allen, and Philip Andrew Luck. 1997. "The Goddess and Power: Witchcraft and Religion in America." *Journal of Contemporary Religion* 12, no. 1: 69.

Shupe, Anson, and David Bromley, eds. 1978. "Witches, Moonies and Evil." *Society* 15, no. 4: 75–76.

Smart, Carol. 1989. *Feminism and the Power of Law.* London: Routledge.

Spanos, Nicholas P. 1978. "Witchcraft in Histories of Psychiatry: A Critical Analysis and an Alternative Conceptualization." *Psychological Bulletin* 85, no. 2: 417–439.

Van Praagh, Shauna. 1997. "Religion, Custody, and a Child's Identities." *Osgoode Hall Law Journal* 35: 309–378.

Vaughan, Megan. 1991. *Curing Their Ills: Colonial Power and African Illness.* Cambridge: Polity Press.

Waccholz, Sandra. 2000. "The Good Mother." In *New Perspectives on Deviance: The Construction of Deviance in Everyday Life*, edited by Lori G. Beaman, 180–191. Scarborough: Prentice-Hall.

Winter, Miram Therese, Adair Lummis, and Allison Stokes. 1994. *Defecting in Place: Women Claiming Responsibility for Their Own Spiritual Lives.* New York: Crossroad.

Wright, Sherry. 2000. "Impact of Religious Pluralism on Designation of Minority Religions." Unpublished manuscript.

York, Michael. 2003 "Defining Paganism." Paper presented at the annual meeting of the Society for Scientific Study of Religion, Houston, Texas, November.

CHAPTER 12

In Defence of Magic: Philosophical and Theological Rationalization

Tanya Luhrmann

magicians need to rationalize their magic, to give reasons for their involvement, which they think that the outsider should at least accept as reasons, because they live in a society in which magic is not taken for granted. Different magicians follow different routes to justify their practice. However, a common tendency emerges. Magicians often argue indirectly for the value of believing in magic, rather than for the truth of magical ideas. That is, rather than arguing for magic as a persuasive account of physical reality, magicians tend to explain why the normal criteria of truth-testing do not apply to magic. Then, they justify their involvement on the grounds of its spirituality, its freedom, its aesthetic beauty, and so forth. Despite the difficulty of arguing by the normal rules, magicians are not willing to abandon their claims. That, one might imagine, would be the simplest solution to cognitive dissonance. But magicians seem to need their claims; the magical claims seem too important as the means to identify and legitimize an activity deeply significant to the practitioners.

Let me quickly reiterate what I mean by the term "claims." The most basic understanding of magic is that doing a magical ritual has an effect that is not due to commonly accepted psychological consequences. Magicians can usually give some account of the way the ritual should work, with the body of ideas described earlier. There are a host of more specific ideas about astrology, tarot, divination, and the like, with which the magician is also probably comfortable. I doubt very much that a magician is always fully conscious of an abstract list of relevant propositions that he calls his "theory"; nor do I think he formulates a propositional assertion about the efficacy of ritual when he performs his rite. However, he probably does think of the ritual as being effective while performing it. And certainly there are times when he explicitly defends the idea that magical rituals can be effective, and asserts what he calls his belief about the rite's power. This commitment to the view that the rituals do produce results, which usually includes some rather fuzzy explanation of why these results occur, is what I mean to identify by the term "claims."

There seem to be four primary rationalizations of magical claims themselves, four different ways of intellectualizing the idea that rituals produce results. I call these approaches realist, two worlds, relativist, and metaphorical. The realist position says that the magician's claims are of the same status as those of "science"; the two worlds position says that they are true, but cannot be evaluated by rational means; the relativist position says that it is impossible even to ask questions about their "objective" status; and the metaphorical position asserts that the claims themselves are objectively false but valid as myth. In essence these are different positions about the truth-standards applied to ordinary discourse and about whether magic fits within them. The first position asserts that there is an objective reality and that magic is valid in its terms; the second asserts the possibility of an objectively true referent for the magical talk of other planes and forces, but says that the claims are rationally indeterminable, not evaluable by ordinary means; the third also claims that ordinary truth-standards do not apply to magic, but not so much because magic is different but because the very idea of truth-standards is itself an illusion; and the fourth, that objective reality is knowable, but that the magical claims are false descriptions of it, failed by a justifiable test. As theories based on different conceptions of objective truth, these positions are incompatible, but as means of asserting commitment they are often employed in tandem.

My sense is that most magicians will give most of these arguments at some time during their magical career. The metaphorical position, probably the most sophisticated philosophical view, is the least frequently used. This may be because it is intellectually comfortable to abandon truth-claims only if there is another very obvious reason for commitment to the practice—and I heard the metaphorical argument almost exclusively from women who were drawn to goddess worship with political concerns. However, it is not at all uncommon for someone to argue both realist and two worlds or relativist positions together, a commitment to the reality of magic along with an explanation of why magical claims seem inconsistent or false. In essence, arguing both that magic is real and that truths are relative amounts to an argument for relativism; however, I am not convinced that the magicians who gave me these arguments were genuinely convinced that the non-magical Christian had as clear a perspective on the truth as a magician. A relativist should think that anyone's views are as valid as his own. But when a magician argues for relativism, he seems to want to justify a view about magic to which he is already committed, and the argument for relativism is a way to end the disagreement with a skeptic. The magician does not arrive at his magical claims by way of philosophical argument. He justifies a position already taken. And yet, there was sometimes a genuine hesitation, and a sense that all knowledge was freely chosen, that there was no final "truth."

This chapter presents the four common positions illustrated through case examples. Then it compares them with the recent arguments in British theology to illustrate the common strategy in this type of defensive argument. Magicians will assert that objective reality is partially or completely unknowable, and that in consequence magical ideas cannot be challenged under truth's banner. They treat magic as set apart, and offer reasons independent of its truth for engaging in its practice. These are the tactics of the modern theologian: the divine is different, it cannot be tarnished by your rational skepticism. The similarity between the two, magic and Christian religion, might not be so obvious—after all, one might initially think of magic more as a pseudo-science of occult vibrations rather than as a religion focused on a transcendent reality. But the thrust of the previous part of the book was to illustrate the spiritual, otherworldly feelings conjured by the practice. Dependent as they are upon ideas of a spiritual reality, magical ideas are hard to defend in the same way that God's existence is difficult to demonstrate. There may be good reasons for that difficulty: claims about transcendent reality are inherently difficult to prove, while claims about racial supremacy may be hard to defend because they are wrong. In any event, the similarities between magicians' arguments and theologians' arguments identify common tactics in defending the unprovable.

THE REALIST POSITION

Magicians who hold a realist position think that there is a knowable objective reality and that magic reveals more of it than science. There are controllable forces, they say, that escape the scientific purview. The magicians who say this might not be too concerned with the accuracy with which they can describe these forces: where they come from, what they are, how they can be directed. They still think that the forces exist on some other "plane," and they still describe them as spiritual. But they rely on accounts of that spiritual plane as being a type of reality that is integrated with material reality. They *will* say that they know that the forces are real in the same ways that they know that tables and chairs are real. You kick chairs to see if they are really there; you do rituals to see if the forces are really there. They might also say that they do not "believe" in magic. They practise, skeptical and intrigued, until they "know" through personal experience that magical power genuinely exists.

*****

Emily had been reading about magic for five years—mostly astrology, herbs, and tarot—when she decided to enter magic practice in earnest. She took a home study course advertised in a magical journal that she found in an occult bookstore, and became involved in discussion groups. She joined the Glittering Sword shortly before I did, and then joined a "women's mysteries" group—the one that performed the Halloween ritual described earlier. During the year in the *ad hoc* group, she performed rituals that she "knew" were powerful. She said about one which she wrote that, "I couldn't remember reading more than a third of it. Something else took over." That ritual was about water. Later, she remarked: "and the results have been amazing. For a week everyone around me was bursting into tears or anger, and then it rained. There was water everywhere." When she went to study groups on divination, she was delighted with the high rate of her predictive success. It was she who thought that a Greystone ritual was powerful, but that the leader's "direction" of the power was wrong because her images were so different from the ones he described. Soon afterwards, alone in her room, she had a vision of the goddess. It was, she said, very much her own view of the goddess, a woman with stars around her head. "But I saw her the way I see you now."

By the end of that year Emily was quite sure that magic had practical effects and that magical forces were part of physical reality. When I told her that some of my academic colleagues had asked if magic was only a hobby, like stamp collecting, she laughed. "They're afraid. And if they only knew that we could really do things, they'd *really* be afraid."

*****

Tom was raised a Catholic. He now gives lectures on computers. Although he says that he was always drawn to religion—"I had a contact and had made a dedication before I knew who or what it was to"—he dropped out of the conventional church in adolescence and became involved with a theosophical group with spiritualist leanings. His marriage ended his occult involvement, but after a divorce, he came to England from his native midwestern America and picked up Knight's mystical, magical training manual in a bookshop. The book contained a leaflet describing the correspondence course. "I knew, when I started it, that it was me. It was exactly right." That was seven years ago; Tom is among a few who have attended every Greystone weekend. He has dropped the course—he got "stuck"—but it has provided his primary esoteric orientation.

When he drove me back to central London from the study group he ran with his magical partner—that night he had lectured on the kabbalistic sephirah Yesod—he said that after the powerful Greystone ritual in May 1983 he had switched from "the necessary suspension of disbelief" to a state of "knowledge." That Greystone meeting was the Atlantean ritual, the culmination of a six-year series of annual ritual workings. The weekend has been described as exciting, upsetting, and extremely powerful by most of its participants. "I'm not sure that even [Knight] was aware of everything that happened." Tom's vivid experience of the ritual power convinced him of the absolute, objective reality of magical forces. He was always predisposed to that conviction—"I always 'believed' in my 'belief'"—but now, he said, "I've had experience, I *know*."

*****

Tom and Emily assert that they know that the magic works, and that the forces are part of a physical reality. This, they think, is objectively true. They have been convinced by the results of their ritual practice. They still rely on experiential, emotional response for the evidence of the rite's success, but they find this evidence compelling: it is, for them, a clear indication of the external magical force. They even distinguish between "knowledge" and "belief" because the latter, they say, implies uncertainty. Knowledge is acquired through experimental practice; belief in faith is something that never can be fully known. Emily uses "knowledge" to indicate her certainty. Tom exaggerates the uncertainty by speaking of the "suspension of disbelief": to experience magic, one must quell a natural skepticism, but after enough experience, one knows. In the philosophical literature, one common definition of knowledge is that it is "justified true belief": knowledge must be true, be believed, and be justified by adequate grounds.[1] Knowledge is more certain than belief. However, the certainty arises because knowledge comprises true statements. These magicians use the conventional distinction between religious belief and scientific knowledge to assert a claim about the ontological status of magical forces.

TWO WORLDS

Those magicians who take what I call the "two worlds" approach talk explicitly about a "suspension of disbelief" in magic, and assert that the objective referent of magical claims is unknowable within the terms of an ordinary, scientific world. No explanation that captured the essence of magic could be comprehended by the rational mind. In this explanation, magicians say that they leave their analytic minds behind them when they step into the magical circle. The experience of magic, they say, stands outside the limitations of the analytic mind and cannot be conceived by it. Whereas Tom and Emily seem convinced that magical forces are real, these magicians are more convinced when they are practising magic than when they are not. They intuitively feel that magical claims are correct, but they do not think that their truth can be rationally verified. This is not quite a relativist position: Subscribers stress an incompatibility between magic and science, both of which they see as somehow "true" but also mutually inconsistent. They do not make an effort to debunk the source of the inconsistency itself, or to take the further step and cast aspersions upon rational analysis. In other words, they do not provide an overarching account of this incompatibility. Indeed, the unprovability of the magic sometimes seems to make them nervous.

*****

Jan and Philip met 10 years ago at university and married; he is now a physician and she, an officer of a pension scheme. They entered magic through an occult workshop, where they met a fellow participant with witchcraft contacts. They became fascinated by witchcraft, with its paganism and magic, and through the occult exercises they began to understand the inner imaginative experience of what was called the "psychic plane": an intuitive, associative use of imagery. Four years ago they found a coven with which they felt comfortable and were initiated. To Jan, the "gut-interpretation" makes the magic real and effective. "In the circle I refuse to ask, 'Is this rational?'" And you cannot challenge or question the circle from outside. "The point is just to let it happen." Philip stressed that this was not a psychological trick, a self-conscious psychotherapy. Magic differs from psychotherapy because the latter works on the self and assumes that the outside world does not change. Within the magical circle you must feel as if you know that your inner imaginative world affects a physical reality. You do not "try" to change an outer world: You assume that you can, and this assumption, if it is genuine, distinguishes the circle from mere theatre and makes the magic work. Inside the circle, the magic is fundamentally real. Outside it, in the mundane world, you acknowledge the possible consequences of the ritual, but retain a healthy skepticism.

*****

To Jan and Philip the abandonment of the analytic, critical mind is the most difficult step in entering the circle, but it is central to the magical experience.

*****

Paul is a witch of some five years' standing. He introduced Jan and Philip to their coven's high priestess and is a primary organizing force behind the sabbat gatherings of some four or five covens in the local countryside. We met weekly in the same study group. Sometimes Paul would lead one of the evening sessions. Once he interpreted the myth of Osiris as creative expansion constricted by form, Osiris locked into a coffin by his malicious brother Set. As we stood in the darkness Paul told us to imagine ourselves as Osiris, toasting the success of our creation and then ensnared by Set. Then we imagined that our spinal column had become the leaden coffin and we were told that throughout our lives action and constraint must be in perfect balance.

A librarian, Paul worked nearby and occasionally we lunched together. When a "textbook" on witchcraft was published, he was scornful and indignant. The authors had presented a kind of dogma, with short essays on witchcraft ethics, symbolism, nudity, and so forth. To Paul the book was idealized and intellectual. The circle is a whole experience, he said, an intuitive merging of action and belief. The very point of the witchcraft was not to analyze. After coven meetings Paul tries to forget about them, to keep the experience undissected and self-contained. "It's the only way I can hold it. When I intellectualize, it disappears." On the evening he had talked to the exercise group about Osiris, he presented ideas from Egyptian, Indian, and Greek mythology through a medium of Jungian and humanistic psychology. His narrative style is intellectually demanding and complex. In the library he is surrounded by books and catalogues. With the witchcraft he feels that he escapes the intellectual strictures that his personality and his chosen work impose upon him. He still writes intellectual pathworkings, but for the most part he feels as if he simply experiences within the circle. But while he thinks that witchcraft is psychologically good for him, he does not think that magic is "only" psychotherapy. He thinks that the rituals work. But he would prefer not to mix his views about magic with commonplace understanding.

*****

When Maria entered magic (she is the pre-doctoral biochemist who was a member of the Glittering Sword) she came to magic, with trepidation, because she could not explain the strange happenings that suddenly seemed to fill her life. There were odd events, usually during her menstrual period, that she interpreted as paranormal: Curtains she had drawn at night stood open in the morning; her dreams had become peculiarly clairvoyant. Most traumatically, she could no longer reproduce a published chemical reaction central to the thesis. Neither her supervisor nor her colleagues understood why the procedure failed, again and again, in different laboratories and in different circumstances.

Maria now thinks that perhaps she has a scientific insight into the nature of the reaction. But in spring 1983 she found it inexplicable and coupled with the paranormal experience, it led her, she said, to casual reading in magic, a correspondence course in natural magic (one I took), and thence to practice. I have seen her develop from a frightened novice into a learned practitioner. We become involved in the same study groups—herbalism, dream interpretation—and were initiated on the same night into the Glittering Sword. We went to Greystone together, socialized together, and together jumped over festival fires in various London parks.

One year after our first encounter, over tea at the Glittering Sword, Maria said that she kept her magical and scientific worlds very separate. "I don't do this with my rational mind." She was not sure whether the forces we invoked were objective or subjective—she could not decide. But the magic worked; the rituals gave results. If a magical rite was performed, it would have consequences, she said, and while at first she had struggled with that notion, she had accepted it by then. Ritual sets things in motion that could not be stopped, and the ritualist must pay careful heed to the words and symbols that he chooses. "The important thing is to define magic by results." She does not find this uncertainty about the objective nature of magical forces irrelevant, as some magicians claim, but because her trained scientific mind cannot accept her magic, she keeps the two distinct. "It's harder for me, you see, because I'm a scientist and agnostic." The original motivation for her involvement has vanished, but she has become progressively more active and interested.

*****

To these magicians, magic violates the acceptable canons of their logical minds. Indeed that may be why Jan, Philip, and Paul find it so enjoyable and so profound. Magic provides a type of experience that their intellectual minds ordinarily deny to them. The attitude is not dissimilar from that of the countercultural sixties: in that discourse, the analytic mind was said to alienate the soul from true experience, suffocating it within rigid, conventional constraints. However, these three magicians express a quite significant difference from the countercultural rhetoric. They did not search out the witchcraft with the specific goal of "dismissing" their analytic minds. That they could have done with LSD. Rather, they say that they became involved in magic and subsequently discovered that involvement demanded abandoning rational analysis. For Jan, Philip, and Paul, it seems more accurate to say that witchcraft may only be experienced outside of barriers of rational skepticism than to say that the removal of those barriers is their conscious aspiration. Nevertheless that aspect of magic may make it deeply satisfying to them.

Maria did not initially see the abandonment of her cautious scientific assumptions as good in itself. Rather, she found it a necessary step in her determination to comprehend her strange experiences. After considerable involvement she decided that the two sets of assumptions, those of magic and science, were not compatible. In her magical work she does not employ her scientific rationality—and thus, cannot provide a "rational," "scientific" explanation for magical efficacy. That it does work, she is convinced. But rather than interpreting her conventional scientific assumptions as wrong, she simply defines them as inapplicable.

The point is that the "two worlds" approach asserts the objective truth of the magical claim while simultaneously expressing its scientific dubiety, and without giving some relativist theory to justify it. Maria felt that she could not explain the magic, but she did feel that it worked, that it gave tangible results. Jan, Philip, and Paul also found it impossible—even self-defeating—to explain the magic by what they call "rationality." Within the circle, at least they assume their claims to be correct. They act effectively on that basis and enjoy the non-analytic experience that this demands. They assume that magical theory is valid; in fact, they assume that the magic will work only if they assume that it works; and certainly, it provides them with the non-analytic involvement that they enjoy.

RELATIVIST

Relativism is a common approach. Rather than arguing that magical claims are not rationally determinable, this argument rests on an overarching philosophy that defines all truth as relative and contingent. Where the two worlds position describes magic as incompatible with scientific norms, this position goes beyond to attack the very notion of those norms. Here magicians say that all people create their own realities, that no knowledge can be certain. Subjective and objective can never truly be unravelled. The magical world of the practising magician is as true to him as is the traffic light to the man in the Clapham omnibus.

*****

Mick is a witch who lives alone with 10 cats in a Jacobean cottage at the edge of the desolate Fens. She calls herself a witch and treats the witchcraft seriously: she casts spells and claims very tangible results. But she also qualifies her claims. In one of my rare taped sessions, she declared: [the statement is slightly abridged]: "Descartes says, I think, therefore I am. Maybe it is, I believe, therefore it is. And if you believe something enough, maybe you make it happen. Maybe I created the witchcraft. But I know that it works for me. I can't prove it one way or the other. It is only what I believe, and my truth is as valid as anybody else's. I mean, truth is like beauty, it's in the eye of the beholder, isn't it? And therefore I haven't got any answers, I haven't got any explanations. I only have my faith and my beliefs, which may or may not be right. But it really doesn't matter because it's what I believe that matters to me. So I am. *I* am. I occupy a little bit of space in a little bit of time, and I am a witch, and whether this is all nonsense or not is totally unimportant. Because if it's true for me then it's *true*. If it's true for me, that's my truth, and my truth is really all that matters to me."

Mick is making two sorts of claims with her notion of truth. The stronger claim is that no absolute truth can be known by man, as implied in her statement that "truth is in the eye of the beholder." The weaker claim asserts that she can't tell if her interpretations are "right"—whether she, in some unknowable empirical context, has the powers that she claims—but that she finds it psychologically helpful to maintain her claims to witchhood. No human, she says, can truly know. "Mankind's got a tiny brain." Although she may not in actuality be a witch, neither she nor anyone else has legitimate authority to dispute a claim that in her own experience she finds bountifully confirmed.

*****

Like Mick, Gareth Knight, the adept, has performed rituals that he "knows" have worked. His goals are always lofty—revitalizing England, uniting Christian and pagan spiritual currents—but he has convinced himself of magical efficacy through the "coincidences" that follow the rites and through his sense of power within the ritual performance itself. Magical power, he says, is real. But he has a sophisticated notion of that reality. In lectures, articles, and in private conversation he attacks the Cartesian split of inner subjectivity and an outer subjective world. (As quoted before) "the most glaring assumption upon which all modern science is based ... is that there is an absolute dichotomy between mind and matter, subjective and objective, observer and observed."[2] Whether or not his characterization of science is accurate, his point is that there are no objective foundations, that subjectivity presents the only truth. He told me that this split is philosophically naive, that observation itself alters the observed and thus renders any concept of objectivity fatuous. Reality, he says, does not lie behind the appearances. It is the appearances—imaginative or otherwise—themselves.

In ways Knight's position is not dissimilar to the realist claim. But where Tom and the others felt they had demonstrated the empirical reality of the spells, Knight does not distinguish between subjective and objective and would be less likely to use the term "empirical." The inner world profoundly alters the interpretation of an unknowable external reality; thus, the magician lives in a different reality from that of the engineer, and his "truth" is bound to differ. His students reiterate this position. "The critical point is when you accept that the imagination *can* be a reality." The speaker is a professional actor. "For me, it's been gradual—but oh yes, the magical forces are real."

*****

Enoch was initiated into Gardner's original coven over 25 years ago and is a person of seniority and status in the magical subculture. He is also a talented computer software analyst, and analogies of rules and patterning permeate his conversation. All life situations, he says, are determined by "game conditions." They are governed by particular rules, circumstances, and assumptions that constrain the actor's creativity and behaviour within ordered structures. Daily work provides one set of game conditions, magic, another. In daily work we experience one "map" of time and space. In ritual that map alters, and indeed one of the most valuable lessons magic teaches is that experiential maps are underdetermined. The raw data of life can be surveyed and mapped in various ways. The magical "adept" can transcend a particular map and see the whole. In that sense there can be no true adepts, for as humans we remain within a given map at any time. But the ideal of omniscient, unfettered comprehension and control is at the heart of magic.

I have heard Enoch play with the metaphor of a plum pudding to suggest the rich diversity of our lives. To bring order into chaos each individual cuts his pudding and draws connections between the random fruits which that slice reveals. The world is infinitely complex, and its interrelations infinitely inter-referential; each map is bound to be good and explanatory. But if you had cut a different slice your map would differ. Sometimes otherwise unconnected maps intersect; they create "synchronicities" in which an event interpreted by one set of assumptions is differently expounded by another. No hermeneutic system can give justice to the whole, and because humans demand structure they may never perceive reality as it is. Meaning emerges through the interstices of the mapped and structured framework. Magic is simply a particular set of maps, an heretical exegesis that heeds different events and has distinctive axioms.

*****

Mick, Knight, and Enoch have different philosophical positions, but each handles cultural skepticism by describing it as a different but not superior account of an unknowable reality. Mick asserts that absolute reality is inaccessible. There is, she says, no privileged viewpoint. Therefore, all viewpoints must be seen as equally valid. Enoch holds a similar but involuted position. Interpretation, he says, relies upon ordered maps based upon adventitious circumstance, drawn with common human standards of coherence and explanatory power. No human is independent of his map, and magicians simply use a different one. Knight asserts that the distinction between subjective and objective experience is invalid. Perception arises through imaginative apprehension and is transformed by the creative imagination. True reality lies in our awareness, and through our awareness we shape our world in interaction with it. They all state, in different ways, that humans have a limited, subjective perception of the world, and they give this account to explain why this unusual view is valid, and cannot be dismissed.

METAPHORICAL

Magicians of the metaphorical position argue that it *is* possible to know an objective reality, and that the claims of magical theory are probably false. But magic is about personal development, spiritual experience, and so forth, and to think in terms of an efficacious magic facilitates these ends. The claims of magic may be false, but claiming them does something that is satisfying and creative in itself. In the magical literature, this is a position largely taken by those who have come to magical practice largely through political concerns. I have heard it argued by practitioners far less often than the other approaches.

*****

Angel had come to magic through her interest in goddess worship and described herself as a committed feminist. She told me that she could not see what ritual magicians spoke about when they talked of "contacts" and "Masters" and "disincarnate entities." To her, "that's like a low-grade spiritualism." Magic had to do with "spiritual experiences and the imagination, and how you conceive of yourself." Once, after a winebar discussion of various magical groups, I asked her if she believed in the magical claims of efficacy. "Belief—that's a loaded term." It was hard not to be skeptical in the ordinary world, she said. But the brain is remarkably complex. Who knows? "We do work for ourselves in the group, but the world is changing for women. I'd like to think that there's a chance that all the goddess groups did something." She's seen things she finds it difficult to explain;

she would like to think that there's something in it even though she often suspects that there is not.

In any event, it is the pleasure in the practical involvement that drew her into practice.

*****

Celine, an expatriate American in her thirties, runs a (different) feminist coven in London. She lives in a beautiful house on Hampstead Heath, with wide kitchen counters and soft cushions in the sitting room; as I left her after morning coffee, she went out with a friend from the BBC for pasta. She told me that she became involved in magic through her political commitments to ecology and to the women's movement, and more specifically through feminist political theatre and its relation to ritual. She talked about the complexity of her religion and how different it was from Judeo-Christianity. She was raised in the Jewish faith, but became agnostic. Now, she describes herself as "believing" in the goddess, but talks about the "duality" in her belief. On the one hand, she thinks of the goddess simply as a personification of the natural world. On the other hand, "She *is* there. I can talk to her." The difference from Judeo-Christianity is that "the Christian god is always out there. He can be in your heart, but he is not you." In witchcraft, she said, there was no goddess apart from the natural world, but you could treat her as a being, and she described this as using "mythology, not rationality" to describe the world. Magic in this setting plays an ambiguous role for her. She performs spells and experiences the rise and fall of the "power," but treats the spells as ways of expressing her feelings about the goddess. Spells are creative, expressive, and they contain a sense of the holy.

*****

Celine and Angel then were both drawn to the practice for political reasons, and both treat the magic primarily as a myth, a way of expressing rather than of doing. Angel would like to retain the possibility that the magic is instrumentally effective, and Celine would also probably concur, but their primary emphasis is upon ritual practice as expression, not as practical act based upon intellectual claims. Yet even though they both recognize that magic may not be real, they are reluctant to admit this.

The striking feature of these four sets of rationalizations is that even though most arguments recognize the doubtfulness of the arguments for magic's validity, magicians are noticeably reluctant to abandon them. Few magicians adopt the position that "magic" is really only a metaphor for very ordinary experiences. Three of the four positions argue about how one can accept the claims, not why they should be accepted—even the realists give personal, inaccessible experience to explain their convictions. The magician does not conclude from a philosophical argument that magical claims could be valid; she gets involved with magic, and argues for the validity of the apparent inconsistency, on the grounds that the outsider's critique relies on misguided standards of truth and objectivity. I am sure that Knight thinks that his views are fundamentally more valid than his neighbour's; however, I am equally sure that he is doubtful that he could convince his neighbour through appealing to what he would see as evidence.

Having explained why the magic is immune from criticism, magicians proceed to justify their practice by other means, with second-order explanations that talk about the value of holding magical ideas to be true, not about whether the ideas are in fact true. For the most part these arguments rest on grounds of morality, spirituality, aesthetics, or psychology. Some of these we have already seen: magicians recognize many of the benefits of the practice, and use these to justify their engagement with it. For example, Fortune remarks that ritual is a system of "pure psychology"[3] and many other magicians describe magic as a psychological practice. Green depicts magic as a psychotherapy: "How can you expect to change the world around you when you aren't even concerned with changing yourself?" An initiate of the Western Mysteries said that "magic is really about coming to terms with yourself: first you work on yourself, and then you become a fit channel for the forces." A witch explained to me that magic drew him because it combined creativity and mystery (he is a professional artist, a painter). He told me (twice) of his trip to Japan and his question to a Japanese potter about what made one pot worth 450 and another pot worthless. "He essentially said that if I did the tea ceremony for 20 years, I would begin to understand." Magic, to him, involved that trained intuitive sense of the aesthetic. Another witch spent her adolescence searching for a powerful goddess in the Virgin Mary and entered witchcraft for its spiritual depth for women; in my encounter with the group of women with whom she was associated, it was clear that this was a common theme. Others felt that magic was morally justifiable, that it forced you to grow up and take responsibility for your actions. Two members of Knight's group told me that the Greater Mysteries—in other words, the "real" magic—was about taking responsibility; it involved spirituality, but it was justified by "the work that must be done." Magic required you to take on adult morality and commitments. Magicians of the two worlds, relativist, or metaphorical positions are arguing that there are alternative reasons besides the "proof" of magical claims that leads them to defend those claims, and they will put forward more reasons along these lines.

These sorts of explanations are used in addition to accounts of how one can accept the magical claims, and as magicians slip from the realist to the relativist position, they rely on the second-order justifications as demonstrations of magic's value within the terms of the skeptic's language. They can move back and forth, from one account to another, so that they need never violate their intellectual integrity. They are able to maintain their commitment, without necessarily being sure of the epistemological status of the commitment.

For example, it is common for a magician to offer a second-order justification for the practice, and then a first-order account to whose validity he refuses to commit himself. He explains first why accepting the theory is a good thing to do, and then offers an account of how the theory might be true. One manual, Starhawk's manual, gives this account of spell-casting:

> Spells work in two basic ways. The first, which even the most confirmed skeptics will have no trouble accepting, is through suggestion. Symbols and images implant certain ideas in Younger Self, in the unconscious mind. We are then influenced to actualize those ideas. Obviously, psychological spells and many healing spells work on this principle. It functions in other spells, too. For example, a

> woman casts a spell to get a job. Afterward, she is filled with new self-confidence, approaches her interviewer with assurance, and creates such a good impression that she is hired.
>
> However, spells can also influence the external world. Perhaps the job hunter "just happens" to walk into the right office at the right time. The cancer patient, without knowing that a healing spell was cast, has a spontaneous remission. This aspect of magic is more difficult to accept. The theoretical model that Witches use to explain the workings of magic is a clear one and coincides in many ways with the "new" physics. But I do not offer it as "proof" that magic works—nor do I wish anyone to drop their doubts. (Skeptics make better magicians). It is simply an elaborate—but extremely useful—metaphor.
>
> ... When our own energy is concentrated and channelled, it can move the broader energy currents. The images and objects used in spells are the channels, the vessels through which our power is poured and by which it is shaped. When energy is directed into the images we visualize, it gradually manifests physical form and takes shape in the material world.[4]

The "real" explanation of magic—magic affecting the physical world—is difficult and a little unclear. You can't give a completely convincing explanation, the author implies: all you can do is to suggest how the magic seems to work, and be convinced, by your results, that it does. In the meantime, even die-hard skeptics must admit that magic does some good. The invocation of psychology assures that even if magic's theory is not acceptable, its practice is vindicated as a worthwhile pursuit. This assurance is terribly important in a skeptical society. It gives skeptics an entry into a practice whose theory they need not endorse until later, and still not think of themselves as wasting time. Magicians often shift back and forth between these first- and second-order explanations, between claims that magic works, and claims that whether or not it works, it is beneficial in some way.

THEOLOGY

Modern theologians face similar difficulties: They must explain and justify their understanding of God to a secular community. Many do so with the same sorts of arguments that magicians use, often asserting that ordinary judgments of truth or objective reality cannot apply to religion, and mixing the defence of the theology's validity with the satisfaction of the theology's practice. Like the magicians, they argue that spiritual reality is somehow different from ordinary reality, and argue for their practice on the basis of its ethical or spiritual value. Theologians are responding to an age-old authoritative tradition. Magicians fly in the face not only of modern science, but of traditional religious beliefs as well. Unlike many theologians, they claim that their rituals have a physical effect. But as we have seen, magicians accommodate to the difficulty of achieving their goals by interpreting spiritual and emotional response as positive evidence and firmly establishing themselves as arguing about spiritual matters. Both modern magic and theology make claims about their different realities, which are difficult either to prove or to disprove. That they share similar strategies suggests that the magician's style of argument springs not from his idiosyncracy but from the general nature of his difficulty—defending a hard-to-defend belief in a skeptical society.

To illustrate the similarity in theological and magical arguments, I turn to some British Protestant theologians of the last two decades. They are not the theological giants of their age—neither are the magicians—but they emerge from a similar social context, and they write books, like the magicians, partly targeted at a secular audience and partly toward those of their persuasion.[5] I cannot claim to have given an exhaustive or even representative survey of theologians; however, those authors that I have encountered argue in ways that resemble these magicians' approaches.

One position, a realist view similar to the knowledge-not-belief position sketched above, argues that the intellectual claims of religion are of the same nature as the intellectual claims of science. They are true statements about an objective reality and those people that do not share them are profoundly mistaken. One recent examplar remarks:

> The intellectual credentials of thorough-going Christianity are very strong, much stronger than is often allowed.... Skepticism, solipsism and nihilism, being philosophies of ultimate negation, cannot be refuted in the ordinary way, but can yet be shown to be paradoxical and unnecessary, while affirmation of alternative absolutes, Marxist, humanist, Freudian or whatever, prove on inspection to be inadequate to fit all the facts.[6]

Another says that a Christian explanation of cosmology is essential because a non-deistic description is simply "inadequate." In his *Existence of God* Swinburne examines the various arguments about the existence of God and concludes that, all things considered, existence is more probable than not. This is an assessment of truth, of things-as-they-are in the world, and his discussion of probability is actually presented in mathematical symbols.

> The only plausible alternative to theism is the supposition that the world with all the characteristics which have I described just is, with no explanation. That however is not a very palatable alternative. We expect all things to have explanations. Above all ... it is probable that things which are inert, diverse, complex and yet show manifold correlations, have explanations.[7]

That there is something, rather than nothing, must be explained. The existence of God is induced from the facts, as an objective rational statement about what is the case. God exists, and he made the world.

Other theologians hold that faith is for the most part a practical experience. Like the two worlds position, this argument contends that the believer must evaluate his faith by experience and not worry too much about its rational inconsistency. The metaphysical claims are still said to be objectively true, but they are not judged as the claims of science or philosophy would be judged—they are not evaluated by intellectual means—but rather by an appeal to the quality of life lived through accepting those metaphysical claims. Some theologians acknowledge the doubtfulness of the claims in a commonsensical world; they still assert the importance of the claims. The magicians who take the two worlds position sometimes say they believe in magic within the magical circle, and tend toward skepticism outside. Nevertheless, their arguments resemble those of these theologians because neither doubts the general validity of real-world, science-validated canons. It is simply that they do not accept that those canons can judge the claims of a spiritual reality.

To Baelz, intellectual doubt is an almost necessary component of faith in contemporary English society. "Once the intellectual difficulties inherent in [the Christian's] belief have been fully drawn to his attention, especially in a culture in which alternative if equally problematic beliefs are widely held by persons whose integrity, insight and understanding he respects, the believer must accept the inevitability of doubt within himself."[8] One possible solution might be to say that the religion does not demand theoretical belief, but is merely a "way of living." Baelz acknowledges but rejects this solution. "I must simply affirm my own opinion that [the solution] fails to do justice to the theoretical and explanatory functions which belief in God has more commonly been thought to include.... Belief in God is theory as well as practice, even if the theory cannot be fully understood apart from the practice."[9] But, he asserts, "there is a sense in which practice may be allowed priority over theory."[10] Baelz articulates this as the "justification by response," and claims that the commitment to faith is a moral choice. What may the doubt-inflicted half-believer believe with integrity?

> The half-believer, disposed to follow the Christian way because he acknowledges in Jesus a manner of life which engages his deepest response, may, I suggest, without dishonesty act on the *assumption* that the basic Church affirmation concerning the way of God is true. To assume that this affirmation is true is not the same as to believe that it is true. It is to accept it as a fundamental working hypothesis.... It is an experiment with life.[11]

Neither demonstrable proof nor indisputable answers are forthcoming to assert the truth of these metaphysical beliefs and if this is the basis of the belief then belief per se must be tentative. Nevertheless, these claims can also not be disproved, and when the rationally inquiring mind cannot judge the answer the potential Christian must assert his choice on the basis of these different factors. Moral idealism, the restructuring of his human experience, the vision and hope of the Christian message, may be allowed to persuade him to accept the claims as a "working hypothesis," and this is the basis for his commitment.

Drury takes a similar if oblique line of argument. Theologians, he says, must tolerate uncertainty. "Life with God, the concern of theology and prayer, is ... a game of hide and seek which is enacted on the brink of the precipice of tragedy with masks and disguises concealing the participants from one another."[12] It is the metaphysical claims themselves that are incomprehensible to the religious individual. He cannot understand them, and therefore must be content to accept that they surpass his rational comprehension.

> The material of theology is the mystery of the intersection of two worlds, so that it too "must contain something incomprehensible." It therefore expresses itself in hints, points and even jokes.... It never reaches the level of comprehension which amounts to mastery over its subject by the abolition of its mysterious material.[13]

In order to understand religion, one must relinquish the demand for objective, delineable metaphysical reality. "Success consists in an alliance of overcoming and letting be, which gives birth to something new, indefinable, and real."[14] It is because there is something new and "real" that the demand to ignore paradox is worthwhile. Again, it is an argument from the quality of life and from the apparent truths that this life reveals. Christians "thread their way through the labyrinth to the source or *datum* of the one who was there all the time, revealing himself and making himself clear in a thousand ways which all added up to something unified and real which they cannot pin down."[15] Baelz stresses the moral satisfaction and quality of life that faith will bring, Drury, the incomprehensibility of its claims. To both, the claims are confirmed through the experience of accepting them, and cannot even be comprehended by rational analysis.

A somewhat different line is taken by theologians who claim

Wittgenstein as their philosophical fountainhead. These theologians, like relativist magicians, say that questions of objectivity cannot even be broached. Metaphysical faith in God is enmeshed in religious language, and one cannot step outside the limits of language to ask if its tenets are true. It is not that the metaphysical beliefs are true but indeterminable, as in the two worlds position; it is that the question of their truth, in relation to the truth of scientific claims, cannot be posed.

For Rhees there can be no "proof about whether God exists as an object. Being religious depends upon using language in a certain way. The use of language in this particular way involves and indeed constitutes religion, and it is not the expression of something distinct that can be articulated. He speaks to the skeptic thus: "you still seem to want to think of the language of religion as though it were in some way comparable with the language in which one describes matters of fact."[16] The language of religion is not the language of matters of fact and cannot be understood as a claim about objective reality. In fact, "objective reality" cannot be conceived at all.

> You say that I "deny that the term 'God' stands for any objective reality in the literal sense." I cannot have said just that, because the phrase "objective reality" is one which I can almost never understand, and I try to avoid it.[17]

"Objectivity" is not one of the things that life provides. One has faith, one is committed to the religion, but the religion can only be understood by, with, and in the language that constitutes it. "There could not be religion without the language of religion."[18]

Phillips, Rhees's student, presents his persuasion similarly. Religious faith is not about the issue of whether or not something is the case. "The point is not that *as a matter of fact* God will always exist, but that it *makes no sense* to say that God might not exist."[19] Like Rhees, Phillips is not making a claim about an "objective" reality. He is rather concerned to emphasize that people who talk about God talk in a context. "If the philosopher wishes to give an account of religious beliefs he must begin with the contexts in which these concepts have their life."[20] Through these contexts particular concepts find their meaning, but without them such meaning does not exist and it is nonsensical to attribute any to them.

> The philosopher is guilty of a deep misunderstanding if he thinks that his task in discussing prayer is to try to determine whether contact is made with God; to understand prayer *is* to understand what it means to talk to God.[21]

Religion cannot be understood outside of the language that envelops it. The religious have faith in certain ideas, but one cannot examine their faith in relation to scientific claims, for to do so would be to step outside the texture of religious language and one cannot do that without destroying the nature of its thought.[22]

Still other theologians wish to preserve religion while simultaneously denying its metaphysical claims. They specifically reject the realist conception of a God who exists in an objective physical sense. Religious language has a function as a myth used to talk creatively about the religious life, as an expression and ideal of its aims. The human animal, they say, is a myth-maker, and its myths are quite important. But the language should be recognized as myth, not metaphysic.

Cupitt specifically denies the realist concept of a God who exists in an objective physical sense.

> God is the pearl of great price, the treasure hidden at the centre of the religious life. The religious claim and demand upon us is God's will, the drama of the religious life within us is God's activity, and the goal of the religious life before us is God's nature. But we should not suppose God to be a substance, an independently-existing being which can be spoken of in a descriptive and non-religious way. Religious language is not in the business of describing really-existing super-sensible objects and their activities.[23]

Religious language does not prevent us from asking the question of God's existence; the metaphysical claim can be denied but the language has a function as myth. Such myths are essential to humans as myth-makers, but they cannot be considered as rational claims.

> I continue to speak of God and to pray to God. God is the mythical embodiment of all that one is concerned with in the spiritual life. He is the religious demand and ideal, the pearl of great wisdom and the enshriner of values. He is needed—but as a myth.[24]

This myth enables one to talk creatively about the nature of the religious life. But it would be foolhardy to make the claim greater than this, for it is not.

Kee subtitled a book "Faith without Belief in God." He proposes "an understanding of Christian faith, appropriate to our secular age, which does not require belief in God as its prior condition."[25] This is not, for him, an attack upon faith in God, but rather an understanding of what faith would be without such a metaphysical claim. He attempts to offer an exploration of faith that does not involve a claim about God. This he describes as the "Way of Transcendence," the comprehension of that which is beyond the human. "There is a life which is natural to man, and there is another kind of life for which he must consciously decide ... paradoxically, we may discover later that the life which transcends our 'nature' may ultimately prove more natural, since in it we find fulfillment."[26] To Kee, the justification of that life by its quality is sufficient unto itself, and the metaphysical claim is explicitly acknowledged as irrelevant. "The mystery is that secular faith in the way of transcendence *is* confirmed by subsequent experience."[27] Religion is justified by morality, by the qualities of life, and evaluated through personal experience.

The most significant difference between the theological texts and the magician's arguments is that theologians rely more heavily upon justification from morality. Magicians seem to expend more effort in explaining why magical theory is impervious to skeptical doubt, whereas these theologians seem to focus more closely on the moral, spiritual gains to be had from the practice. There are good reasons for the difference: Theologians write within a dense tradition in which spiritual life is possessed of moral value and in which the ethical worth of the religious life is widely credited.

Magicians, by contrast, do not have such a culturally approbated tradition, nor is the moral worth of their undertaking immediately obvious. Their practice, moreover, is associated with a particular set of ideas about the physical world that is widely perceived to be false, and they struggle for intellectual legitimacy without the benefit of traditional cultural acceptance. It is also less obvious that the magician's claims are unprovable than the theologian's: Certainly the magician is more likely to compare her practice to a science than is the theologian, and it is characteristic of a science that its ideas are meant to be testable. However, the magician does use many theological strategies, marking off the magical as insulated from skeptical attack but valid for the benefits of engaging in its activity.

The similarity between theological and magical arguments highlights an important characteristic: that the claims of both enterprises, difficult to defend as they are, are seen as central by the practitioners, and once practitioners are deeply involved in the practice, they use a variety of different methods to patch together the apparent rift between the practice and an outsider's skepticism of its conceptual frame. It is surprising that the magical concepts *are* so important to its practitioners. To the observers, it seems that magicians cling to their magic ideas—that rituals affect reality—and assert the possibility of their truth more to mark off and legitimize a set of practices than for their content. Magicians do not exclusively, or even primarily, attempt to prove a theory within an established intellectual realm: They are willing to argue in ways that stretch the conventional criteria of intellectual validity. Somehow, the claims are sufficiently important to the practitioners that they will not abandon the possibility of their truth, even if that truth seems difficult to demonstrate in a conventional, reliable manner.

Magicians use a variety of odd-job methods to argue for their practice. Rather than arguing for the theory directly, testing it by methods that seem satisfactory when arguing about whether the house has termites, they explain that magic is different, that it does not interfere with other claims (two worlds), is of the same status as all other claims (relativist), is not science-like but myth-like (metaphorical). Then, they justify holding it. These justifications by morality, aesthetic pleasure, therapeutic efficacy, allow the magician to make sense of his practice with justifications shared by the wider society without sacrificing the magical theory that the society would reject, or even holding that claim up for scrutiny. Magicians can shift back and forth between first-order and second-order claims, between justifications by truth-testing and justification by effect of faith, depending on their audience and their needs.

To reach this *modus vivendi*, the magician must be able to abstract his magic, to treat it as a way of thinking different from other ways. He must be able to understand what it is about it to which the skeptic objects. He meets the skeptic's argument by asserting that it is irrelevant; he transcends the conflict of particular claims by giving a meta-argument, explaining why holding those claims is personally valuable, whether or not they are true in the disbeliever's eyes. This calls for a high degree of abstraction, and a marked ability to move conceptually between being involved, and referring to your involvement. Magicians develop this skill of distancing themselves from an activity that they care for deeply, and doing so in a way that justifies their involvement without calling it into jeopardy. They are aided by conceptual "tricks" to underline a difference between the magical and the mundane: special names, clothes, space, a metaphor of separation, tricks that enable them to treat the magical involvement as something set apart.

Magic leads its magicians into a world of symbolism and fantasy that is hard to talk about but that becomes quite important to its practitioners, and its personal significance forces them to make sense of it in terms that at least relate to those of the wider society. They rely on this claim of efficacy: They are not willing to abandon it if it seems unacceptable within conventional canons; they adjust their view of the canons in order to make it fit. Then, by marking off their magic with elaborate theatre and metaphor, they can defend their involvement in ways that they think that the wider society can also understand. This is no different from the theologian's defence of his faith. But it does present an image of human as tool-user rather than as coherent rationalist: if a practice is important to someone, he will explain away its intellectual disjunctions when he must—locally, haphazardly, with the intellectual tools that come to hand—rather than evaluating its claims as intellectual end in themselves.

There is an important concluding remark. Most magicians take their claims and practices seriously and when they give relativist or two worlds arguments, they seem to be defending their practice using the best means available to them. However, their wavering to and fro, this shifting of positions and defences, is not without its effect. Most practitioners do question the rational canons that seem to undermine their practice, and while they are committed to their practice, they are also aware of the idiosyncratic, personally relevant manner in which they have constructed their interpretations. I think that many of them are genuinely aware of being in a paradoxical intellectual position, in which they both adhere to a set of ideas, and are also conscious that their adherence owes as much to choice and circumstance as it does to any "truth." This seems to be an intellectual attitude endemic at least to modern magic: that magicians affirm their practice and its claims by attacking the notion of rational standards, and while they take their claims to be valid, they are sometimes painfully aware of the limited nature of any claim to "truth."

NOTES

1. E.g., Ayer (1956:35).
2. Knight (1981:II, 20).
3. Fortune (1935:306).
4. Starhawk (1979:111–112).
5. There are other authors, with somewhat different and quite sophisticated theologies, within the Roman Catholic Church: e.g., F. Kerr and H. McCabe.
6. Packer in Stacey (1981:65).
7. Swinburne (1979:287–288).
8. Baelz (1975:134).
9. Baelz (1975:137).
10. Baelz (1975:137).
11. Baelz (1975:138–139).
12. Drury (1972:138–139).
13. Drury (1972:94–95).
14. Drury (1972:94).
15. Drury (1972:96).

16. Rhees (1969:120).
17. Rhees (1969:114).
18. Rhees (1969:121).
19. Phillips (1965:14).
20. Phillips (1965:27).
21. Phillips (1965:38).
22. Hesse made a similar point, more closely argued with respect to recent accounts of metaphor and critical theory, in the 1979 and 1980 Stanton lectures, which exist only in typescript, and in a more recent article on metaphor (1984).
23. Cupitt (1980:164).
24. Cupitt (1980:166).
25. Kee (1985:20).
26. Kee (1985:37).
27. Kee (1985:270–271).

REFERENCES

Ayer, A.J. 1956: *The Problem of Knowledge*. London: Macmillan.

Baelz, P. 1975: *The Forgotten Dream*. London: Mowbrays.

Cupitt, D. 1980: *Taking Leave of God*. London: SCM Press.

Drury, J. 1972: *Angels and Dirt*. London: Darton, Longman and Todd.

Fortes, M. 1966: "Religious Premises and Logical Technique in Divinatory Ritual." In *A Discussion of Ritualization of Behavior in Animals and Man*, edited by J. Huxley, 409–422. Philosophical Transactions of the Royal Society. Series B, no. 772, vol. 251. London: Royal Society.

Fortune, D. 1935: *The Mystical Qabalah*. London: Ernest Benn.

Hesse, M.B. 1979, 1980. "The Stanton Lectures." Unpublished text. Cambridge, Whipple Library.

———. 1984. "The Cognitive Claims of Metaphor." In *Metaphor and Religion: Theolinguistics*, vol. II, edited by J.P. Von Noppen, 27–45. Brussels.

Kee, A. 1985. *The Way of Transcendence*. London: SCM Press.

Kerr, H., and C.L. Crow, eds. 1983. *The Occult in America*. Urbana: University of Illinois Press.

Knight, G. 1981. "The Importance of Coleridge." *Quadriga*. Part I: no. 17 (Spring): 3–13; Part II: no. 18 (Summer): 14–22; Part III: no. 20 (Winter): 13–15.

Phillips, D.Z. 1965. *The Concept of Prayer*. London: Routledge and Kegan Paul.

Rhees, R. 1969. *Without Answers*. London: Routledge and Kegan Paul.

Stacey, D., ed. 1981. *Is Christianity Credible?* London: Epworth.

Starhawk. 1979. *The Spiral Dance*. New York: Harper & Row.

CHAPTER 13
Witch Wars: Factors Contributing to Conflict in Canadian Witchcraft Communities[1]

Síân Reid

neopagan witchcraft is often portrayed, in books directed at practitioners and by the practitioners themselves, as a tolerant religious or spiritual movement, in which a wide range of beliefs and practices coexist without normative prejudice. However, when one actually speaks to neopagans about the Craft, and what they like and dislike about it, almost invariably the subjects of "politicking," "bashing," and "witch wars" arise. These terms reflect the perceived presence of conflict between neopagan groups. When I conducted research among contemporary witches between 1995 and 1998, participants cited this as one of the things they liked least about the Craft. "I hate the trad bashing. And I hate the eclectic bashing. You know, I don't see this as being anything else but drawing virtual lines in virtual sand. It's so silly" (Francine).

This animosity is visible not only to those inside the movement, but also to those approaching from the outside. Kevin Marron, a Canadian journalist who, in 1989, published *Witches, Pagans and Magic in the New Age*, based on interviews with neopagan witches across the country, notes,

> ... the present day Craft is beset with factional differences. There are many versions of witchcraft and the followers of each often engage in disputes over strongly held philosophical conflicts. This tendency towards infighting is notorious among witches. (91)

As some measure of conflict is inevitable in human interactions, it is interesting that participants should single it out over and over again as a particular problem in the neopagan setting. Available data suggest that there is a certain construction of "ideal" interaction, which, combined with structural features of neopaganism and characteristics of the neopagan population more generally, acts to make conflict particularly evident and particularly difficult to contain.

Data for this paper come from a range of sources, including books published by, for, or about neopagan witches, as well as 187 survey responses collected from a non-representative sample of neopagans across Canada, 18 semi-structured interviews designed to supplement the survey information, and countless conversations with neopagan practitioners during my many years of involvement with the movement, as a student, teacher, priestess, resource person, occasional occult store employee, and, most recently, as a sociologist and a researcher. I have set out, in this paper, to generate somewhat general observations and broad linkages that could be refined through subsequent fieldwork in specific communities or locations.

For the purposes of this discussion, "neopagan community" will be considered to be two or more neopagan groups who are engaged in sustained interaction at some level. Conflict within a single group, although it certainly occurs, requires a different level of analysis than the one I am proposing here. Similarly, two groups in geographical proximity who are not interacting in any way are part of the same "community" only in a much broader sense than is meant here. A "witch war," as opposed to other kinds of conflict that may also be prevalent in any given community, tends to display two central features. First, the conflict is conducted in a fairly open and public manner that is visible to the community members; second, it permeates and polarizes the community to such an extent that community participants are left with two choices: either to choose a side, or to withdraw from participation in the community until the conflict finds some resolution. These are not arbitrary definitional distinctions on my part, but abstractions arising directly from the usages of participants, who only describe some conflicts as "witch wars," although they themselves are often not entirely certain why some things seem to "qualify" better than others.

This paper will suggest that "witch war" type conflicts in neopagan communities are the result of the difficulties experienced by practitioners in negotiating successful interaction between groups and individuals with competing visions of witchcraft, in situations that are perceived to involve authority or legitimacy. There are three main types of factors that contribute to the proliferation of different visions of neopagan witchcraft. The first is structural, the second is ideological, and the third is personal. Each of these will be discussed below.

ELEMENTS OF NEOPAGAN "COMMUNITY"

Neopagan witchcraft is not a homogeneous movement. In fact, there are three broad categories of groups, which can engage in considerable amounts of borrowing and overlap in both ideology and practice: traditionals, goddess-spirituality groups, and eclectics.[2]

The fundamental unit of neopagan witchcraft is the individual. Solitary practice is not uncommon and is seen as a legitimate mode of spiritual development in most strands of the Craft, especially the more eclectic ones. Most witches will practise alone at some point, either by choice or circumstance. The fundamental unit of social organization in neopagan witchcraft is the coven. Covens are generally small, rarely exceeding 13 members, and strive to maintain a high level of intimacy, trust, friendship, co-operation, and contribution among members. They are intended to be fully autonomous entities, regulating themselves and organizing their practice according to the needs and wishes of their membership, not accountable to any "wider" body or organization. Even among traditionals, who tend to maintain more of a sense of connection with others in their own tradition, there is a very specific acknowledgment that once practitioners are senior enough to found an independent coven, they are no longer subject to regulation by their initiators if they choose to do so (Farrar and Farrar 1985:22).

Some urban centres, in addition to covens, which are small and private, have "churches," "groves," or "temples" that are open to the public and are usually the extension of a vision of a more accessible neopaganism that might eventually be able to get some form of legal standing with the Canadian government. Groups of this type include the Wiccan Church of Canada (Ontario), the Covenant of Gaia (Alberta), and The Aquarian Tabernacle Church (B.C.). These are not ecumenical assemblies of previously existing groups, but rather are modified and extended versions of a coven, inasmuch as they train and initiate their own priesthood and set their own standards independently.[3] However, like more mainstream "churches," and unlike the case with most covens, members of these larger pagan organizations are not required to make an explicit commitment to the group in order to participate in the classes and rituals that the group runs for the public.

The prominent public position of these large pagan organizations, however, is often a source of irritation and conflict in those cities where they are found. Media outlets frequently go to the representatives of these organizations when they need comments from "a witch," with the result that their version of "witchcraft" is presented to the non-pagan public as "witchcraft," period, without any acknowledgment that there are other groups or beliefs around. Sometimes this represents a real attempt by the larger organization to assert a hegemonic vision, but other times, it is more the result of reporters' agendas and editorial practices. In addition, the fact that these organizations are numerically so much larger than any individual coven means that they can often "swamp" events that were intended to be ecumenical, leaving the members of other groups feeling marginalized or excluded.

The decentralized nature of neopagan witchcraft, combined with the principle of group autonomy, means that "community," in the sense that I have described it earlier, is not an inevitable and natural outgrowth of the movement itself. The development of "community" requires a focus, a reason for bringing groups together. These foci can have primarily religious, social, or practical goals, and are most often a combination of all three. However, any sustained intergroup activity requires a continual negotiation of interaction. It is by no means guaranteed that the norms, values, and practices that are taken for granted by one coven will be shared by, or agreed to, by another coven, group, or individual. Compounding this difficulty is the fact that many witches use precisely the same language to represent related concepts with different underlying content.

The word "Wicca" is a particularly good case in point. Traditionals, Alexandrians and Gardnerians in particular, tend to reserve this word exclusively for their style of practice. In Britain, where the bulk of witchcraft is of this type, this usage of "Wicca" is taken for granted in books and other publications. Other styles of practice are simply referred to as "pagan," and "traditional" refers to those family traditions of witchcraft that cannot be reliably traced to Gardner. In North America, however, "Wicca" has been adopted by many branches of eclectic witchcraft as an interchangeable and less controversial term for neopagan witchcraft more generally, while being retained by the Alexandrians and Gardnerians as a word exclusively denoting their practice. This creates tension between people with very different visions of "Wicca" as well as a kind of territorial dispute over the "entitlement" to the label. A couple of my "traditional" respondents made comments to the effect of "You know, I don't really care what the pagan community does with itself; I just wish they wouldn't call it Wicca!"

The difficulties of a shared vocabulary without shared connotations are exacerbated in the case of larger pagan organizations, where the demands of their larger size and public presence require very different emphases in structure and practice than those that are utilized in covens. Language touching on authenticity (what is a "real" witch), legitimacy (what is a "real" initiation), and authority (who is qualified to do what, and on what basis) tends to be particularly contested, and it is on these issues that most "witch wars" hinge.

In the context of any individual group, generally some, often implicit, consensus has been reached on the content of such concepts as "priesthood" and "initiation"; members understand the roles and requirements of their negotiated structure, and express their agreement with the group's organization and procedures by staying within it. There is generally some understanding about how conflicts and disagreements within the group will be handled, and even in the cases where there are no explicit guidelines, members are always free to leave if they are dissatisfied and, in fact, are often encouraged to do so (Valiente [1978] 1983:176). In a "community" setting, there is no consensus on the meaning of key concepts, and there is generally no structure or procedure through which disagreement and conflict can be mediated. This leads to a situation where groups and individuals with competing visions of witchcraft are trying to establish their authority and authenticity in an unregulated environment, where the language used by all parties, although superficially similar, often has very different connotations.

The different emphases, styles, orientations, and "standards" of witchcraft groups, although all perfectly legitimate in their own contexts, can pose problems when groups try to join forces for "community" events. Those events that specifically involve "theological" concerns and those in which a status-based hierarchy are implied are particularly volatile. As one witch noted, there does tend to be a shared value orientation in the Craft, but it can be obscured by the plethora of liturgical minutiae that differentiates groups, especially when those groups are trying to negotiate which of their stylistic peculiarities is going to be incorporated into an intergroup ritual.

> And I think, no matter which of the traditions of, of paganism one deals with, and no matter how, you know, how twisted the shorts may get about what they do, how they do it, when they do it, what colour the candle has to be, if you sit them down over a coffee or a scotch or whatever, and you get them to talk about the Gods, you will find the same underlying world view ... (Judith)

Situations that force neopagans to confront their differences in a manner that is concrete and requires consensus or resolution, and those that explicitly focus on people's individual practices and opinions about what is "right" or what works "best" in the Craft, are always going to hold the potential for conflict, as the parties involved advance positions in which they have placed considerable emotional and intellectual investment. Among these situations of high potential conflict are the organization of intergroup rituals, festivals, and classes, where "qualification," "legitimacy," and gatekeeping can become issues, and in discussion fora, such as some newsletters and more recently online newsgroups, Web site bulletin boards, and chat rooms that highlight theological issues.

NEOPAGAN IDEOLOGY AND "IDEAL" COMMUNITY

Clearly, the decentralized nature of neopaganism in general acts as a crucible for conflict. However, the ideology of neopagan witchcraft is such that conflict "should" not occur because a whole range of beliefs and practices are accepted as valid and legitimate.

> I think that everybody needs some sort of philosophy or spirituality. Religion is the structure and the trappings that we place on the mystical and spiritual practices, and those are just tools, it's the mysticism and the philosophy and that that is the most important aspect of it all. (Beth)

> Wicca happens to be our own particular Pagan path, our way of ritualizing and living the basic philosophy, but we share the general Pagan view that different paths have equal validity, one's choice depending on one's personal wavelength. It is the philosophy itself which matters. (Farrar, Farrar, and Bone 1995:3)

Individuals are expected to develop their own understanding of the meaning of their practice, and come to their own conclusions about appropriate morality and ways of "being" in the world. There is a widely expressed and almost postmodern belief that these are very personal decisions and choices, and that although they can be "different," it is difficult to characterize them as "wrong." So, although there is no prescriptive text or practice to which all neopagan witches can refer for their vision of the Craft, normative visions still emerge on a small scale, for an individual, negotiated by a group, or presented by an author. Although it may not be possible to say that there is a "right" way to do something for everyone, in practice, there is still a sense that there is a "right" way for me, or for my group. These visions, however, are theoretically bounded, restricted to the individual or the group, because the underlying ideology is that no one is empowered to impose their version of the Craft on other people.

Many people involved in neopagan witchcraft encounter this ideology of tolerance, diversity, and respect that the movement is supposed to embody before they encounter other neopagans or the enacted realities of neopagan communities. A third of the people who responded to my survey indicated that their first awareness of the Craft came through books; in addition, about the same number said that they first became involved in the movement through books. The authors cited most frequently as having been particularly influential by my respondents were Starhawk (*Spiral Dance*, 78 out of 187), Scott Cunningham (*Wicca: A Guide for the Solitary Practitioner*, 40), Janet and Stewart Farrar (various, 37) and Margot Adler (*Drawing down the Moon*, 21). Of these, Starhawk presents a feminist eclectic perspective; Cunningham takes a different, but also eclectic approach; Janet and Stewart Farrar are traditionals; and Margot Adler's book tries to present the range of neopagan approaches prevalent in the United States. All use some or all of the words "pagan," "neopagan," "Wicca," and "witch" in ways that may seem almost interchangeable (and, in some cases, are interchangeable), and can leave the novice with the impression that the movement is far more cohesive than it actually is. Adler, in particular, creates the impression that there is a "pagan community" that somehow encompasses all of the groups that claim the labels "pagan," "neopagan," or "witch." She writes,

> Individuals may move freely between groups and form their own groups according to their needs, but all the while they remain within a community that defines itself as Pagan. The basic community remains, although the structures may change. (1986:33)

Kevin Marron notes, "'Perfect love and perfect trust' are the traditional passwords for initiation into a coven. The phrase represents the kind of total understanding and acceptance that witches feel they must have in order to work together" (1989:91). It is also, I believe, the unspoken and somewhat naive expectation of those venturing into neopagan "community" for the first time, and helps to explain why conflict between groups is singled out as a problem. The levels of agreement, consensus, and intimacy that are possible within the confines of a coven do not translate well to larger, more diverse groups. That is precisely the rationale that most authors give for keeping covens small, but the coven experience somehow becomes "typical" of the kind of interaction one should be able to expect in neopagan witchcraft, and that leads to disappointment and even disillusionment when one steps outside the coven boundaries.

The contrast between the portrayals of neopagan witchcraft as tolerant, diverse, and unified around some vaguely articulated core of "values" and the reality of bickering, sniping, and status games creates the perception that the latter is somehow an unfortunate aberration, and causes it to stand out. People know that the same thing happens in other kinds of groups, in the workplace, in society in general, but somehow they still cherish the belief that those involved in neopaganism should be "above" or "beyond" that kind of thing. In fact, the composition of the neopagan movement may well make it particularly susceptible to conflict centring around issues that touch upon people's religious beliefs and practices because these tend to be tightly bound up with people's sense of identity and their relationship to authority more generally.

CHARACTERISTICS OF NEOPAGAN WITCHES

When I surveyed Craft practitioners in 1995–1996, I asked both how long they had been involved in the Craft, and how old they were when they first became involved. What I found was that, of 183 people who answered the first question, half had been involved for 5 years or less, an additional quarter had been involved between 6 and 13 years, and the remaining quarter had been involved for more than 13 years. In terms of age at first involvement, of 186 people who answered, half were involved by the time they were 22, another quarter by the time they were 30, and fully 90 percent of my respondents were involved by the time they turned 40. This suggests that the Craft contains a much larger proportion of young people than most other religions.[4]

These also suggest that people in their mid- to late twenties may have, in many cases, been actively involved in their Craft practice for almost a decade, giving them a level of "seniority" and a claim to leadership that they would not have in more institutional religions. Notes one respondent,

> ... our "elders" either draw their eldership from being thirds, or seconds, status-oriented, adept-level stuff, or they draw it from "You know, I've been in the Craft for ... how long have you been in the Craft?" So I'm "older" than you .... (John)

Unfortunately, extensive experience with meditation, visualization, trance work, ritual writing, and the many other skills that are associated with the practice of neopagan witchcraft do not, in and of themselves, confer the interpersonal skills necessary to manage harmonious and productive relationships among a group of people with diverse views and interests, particularly when many of them say that they were marginalized, or "loners" growing up. People in adolescence and early adulthood are engaged in the process of establishing themselves as independent and autonomous individuals with the ability to develop their own beliefs and identity in line with the values to which they subscribe. Many are disinclined to merely accept the authority or pronouncements of others, preferring to decide for themselves, or find their own way. In addition, older people sometimes find it difficult to accept the leadership of those significantly younger than themselves.

A highly individualistic attitude is not confined to the younger or newer members of the movement, however. In the survey, I asked people to tell me what the three things were that appealed to them most about the Craft when they first became involved, and what appealed to them now. Just shy of 20 percent of all the responses I received to the first question had to do with the individual and personal orientation of the Craft: the flexibility of the beliefs; the requirement for the individual to take full responsibility for his or her morality and life choices; the requirement to engage in self-reflexive and personal development practices; the empowerment of the individual to make choices and changes in life; and the facilitation of a deeply personal relationship with the sacred, unencumbered by intermediaries. Twenty-three percent of the responses I received to the second question highlighted the same elements. Most of those involved in neopagan witchcraft do not *want* a vision of the Craft that is presented to them as a *fait accompli*; the level of personal and spiritual autonomy that is provided is a central appeal of the practice.

> I think that people who feel really stifled by people telling them what to do all the time like the Craft. It demands a lot from you, in terms of responsibility and discipline and work, but at the end of the day, it's yours. You own it, and no one can take it away from you. (Carrie)

In addition, when interviewed, many respondents described their disillusionment with their previous religious identification—and three-quarters of my survey respondents had some previous religious identification—as arising out of perceived restrictions on their ability to hold certain beliefs, act in certain manners, or play certain roles.

> ... it's [the Craft has] allowed me to grow as a person ... in a way that I don't think that Judaism, that's the religion I was part of and the culture I was part of before I made the change, would have allowed me to.... (Beth)

> I saw no reason that as an adult heterosexual woman, I could not be religiously involved in the practice of my parish. When that was denied me, it was literally as though I'd been thrown out of doors. I did feel dispossessed. I felt disinherited and it's wonderful that I can more openly express the mysticism I do feel [in the Craft], let's put it that way. (Francine)

> ... If you want to understand what's happening, you have to go to the priest, and the priest will interpret it for you officially, and this is the one true way that it can be interpreted, which is, I mean it's one of the reasons that I left Christianity—all of those bullshit kinds of interpretations ... and I think that there's a lot of that. It's power over meaning—meaning and behaviour construction. (John)

It is not unreasonable to expect, then, that many people who are drawn to witchcraft are already predisposed to resist normative constructions of their spirituality and spiritual practice, and are likely to take umbrage at the suggestion that perhaps they are not a "real" witch because of differences in viewpoint, practice, or standards with somebody else. Noted one respondent of her interaction with a large pagan organization after having been solitary for a few years,

> And they talk about how you have to be a third level initiate, and all this other stuff, and I'm going, "No, I've never been initiated by anybody, I self-initiated myself because there was no one around at the time," and well, I'm not sure I'm "qualified" to do anything yet, but at the same time, I feel I'm very connected.... And yet, at the same time, compared to some, you know, if I was going to go talk to someone from a different sphere, you know, like [pagan organization], they'd be like, "No, you have to go through this level of initiation, and you have to do this and you have to do this ..." And I'm going, "Well, no I don't." I don't have to do any of that kind of stuff.... (Sarah)

The tendency to take these differences of opinion very personally, and to respond to them defensively, which is one of the factors that contributes to the escalation of conflict in a community once it has begun, is, I believe, bound up in the central identification that practitioners make between their Craft and who they are. In interviews, many people expressed the sentiment that neopagan witchcraft reflected the essence of who they were, and who they had always been.

> I've had beliefs affirmed, challenged, but certainly not imposed on me. There was never an "Ah-hah, that's what I need to be doing," rather "Ah-hah, there are others who do it too!" (Francine)

> All my life I have been involved, I just didn't know it consciously until around 1988, when I finally found the name and more of a manifestation, and I said "Ah! that's what it is! ..." (Martha)

Some also expressed the idea that they could not possibly do or be anything else, and that people who choose the Craft do so almost inevitably, following what, if it were occurring in a Christian context, might be termed as a sense of "vocation."

> It's what I am. Fundamentally, it is the fabric of my being. I couldn't *not* be Craft. It's shaped and fostered my relationship with the Divine, and it's developed me as a human being and an adult.... In celebrating the Mysteries inside the Craft, I am doing what I have to do, and what I feel as though I was meant to do. (Andrea)

When the authenticity or legitimacy of an individual's religious practice is challenged, in this context, it can also be experienced as a challenge to them personally, as a belittlement or disparagement of who they are, even if that was not the intent.

Finally, it has been the observation of many of those to whom I have spoken that many people come into the Craft with weak interpersonal skills. I am not prepared, in this paper, to challenge the accuracy of their perceptions, or to make any assertions about whether this is any more common in witchcraft than it is in other religions or segments of our society. But, like "witch wars," it is something that many participants highlight when they speak about their experiences with contemporary witchcraft.

> ... Because so many of the people in the Craft that I have met, in my studies and my travels, because I've now been to the U.S., Canada, and Europe, and met large numbers of Craft people from numerous traditions, an awful lot of them are as I was, except I was much younger

> when I got in, a lot of them get introduced in college, or even after university, [and they] are socially maladroit. Many of them don't know how to deal with, don't understand concepts like constructive criticism. They don't understand things like social interaction, as compared to demanding things or manipulating for things.... (Judith)

> I mean people with really low self-esteem, people who have trouble making commitments, people who are immature, much more immature than they should be, people who lack even the most basic social skills, people who have had terrible childhoods, or suffered horribly abusive relationships ... all of that. (Andrea, describing the many "walking wounded" she has encountered in the Craft)

When confronted with a disagreement or dispute, especially one that centres around miscommunication, many of these people may not have the skills or experience to deal with it constructively. Instead of being resolved quietly at a fairly early stage, as might be the case if there were some formal mechanism in place, the disagreement can escalate and become not only polarizing, but also the focus of other tensions that might not, by themselves, be sufficient to cause a conflict.

> And so a lot of these things don't get fixed, and you have long-standing, you know, "My coven doesn't talk to your coven" stuff, or "Fifteen years ago you said this about me and so I hate you" and it continues.... So there's this, this, it's ... because it's a small, somewhat networked group of communities, what might look like a small ant to you becomes "godzilla who stomped on New York City" within the community, because it becomes very large, and it stays, and these people don't know how to forgive, they don't know how to work through these issues.... (Judith)

CONCLUSIONS

"Witch wars" are polarizing conflicts that may occur when neopagan witchcraft groups interact. They are most often centred around issues of authenticity, authority, and legitimacy, and triggered by some perception that an individual or group is attempting to impose their particular vision of the Craft hegemonically. Various structural and ideological features of the neopagan witchcraft movement, combined with some of the features of participants, can both provide fertile ground for these conflicts and make them difficult to resolve.

Structurally, the most significant change going on in neopagan witchcraft right now is the push by some large pagan organizations to acquire legal standing as "churches" with the federal and provincial governments. This would allow these organizations to benefit from tax treatments available to other religious bodies, as well as to offer religious services, such as marriages, in a legally recognized context. Despite the generally well-intentioned motivations behind these activities, they are likely to increase conflict rather than decrease it. The perception of many witches is that if such recognition is given to the large organizations, it will reside with them exclusively, effectively creating two classes of witches: those whose practice has legal standing and those whose practice does not. This will force those who want the benefits of legal standing to affiliate with and conform to the practices of the larger organizations, which is unlikely to sit well with those who already feel that the large pagan organizations are attempting to assert a kind of hegemony. These concerns about a certain lack of transferability are legitimate, given the way in which legal recognition is organized (Reid 1994).[5]

> Yeah, they're [organization] actually recognized by the state, and there's a hierarchy, in there.... They're becoming very, very stuck on themselves. They're becoming very "This is the way we do it," very dogmatic, I guess. And I found that that was one of the things that really, really attracted me to the Craft, was that there wasn't a lot of "This is how it is, this is the only way that it is, and there are no other options," kind of thing. (Sarah)

> They [organization] sent word around that, that we could have, that they were going to get legal status and, legal status, and that if any of us wanted that legal protection extended to us, they would do that, provided that we handed in our Books of Shadows to them. (Deanne)

In many ways, it could be argued that the pagan organizations are in a "no win" situation here. If they go forward to obtain legal standing, they reinforce the perception among many other pagans that they are seeking a hegemonic position, when in fact, it is the governments' constructions of legal recognition that produce much of the apparent hegemony, not the intentions of the pagan organization. This source of conflict is likely to become more pronounced as more pagan organizations obtain legal standing.

Another clash of visions that appears to be deepening is that between traditionals and eclectics. Kevin Marron also notes this division, although he highlights the politically and environmentally activist eclectics, whom he calls "radicals," in particular.

> These two groups are on a collision course. The radicals tend to see the traditionalists as failing to live out the principles of a religion based on respect for nature, which should oppose a society that exploits the earth. The traditionalists regard the radicals as people who have latched onto Wicca for their own political ends. (1989:94)

When I have spoken with witches, the "activist" tensions have been less apparent than tensions based around the focus of the practice itself. Traditional Craft constructs itself very much as a mystery tradition and puts a relatively greater emphasis on the esoteric and mystical aspects that are highlighted in their received material than do most eclectics. Eclectics are far more likely to focus on the creative and celebratory aspects of the practice, with the esoteric and mystical components being available, but not essential, elements of the spiritual practice. This leads to tensions between the two groups because of the way in which each constructs and construes the other's practice. Eclectics often perceive traditionals as hidebound, hierarchical, and slavishly adhering to received material, while traditionals view eclectics as fundamentally missing the point of the entire practice, diluting the mystery tradition to the point of unrecognizability with "surface" rituals.

> Things I don't like about it. Well, the way some of the rituals are set up. The way it, it's very ... in some traditions anyways, that I've read about ... they're very strict as to "You have to do this, and you have to do this, then you have to do this, then you have to do this," and, you know, all that kind of stuff.... (Sarah, eclectic)

> I think that the proliferation of so-called "traditions," mostly started by people who have had some British traditional training, really dilutes the mysteries. There's nothing to prevent people who've only had part of their training from setting up shop and taking students, and those students may be honestly looking for Wicca, and willing to train and willing to work hard, but they just aren't going to get the whole picture. And people who would really benefit from being Gardnerian or Alexandrian either don't find it, or find it late when they've picked up all sorts of bad habits. (Andrea, traditional)

Because the numbers of people involved in eclectic practice are increasing at a much greater rate than those involved in traditional groups, these tensions are unlikely to vanish. Some traditionals are dealing with their disapproval of "eclectic neopagandom" by withdrawing from community interaction, which prevents the eruption of conflict, but also deepens the division. Again, there is no easy resolution to these differences. The traditionals are entitled to hold whatever views they wish, but as long as there is a perception that the traditionals' view is that everyone else is practising a "debased," and therefore less legitimate and authentic, form of the Craft, tensions will exist whenever people from both persuasions try to work together in any setting that highlights theology and practice.

One of the most successful ways to minimize the possibility of "witch wars" is to develop community in arenas that are not inherently "theological," that do not require an authority structure and are not subject to gatekeeping on the grounds of legitimacy, but only on grounds of respectful behaviour toward others. Social settings, such as brunches, pub moots, and coffee klatches, in which people participate voluntarily as individuals rather than as members or representatives of groups, allow neopagans of various traditions to meet one another, interact, and trade ideas without any intrusion onto what could be considered the territory of "coven autonomy." The individual nature of participation in these events allows people to get to know one another as people first, and as traditionals, or eclectics, or whatever, second. This means that people are less likely to react first out of the stereotypes that they carry about other types of practice because it is not immediately obvious, or even necessarily relevant, what the particular practice of the other party to the interaction is. Once social interaction is established and people know each other and are familiar with the peculiarities of the way they communicate, then it may well be possible to organize a "community" ritual or a festival, or another more theologically invested event, with a greatly reduced likelihood of outright war breaking out on the organizing committee. Those individuals who feel particularly strongly about the value of intergroup interaction might consider getting some training in mediation, conflict resolution, or other peer-focused techniques so that the resources will be available to recognize and address incipient conflicts before they become polarizing and cause long-term damage to relationships within the community.

Although maintaining strict separation between groups is certainly a guaranteed way to almost eliminate open intergroup conflict, being able to participate in a broader community has real advantages for neopagans. It can allow them to trade ideas, techniques, songs, and fragments of liturgy. It can give them a wider group of people to discuss the various challenges they encounter in being pagan in a non-pagan culture. It can provide a market to those people who enjoy making tools or robes or other paraphernalia, and who may have previously done so only for their own group. It can make setting up co-ops for buying supplies, or babysitting, possible. Most importantly, though, it reinforces the idea that people are not alone in their beliefs, practices, values, and orientations to the world.

> [The Craft] is something I can live as part of a community, where I don't have to justify the fact that I believe in, and want to act in, certain ways. (Francine)

> I think that there's a real importance for people to have a healthy sense of community in their spiritual practice. That's one of the

things that I've learned from it is that creating a healthy environment and community allows a person to grow in ways that are not possible in any other context. (Aidan)

Neopagan communities are constituted and reconstituted on an ongoing basis as their memberships shift and change. Individuals leave and other individuals arrive on a continuing basis. In the "best case" scenarios, the regular events, locations, and interactions around which the community exists can survive this personnel "churn"; in the worst case, interaction must be negotiated again from scratch every time a key organizer withdraws his or her participation. However, as long as the notion of "community" retains some practical or ideological appeal for participants, efforts to initiate and support it will continue to occur. The success of these would seem to be dependent on the participants' abilities to find and maintain a type of interaction that does not entail giving any of the participants the right, or the perceived ability, to dictate to others. For although neopagan communities will often come together to combat pressures and challenges from the "outside," the bonds within the communities themselves are nonetheless fragile, and will disintegrate if any one part pushes too hard on any of the others.

NOTES

1. A draft version of this paper was presented at the Qualitative Analysis Conference in Fredericton, N.B., May 1999. A shorter version was published in *The Pomegranate* 11 (February 2000).
2. These terms are being used to mean: (1) Gardnerians, Alexandrians, and other mystery-based traditions that have persisted for more than a single generation, but that cannot be reliably attributed to Gardner; (2) groups, generally eclectic in style, that are distinguished by taking a more explicitly woman-centred approach, often privileging the goddess over the God, or omitting the God in worship entirely, frequently restricting ritual celebrations to women; (3) the broad residual category of individuals and groups who do not fall clearly into one of the preceding categories.

3. "The Grove" in Montreal is an ecumenical assembly, and relies upon priesthood from other traditions to conduct its rituals. The Pagan Federation/Federation Païenne Canada (PFPC) is an organization that facilitates efforts by neopagans to combat discrimination, to provide accurate information about neopaganism to government authorities, and to facilitate prison ministry and other similar programs. They neither hold rituals nor train priesthood and are the organization in Canada that is the most strongly similar to the Covenant of the Goddess (COG) in the U.S.

4. I also included a question on the respondent's year of birth, which indicated to me that about 40 percent of my respondents were under 30, and the majority of them, about 60 percent, were between 20 and 44. I consider this question to be a slightly less reliable indicator of the general composition of the movement, however, because I suspect that it reflects, in part, the ages at which people are likely to be aware of and purchasing the kind of neopagan periodical in which my survey ran.
5. The Pagan Federation of Canada (PFPC) is engaged in a struggle to prevent just such an outcome by lobbying government departments to treat pagans in the same way that Quakers and Native Aboriginal elders are treated, as these are similiarily decentralized groups.

REFERENCES

Adler, Margot. 1986. *Drawing down the Moon*. Boston: Beacon Press.

Clifton, Chas, ed. 1993. *The Modern Craft Movement: Witchcraft Today*. St. Paul: Llewellyn Publications.

Crowley, Vivianne. 1989. *Wicca: The Old Religion in the New Age*. Wellingborough: Aquarian Press.

Cunningham, Scott. 1988. *Wicca: A Guide for the Solitary Practitioner*. St. Paul: Llewellyn Publications.

Farrar, Janet, and Stewart Farrar. 1985. *The Witches' Way: Principles, Rituals and Beliefs of Modern Witchcraft*. London: Robert Hale Publications.

———, Stewart Farrar, and Gavin Bone. 1995. *The Pagan Path*. Custer: Phoenix Publishing.

Kelly, Aidan. 1991. *Crafting the Art of Magic: Book I.* St. Paul: Llewellyn Publications.

Marron, Kevin. 1989. *Witches, Pagans, & Magic in the New Age.* Toronto: Seal Books.

Reid, Síân. 1994. "Illegitimate Religion: Neopagan Witchcraft and the Institutional Sanction of Religion in Canada." Paper presented to the Annual General Meeting of the American Academy of Religion, Chicago, unpublished.

Starhawk. 1979. *The Spiral Dance: A Rebirth of the Ancient Religion of the Great Goddess.* San Francisco: Harper & Row Publishers.

Valiente, Doreen. [1978] 1983. *Witchcraft for Tomorrow.* London: Robert Hale Publications.

CHAPTER 14

Constructing Identity and Divinity: Creating Community in an Elder Religion within a Postmodern World[1]

Jenny Blain

INTRODUCTION

As an increasing number of people are drawn toward earth-centred ("alternative" or "pagan") religions, the ways in which they seek for information are as diverse as the people themselves, and the goddesses and gods whom they name. Many practitioners, particularly within the women's spirituality movement, state that they look primarily to "ancient" religions and practices as suggested by archaeological findings from the Bronze Age, Neolithic, or even Paleolithic periods. A further group relate their beliefs and practices specifically to mythologies and mythological texts (such as the *Mabinogi*, or the Icelandic *Edda*), and archaeological findings from western Europe in a period of approximately 1,000 years, from the fourth to the fourteenth centuries of the Common Era. Others may gather information on particular deities without being historically, geographically, or temporally specific about practices, so that they might use staves of the Anglo-Saxon runic alphabet for divination, while invoking the Irish goddess Brigid before an altar statue of the Venus of Willendorf.[2]

Various terms can be used to refer to the beliefs and their adherents, including "earth religions," "paganism," "alternative religions," and "pre-Christian religions." These cover many different approaches to spirituality and belief, whose adherents in general do not consider that their approach is the only "correct" one. Most pagans see others' forms of paganism as valid. Within this varied and varying mix of spiritualities, groups and individuals draw on narratives of (for instance) ancient goddess worship, or ninth-century heathenry, to demarcate who they are: to not only establish authenticity, precedents for practices, and status for group members, but to provide individuals and groups with ways in which they relate discursively to goddesses, gods, earth, and community. Perceptions of earlier "indigenous" pagan religions provide reference points for identification and credentialling of not only group and individual practices and organization, but cosmologies and mythologies.

Earlier in my research on pagan and reconstructionist-polytheist spirituality, I differentiated three major sets of narratives, which provide a means to categorize the uncategorizable. First are narratives based on assumptions of an unbroken chain of practice, disrupted, and driven underground by the period of European "witch burnings": while such assumptions are not substantiated by evidence, and discounted academically, they still appear in discourses of some practitioners. Second are accounts of practices as modern and as deliberately created, but as derived from, influenced by and possibly including survivals of early practices. This group of narratives includes accounts constructed from interpretations of archaeological findings, such as Gimbutas's concept of "Old Europe." Third are deliberate "reconstructions," though within a present-day context and with present-day meaning, of such practices that are described in surviving documents, generally written during the Middle Ages, in which Celtic or Norse mythologies are detailed. A late twentieth-century overview of the range of "paganism" available within Britain was given by Harvey and Hardman in their book *Paganism Today*, and by Harvey in *Listening People, Speaking Earth* (Harvey 1997). The North American scene was described by Adler (1986) in *Drawing down the Moon*, which received both plaudits and criticism for its range, though many descriptions may now be outdated. The group I will describe in this reading often consider that while Adler's work is valuable, it gives a highly distorted picture of their community.

This piece is an examination of discourse and community formation of those often described as "reconstructionists," who trace their beliefs and practices to the literature and archaeological findings of the Nordic and Germanic cultures of northern Europe. As such, it draws particularly on earlier work among heathens in Canada and the U.S. in the late twentieth century (Blain 1996; 1999), while making some reference to my more recent work in Britain in the twenty-first. Here I intend to examine how heathen reconstructionists not only draw on "public narratives" but use these with deliberation in the construction of community.

Heathen reconstructionist Nuallë defines the term by saying:

> By "Reconstructionist" I mean that I try by scholarly study to put together an understanding of the ways that those who historically worshipped the Gods I worship lived and practiced their worship. I then try to live and practice in the same ways, so far as that is possible and/or feasible while living in the real near-twenty-first-century CE world.

In general, the expressed aim of reconstructionist[3] groups is not to recreate pagan society or ritual exactly as it was, but to use sources from the past to aid in the creation of religious, spiritual, and ritual experiences and structures that suit the present day: to draw on the understandings of the past for an improved understanding of the present. While there are reconstructionist groups that trace cultural links to religions of many parts of the world, the groups I am studying look to northern Europe, to the rich sources of Nordic or Germanic mythologies, for their primary information (see Blain and Wallis 2004). In drawing upon evidence from archaeology and literature, they will engage in lengthy debates over the interpretation of particular passages of "ancient" material, and how these shed light on their spiritual ancestors' concept of soul and spirit, or religious practice, or indeed how these inform their own responses to questions that concern present-day people (such as child-rearing, education, individualism, gun control, or social policy). All the reconstructionists I have met or spoken with are relatively well read, regardless of their level of formal education.

Reconstructionists, then, are attempting to uncover previous rituals, philosophies, and theologies, and adapt these to a present-day setting, creating religious philosophy and practice that they consider appropriate. They generally define themselves as belonging to specific faiths relating to culturally specific goddesses and gods: in the case of the Norse heathens described in this chapter, the Æsir and Vanir, the deities of the Germanic-speaking peoples of Europe. Several organizations exist, in North America, Europe, and elsewhere, whose objectives are not only to bring together like-minded people to practise religion, but to conduct the necessary background research to expand such practice. Not all reconstructionists are members of these organizations, and indeed the majority are probably not members, though many may belong to local groups that have connections or affiliations with national or international organizations. However, for many heathens, particularly in Britain, loose networks founded in friendships and e-mail groups form the basis of communication and sharing of techniques, information, and discourse.

DEFINING ÁSATRÚ

Heathenry or (more specifically) Ásatrú is defined by its adherents as the set of religions of the Germanic-speaking peoples of Europe prior to Christianization, basically the beliefs and practices of northern Europe. Present-day Ásatrú is an attempt to find ways of reconstructing heathenry within a late twentieth-century setting. While "Ásatrú" is the name most commonly used, some prefer "heathenism" (in the U.S.) or "heathenry" (in Britain and Europe). In Britain the term "Odinist" is used by some groups, though both there and in much of North America this term may be rejected, at least by the groups with whom I have contacts, for two reasons: First, it is seen as referring primarily to one deity, one, moreover, who is not universally liked and often feared. It is therefore seen as more appropriate for those who regard Ó›inn as their patron deity, who could describe themselves as Ó›innists within Heathenry.[4] Second, the name "Odinist" is seen as associated with factions of the right wing (some of whom have very little to do with Heathenry as the word is understood in this chapter), and has in some quarters taken on the association of "racist" and at times "Nazi." Increasingly there is a preference for "heathenry," and I have indicated a possibility for heathenry to describe practices, people, and communities, heathenism to relate to underlying philosophical or cosmological principles.

The earlier history of the heathen revival has been outlined within North America by Kaplan (1993) and within the U.K. by Harvey (1996, 1997). Both point to problems of definitions and divisions within heathenry, some of which will be met with later in this piece. Also in each case the movement attempts to differentiate itself from the wider pagan community, and particularly from Wicca. Distinctions between Heathenry and Wicca are very apparent to heathens, not necessarily so to outsiders—or to many Wiccans, who use a more universalizing set of discourses. The phrase "all the goddesses are one goddess," quoted also by Harvey (1996:62), used by many Wiccans, is to most heathens unacceptable, and they will point out that not only is Frigga culturally, cosmologically, and mythologically distinct from (for instance) Isis, she is distinct and separate also from Nerthus or Nanna, both goddesses who are found within Ásatrú cosmology. Nevertheless, Wiccans or eclectic pagans attending Ásatrú rituals will seek to describe events and deities in terms of how "really" the goddesses, or gods, are "all the same" or how "really" the ritual took place within a magic circle, regardless of whether the practitioners considered they had cast one. The need to distinguish itself and its specific practice from Wicca therefore becomes the first task of the discourse of heathenry, though not, as we will see, necessarily the most important task it faces in distinguishing itself from other forms of practice in today's complex North American society.

PUBLIC NARRATIVES OF HEATHENRY

There seem to me eight major or "public" narratives[5] within the Ásatrú and heathen community that are used by heathens to identify themselves and demarcate their practices and beliefs. These are:

(1) References to myths and stories of the Æsir and Vanir, for instance to explain the characteristics or personalities of the gods. Followers of Ásatrú index specific pieces of what is referred to as "the lore." Knowledge of this material forms a backdrop to ritual and other events, and to discussion. Most Heathens consider that people do experience the deities in their own ways, and personal revelations (see 4, below) are known on one e-mail list as Unusual Personal Gnoses (UPGs), which can be checked against, and remain secondary to, "the lore."

(2) A concept of polytheism (as distinct from monotheism or duotheism, and from at least the more popular conceptions of a Jungian discussion of "archetypes"). The gods are spoken of as real entities, separate and distinct, with rounded personalities and *different* from, for instance, Celtic or Greek or Native American beings or deities.[6]

(3) Along with this goes a sense of *cultural specificity.* Blót and Sumbel, the ritual forms of Ásatrú, are spoken of as suitable ways to worship or honour the Æsir and Vanir, and as distinct in kind from, e.g., a Wiccan circle. Again, they are drawn from "the lore."

(4) The possibility of direct communication with these beings, to both speak with them and gain various forms of knowledge. This narrative is possibly the most difficult for many non-Ásatrú readers to understand, as it diverges sharply from the rationalist discourse of Western academia. Other pagans can more easily accept it, while complete "outsiders" may tend to dismiss it. However, in interviews with many Ásatrú practitioners and theologians, this narrative of communication appears as an explanation of how they "know" about their deities and why these deities appear so "real" to them. Direct communication is a means of achieving personal gnosis (UPG).

(5) The possibility of manipulation of consciousness or "reality" by deities, or through magic inspired by them or given by them to their followers: including *Galdr* (chanted magic), runic magic, and *spae*-working or *seidhr*. Not all Ásatrú folk practise seidhr or attend sessions, but it is growing in its following. The practice of *spae*-craft is referenced in "the lore," for instance in the *Saga of Eirik the Red*. More Ásatrú folk, probably the majority, engage in rune-divination or rune-magic, often including *Galdr*. However not all practitioners of Ásatrú engage in, or give credence to, magic as something they can perform, and in this Ásatrú diverges from some other popular forms of pagan practice, such as Wicca. While magic may often be a part of religious practice, not all ritual is magical.

(6) Discussions of "the lore" and "the goddesses and gods" is, however, not engaged in solely for its own sake. A sense that spirituality is not separate from everyday life, but informs it, and what people do, and how they relate to each other, is in turn part of heathen spirituality. Many Ásatrú folk place a high value on skills of daily living, which are mentioned in "the lore" or known from archaeology or from later folk practices—woodcraft, fibre crafts, smith crafts, and brewing are only some. A craft fair is an important part of an Ásatrú gathering. Part of this is the relation of Ásatrú folk with earth (focused on by some more than others, though all see earth as living, or speak of her as personified by a deity).

(7) A sense of individual merit and responsibility, combined with community worth. Some Heathens focus on moral values or strictures, listing these as the *Nine Noble Virtues*. Others talk about individual responsibility and "being true" in more general terms. In general, heathens point out that people have a choice in what they do, and need to accept responsibility for their choice. They contrast this with perceived Christian concepts of either "God's will" or "being tempted into sin" (a word that Ásatrú folk do not use otherwise).

(8) This general sense of responsibility goes hand in hand with an elaborate concept of "soul" and "self," which is currently being explored by some Ásatrú researchers—with reference, once again, to "the lore." With this goes a concept of personal or family fate or *ørlög*,

which people, and the Norns, weave. This concept is less generally discussed than the others listed here.

A ninth discursive concept would be that the Elder Kin (deities) also are subject to the workings of Wyrd or fate, but this entered much less into the interview data or general talk that I observed in earlier research, though it may underpin it: in today's heathen discourse in the U.K., this concept is appearing more centrally.

Within earth-centred religions today, Ásatrú practitioners are using these narratives to distinguish themselves and their religion from a host of others. Their religion appears more theorized—or theologized—than some others, notably than the general collection of spiritualities known as paganism or eclectic Wicca. This is in part deliberate, with emphasis both on learning the lore and on being able to explain it to others. However, the sense of being linked with a complex body of knowledge, full of interconnections and complex meanings, appears to be one of the attractions for newcomers, and a central focus even for those Ásatrú folk who do not themselves attempt to theorize the material, so that even those who do not speak of divisions of the soul, or recite from the *Eddas*, will debate the Gods and their personalities and characteristics, and know something of how their stories have come down to a late twentieth-century world.

Many followers of Ásatrú ground their concepts of deity in the old literature, the Icelandic *Eddas* and Sagas. Others prefer to rely on their intuitions, on what "comes to them," though usually specifying that these are personal and pertain only to themselves. The acronym UPG, coined by a heathen on an e-mail list in the 1990s, has persisted and indeed been adopted among polytheists more generally, to refer to "unusual personal gnosis" or "unsubstantiated personal gnosis," that is, not found in the lore. Many polytheist reconstructionists will point out that "lore" (whether *Eddas*, folktales, Greek myth, etc.) was "originally" UPG that, by making sense to other people where it chimed with their own UPG or knowledge, became accepted. Nonetheless, most heathens follow broadly similar patterns of ritual, and most will, if pushed, seek to trace back their practices to *Edda* and Sagas, whether through their own reading and research or through the research of those whom they see as authoritative or knowledgeable practitioners. Ásatrú boasts a number of adherents who are either fully capable of reading materials produced by scholars of Norse or Germanic religion literature, folklore or anthropology, or are themselves members of these disciplines. In other words, there is some direct connection between religious practice and scholarly debate.

In practice these narrative strands are woven together in the discourse of Ásatrú practitioners. Some examples come from an interview with a Canadian Ásatrú woman known as Valkyrja.[7]

JB: What is the most important focus of the religion for you?

Valkyrja: The moral and ethical values. The fact that it's unwavering, and also, I mean for lack of a better term the Raven's Kindred's "Nine Noble Virtues" I find very nice. The self-sufficiency and the non-subservient relationship to gods. You know, as far as I'm concerned, other religions can have the grovellers. I don't think they want us to grovel, and I know a lot of people think it's arrogant, but I honestly believe they treat us as equals. Equals with a little less power, but equals nonetheless. We can do things they can't, even though they can do a lot of stuff we can't.

... It's a partnership without being unequal, which I like, really like.... And it's the same way with friendships as well, it's equal give and take, or it's nothing. But you don't keep score. There's equal give and take, but it's not "Well, I did something for you, now you gotta do something for me." Oh *excuse me.*

JB: How about [...] as the *Hávamál*[8] has it, a gift looks always to a gift, not in the sense in that it's kept score, but that it's expected to come around.

Valkyrja: Yeah, and [...] in the way I look at it is, if I do something for a friend of mine, they may in turn do something for somebody else, and it's a what goes around comes around

> kinda thing. It doesn't have to automatically come back to me, 'cause eventually it will, and even if it doesn't, someone has taken notice.

Several points appear in this dialogue: The narrative of self-sufficiency blends with that of regarding the deities as real, as beings who can do certain things that people cannot, but before whom people do not bow. The sense of "equal give and take" comes from the lore and becomes part of the concept of responsibility, as pointed to by heathens on two continents.

The emphasis on "the lore" means that, when asked, Ásatrú folk are able to give accounts of cosmology, which, though individual, are recognizably patterned on the shared mythological basis. In my experience of interviewing, this does not happen with, for example, Wiccans, who give accounts that seem to bear little relationship to each other. The following account is from Steve, leader of a kindred in Kentucky, who was asked to explain his cosmology.

> I'm an avid reader of myths and then taking the myths and interpreting them in terms of modern scientific work.... I'm not a literalist with the Norse mythology ... but I find the Norse mythology very rich, and very rewarding way of looking at the development of the universe, the creation of the universe. I feel that the universe sprang into being, perhaps out of some unknown and unknowable tension between polarities that we can't really understand, we can only accept on a very basic level. So in other words, the story of Ginnungagap and Muspellheim and Nifelheim just fits right into that ... and the tension and the dance between these polarities bringing things into being. I've talked to a lot of people about the story of Ymir coming into being spontaneously from the centre action of these poles, and I look at Ymir as being raw chaotic matter/energy, that sort of flux-like state that we now know exists in the laboratories. And at the same time Au›umbla coming into being represents to me a sort of an intrinsic shaping principle that exists in the Universe, um, things want to be ordered. And I find it interesting that Ymir comes into

> being spontaneously from this material, Au›umbla shapes Bor from the same material, so you have raw chaotic matter and then you have the raw chaotic matter shaped into some order, and it's from this shaped being that the race of gods springs.

Steve here indexes accounts of the creation of the worlds from the *Edda* of thirteenth-century scholar Snorri Sturluson, and from the earlier cosmogonic poem *Vafflru›nismál*, in the *Poetic Edda* (as is the poem *Hávamál* referred to previously). Steve links these accounts to the accounts of present-day science, and finds that each helps in an understanding of the other. Few Ásatrú folk that I have met interpret the stories totally literally. While "the god/desses" are "real" and are in some ways "kin" to people, this does not mean that they are merely some kind of super-people, but rather that the poets who gave us the stories used human analogies or metaphors. The *Eddas* are not a "revelation" and are not "factual." There is speculation that some of the poems may have been used as ritual drama at the time of their composition, and this speculation has been shared by at least some Eddic scholars (e.g., Haugen 1983; Gunnell 1995).

Not only cosmology, but everyday things such as food preparation are linked with spirituality and with relationships of individuals and groups to the earth.

> *Valkyrja:* When I go out and pick vegetables, without making a big elaborate production of it, I'm consciously playing or paying respect to, you know, the land, woods, and the sun and the air, and the time and energy that people have put into making these things. If I'm out in the forest and I'm picking flowers or mushrooms or some herbs or something, it's more of a I didn't grow this, yet this [is] here when I need it, so thank you, kind of thing, and same thing when I'm cooking. When I'm cooking I'm [...] embodying everything that I believe that should be good about the food into it.... When I hunt, [...] I feel more that it's better than going to the grocery store and

> picking up a piece of cow. I don't know if that makes sense, but I'm going out, I'm doing the work, I'm tracking it, I'm killing it, and I am personally returning its spirit back to where it came from. And then the poor animal isn't in the slaughterhouse with 50,000 other ones. That's just a personal thing, but that's part of it.... I'm taking the whole thing for need and use, [...]and if I don't get close or I don't get an animal, then it's still the same kind of experience. It's just the balance of life and death [...], you know.

Ásatrú folk become exposed to the discourse through reading and through meeting with other Ásatrú folk, whether at gatherings or events, through membership in a local group (often called a kindred or a hearth, emphasizing the local and "family" dimensions of heathen practice), or through the electronic means of Internet web pages, e-mail and mail lists, and usenet news. Some find the practice of Ásatrú through an acquaintance with the mythology, discovered as an adult or as a child. For others the entry is through other means. For instance, Asvard, a gó›I (priest) living in Toronto, describes his entry, over a number of years, from an original concern about anything "occult," through a later reading of the work of feminist pagan author Starhawk and discovering that he shared many of the ideas she promoted, so that "paganism" became acceptable to him, to being given a set of runes and deciding to read about the culture that had spawned them. This led to his first experiment with ritual.

> *Asvard:* I did a blót with Freyja and Freyr. That was the first two gods that I ever contacted, and I was filled with such a sense of welcome, like it's sort of like coming home for the holidays kind of feeling that you get from your family, and from then on I was hooked. I couldn't get enough of [...] books on the subject, and I read everything.

CREATING COMMUNITY: GATHERINGS AND DISCUSSION

Whereas many people come to an understanding of themselves as Ásatrúar from reading, they also say that the direct interchange with other Ásatrúers, and attendance at rituals, is an important part of learning the practice and discourse. Alissa says:

> I learned by doing it because even though you can read them up in the books, you really have no clue what's goin' on. 'Cos you can say, well a Sumbel is when you do this, but you have no idea, well, what kind of things to say, and what's it about, and what does it mean. [...]When doing it you get to interact with other people, and then you understand.... One of my first Sumbels was with Slowfoot, and he made a point of saying, "Anything you say, this horn represents the well of Wyrd. Anything you say continues on, it means something, it's important, so make sure your words aren't petty, and your words are true." And you know, just understanding that is important.

William Bainbridge, a former elected leader in The Troth (an international heathen organization), points to the importance of gatherings not only as instruments of teaching people practices, but of developing practice and culture and, through these, developing community. As he explains it, a religion exists within a community. In pre-Christian times, religion existed within a cultural setting, and varied from one group to another. Present-day Ásatrú is being created deliberately by "converts" all of whom are rather self-conscious about their beliefs and practices. To develop as a serious religion, Ásatrú must become "organic."

> *WB:* The idea of people [...] reading a book on a religion, forming beliefs inside their own head, and then suddenly declaring themselves to be something is a very modern phenomenon. People in traditional societies simply didn't think that way. They didn't act that way and that's not

> how they developed and acquired their spiritual orientations. And if we are serious about practising a heathen, traditional, an indigenous religion, or making what we're practising into one of those, we need to realize that the community dynamic was part of that back then and therefore it probably needs to be part of it now.

When people read a book on Ásatrú and come to an event or a gathering, they often come to learn. The expectation is that they will find people there who are "experts," but as Bainbridge says:

> There's a great expectation among newcomers to the religion that they will be presented with a finished work, with something just like Christianity, which, of course, is developed over a number of centuries, that will answer the questions, that will function efficiently, in which every person knows their place, and [...] knows what's expected of them and so forth, and the realities in really any organization, group, or other set of collective activities that I'm aware of, are the realities that this simply is not the case. All of us, whether we admit it or not, are still seeking for the proper way to practise this religion, in modern context because, of course, our sources come from a very ancient context....

Through gatherings and meetings, and Internet discussion, the discourse is not only being reinforced but actively being created. There are many groups within present-day Ásatrú, some small, some relatively large, some international. Although the groups tend to share and use the public narratives I listed previously, different groups will put differing emphases on lore versus personal gnosis, or on individual versus community (and indeed these words "individual" and "community" are interpreted in diverse ways within Ásatrú). Further, the discourse of "individualism" makes it unlikely that many groups will want to be "taken over" as part of a large organization. For these reasons alone, it seems unlikely that any one group can "organize Ásatrú," and, especially given the emphasis placed on self-reliance and independence, there is some suspicion of anyone who looks as if they might claim to be "Ása-pope." However, many smaller groups are associated with larger ones, attending their gatherings. Orjon, a heathen from the Midwest, makes a plea for discussion and "bonding" between heathen groups.

Orjon: If we don't have healing, if we don't have bonding between kindreds—my kindred is a free kindred, we don't belong to any organization, however, we are bonded with several kindreds. If we don't have that, if we don't have bonding on a national and international level, we're not going to survive. I'm one of the old ones. I'm 57 years old. If we don't bring the young ones in, if we don't give them a good grounding in the old gods, in magic, in spirituality, not the doctrines, but worship of our gods, our cultural gods. If we don't bring them in, if we don't bring these groups together, we won't survive. I think the gathering [Trothmoot '97, at which he was interviewed] was wonderful, it just was totally enlightening to me. I was so happy that Frigga's web was so active this weekend....

Here we can turn to the question of why people are drawn to Ásatrú (or any non-mainstream religion) and how they construct meanings around it. Clearly not all heathens derive the same meanings, and it seems that not all can "bond" together. Young though it is, present-day Ásatrú has a history, in part mapped by Kaplan within the U.S. This history includes growth, but also division. This is perhaps inevitable given the diverse meanings that people create and the different reasons that have attracted them in the first place. Many are drawn by the stories of "the lore" or by the concept of independence and self-reliance. A small proportion, however, are attracted by quite another factor.

IDENTITY AND POLITICS

> Ásatrú has its right-wing nuts. So does Christianity. Right-wing Odinism bears about the same relationship to mainstream Ásatrú as Christian Identity does to the United Church of Canada. And some of them are *the same* right-wing nuts.

I am quoting myself here when I was asked to summarize the situation of "mainstream Ásatrú" with respect to those who used concepts and symbols from heathen lore or art for political, usually right-wing, purposes. The above quote was a compilation and distillation of comments made by Ásatrú folk interviewed in Canada and the U.S. It encapsulates a situation that some Norse heathens see as the greatest problem facing Ásatrú in the twenty-first century, and that consumes the energies of many organizers. To outline the situation, I will draw on the work of Jeffery Kaplan, whose explorations within Ásatrú have been made from a different perspective, and hence with different emphasis and conclusions, than my own. More recently, Matthias Gardell (2003) has addressed some of the same issues.

Kaplan, in outlining the history of Norse-heathen religions in North America to the mid-1990s, distinguishes between "Odinism" and "Ásatrú." In this usage, Odinists are people looking for a "White" religion, and Kaplan traces its construction from the Germany of the Weimar republic, through the writings of an obscure Australian, Alexander Rudd Mills, and their adoption by members of the American post-war extreme right-wing, to associations with present-day National Socialist groups (1993:200). I do not intend to further explore these connections, but to note them for future reference, and to note that today some members of hate groups, including Christian-based hate groups, call themselves "Odinist."

Kaplan also traces the history of Ásatrú within North America, at least in terms of its formal organization from 1973, with the formation of what would become the Ásatrú Free Assembly, through its dissolution in 1987 and the arising from its ashes of two competing organizations, The Troth (known also as the Ring of Troth) and the Ásatrú Alliance. The split was in part over questions of who could consider themselves "Ásatrú"; that is, what kind of people were acceptable as members of kindreds or groups. Those who felt called by the god/desses? Those who were interested in the mythology and cultures of northern Europe? Those who were descendants of northern Europeans—or those who were descended *only* from northern Europeans? The two resulting groups took different stances, The Troth maintaining that membership of the organization, and participation in rituals and festivals were open to all "Trú folk," whomsoever these might be, regardless of background, race, gender, or sexual orientation, while the Ásatrú Alliance held that individual kindreds had the right to determine with whom they would worship, and accepted that some members would not wish to worship with those who were "other" than themselves (in a number of ways, chiefly "race" and sexual orientation). Both organizations claimed to be the inheritors of the Ásatrú Free Assembly, and appear for some years to have functioned by essentially refusing to recognize each other's existence. However the Alliance was an alliance of kindreds (small groups), each setting their own policy, whereas The Troth was a collective of individual members, and in practice many individuals belonged to Alliance kindreds, but were themselves members of The Troth. In addition, a number of "independent" kindreds had arisen, some fairly closely associated with the Troth and in sympathy with its goals, but remaining "independent" because of the various organizational and other problems that plagued The Troth (many of which appear common to alternative religious groups within North America, as Kaplan points out).

In the years since 1993 (when Kaplan completed research for his thesis), a number of factors have complicated the scene. The Troth, focusing on scholarship and in pursuit of a goal of providing trained and knowledgable "clergy" to the Ásatrú community, published its 700-page volume *Our Troth*, now available only on the Internet, in 1993, and revised its clergy programs to be (in theory at least) more manageable than those outlined by Kaplan; the increased growth of the Internet enabled increased development of international links, and vastly increased dissemination of information; some "independent" organizations have grown and developed their own clergy programs, so that there are now more "players" on the scene than merely The Troth and the Alliance; and Steve McNallen, original founder of the

AFA, has created a new organization with the same initials, the Ásatrú Folk Assembly, whose status has seemed to vary between that of a kindred of the Alliance and that of a national U.S. organization with its own links with overseas.

These groups later did acknowledge each other's existence, though not always amicably. In general an awareness arose that Ásatrú does not constitute one community. Instead debate centred over whether "non-racial" Ásatrúshould be in dialogue with "folkish Ásatrú." *Idunna*, the magazine of the Ring of Troth, ceased to carry advertisements for *Vor Tru*, the magazine of the Ásatrú Alliance, the latter having some "folkish" kindreds. As William Bainbridge told me:

> I know in The Troth ... we developed the principle that we are the non-racial approach to heathen religion; that is, we do not believe in or accept theories that spirituality is racially determined and we absolutely do not tolerate discrimination on the basis of race.

This principle has been shared by a number of smaller groups and individuals, and in the U.K. is basic to most heathen practice, though some leading members of the Odinic Rite have continued to maintain that theirs is the true native religion of Europeans. Indeed on both sides of the Atlantic, there are some kindreds or groups that officially hold the line that spirituality is inherited (a doctrine known as "metagenetics," outlined by Kaplan). An increasing understanding among some members of The Troth and some of the "independent kindreds" that attend their gatherings in North America, and most of "mainstream" heathenry in Britain is that "folkish Ásatrú" does exist, does attract some people (notably from among the prison population), and will continue go its own way. Its members are not likely to be converted, and its presence can be a liability—particularly if a link is perceived between the "folkish" doctrine of metagenetics,[9] and some of the more bizarre Odinist pronouncements. This understanding implies that it is up to members of non-racist or anti-racist organizations to proceed with their own creation of community, accepting that not all those who term themselves "Ásatrú" can or will be part of this.

IDENTITY AND THE WIDER SOCIETY

Ásatrú or heathenry exists within a social context of late twentieth-century and early twenty-first-century social discourse and politics. Racism, at times virulent, is part of that context, as is awareness of recent history, and these impact on Ásatrú in a number of ways. The U.S. popular press is aware of Ásatrú, and periodically indulges in articles such as *Time*'s "Can Thor Make a Comeback?", describing a "folkish" site on the Internet. The people who see themselves as "mainsteam Ásatrú" perceive themelves as constantly engaging in damage control. An article in *U.S. News* of December 29, 1997, by David Kaplan and Mike Tharp, states that

> ... another strange sect attracting the radical right is the Odinists, who espouse a form of ancient Scandinavian mythology. Odinist practices include witchcraft and paganism, and the sect has attained a strong following among new-nazis and racist skinheads, who blend in white supremacy beliefs....

This was all strictly true, in Kaplan's terms, but highly problematic for Ásatrúars (both mainstream and "folkish") as the unstated implication was that all followers of "ancient Scandinavian mythology" were "racist Odinists." It sparked a number of letters from Ásatrú followers, explaining differences between mainstream Ásatrú/Norse heathenry and whatever these "racist skinheads" might be practising. At least one was printed, from Ann Sheffield, which included the following statements:[10]

> ... I appreciate your pointing out that "most Odinists are not dangerous," but I fear that your article may still leave the impression that racist views and terrorist sympathies are the norm among those who practice modern forms of ancient Scandinavian religion. Like any religion, including Christianity, we have our lunatic fringe, but it would be a mistake to think that the fringe is typical or in any way represents the beliefs and practices of most believers.
>
> I am a follower of Ásatrú, a form of reconstructed Norse polytheism. I, and the majority of my co-religionists, view racism and

> terrorism with the same abhorrence shared by all decent people. Ásatrú is open to all, and white supremacism is morally repugnant to me....

Periodically, requests circulate within mainstream Ásatrú groups for people to respond to "watchdog" organizations and to the popular press, to inform them that "we're not racist." Several Ásatrú folk have reported that even members of other pagan groups made them feel unwelcome, or refused to discuss Ásatrú or attend Ásatrú rituals because of such a perception equating heathenry and racism.

The perception of outsiders and the existence of "Odinism" have caused Ásatrú to devote considerable time and energy into articulating theories of culture, inheritance, and spirituality. Some of this exercise has been divisive. However, the effect has been to problematize concepts that, within many other earth-centred religions, have gone unexamined. Some members of Ásatrú groups are now on interfaith councils, or assisting "watchdog" organizations; others are engaged with press and public in ways similar to the writer of the letter to *U.S. News* quoted above. The range of expression on ethnicity, "race," and, generally, inclusiveness varies from The Troth's statement that "race" is not a factor and discrimination is intolerable, through to a sense that those people most likely to be drawn to Ásatrú will have some descent from the peoples of northern Europe, but almost all make plain that they regard concepts of superiority and "White supremacy" with the same distaste as the writer of the letter. Deep divisions within Ásatrú, some indicated by Gardell (2003) in the U.S., lie between the view that says "to each their own" and The Troth's position, which comes closest to sociological theories on the construction of ethnicity and "race." This range of views parallels that of mainstream North America, or indeed other areas such as Scandinavia, Britain, or Europe.

COMMUNITIES AND CULTURE

To conclude, followers of Norse Heathenry within North America and elsewhere today are attempting to construct for themselves some sense of who they are with respect to the wider community, both of other earth religions and of society in general. They are constructing the boundaries, through discourse and practice, that indicate what Ásatrú is and what it is not. Some of these boundaries are set by referral to "the lore" and shared concepts of ritual practice. Some of the boundaries are set by referral to social assumptions and expectations. Heathens are endeavouring to ensure that these boundaries are set through their own active definitions: They claim the right to define what they are, rather than have this done for them by outsiders. In doing so, they are constructing a set of overlapping communities of shared perceptions and shared discourse.

This construction of community cannot be forced, and cannot be entirely, or even largely, directed by the current leadership. As William Bainbridge says:

> ... today we are dealing with so many individuals, who have thought deeply about religious matters for a number of years, who have developed their own ideas on spirituality and their own expectations from spirituality, that we are not working in a context where our leadership can profitably tell people how the religion should be practised, and expect them to simply do it that way. We have to be a lot more indirect and we have to be a lot more artistic in the way we go about things because a lot of what we are really trying to do is allow people's own creativity to come through enough, so that it's recognizable to other people, and in this way when we start recognizing these deeper and more creative aspects of, of our own spirituality, people will start to recognize one another, to recognize common approaches, to recognize the people with whom they feel comfortable working, the people with whom they should be working, and organizations really will start assuming the character that reflects the deeper motivations and character of the people.

Whether this can occur when the "community" is widespread, without daily contact with individuals, is not yet evident. If heathenry is to be treated seriously as a religion by others than its adherents, it will have to be seen as an expression of community spirit and feeling. When I first drafted this article, I concluded by describing Heathenry as still in an experimental stage. Today it may be going beyond that stage, to reflexive positioning that is no longer driven only by a need to distinguish practitioners, as individuals, from dominant religions. To become "indigenous," it will require an orientation of practitioners to landscape that we are starting to see emerging in British practice, and a thoughtful sharing and debate of how concepts, UPG, and technique, construct the overlapping communities and sets of understandings that may be emerging. Can this happen in North America? We shall see.

NOTES

1. An early version of this chapter was presented at the Qualitative Methods conference, Toronto, August 1997, Interdisciplinary Perspectives: Using Qualitative Methods to Study Social Life.
2. I have outlined some categorizations of pagan religions in an earlier paper, given at a conference on "The Middle Ages in Contemporary Popular Culture" (Blain 1996).
3. I use the word because it is convenient. Some adherents of heathen or other (including Celtic) practices, however, dislike it, and I am currently searching for a better word that covers the same range of meanings.
4. As others might use the terms "Thorswoman," or "Tyrian," or "Freyasman," in each case referring to a deity who has their primary allegiance. Many Ásatrú folk will avoid the word altogether, so that a woman might say something like "I am a heathen and an Ó›insgy›ja," in referring to herself as a priestess of Ó›inn.
5. Note that these are further discussed in Blain (2002) and subsequent work, with more details on discourse and narrative analysis.
6. Some heathens do talk about archetypes, though those engaged in constructing theology generally do not. It has been pointed out that individuals use the word "archetype" in diverse ways and that Jung's own meaning may not be too far from an Ásatrú conception of deities. In a recent debate via an e-mail discussion list, it was

pointed out that newcomers to Ásatrú speak of the god/esses as archetypes, while "old hands" speak of them as "real." From the point of view of discourse analysis, part of this may be that exposure to Ásatrú discourse "permits" a person to come to speak and think of deities existing independently of people without feeling they will be regarded as "flaky." In my interviews, some do use the concept of archetypes, and it seems that they do so to express something that has its being on a cultural or social level, rather than uniquely within the individual psyche (which is how the word is chiefly used by Wiccans).

7. Many practitioners suggested a pseudonym by which they could be known for this study, sometimes a name they use for religious purposes only, or on occasion an Internet user name. Some, particularly community leaders, wish to be identified by their own names, and this is done most obviously in the cases of writers in the field or publicly known leaders who are speaking as such, e.g., William Bainbridge, who is quoted later in this chapter.
8. A poem of the *Poetic Edda*, the Words of the High One (O›inn).
9. Eavesdropping on the Internet newsgroup alt.religion. Ásatrú leads one to ponder the possibility that the only proponent of "metagenetics" who can actually discuss the concept may indeed be Mr. McNallen himself. (In this I am in accordance with Kaplan.) The theory is very little discussed, and mostly used as a reason people might want to restrict membership of their groups. Alt.religion. Ásatrú is mostly occupied by the slinging of insults between groups and individuals, as the newsgroup serves as a chief point of contact between those who use heathen discourse and practice as a way of proclaiming superiority and those Ásatrú folk who are willing to "talk with racists," usually in order to demonstrate to other readers that Ásatrú is about other things than race. Serious discussion of points such as those enumerated in this paper occurs in other forums.
10. Quoted here with permission of the author.

REFERENCES

Adler, Margot. 1986. *Drawing Down the Moon*, 2nd ed. Boston: Beacon Press.

Blain, Jenny. 1996. "Witchcraft, Magic, and Religion: Some Discursive Reconstructions of Belief and Practice." Conference on "The Middle Ages in Contemporary Popular Culture," McMaster University, Hamilton, Ontario, March 1996.

———. 1999. "Presenting Constructions of Identity and Divinity: Ásatrú and Oracular Seidhr." In *Fieldwork Methods*, edited by Scott Grills, 203–227. Thousand Oaks: Sage.

———. 2002. *Nine Worlds of Seid-Magic: Ecstasy and Neo-Shamanism in North European Paganism*. London: Routledge.

———. 2004. "Tracing the In/authentic Seeress: From Seid-Magic to Stone Circles." In *Researching Paganisms: Religious Experiences and Academic Methodologies*, edited by J. Blain, D. Ezzy, and G. Harvey, 217–240. Walnut Creek: AltaMira.

———. 2005. "Heathenry, the past, and Sacred Sites in Today's Britain." In *Modern Paganism in World Cultures*, edited by M. Strmiska, 181–208. Santa Barbara: ABC-CLIO.

———, Douglas Ezzy, and Graham Harvey, eds. 2004. *Researching Paganisms*. Walnut Creek: Altamira.

———, and Robert J. Wallis. 2004. "Sites, Texts, Contexts and Inscriptions of Meaning: Investigating Pagan 'Authenticities' in a Text-Based Society." *The Pomegranate* 6, no. 2: 231–252.

———, and Robert J. Wallis. 2006. "Ritual Reflections, Practitioner Meanings: Disputing the Terminology of Neo-shamanic 'Performance'." *Journal of Ritual Studies* 20, no. 1: 21–26.

Gardell, M. 2003. *Gods of the Blood: The Pagan Revival and White Separatism*. Durham and London: Duke University Press.

Greenwood, Susan. 2005. *The Nature of Magic*. Oxford: Berg.

Gundarsson, Kveldúlf, and R. Hagan, eds. 1993. *Our Troth*. Seattle: The Troth.

Gunnell, Terry. 1995. *The Origins of Drama in Scandinavia*. Woodbridge: D.S. Brewer.

Harvey, Graham. 1996. "Heathenism Today." In *Paganism Today*, edited by

Graham Harvey and Charlotte Hardman, 49–64. London: Thorsons.
———. 1997. *Listening People, Speaking Earth: Contemporary Paganism*. London: Hurst.
———, and Charlotte Hardman, eds. 1996. *Paganism Today*. London: Thorsons.
Haugen, Einar. 1983. "The Edda as Ritual: Odin and His Masks." In *Edda, a Collection of Essays*, edited by Robert J. Glendinning and Haraldur Bessason, 3–24. Winnipeg: University of Manitoba Press.
Hutton, Ronald. 1999. *The Triumph of the Moon: A History of Modern Pagan Witchcraft*. Oxford: Oxford University Press.
Kaplan, Jeffrey. 1993. "Revolutionary Millenarianism in the Modern World: From Christian Identity to Gush Emunim." PhD thesis, University of Chicago.
———. 1997. *Radical Religions in America*. Syracuse: Syracuse University Press.
Wallis, Robert J. 2003. *Shamans/Neo-Shamans: Ecstasy, Alternative Archaeologies and Contemporary Pagans*. London: Routledge.

CHAPTER 15

Weaving a Tangled Web? Pagan Ethics and Issues of History, "Race," and Ethnicity in Pagan Identity

Ann-Marie Gallagher

INTRODUCTION

On March 25, 1997 a witch, Kevin Carleon, got into Stonehenge and at dawn unfurled and flew the Union Flag. This was in protest at a theory published in the *Wiltshire Archaeological Magazine* that Stonehenge and Avebury may have been built by insurgent peoples originating from the west of what is now France around 4,500 years ago. Carleon explained his protest by declaring, "It is my theory that those living in this country invaded Europe—and not vice versa."[1] The deployment of a Union Flag in the circumstances seems somewhat anachronistic, given that it did not exist in its present form until 1801 and the idea of "nation" in its contemporary sense did not exist before the eighteenth century (Robbins 1989; Hobsbawm 1990). But this is just one example of a whole range of misconceptions, and arguably misappropriations, of concepts of history, nation, "race," and ethnicity that seem to exist within popular pagan lore. It is the purpose of this article to hold up to the light, from an academic and pagan participant perspective, a number of issues arising from the continuing evolution of pagan identities in Britain at the end of the twentieth century. Some of these are named in the title of this short piece; all, it will be suggested, arise from a number of as yet unaddressed assumptions about the place that pagans occupy in our current historical, social, and political situation(s). These assumptions are articulated in a number of ways: in the opinions, philosophies, texts, and vernacular expressions of pagan culture, and they occur with a regularity and variety that is almost dizzying when one seeks to catch at their sources and their boundaries. In order that the varying emanations of ideas around history, gender, "race," identity, and ethnicity and other issues do not slip the net, I will be seeking to identify the nodes each presently occupies on the web of pagan culture and to name the points at which this web is becoming entangled with that of the more dominant social structures in which pagans also participate. This piece will argue that current pagan praxis has the power to transform both, and to point the way toward a pagan ethics that would support this mutual transformation, but this first requires acknowledging the links between the two identities and meanings being allotted and ascribed to an ongoing construction of current pagan identity that may make that identity appear more fragile and contingent.

"HISTORY" AND POPULAR PAGAN TEXTS

> The dead are not always quiet, and the past will never be a safe subject for contemplation. (Hutton 1996)

A survey of popular pagan texts published by Aquarian Press, Thorsons, Element, and Arkana turned up an arrestingly unproblematized relationship with ethnic, historical, national, social, and political boundaries.

Among the very popular titles surveyed, there was a markedly lackadaisical attitude toward historical periodicity. This was particularly the case in titles that invoked historical precedent as the foundation of both the authority of the information contained in the book about contemporary pagan practices and, significantly, the basis for present-day pagan identity. The examples I analyzed were peppered with invocations of "Ancient times ..." and began seemingly authoritative pieces of information with "In the past ..." invariably failing to identify era let alone dates, cultural context, or cite provenance. Admittedly, none of the books I looked at claimed to be an academic text, although one of the worst offenders did, somewhat ironically, deplore the "flimsy scholarship" on which many books detailing various magical traditions are based (Green 1995). I would argue, however, that neither the lack of claims to scholarship nor the disclaimers about it that some texts occasionally carry exonerate them from blatant inaccuracy or unaccountability. The influence of popular pagan texts should not be underestimated; most self-identifying pagans in Britain, northern Europe, and North America are first-generation pagans (in the contemporary sense at least!) and the majority either have first contact with paganism via these texts or consult them for follow-up information after initial person-to-person contact with paganism. Moreover, in my experience and from the evidence of other similar sources cited in the texts themselves, the information and ideas generated by these books is often enthusiastically picked up on and quoted, taken as given and often, as I will go on to argue, reapplied somewhat problematically.

PAGAN "ETHNICITIES," CELTICISM, AND CROSS-CULTURAL COMPARISONS

A concept that appears to span some particularly woolly ideas around some of the issues mentioned is the often uncritical and unproblematized application of the term "Celtic" (cf. Bowman 1993). What has effectively been a salvage job around previously suppressed, silenced, and overlooked aspects of past and present cultures of the British Isles has been a positive consequence of the so-called "Celtic revival" and has gone some way to challenging the myth of Anglo-Saxonism first imposed within ideologies of racial hierarchies in nineteenth-century England. However, the current wave of popular "Celticism" stands in danger of propagating myths with similarly denigrating effects. Courtenay Davis, in the introduction to his book *Celtic Design*, uses the term "the Celtic nation" (Rutherford 1993)—one of the problems related to which I have already pointed out. But the frequency with which the rhetoric of Celticism abounds, for example, "the Celtic civilization," "the Celtic people" places it in favour of an homogeneous "Celtic" history and identity. Only one of the samples of books on the Grail Mysteries that I looked at, for example, contained any element of differentiation in terminology. John and Caitlin Matthews do pause at the beginning of *Ladies of the Lake* to deplore what they term a "growing tendency to confuse 'Celtic,' 'British,' 'Welsh' and 'Gaelic.'" However, they go on to say that when they are talking about "Celtic," they are "speaking broadly about the traditions of Britain and Ireland combined, since both countries share many common themes and stories" (Matthews and Matthews 1992). Notably, both authors employ the term "Celtic" unproblematically and without even as much differentiation as this in a number of their other works. So what we have, effectively, is a large number of popular texts invoking a cultural specification without ever specifying whose culture, or when or where it is or was.

WHAT DOES THIS FINE DISREGARD FOR CULTURAL AND HISTORICAL SPECIFICITY SIGNIFY?

Perhaps we could paraphrase the historian Renan by applying his assessment of the tendencies of forming nations to present-day pagan identity. He claimed that "getting its history wrong is part of being a nation" (Hobsbawm 1990). Perhaps getting our history and occasionally our geography wrong is part of constructing a pagan identity. But what might the consequences of such myth-building be? Might not the construction of our ideas about, for example, Celticity actually be "culture-u-like" with knotwork, and undermine those voices struggling to be heard below the surface of that lumpenmasse identity; fighting for land rights in Scotland, against racism and poverty in Wales, against war in Ireland, absentee landlords in Cornwall, and against the demise of the Manx language in Vannin? To what extent, when an author claims and a reader believes that building a mound in your garden is a "very Celtic thing," are we essentializing racial characteristics, positing an "inside track" on spirituality in place of recognizing human rights issues and lack of power? Stereotyping, even when it appears to be awe-struck and benevolent, actually denies and "disappears" self-autonomy. Claims toward "Celticity" or any other identity that ignore the real history and material conditions of those with whom we are declaring affinity becomes another form of abuse; whether this takes the form of ripping off identities that are not ours, or the strip-mining of the spirituality that may be the last dignity some peoples have remaining. All pagans have a responsibility to act ethically in relation to oppressed peoples—that means respecting their history and present struggles, not constructing a "Stage Oirish" spirituality.

Romanticizing minority-ethnic cultures is a concurrent issue occurring within the recent interest in Native American spirituality. This has had a devastating effect on Native Americans, as Andy Smith, a Cherokee woman, points out in her essay "For All Those Who Were Indian in a Former Life" (Smith 1993). She points out that Native Americans are told they are greedy if they do not choose to share their spirituality, and gives the example of White women in search of spiritual enlightenment appealing to female solidarity in order to glean some "secret" knowledge from Native American women. She notes that she can hardly attend a feminist conference in the United States without the only Native American presenter being the woman who opens the conference with a ceremony. Because of this romanticization of indigenous peoples' spirituality, the real oppression of Indians [*sic*] is overlooked, even trivialized; "Indian women are suddenly no longer the women who are forcibly sterilized and are tested with unsafe drugs such as Depo Provera; we are no longer the women who have a life expectancy of 47 years; and we are no longer the women who generally live below the poverty level and face a 75 percent unemployment rate. No, we're too busy being cool and spiritual."

An analogy between what has happened to Native American spirituality and the situation with the new Celticity in Britain is drawn, albeit unwittingly, in a book on Celtic lore. In a section where "past" "Celtic" oral culture is discussed in relation to storytelling traditions, the author inserts an amazed footnote:

> There are still peoples who retain an oral tradition and possess memories which are, to us, startling. An example of this is the Navajo Indians. A writer in the *Independent Magazine* in August 1990 records a visit to a restaurant in Navajo country. The waitress went from packed table to packed table taking orders without the benefit of written notes, then returned with laden trays bearing the correct dishes. (Rutherford 1993)

Since all that can be said with any certainty, given the evidence, is that this woman has an extremely good memory, it is difficult to conclude whether the author really believes this woman lives wholly outside the rest of American culture in spite of the fact that she is found waitressing in a restaurant, or that she somehow embodies an essence possessed by all Navajo. It is clear, however, that in his enthusiasm to point out the difference of oral cultures from literary ones, the author is keener to attribute the ensuing abilities of the former to groups of peoples than he is to engage with the social contexts of their lived realities.

Essentializing, romanticizing, and imbuing with mysticism is, in fact, racist. John H.T. Davies, a Welshman writes,

> I do not want to see what has happened to the native Americans, happen to the heritage of my own people. I do not wish to see us marginalized as the "Dreamtime People" of Europe.... To value us only for our dreams is extremely patronizing. (Davies 1995)

He goes on,

> I do not wish to encounter your expensive workshop leader who can't even pronounce, let alone speak, any Welsh; whose only qualifications are a set of distinctly cranky ideas, assembled from fragments torn loose from our heritage. (Davies 1995)

While it is possible for me to agree heartily with the sentiments and warnings expressed in this plea, the linkage made between land, heritage, and spirituality provokes another important question. The pagan movement is a predominantly White movement. Are we passively or even actively excluding Black and Asian participants because of the store we are setting by indigenous British traditions? And what are we defining as "British," or even as Cornish, English, Irish, Manx, Scottish, and Welsh? One finds, for example, the rare text that appears at least to acknowledge that Britain is multicultural, by declaring appreciation of the cultural "gifts" successive "visitors" have brought to British culture. Needless to say, caveats of this type are clearly defining "British" culture as something core and pre-existing those "visitors" and defining the "gifts" as added extras (Matthews and Matthews 1988). This seems to situate "British" pagan antecedents as part of an historical identity that actually excludes all those communities and ethnicities arriving after a given date. At one level this indicates a measure of social unawareness around, for example, Black and Asian Britons, whose "own" culture is Black and Asian British. At another it connotes an inadvertent racism, the message of which is the spiritual equivalent of "These roots are not yours."

CONTEMPORARY PAGAN "ETHNICITIES"

Given the expressed importance of historical precedence and provenance to contemporary pagan identity, one is not surprised, then, to find that contemporary paganism in Britain is a predominantly White movement, particularly given the additional tendency to essentialize certain spiritual attributes as the gift of given peoples. However unintending, and for whatever reasons, there do seem to be a number of exclusionary definitions operating around the construction of pagan identity in the British context. Oppressions often work multiply and are rarely without complexity, but it seems that there is a good deal of difference between a person of colour resisting what Davies identifies as "spiritual strip mining" and a predominantly White movement in a racist culture steering clear of Black or Asian participation. It is perhaps the case that White ethnicities (and I would include among these British pagan ethnicity) are selective in which inequalities they seek to redress. As one Manxman wryly put it when I began to enumerate the loss of many Manx traditions, "and don't forget the alarming demise of bigotry, including sexism, racism, homophobia."[2]

ASPECTS OF PAGANISMS AND UNIVERSALITY

At the very least, there is currently a good deal of ambivalence expressed within the pagan community regarding certain forms of oppression and here some of the more troubling aspects of these tendencies open up in relation to ideas regarding, for want of a better description, issues of "fate" and personal responsibility. There is a tendency, which expresses itself in a variety of ways, to place responsibility for the conditions of one's life at the feet of the individual. This is often taken up and applied uncritically and regardless of the specific context of the individual's life and the extent to which they may control events governing their situation. This conviction comes across quite strongly in a number of popular pagan texts, although the strength of this underpinning credo is perhaps felt more in its accumulative effect, both within an individual text and in seeing it reiterated in a range of similar texts. Consequently the examples below, which have been selected from two of the more popular texts analyzed for this study and which are based in the Western Mystery Tradition, appear on the face of it to be relatively harmless:

> If you have lost a lover you must ask yourself; "In what way did I fail to meet her needs/passion?" The fault lies with you. (Green 1995)

> If you have no love in your life, magic will not supply it, until you learn why you are not loveable. (Green 1990)

If this philosophy stays where it is put, it may be regarded as little more than a rather callous homily for broken-hearted ex-lovers. However, the basis of this rather uncomplex theory of unconditional personal responsibility is often reapplied and extended to global problems and both natural, and often unnatural, disasters. The suffering of the people affected by starvation and disease following the war in Rwanda was theorized by one pagan as: "... the earth getting rid of her surplus. There must be a life lesson in it for them, mustn't there? We all have to take responsibility for what happens to us."[3] And so presumably the same applies to a raped woman, a tortured man, an abused child, a beaten pensioner, and so on. It seems quite significant, moreover, that the philosophy is so readily applied to people of colour who live "over there." But the crucial thing here is that a self-motivating philosophy applied to an individual living in the West, who to a certain extent enjoys the type of autonomy not experienced in other cultural contexts, is not appropriate for projection onto what is the result of political interventions, often by the Western powers, whose freedoms that individual enjoys.

Another typical, if troubling, pagan response to suffering is to attribute it to a mysterious spiritual malaise that is felt globally:

> The Wasteland is growing, both on the face of the planet and in the minds of the people. Many have sunk so low through poverty, homelessness, sickness, deprivation or disaster that they have lost hope of things getting better. They have even become so hopeless that they are not able to take advantage of any good which may come their way. (Green 1995)

One of the corollaries of this type of stream-of-consciousness universalism is that it substitutes blanket explanation for any attempt to focus on the particular causes of specific sufferings. It also raises the question of how appropriate a response to privation it is to map onto the events of one geographical and historical location the symbols and metaphors of the historically and geographically located tradition of another. At this particular node of the web the tension between the universal and the specific mirrors that which snags where a philosophy that motivates the individual is applied to the general to produce a theory of inaction. At these points, the two webs, that of pagan identity and that of the wider social web against which it occasionally strains, become entangled. This may, in part, be due to the internal entanglement that some paganisms have with philosophies that could more accurately be defined as New Age. However, the distance often placed between the political and the spiritual in both mainstream and pagan culture is a predisposition both to this type of entanglement occurring and, significantly, the catching of something nasty in the web.

PAGANISM, RACISM, AND NEO-NAZISM

The occult-fascist axis often posited by historians of the German Nazi movement of the 1930s and 1940s is perhaps the better known of the interludes where paganism has proved a rich hunting ground for fascist groups looking for symbols of *volkisch* unification. This specific connection in fact had a much longer history, but I am more concerned here with present connections being made.[4]

Initial analyses of alleged connections between pagan groups and neo-Nazis being made from within the anti-Nazi movement led me to regard some of the claims with a measure of skepticism, partly because some of the rhetoric tended to be either anti-pagan or rather confused in conflating all occult interests of known neo-Nazis into "paganism." However, a close examination of neo-Nazi literature available in Britain makes it quite clear that paganism is being pressed to the cause of spiritual Aryanism in Europe, through groups such as ANSE (Arbheitsgemeinschaft Naturreligioser Stammesverbade Europas or European Racial Association of Natural Religious Groups) and the Thule Seminar and others currently operating on the Internet.[5] Indeed, there are a number of neo-fascist initiatives operative in most parts of Britain and some of these appeal to what they perceive as pagan "values" within the extreme right. These values are those mobilized around notions of history, race, and nationhood. The edges of some pagan philosophies blur dangerously with those that support racism and warn against what they see as racial and spiritual "miscegenation." The links made between fascist aspirations and paganism appear to come from the provision, within the formations of pagan identity in Britain, of the racial specificity of what some pagans perceive to be their past and their cultural antecedents.

An example of the way in which pagan discourses of history, "race," and nationalism can be diverted and appropriated is found in the (undated) desktop-published newsletter *Valkyrie*, which advertises itself as the "voice of the Patriotic Women's League." The League is based in the northwest of England. *Valkyrie* is replete with Celtic knotwork and symbols and contains advertisements for the "Church of Thor-Would" and for the neo-Nazi band "Celtic Warrior." It also carries a list of publications, organizations, and bands that have links with the League, including titles such as "Renewal of Identity," "Aryan Sisters," and "Blood and Honour." As well as featuring strong imagery referring to a pagan past, including a blonde-plaited child regarding a stone dolmen, it posits a warrior goddess dubbed "Mother Europe." This figure is juxtaposed with a diatribe against non-racist and non-sexist educational materials that reiterates the theme of preservation and a mythical all-White heritage found elsewhere in the magazine. The message of a photograph of a White mother teaching her White child on the page opposite that of the goddess-figure "Mother Europe" emphasizes the role of both mother and goddess, whose fiercer intentions are focused upon "defending" Europe from multiculturalism by invoking a veritable confusion of Celtic and Nordic knotwork. At the same time, this sacralizes the task being set here for all White mothers, exhorting them to play this role within the home.

Other neo-Nazi magazines and newsletters indicate that several more pagan organizations are actively supportive of neo-Nazi aspirations. The latter are entirely commensurate with those of ANSE and the Thule Seminar, both pagan fascist organizations with the philosophies of hatred and denial that appear on the agendas of fascism globally. The blurring of pagan affinities and neo-Nazism to the point where neo-Nazis are as at home in the former as they are in the latter is a cause for grave concern. At which point does a badge declaring "Albion for Pagans" or "the Pagan State of Albion" (found on stalls at a Pagan Northwest Region conference and in a number of shops selling New Age and pagan paraphernalia) become "England for the English" or "Keep Britain White"?

The nature of the highly particularized standpoints that fund ideas of pagan identity, historical rights, and future aspirations is that they emanate from a new, minority perspective that is fundamentally in flux around issues of identity. Accordingly, notions of history, authenticity, and provenance are often seen as paramount in the task of constructing an "authentic" identity to such an extent that where these are contested, any newly forming ideas around identity are considered under threat (cf. Bowman 1995). Similarly, ideas that are seen to smack of "political correctness" are given short shrift, partly because of the challenge to the pagan love affair with "nature" and the organic, both of which are seen as ontologically integral to the past(s) to which we refer, distinctive aspects of our spiritually led identities. In this context, what appear to be challenges to the exclusionary nature of what are actually reconstructions of past ways of life and socio-cultural constructs of "nature" are seen as joltingly modern (if not postmodern), interventionist, and as wishful thinking. The search for authenticity in the formation of contemporary pagan identities does tend to lead to quite reactionary stances on issues of social concern; the will to change social inequalities is seen as being out of step with the "realities" of past societies and out of step with the organic, with the "nature" from which past pagan societies emerged. That our ideas about the past and about nature are largely social constructs doesn't seem to bother anyone overmuch, judging by the survey of popular pagan literature and participation in pagan communities.

The predisposition toward misappropriation by fascist and neo-Nazi groups is in fact coming from the very bases ("history" and "nature") upon which the anxious construction of pagan identity appear to be resting, and is further adumbrated by notions of the collective "fate" of people who, paradoxically, are deemed responsible for their own troubles. "Destiny," it should be remembered, was a very good friend of British imperialism. It could be argued that pagans are not responsible for symbols and identities hijacked from our movement. After all, we can't actually stop anybody doing this. But unless we are to be associated with these agendas calling themselves "pagan," we have to examine what they are finding so attractive and make a positive statement that irrevocably dissociates us from them, whoever "we" turn out to be. And this brings us back to disposing with the idea that spirituality has nothing to do with the political, with power.

PAGAN PRAXIS AND CHALLENGES TO RACISM

Given that paganisms often abhor dualistic separations, our embodied spiritualities, our notions of immanence, and our sense of the interconnectedness of things are particularly fitted to provide models of interrelationship, gradation, and flow. Within the structures of our practices and symbols, our acknowledgment of tides, cycles, and seasons, lies the potential to challenge political hierarchies and provide an agency for positive change in our society and on our planet. This means acknowledging diversity—of needs, of experience, of the cultural, social historical, and geographical contexts of people's lives. One of the most compelling and powerful symbols we have is that of the web. It is a symbol that has been deployed with amazing success both metaphorically and physically at Greenham; it provides a model via which we might see varied forms of oppression, different spiritualities, economic means, and different identities as contingent upon each other and touching at various nodes of the web. But perhaps we may see it as many webs, each touching and interconnecting but varying with location, experience, political agenda, and world view.

As a spiritually led identity we may occasionally see ourselves as an oppressed group; for example, our spiritualities provoke fear and hatred among other groupings (both religious and non-religious) to the point that the fear of child-kidnap by misinformed social workers is still real. But the acknowledgment of our own oppressions carries the responsibility of acknowledging both our own privileges and the oppressions of others. Fighting for our own rights need not mean that we privilege our community's needs by ignoring or trivializing the day-to-day prejudice that other oppressed groups experience. The principle of interconnectedness, signified within this article as a web, lies at the heart of pagan spirituality. It is not a philosophy that espouses sameness as oneness. By definition, it interconnects and coalesces by recognizing diversity.[6] Given what I have had to say about the inappropriateness of projecting specified and located symbology as universals, this may be a surprising proposition. But the point about interconnectedness as a touchstone is that it recognizes and situates "me" and "us" and "others" as contingent and located.[7]

CONCLUSION: TOWARD A PAGAN ETHICS OF DIVERSITY

A pagan ethic that acknowledged the proximity of the wider social web to that of its own communities would go some way to disentangle the prejudices of the one from the spiritual declarations of the other. But as I have indicated, there are other pressing and compelling reasons why such an ethic would need to be developed. This brings us full circle to the issue of identity, which began with the Union Jack being flown in Stonehenge at the beginning of this paper. Who are "we"? Where and when are "we"? Who and what do "we" embrace; who and what do "we," should "we," exclude?

On the issue of exclusivity in term of heritage, history, tradition, some words from Caitlin Matthews:

> ... there are no rightful bearers of tradition, only bearers of tradition. However we are welcomed into our tradition—whether it be by formal training, ritual initiation or long personal meditation—we become bearers of that tradition by desire, aptitude and dedication. (Jones and Matthews 1990)
>
> To this I would add the quality of committed understanding, and that would include the criteria that we are prepared to accept and find out why it is more useful to some oppressed groups that we respect their traditions from the sidelines rather than attempt to enter them from certain given positions of social privilege.[8]

As for the issue of legitimate exclusion and dissociation, this depends upon the will to develop an ethic that would positively undermine those predispositions that make our philosophies so tempting to some of the more malevolent tendencies currently misappropriating pagan symbols and philosophies. What such an ethic might eventually look like depends to a certain extent on the passage of time, on the growth of the movement, and its ideas. Given the very real threat of the misappropriation by the New Right of both, however, it is critical that it is not left entirely to time. More than the future of the pagan movement is at stake here. If we acknowledge that the web of our culture connects with that of a larger, dominant social web, we do not simply disentangle ourselves from its worst tendencies, but have a position of agency, a potential for transformation that can spread from our web to others. Change is a multidirectional process; enchanting the web with a commitment to ending oppression means not only holding up a mirror to ourselves, but becoming, in turn, a reflection in which others may see something worth emulating. If we believe in a web of life, one in which everything is interconnected, then we must believe in the reverberating effects of a conscious disentanglement, a conscious awareness of privilege and oppression, and the outflowing change the ownership of that awareness can bring to wider contexts than ours.

The question that a pagan ethic might address could be something close to the thought on which I would like to close the discussion here and open it up elsewhere and the question that the poet-philosopher June Jordan suggests we constantly ask of ourselves: "How is my own life-work helping to end these tyrannies, the corrosions of sacred possibility?"[9]

NOTES

1. *Psychic News* (April 12, 1997). *Fortean Times* (August 1997). Reports of the findings published in the *Wiltshire Archaeological News* can be found in *The Guardian*, *The Independent*, *The Times*, and the *Daily Telegraph* on March 1, 1997.
2. This particular Manxman has asked not to be identified, so I send my thanks to him in his anonymized form!
3. Here, perhaps, is evidence that paganism currently experiences overspill from what some commentators would term "New Age" philosophies.
4. *Searchlight* (August 1997): 17–18.
5. Ibid.
6. It has this in common with some ecofeminist perspectives; see, for example, Lori Gruen's essay "Toward an Ecofeminist Moral Epistemology," in Warren (1994); and Karen Warren's essay "Ecofeminism and the Spiritual" in Adams (1993).

7. A good example of thinking around difference in this way is found in Keya Ganguly's essay "Accounting for Others: Feminism and Representation" in Rakow (1992).
8. See Elizabeth Brookes's (1993) section on "Ethics" in *A Woman's Book of Shadows*; and Smith (1993).
9. June Jordan has published a collection of her essays in a volume (1989) entitled *Moving towards Home: Political Essays.*

REFERENCES

Adams, C., ed. 1993. *Ecofeminism and the Sacred.* New York: Continuum.

Bowman, M. 1993. "Reinventing the Celts." *Religion* 23: 147–156.

———. 1995. "The Noble Savage and the Global Village: Cultural Evolution in New Age and Neo-Pagan Thought." *Journal of Contemporary Religion* 10, no. 2.

Brookes, E. 1993. *A Woman's Book of Shadows.* London: Women's Press.

Davies, J.H.T. 1995. "The Celtic Tradition." In *The Pagan Index.* London: House of the Goddess.

Green, M. 1990. *Elements of Ritual Magic.* London: Elements Books.

———. 1995. *Everyday Magic.* London: Thorsons.

Harvey, Graham. 1997. *Listening People, Speaking Earth: Contemporary Paganism.* London: Hurst.

Hobsbawm, E.J. 1990. *Nations and Nationalism Since 1780: Programme, Myth, Reality.* Cambridge: Cambridge University Press.

Hutton, R. 1996. "Who Possesses the Past?" In *The Druid Renaissance*, edited by Philip Carr-Gomm. London: Thorsons.

Jones, P., and C. Matthews, eds. 1990. *Voices from the Circle: The Heritage of Western Paganism.* Wellingborough: Aquarian Press.

Jordan, J. 1989. *Moving towards Home: Political Essays.* London: Virgo Press.

Matthews, C., and J. Matthews. 1988. *An Encyclopaedia of Myth and Legend: British and Irish Mythology.* Wellingborough: Aquarian Press.

———. 1992. *Ladies of the Lake.* Wellingborough: Aquarian Press.

Matthews, J. 1986. *The Grail Seeker's Companion: A Guide to the Grail Quest in the Aquarian Age.* Wellingborough: Aquarian Press.

Rakow, L., ed. 1992. *Women Making Meaning.* London: Routledge.

Robbins, K. 1989. *Nineteenth-Century Britain; England, Scotland, and Wales: The Making of a Nation.* Oxford: Oxford University Press.

Rutherford, W. 1993. *Celtic Lore: The History of the Druids and Their Timeless Traditions.* London: Thorsons.

Smith, A. 1993. "For All Those Who Were Indian in a Former Life." In *Ecofeminism and the Sacred*, edited by C. Adams. New York: Continuum.

Warren, K.J., ed. 1994. *Ecological Feminism.* London: Routledge.

QUESTIONS FOR CRITICAL THOUGHT

Chapter 9: Harvey

1. How is Harvey's description of an ovate similar to Davy's description of a shaman? How are they different?
2. Harvey seems to believe that druidic borrowing of Native American techniques and beliefs is more acceptable than "New Age" borrowing of those same customs. Do you agree with him?
3. Many contemporary pagans work alone, by choice or by circumstance. Harvey describes druidry as fundamentally embedded in the idea of community. Is it possible to be a solitary druid? Why or why not?
4. The stereotype of a druid is male. Eighteenth- and nineteenth-century druid orders were exclusively male. Is contemporary druidry, as Harvey describes it, destined to become "patriarchal paganism"? Why or what not?

Chapter 10: Berger

1. The wiccaning ritual that Berger describes is a life-cycle ritual, one that celebrates a significant event in a person's life. This sort of ritual, also known as a rite of passage, marks the point of transition between one state and another. What change is this ritual marking? How do you know?
2. Berger describes the tension between the idea that the Craft should remain a religion of converts, an exclusive model, and the idea that it should inform all aspects of life from the earliest years, an inclusive model. What are the strengths and weaknesses of each of these models of religion? Can the two models be reconciled?
3. Berger discusses some of the dilemmas pagans face in integrating children into rituals designed for adults, and seeing to the religious socialization of children. These are not difficulties unique to neopaganism. How do other religions address these issues? Do you think that these solutions would work in a neopagan setting? Why or why not?

4. What are some of the techniques that parents try to use to lessen the stigma of being pagan for their children? Do these have the capacity to suggest to children that the religion of their household is somehow bad or wrong because it has to be kept hidden or secret?

Chapter 11: Beaman

1. Beaman suggests that one of the reasons Wicca is disqualified from full social acceptance is because the majority of its adherents are women. Do you think that this is a credible argument? Why or why not?
2. How does a hierarchical organizational form, absent on a large scale in Wicca, facilitate recognition under the law?
3. How does lack of public understanding about Wicca contribute to the marginalization of it as a practice recognized to be "religious" or spiritual?
4. Why is it problematic that members of mainstream, non-pagan religious traditions are called upon by the courts to verify the spiritual basis of Wicca? How might this be addressed in the future?
5. In what ways would it be beneficial to Wiccans to have their religion legally recognized? In what ways might it be detrimental?

Chapter 12: Luhrmann

1. From Luhrmann's perspective as a researcher, does it matter if magic has an objective existence? Why or why not?
2. Given Luhrmann's descriptions of the four types of philosophical claims made to justify magic, does magic have to be "true" to be effective?
3. Why might it might be difficult for a skeptic to "talk someone out of" their magical beliefs and practices? What kind of evidence might they have to produce for each of the four rationalizations?
4. How can the metaphorical position claim that magical claims are probably false, but that its practice is valuable nonetheless? How can disbelief contribute to efficacy?

Chapter 13: Reid

1. Reid suggests that one of the factors contributing to conflict in neopagan communities is a shared vocabulary that is not

understood in the same way by all parties. Do you think that this is as much of a problem in other religious groups? Why or why not?

2. Why does the idea that "there is no one right way" reinforce, rather than de-escalate, conflict in neopagan communities?
3. Would fuller institutionalization of neopagan witchcraft be likely to increase or decrease levels of tension in a community, given Reid's hypotheses?
4. Can a religion in which every individual is presumed to be the final authority over his or her own beliefs and practices ever form a stable community? Why or why not?
5. How can forces outside of the neopagan community contribute to starting or escalating a witch war?

Chapter 14: Blain

1. What characteristics does Blain cite that differentiate between reconstructionists and other pagans?
2. The tone of Blain's article implies that community formation in Asatru is more challenging than in many other religions. What factors might contribute to this?
3. Blain notes that reconstructionist pagans are not so much wanting to recreate the social or material conditions of the pre-Christian culture upon which they focus as they are trying to recreate the ethos of that culture. What difficulties might they encounter in this process?
4. Blain lists eight "public narratives" of heathenry. Which of these might be considered consonant (in harmony) with mainstream narratives, and which are dissonant? In what ways?
5. Do other religious groups need to engage in "damage control" to the same extent as Ásatrú? Why or why not?

Chapter 15: Gallagher

1. In what ways does Gallagher argue that pagan culture prefers universality over specificity? How is this potentially essentializing?
2. Is Gallagher arguing that paganism is intrinsically racist?

3. Pagans often speak of the stories they tell about themselves and their relationships with the past and with history as "mythic"—that is, that they are not considered to be literally true. Given that, can pagans be excused their inaccuracies?
4. Would Gallagher's arguments about the interconnection between land, nation, race, ethnicity, and identity in paganism hold up in the North American context, where there is no way that paganism can be considered an "indigenous spirituality"?

SUGGESTED READING

Cowan, Douglas. 2005. *Cyberhenge: Modern Pagans on the Internet.* New York: Routledge.

Cowan discusses modern paganism through the lens of the Internet. He argues that the Internet has become an integral part of the pagan community as a forum for networking, discussion, and information exchange, as well as being a performative venue in which pagan identity can be developed and rehearsed.

Greenwood, Susan. 2005. *The Nature of Magic: An Anthropology of Consciousness.* Oxford: Berg.

Greenwood's book combines the results of extensive anthropological fieldwork and participant narratives with a discussion of the relationship between nature, magic, and consciousness. This discussion is set against a critical examination of existing theories of magical consciousness, which tend to portray it as less developed and sophisticated than rational consciousness. Greenwood suggests an alternative interpretation of magical consciousness, which roots it less in socio-cultural conditions, and more in the realm of expanded consciousness.

Jennings, Pete. 2002. *Pagan Paths: A Guide to Wicca, Druidry, Asatru, Shamanism and Other Pagan Practices.* London: Rider Books.

This is an easy-to-read, non-academic book giving brief overviews of each of the spiritual forms discussed in this section. It is a good jumping-off point for further research.

Magliocco, Sabina. 2004. *Witching Culture: Folklore and Neo-Paganism in America*. Philadelphia: University of Pennsylvania Press.
Magliocco's book gives a brief review of the "invention" and emergence of modern paganism, and discusses how, as spiritualities centred in practice rather than in belief, modern paganisms use ritual as an expressive art form. She traces the reclamation of mysticism through a discussion of historical and socio-cultural currents from the Enlightenment to the present. She also discusses the syncretic nature of modern paganism and its relationship to new conceptualizations of identity.

Rabinovitch, Shelley, and James Lewis, eds. 2002. *The Encyclopedia of Modern Witchcraft and Neo-Paganism*. New York: Citadel.
The contributors list of this volume reads like a "Who's Who" of modern paganism. Both academics and practitioners contributed to this volume, designed as a reference for non-specialists. Entries range from biographical pieces on key figures in the rise of contemporary paganism, to short entries demystifying the jargon, to essay length pieces on important topics and themes. The bibliography is a rich resource for those looking for additional source materials.

GLOSSARY

Cognitive dissonance: The uncomfortable state produced in an individual trying to reconcile an inconsistency in feelings, attitudes, experiences, or beliefs that appear at first to be incompatible. Individuals ordinarily try to reduce or resolve the dissonance by reinterpreting some aspect of their experiences or beliefs to make them compatible with the others.

Cosmology: World view; beliefs about the nature, origin, and operation of the universe, and about one's place within and relationship to it.

Discourse: The constellation of written and spoken language used to enact or characterize a phenomenon. The discourse of a group is how that group represents itself in speech and writing, as well as language that is specific to the group. For example, you can speak of "legal discourse" or "medical discourse." In the work of Michel Foucault, upon whom many sociologists draw when they use this term, discourse is a system of knowledge that expresses itself in a specific vocabulary. This significance of it is that it is used to legitimate the exercise of power by some people over others by characterizing those others as the legitimate targets of domination.

Hierarchy: An organized system of ranking within a group or organization in which some people are subordinate to others, usually culminating in a single figure at the top.

Routinization: The systemization and regularization of what was originally spontaneous and charismatic.

PART IV
Feminist Spirituality and Goddess Worship

feminist thinking has been an important element in the construction of paganisms in North America. This is different than the situation in England, where witchcraft and druidry both originate. In England, widespread feminist incursions into paganism began in the 1980s, in a witchcraft community that had existed for almost 50 years. Feminist-oriented paganism is the exception rather than the rule in Britain, while it is rare to find a North American pagan group that has not wrestled with issues of sex and gender. Authors such as Carol Christ and Starhawk fused their feminist agendas with their pagan theological writings. *The Spiral Dance*, Starhawk's 1979 book about the practice of witchcraft, is still on most North American covens' "must read" lists. Paganism developed alongside of feminism in North America and was greatly influenced by it. Feminists saw in paganism the opportunity to construct a religion in which they could perceive their own true divinity, and develop female-positive sacred narratives and symbol systems that would reflect women's experience, something they feared mainstream "patriarchal" religions would never provide.

Lucie DuFresne's article, which opens this section, is a reflection on her experience, and the experience of others she has encountered, with the dangers of a female-positive symbol system when one particular aspect becomes dominant. DuFresne argues that goddess worshippers often use the images, narratives, and symbolic references to the goddess as mother in a way that becomes hegemonic and normative. This, she says, however unintentionally, disenfranchises both men who want to worship the goddess and women who do not identify themselves as "mother." While the symbol of mother is meant to convey creation of all sorts, whether it is reproduction, artistic, or musical production, or work that expands people's horizons of possibility, the actual usage made of the symbol is often biologically essentializing—it tells women what they must be, and men what they cannot be. DuFresne brings men's voices into the debate over what the goddess is, and for whom. She problematizes the idea of goddess worship as "women's religion" and suggests that to establish a hegemonic religious system in which men and men's experiences are excluded is to indulge in "patriarchy in drag." In short, DuFresne calls on men and women both to work toward a religious system that will reflect a broader range of the human spectrum of experience, and to avoid being limited by the symbols they have constructed for themselves.

Wendy Griffin also discusses the transformation of religious symbols in feminist goddess worship, but her focus is more on how they liberate and empower rather than how they exclude and marginalize. Through her participant observation research in three groups, a feminist witchcraft group, a goddess group, and a drumming group, she is able to describe the ways in which the sacred imagery and narrative used by these feminists break down the cultural dichotomies with which we were socialized: the spiritual and the material; the active, strong male and the passive, dependent female; the centrality of youth; and the marginalization of age. She notes that in the rituals in which these feminist mythic narratives emerge, the "spiritual" goddess figure is manifested through the materiality of women's bodies and women's experiences, and calls attention to women's potentials and capacities.

She argues that these women are not just changing a religious form or a symbolic narrative, they are engaging the demolition and renovation of culture. Mary Daly, Carol Christ, Naomi Goldenberg, and many others have long suggested that sacred narratives provide a normative framework for the relationships in society. By creating new narratives that reflect women as fully realized human beings and not simply the embodiment of social roles, Griffin suggests, these women are transforming the way they choose to relate to other women and men and take action in society. To what extent these new self-understandings will hold up under the relentless, disconfirming pressure of the dominant culture, Griffin is not able to say, but she does believe that the enlistment of religion in the feminist struggle is a significant move toward the possibility of cultural change.

In the next chapter, Ron Hutton examines the Goddess of the witches from a historical and literary perspective. Writing in England, where witchcraft is less influenced by the feminist movement, Hutton traces the evolution of the Goddess figure as understood by witches. While the names used to evoke the Goddess may be thousands of years old, Hutton argues that the concept of "the Goddess" upon which witches draw more generally is of a far more recent vintage. Specifically, he locates it in the Romantic movement of the nineteenth century, which saw the shift in the attribution of characteristics of many goddesses change from their traditional and medieval forms to new ones emphasizing the goddesses' connection with the earth, the seasons, the sea, and the moon. This is also the period during which the amorphous figure of "Mother Earth" or "Mother Nature" appeared.

These literary developments coincided with an academic debate on the nature of primitive religions. Did they exemplify the essential characteristics of all religion, as Emile Durkheim believed? Were they the fictional products of ignorance and fear? Did they contain important truths that Western civilization had lost over the course of its evolution? Out of this debate and discussion emerged the suggestion that the earliest societies were matriarchal, and that the religions of those societies would have mirrored the social arrangements, having a goddess as primary. This image of the goddess as the earliest of all deities, and as the spiritual form of the living earth, is the one that would have been most readily available to

Gerald Gardner, contemporary witchcraft's chief founder, in the 1930s. By the time Doreen Valiente had arrived on the scene in the late 1940s, Robert Graves's *The White Goddess* had also been published. Graves collected much of the Great Goddess theory together in one book, augmenting it with his own poetic elaborations. Graves's *White Goddess* has three aspects—maiden, mother, and crone. She is the giver of both life and death, and is, as Valiente's *Charge of the Goddess* asserts: "the beauty of the green earth and the white moon among the stars and the mystery of the waters.... I am the soul of nature who gives light to the universe. From me all things proceed, and to me all things must return." Graves's goddess became Valiente's, and diffused throughout the contemporary witchcraft movement.

Cynthia Eller's chapter, "The Roots of Feminist Spirituality," moves the lens further out, and allows the reader to see feminist neopaganism and goddess worship in the broader context of the feminist spirituality movement. Eller argues that while feminist spirituality did not begin within the small, alternative practice that was contemporary American paganism in the 1960s and 1970s, it eventually found its most comfortable home there. There are two main non-pagan avenues through which she claims women journeyed into the religious environment of feminist spirituality: secular feminism and Jewish and Christian feminism.

For some secular feminists, their feminist stance took on the role of what an introductory sociology text would call a "master status"—everything they now experienced was refracted and interpreted through their feminist understandings. Definitions of religion often refer to the provision of meaning, and the integration of the universe of experience in a meaningful way, as being one of the key functions played by religion. For these women, their reinterpretation of the universe in feminist terms became an organizing narrative, and their explorations of this universe through consciousness-raising groups gave rise to the dimension of shared experience that Emile Durkheim, one of religion's earliest sociological examiners, regards as essential.[1]

Jewish and Christian feminists, already accustomed to thinking within a religious framework, took a two-step process to reach alternative religion. Eller suggests that, in the beginning, these women looked to reform their own traditions by calling for particular changes such as inclusive language, and admission of women to all church offices and orders. As they explored their religious tradition, however, it became evident to them that it was not just the institutions of the religion that were patriarchal, but that the texts, values, and viewpoints offered by their tradition were steeped in patriarchy to such an extent that any attempt to excise them fully would leave no element of the tradition intact. While some of these women remained within the Church and struggled to reinvent it, others removed themselves from their institutions and struggled to find a more consonant expression of their religious values. These women, too, entered into the alternative religions' sphere.

Eller notes that while the initial points of contact between existing pagans and the feminist "interlopers" were sometimes contentious, 30 years later, pagans and feminists have come into a comfortable accommodation with each other. For the most part, this is because each group has been socialized with overlapping values—feminists coming to adopt some of the theatrical and ritualized aspects of pagan practice, and pagans learning to espouse a radical gender equality that goes beyond the sex-stereotyped roles that can be seen in some of the 1940s and 1950s elaborations of witchcraft and paganism. Eller concludes that both groups have ultimately benefited from this cross-fertilization.

Chris Klassen takes a more critical view of this overlap, particularly as it is expressed within feminist witchcraft groups. She argues persuasively that the sacred narratives constructed within feminist witchcraft are founded on the discourse of colonization and persecution. Taking as their starting point the myth of the Great Goddess as espoused by the nineteenth- and twentieth-century Romantic folklorists, they create a history of a peaceful society of sexual egalitarianism and sometimes even matriarchal society that was overrun and suppressed by patriarchal invaders. Feminist witchcraft, then, is an act of defiance and reclamation of something that was stolen and/or lost, in the same way that other present-day oppressed minorities are fighting to reclaim their cultural heritages.

Klassen points out the ironic nature of this post-colonial construction. Like feminism, post-colonial discourse challenges foundational myths—in feminism, the idea that men are always and everywhere superior to women by virtue of their sex, and in post-colonialism, the idea that White European society was justified in "civilizing" the non-European cultures they encountered in their race to stake out land and resources. The conflation of sexism and racism in some streams of feminist witchcraft narrative is ironic simply because the majority of practitioners are White women of European origin. Their construction of themselves as the oppressed, and thus equivalent to other indigenous and non-indigenous disenfranchised minorities, allows them to brush off the culpability for the White privilege they enjoy. In contrast to many narratives, Klassen points out, Starhawk's position is refreshing in that it problematizes the role of both victim and oppressor, arguing that these are not absolute, and that every heritage, regardless of its basis, will have partaken of both. Rather than taking the role of victims demanding restitution, Starhawk says that it is only in accepting responsibility for the conditions that exist now, conditions that no one now living created, that people can acquire the power to enact social change.

NOTE

1. "Religious beliefs proper are always shared by a definite group that professes them and that practices the corresponding rites. Not only are they accepted by all members of the group, but they also belong to the group and unify it. The individuals who comprise this group feel joined to one another by the fact of common faith." Emile Durkheim, *The Elementary Forms of the Religious Life*, translated by Karen Fields (New York: The Free Press, 1995), 41.

CHAPTER 16
Mother and Goddess: The Ideological Force of Symbols

Lucie Marie-Mai DuFresne

central to contemporary North American goddess worship, especially as it is experienced by women, is the symbol of the Mother Goddess. This hegemonic representation of the female divine is not without danger for the men and women who worship it. Even though it is only one of many ways the goddess is represented, its symbolic strength is such that it silences and constrains other possibilities and in so doing alienates some worshippers from the object of worship.

Within the local Wiccan or Craft community in which I work, study, and worship, I have been witness to and/or a participant in a number of rituals and discussions (not to say arguments) that I now see exemplify aspects of the ambiguous nature and the ideological force of the symbols *of the goddess, the mother,* and *the goddess as mother.*

Wicca or Craft (from witchcraft) are synonyms used by male and female individuals who self-identify as believers in a goddess and/or god-based religion (Rabinovitch 1992) and who hark back to what they believe was an original form of nature-based fertility cult, identifying themselves with the figure of the historical witch as an outsider with power (DuFresne and Rabinovitch 1996).

The particular Wiccan community I belong to is centred in Ottawa, but extends from Montreal to Toronto. This geographical area encompasses the area of interaction of participants in Rainbow Gathering (Minifest), an annual Wiccan/pagan festival held on private land in MacDonalds Corner, Ontario.

Most telling in our discussions have been strongly felt statements made by male ritual participants and members of the priesthood of several traditions[1] about how threatened they feel by goddess monotheism especially as it is theorized and lived by some of their female co-worshippers. I defend my presenting these male objections *because*, let us not forget, these are men who have invested much self-definition and personal spirituality in being, themselves, goddess worshippers. Furthermore, these men, thealogists[2] all, are underrepresented in the literature of goddess worship and in our own women's discourse because of some women's perception of the intrinsic political incorrectness of the male voice in the discourse of female spirituality. So, I recognize my iconoclastic and anarchist positioning and welcome the debate that, I hope, my words will provoke.

A second impetus to including these male voices is my recognition that in this local community of worship, theirs have been some of the most vocal, critical, and thought-provoking statements regarding the apparent unself-conscious and uncritical use of the goddess in a monotheistic, archetypal, and monolithic way.

As an aside, let us remember that, as much or as little as *she* embodies our experience, as *she* is immanent in all of us, *she* is also and foremost an artifact of our own need for *her*. Therein lies the problem. In searching and finding *the goddess*, we have reified the artifact of our own need.

Having done so, have we done ourselves a disservice? What do the men say? They ask: Why is the goddess alone? Where is the god? What happened to complementary duality, a basic tenet of Wicca and neo-witchcraft? Non-Dianic forms of Wicca all *conceive* of the immanent divine as realized in gendered form, both female and male.

This divine couple is seen as both aspects of the same ungendered divinity and as a relational pair that are complementary and sexually in relation to/with each other. Why do women appear to deny access to the female godhood and experience to men? It is true that some women of non-Dianic traditions choose to meet at the full or new moon for worship of the goddess? These "women's circles" are not open to male participation except by infant males with their mothers. The reason given for the existence of these women-only groups is that women need to discover for themselves what worship means and what a gendered divinity in their own image means for them. They seek a non-male-mediated religious environment and experience. Many men feel threatened by this as they see it as exclusion and heresy. On the other hand, no impediment exists within Wiccan theology to prevent or condemn gender-based worship groups. The women have invited the men to form their own "men's circles" devoted to the worship of the god-based on the same empowerment strategies as the women's groups. So far, the men have either refused or have been unable to foster a men's circle for more than a few months at a time. Some Ottawa women's circles are now close to 10 years old.

Putting aside questions of "new" traditions such as Dianic thealogy, of the rewriting and reinterpretation of traditional sacred texts by women (see Eller 1995; Spretnak 1994), and of the selective blindness some men exhibit to the limits of the doctrines they promulgate, men are correct when they speak of a female-dominated and controlled hegemony, of a new stereotyping of the possible, of a new thought control: the political correctness of worship.

Their pain, anger, and sense of betrayal are real and cannot be dismissed simply for being male. To do so would be to indulge in patriarchy in drag. Furthermore, their profound sense of unease and dismay echoes that of some women. Many of these could be described as marginal if one were to ascribe to the norm as being White, middle-class, anglophone, heterosexual, and fertile. These "other" women also have expressed dis/ease in being forced to identify with a conception of the divine apprehended as female that does *not* embody their experience, that is *not* immanent in them. As one childless woman cried, "How do I connect with a goddess which denies my existence? How can I feel that I belong when even the goddess betrays me?" These are fundamental questions for which I have no answers. Nevertheless, to counter the pervasive nihilism of my comments so far, let me say that I do worship the goddess (no capital letters) and in her worship I find comfort and sustenance. She has been the mother I never had, she has mothered and accepted me as I never was, I have found sisters in her motherhood, and I have found in her aspect as Bride/Bridget[3] a model of mothering other than the biological: word smyth, mother of healing waters, forger of metals, and embodied flame of life.

If she is immanent for me, if she truly embodies my experience, among a multitude of others, she must then be multiple and multiplex. She must be a process of being, a locus of action. She must change, and be, and become relevant and in relevance to my life. She must be unbounded, permeable, changeable. No longer god, god-hood, or god-like, but my own process of living god-ness.

NOTES

1. Wiccans who care to do so recognize various "traditions" within their faith. These traditions have recognized founders and follow standardized liturgical texts and formats in their rituals. Most of these traditions were founded in Britain after the 1950s. Some North American traditions reject canonical texts and identified founders/leaders for a more individualistic and "eclectic" way of worship, thus the name. One North American tradition developed out of the 1970s feminist movement. It advocates goddess monotheism and gender-based ritual segregation for worship. This tradition is called "Dianic" from the name of the Roman lunar goddess Diana.
2. Thealogy, from "thea" goddess, is a term first used in print by Naomi Goldenberg in *Changing of the Gods* (1979) to identify a "theology" of the goddess.
3. Bride/Bridget is a Celtic pre-Christian goddess who has been Christianized as St. Bridget of Kildare.

REFERENCES

DuFresne, Lucie Marie-Mai, and Shelley TSivia Rabinovitch. 1995. "Which Witch Is Which? Recasting Historical Nightmares as Utopian Visions." Paper presented at "The Middle Ages in Contemporary Culture Conference," McMaster University, Hamilton, March 29–31.

Eller, Cynthia. 1995. *Living in the Lap of the Goddess: The Feminist Spirituality Movement in America.* Boston: Beacon Press.

Goldenberg, Naomi. 1979. *Changing of the Gods: Feminism and the End of Traditional Religions.* Boston: Beacon Press.

Rabinovitch, Shelley TSivia. 1992. "'An' Ye Harm None, Do What Ye Will': Neo-pagans and Witches in Canada." MA thesis, Carleton University, Ottawa.

Spretnak, Charlene, ed. 1994. *The Politics of Women's Spirituality: Essays on the Rise of Spiritual Power within the Feminist Movement.* New York: Doubleday.

CHAPTER 17

The Embodied Goddess: Feminist Witchcraft and Female Divinity

Wendy Griffin

INTRODUCTION

although individual feminists in this country have long been concerned about the treatment of women in mainstream religions (see, for example, Stanton 1895), the first contemporary indications of group challenges to mainstream religious misogyny appeared in the early 1970s. In November of 1971, Mary Daly led "hundreds" on an "Exodus from patriarchal religion" (Daly 1992:7) by walking out at the conclusion of a sermon she delivered in the Harvard Memorial Church. A few months later, in 1972 in Los Angeles, the first coven of feminist witches that practised "the Craft" as a religion began to meet under the guidance of Zsuzsanna Budapest. Within a few years, these witches were gathering with several hundred women in the mountains to celebrate their visions of female divinity in religious rituals (see Budapest 1989).

To date, the goddess movement, which evolved from these early initiatives, has been studied primarily by theologians and psychologists, but has been relatively ignored by sociologists (for rare exceptions, see Jacobs 1990; Lozano and Foltz 1990; Neitz 1990; Finley 1991). As a result, relatively little is known about the way these groups function, who participates and at what level, and how the world view of the practitioners is developed and shared.[1] In this paper, I use a phenomenological approach and descriptive analysis to demonstrate how those who practise feminist witchcraft and/or participate in "goddess rituals" use consciously constructed mythopoeic images in religious ritual to create a framework of meaning that seeks to define a new ethos. This ethos is intended to "revision" power, authority, sexuality, and social relations. As in many other new religious movements, the relationship between the spiritual and the material is being redefined (see Beckford 1986), but in the goddess movement the material is firmly rooted in the female body. In the discussion that follows, I describe this redefined relationship and the significance it has for practitioners by drawing on three mythopoeic images from local rituals and my interviews with feminist witches.

METHODS

The arguments in this paper are based on four years of research that began when one of my students invited me to attend a religious ritual organized by her coven of feminist witches. A colleague and I attended this first ritual together, and then sought and received permission from the coven to do participant observation, using a triangulation of ethnographic techniques that included written and tape-recorded fieldnotes on all events we were allowed to attend, semi-structured, in-depth recorded interviews and, when possible, original photographs and videotapes. These events consisted of both private and public (or open) rituals, camping weekends, planning meetings, several religious services marking significant life events for specific individuals, and occasional social gatherings. We collected data for a year and a half on this group, which we call the Coven of the Redwood Moon. Although it is clear we were accepted as peripheral members (see Adler and Adler 1987), we did not ask to apprentice and did not join the coven. After this time, my colleague relocated and I began to do individual research on a local "goddess group" I call Womancircle, returning to Redwood Moon only occasionally for public ritual.

The initial contact with Womancircle was also made on campus, though I quickly discovered that I had met several of the core members or "circle sisters" at public ritual and workshops with Redwood Moon. I used the same triangulation of ethnographic techniques as with Redwood Moon: participant observation, extensive fieldnotes, photography, and interviewing of core members. Several of the members were also in a large, loosely knit group of women drummers, which I joined. During the following year, many of the original drummers drifted away and the scaled-down group began playing occasionally at coffee houses, neopagan craft fairs, and Womancircle rituals. These occasions provided me with a different kind of entree and opportunity to collect data. Although I am a core member of the drum circle, I am not a core member of Womancircle. When "feelers" were sent out to invite me to participate at that level, I discouraged them. I have attended a few of their planning meetings in my dual role as drummer and researcher, and some social events in my role as friend and drummer.

The goddess movement and feminist witchcraft are routinely criticized as being "White women's movements," and while Caucasians are in the majority, the criticism is not valid among the core members in the two groups I studied. Of the seven women who were members of the Coven of the Redwood Moon during the study, one was Chicana and another African-American. Womancircle's nine-member core also included a Chicana and an African-American. Not surprisingly, both groups made a point of including images of goddesses of colour in religious ritual.

Although the age range was similar in both groups, from the late twenties to mid-fifties, there were marked demographic differences between the two groups. Almost all of the Womancircle members had at least a four-year college degree and worked in professional or semi-professional occupations. Most of Redwood Moon's witches did not attend or had not finished college and had working-class jobs. In addition, the majority of the coven members tended to be lesbian, bisexual, or celibate. Only one was in a heterosexual marriage and none of them had children at home. In contrast, two of the Womancircle core were married and had small children living at home and several others were married or were in heterosexual live-in or dating relationships during the study. Only one was a lesbian.

All of the women in both groups identified themselves at one time or another as feminist witches, but there were organizational differences between them. Circle of the Redwood Moon is a radical feminist coven and members are trained through reading assignments and discussions to do a radical feminist analysis of gender and power. Called "Dianics," after the Roman goddess Diana, they are similar to other neopagan groups in the United States and Britain in that they celebrate "sabbats" or holy days based on seasonal cycles, require an apprenticeship and training in ideology and the practice of magic, value female leadership and divinity, and share the one law of the Craft.[2] They differ from most other neopagans in their feminist analysis, political activism, and in that most of them acknowledge only an autonomous female principal and reject the concept of a male divinity. Men are very rarely invited to participate and are not allowed to become members of Dianic covens.[3]

During the time of this study, Redwood Moon held occasional rituals that were open to the public and an annual weekend camp that was locally advertised and attended by 35 to 60 women. In addition, they sometimes participated in gatherings with non-feminist neopagan covens.

Womancircle was much more loosely defined and more typical of the larger goddess movement. Although some of the women in the movement belong to covens and some have even been trained by or have been Dianics, others prefer less structured groups that demand less commitment and may be less separatist. Still others belong to no group but show up occasionally for public ritual, and some are active members of the Unitarian Universalist church, which has a national educational program on the goddess and feminist witchcraft.[4] There is no apprenticeship or required training, although workshops are frequently offered on topics that are believed to empower women, such as meditation and visualization techniques or discovering the "goddess within" (for example, see Bolen

1984). As in feminist witchcraft, the spiritual focus is on an autonomous female divinity and the creation of powerful female images, and the group holds rituals to celebrate the seasons. Many women in the goddess movement practise witchcraft and magic in a manner similar to Dianics and neopagans, although many of them tend not to call themselves witches and to prefer the word "spirituality" to "religion."

Of the nine core Womancircle members, one was formerly Dianic and another still identified herself as such. Three more had taken structured "witch classes," conducted by Dianics outside of their own group, which used feminist analysis, and all of them had attended Dianic rituals. The group organized public rituals five times a year, two solstice fairs, and occasional workshops. Men were welcome at almost all of these events. They also had retreats and workshops for the core members, which I did not attend. Their rituals tended to draw fairly large crowds—40 was the smallest I observed and over 200 the largest—while 1,000 people may stop in at their solstice fairs. They have a current mailing list of 1,300 people who have attended at least one event and want to be apprised of future ones.

Women in both core groups appear to accept uncritically the belief in prehistorical "goddess cultures" where women and "women's values" were a major part of the societal ethos (see Eisler 1988). In Womancircle and, to a slightly lesser degree, Redwood Moon, there was a tendency to consider femininity and masculinity as innate characteristics rather than as social constructs. Many of the women have been involved in feminist activities in the community, such as rape crisis centres, family planning centres, and resource centres. Although the witches in Redwood Moon are much more likely to discuss the political ramifications of religion, all the women in both groups consider public ritual to be a political act.

MYTHOS AND SOCIAL RELATIONS

Anthropologist Clifford Geertz (1973) argues that religion actually shapes social order and psychological processes and that the symbols in rituals and myths are believed to sum up what is known about the world and to teach people how to react to it. This means symbols and myths have both psychological and political impact because they create a framework of meaning through which people learn to accept certain social arrangements and reject others. Geertz's argument is supported by Sanday's findings that the secular power roles of women and men *derived from* sacred concepts of power seen in origin myths of the 150 cultures studied, rather than the other way around (Sanday 1981).

Mythos, then, may be partially understood as a cultural vision of the world, one that "links the individual self to the larger morphological structure" of society (Campbell 1988:72). If not reinforced through the regular performance of religious ritual, myths run the danger of being forgotten or reduced to "mere" literature or art (Priest 1970; Campbell 1988). Myths also lose their vitality when they fail to reinforce the link between the self and the experienced world. Sometimes in times of crisis, a new mythos is created that speaks to the devitalized or faded myth, as Wilder (1970) has demonstrated occurred with the rise of Christianity. The new myth and its symbols come into immediate conflict with existing social institutions and authority.[5]

Feminist witchcraft sees women's oppression and environmental abuse, which they argue are intimately linked, as firmly rooted in patriarchal religions. They claim that the mythos of God the Father and Creator of everything is a devitalized one that fails to address the experience of women's lives, and so cannot possibly link them to the larger social structure. In particular, they focus on the differences between the mythic image of a female divinity who creates life alone in an act of parthenogenesis by reaching within her own body in a physical, material act, and that of a transcendent, celibate male divinity who created life with a thought or a word and who is above and apart from his creation. They talk about the "patriarchal thought-form" based in the latter image and point to how this influences the way we understand the world and human experience in two important ways.

First, feminist witches emphasize the similarities in the hierarchical structures of the world's five major religions, reflected, for example, in angels, saints, jinn, and demi-gods. Mageara, Redwood Moon's priestess of ritual magic who does occasional presentations on witchcraft, says this model trains people to defer their power and responsibility upward. It is reinforced by hierarchical value systems that rank the material, the emotional, the intellectual, and the spiritual in ascending order. Women and femininity are identified with the material and the emotional, the lower half, and men and masculinity are identified with the upper and "superior" half, consisting of the intellectual and the spiritual.

Second, feminist witches point to the linearity of patriarchal myths and intellectual constructs. It is because the material and emotional are devalued in relation to the intellectual and spiritual, they say, that patriarchal religions teach us that "Life is a vale of tears." In order to ascend the hierarchy of values, the material and emotional must be overcome. The body must be disciplined, even mortified, they say, and desire conquered. These religions tend to be salvation-oriented, speaking of a linear lifetime with the goal of moving up and beyond to an afterlife, to a sacredness outside of the world. Even when life is understood as a process of reincarnation, the goal is still to move elsewhere, to move beyond the material and break free of the cycle of rebirth. The enlightenment and experience of the divine is one of transcendence. Mageara argues that:

> Out of infinite possibilities, this belief system creates social relations that will conform with, reinforce, and maintain itself. This thought-form conceptualizes power as power over, rather than power to do or to be. It turns human activity into forced productivity that leads to the abuse of the earth and women because it compartmentalizes the material, separates it from, and places it beneath the spiritual.

THE MYTHOS OF FEMINIST WITCHCRAFT

Max Weber wrote that the world became "disenchanted" when sacredness was removed from everyday life and moved out into another realm where the divine dwelt.

> ... the sense of sacredness was gathered up from the countless tree and water spirits, like so many scattered rays of light brought to focus in a lens, and was concentrated in a nucleate ... concept of the divine. (in Geertz 1973:173–174)

But the goal of transcendence and the concept of sacredness being separate and external to the self are alien to feminist witches, who draw heavily on ideas explored by Chodorow (1978) and Gilligan (1982) and who emphasize the female experience of continuity and connection. Instead of transcendence, the goddess represents immanence, which they visualize as the flow of energy that connects all things. Through religious ritual and magic, feminist witches and women in the goddess movement attempt to link what they believe is the divine within them to the divine around them in the natural world. To them, the goddess is "the normative image of immanence" (Starhawk 1988:9), the mystical experience within of everything that exists without.

Their concept of the trinity, the dynamic cycle of birth, life, death, and rebirth as represented by the goddess's three aspects of maiden, mother, and crone, reflects and reinforces their belief in connection and immanence. The triple goddess is a metaphor that supports cyclical time, like the seasons. As Mageara says:

> What comes around goes around and everything is connected. There's no deferring of power or responsibility upward, no linear plane to transcend, no getting off the wheel. Instead of working toward transcendence, the goal is to accept where in the cycle you are and really BE there. You might as well. After all, this is it folks!

Instead of the basic hierarchy of material, emotional, intellectual, and spiritual of patriarchal religions, the symbol used by feminist witches is a circle that contains and balances the intellectual, emotional, material, adds energy as a fourth element, and represents the whole union as spiritual because the whole is greater than the sum of its parts.[6]

Having rejected "patriarchal thought-forms" as failing to reflect their own experience of reality, these women also reject the core values they grew out of. The four core values emphasized by witches in my interviews were the same as those discussed by Christ (1982) as being typical of goddess symbolism, including affirmations of female power, body, will, and of women's heritage and bonds. Just as it has been argued that the symbols and mythos in Judeo-Christian tradition have reinforced the interests of men in patriarchy (for examples, see Daly 1973; Stone 1976; Christ 1982; Baring and Cashford 1991), the women argue that the symbols and mythos of the goddess shape a new ethos and cultural vision of the world. This mythos uses a definition of power they believe to be free from the dynamics of domination. As Mageara argues, "female power isn't about power over, it is power to do, power to be." It is an articulation of power that, according to recent research on gender differences (Hale and Kelly 1989), is similar to the way that many men and women tend to actually use power in the secular world. Thus their gendered understanding of power and their cultural vision are firmly rooted in the female body and experience, and they believe this presents a serious challenge to patriarchal relations.

FEMINIST MYTHOPOEIC IMAGES

Traditional religious iconography offers one major mythopoeic image for women, that of the mother. Whether she is portrayed as the young virgin with child or the grieving madonna of the Pieta, she is young, she is beautiful, and she is defined by her relationship to her son. In contrast, the triple goddess defines herself and each of her three aspects as a mythic image that is capable of standing alone. This can be illustrated by examining the use of mythopoeic imagery in three public rituals of Womancircle and Circle of the Redwood Moon.

The first was created by Hypatia, Dianic witch and priestess in Redwood Moon.[7] The coven sponsored a weekend of workshops, discussions, and rituals in which I participated along with a group of some 60 women camping in the mountains. My notes describe the scene.

> The second night out was a full moon and we waited impatiently for the moon to crest the tall pines so that the ritual could begin. Finally, we saw two flames winding down the mountain path. As they neared, we saw that these were torches, held by priestesses in silver gowns which caught the light from the flames and glittered like pieces of the moon herself. The priestesses paused in the south, and then I noticed the enormous shadow thrown against the hill. It is Diana who comes behind them. Rationally, I know it is Hypatia, but I also "know" it is Diana. A heavy green cape is swept over her shoulders and matches her baggy pants. Her huge breasts are bare, and her chest is crossed with the leather straps that hold her cape and the quiver of arrows on her back. She carries a large bow and her face is hidden behind a mask of fur and dried leaves. Deer horns spring from her head. There is no face, not a human one, anyway.... The Goddess pauses between the torches and fits an arrow to the bow. She draws it back and with a "twang" shoots it into the darkness. The sound is a catalyst. We are released like the arrow and begin to cheer. (August 24, 1991)[8]

Hypatia told me later she neither "became" nor "invoked" Diana, phrases that would suggest that the goddess was external to her priestess. Rather, Hypatia "manifested that part" of her that *was* Diana. But this was no fleet-footed, pony-tailed chaste young goddess of the woods and dells. Hypatia is a powerful-looking, obese woman whose presence in her secular life often intimidates people who do not know her well. As Diana, this sense of power was dramatically enhanced. This was a Diana who looked like she could strangle a boar with her bare hands. But her strength was more than physical; there was a drama in her presence and authority that seemed to stem from within. This is described by a woman in her mid-twenties who was a feminist new to goddess ritual.

> Other images of Diana are all sexualized from a male point of view, kind of a scantily clad Playboy bunny in the woods. But when she came walking up and I realized who she was, it was really different. It was really kind of overwhelming and shocking. But after the

> initial shock, she *was* Diana. This was a female who radiated power with her body and costume. Her unself-consciousness about her body was powerful and the way she walked was almost majestic. I'll never forget it. *This* was the Diana I want to relate to.

Later in the ritual, Diana asked who was "on her moon time" or menstruating. On those women who were, she pinned a sprig of herbs tied with a red ribbon. This same young woman found this wonderful.

> Moon time! What a beautiful concept! If you were menstruating, you were special. You had this incredible gift that your body has given to you, something to be proud of! And we got to wear red ribbons so that everyone else would know and be proud of you too!

This was a goddess who was a virgin in Goldenberg's (1979) sense of being independent of her lovers, not one who was necessarily by nature sexually inactive, a definition popular with feminist witches. With her attire and gift of moon ribbons, she celebrated the female body in a uniquely female way. This was a totally different image of Diana than the one with which we are familiar. This was the goddess of the moon and the lady of the wild things. With this powerful image, Hypatia manifested the strong, independent maiden that the witches argue may be found in all women, a natural part of the female self that has been denied and suppressed.

The second mythopoeic image was presented by a priestess from Womancircle. Almost 200 people had gathered in a rented church hall to celebrate the winter solstice and were seated on blankets and jackets on the floor in a semi-circle around a large round altar decorated in reds and greens and many small goddess figurines. About two-thirds of the people were female, and infants and small children were scattered in the crowd. Light seemed to dance in the air around the altar from the many candles people had brought as offerings. It was well into the ritual when three figures stepped out from the shadows. Like Hypatia's Diana, each figure was a priestess/goddess. The first was a Black Isis, with a large feathered shawl. The second a Chicana Tonatzin with rattles and beads and feathers. The third was a pale Virgin Mary, draped in white and blue. Each moved slowly around the altar, explaining who she was and why she was there. The image of diversity, the multiple faces of the goddess, was a striking one, and in itself part of the new mythos. But it was the words and actions of the pale Mary that present the particular challenge to patriarchy explored here.

As she circled the altar, her robes swirling gently around her ankles, Mary smiled and said she too was the goddess. She told us that we had been taught many things about her. Some of them were true, some of them were lies. She said that being the mother of a child was not all that *any* female was, no matter how important the particular child might be. There was much more to Mary then her chaste visage might suggest. My fieldnotes record what the priestess/Mary said:

> "The Church Fathers and their artists always dress me in blue and white. What they never tell you is that under my robes I wear a red petticoat," and she lifted her drape to her knees, revealing a bright red petticoat with flounces! People laughed. (December 22, 1990)

The laughter was immediate and spontaneous. Several people told me that they had been momentarily startled by the sight and that was why they laughed. Later, a young woman who had read about the goddess but was new to ritual told me why she laughed.

> It was kind of shocking because it reminded us that the Virgin *had* a body.

And a middle-age woman told me she laughed,

> ... in recognition. It's [the petticoat] a symbol of joy and happiness and sexuality. Life under something else. It's there even if you don't see it. It's like an inside joke. Like lifeblood.

The priestess who had "been" Mary was more specific.

> I see many, many connections that can be made between the image of Mary ... and the denigration of women. One of the things that they have done to Mary, they've taken away her sexuality. She was a mother and yet had no sex. She was not a woman, she was just a role. And I see this personified in our relationships with our own earthly mothers. We have this idea of what they should be, but we don't let them be women. So when I said that Mary had a red petticoat underneath, I meant that under her image of serene mother and chaste virgin, whatever, she was a woman with lifeblood, with sexual blood. Kind of reclaiming her sexuality, it was symbolic of that to me.

The small gesture of raising her robe was intended to uncover a new Virgin Mary. Her red petticoat was a metaphor that served to establish a link between the *female* body and the divine, in other words, between the material and the spiritual. Instead of denying the body, this image celebrated it.

The Virgin Mary in this ritual was a mother goddess who had a material, female body, who birthed and created life out of her own flesh and blood, who might still be sexually active even after giving birth, and who, in raising her petticoat, metaphorically redefined what it means to be female and to be spiritual. This Virgin Mary did not give the impression she would ever utter the words, "be it unto me according to thy word" (Luke 1:38). Thus "re-visioned," she reclaimed her sexuality, her fertility, her autonomy, and her divinity.

The last image was consciously constructed by several Womancircle priestesses and unaffiliated women in the community. An announcement had gone out to the community that a six-month series of workshops would begin to focus on the crone aspect of the goddess. The culmination of these was a ritual in late October, where the women who had attended the workshops publicly "claimed their cronehood."

Inside the dimly lit rented church, almost all of the 100 attendees wore black. There were men and children here and there in the crowd that circled two round tables in the very centre of the hall. These tables had been placed together and draped in purple velvet, and the effect was a horizontal figure eight, the symbol of infinity. One lone white taper burned on this dark altar; other than that, it was bare. The community of celebrants had been dancing to a small group of drummers, a wild, wide spiral dance that filled the church as people awaited the coming of the crones. The "handmaiden" who had been sent to invite them into the hall returned, and the dancers stopped in place, forming a large double spiral that led up to the altar. The drums beat slowly as the handmaiden scattered rose petals in the path of the crones. First came two together, carrying between them a large cauldron symbolizing wisdom, death, and rebirth (see Walker 1985). Behind them, the other crones glided in one by one. They were dressed entirely in black, their faces partially hidden behind black veils. They carried candles specially made for the occasion, beeswax dipped in black, purple, and red. Some of them carried flowers in their arms, several had small goddess figures in their hands. The veiled figures circled twice through the human spiral as people spontaneously cried out small encouragements. "Welcome, crones!" "Hail, crone!" "We love you!" "The world needs more crones!" One of the crones told me:

> It was close, very close. People didn't touch us as we passed through, but we felt emotionally touched.... It felt like we entered the body of the goddess and were birthed as crones.

The line of crones reached the altar and encircled it, forming a circle within a circle. Several "called in" their favourite crone goddesses—Hecate, Lilith, Medusa—inviting them to join the circle. One by one the women went to the altar candle and used its flame to ignite their own, which they placed around it, along with any flowers and statuettes they carried. When they had all completed this act, they lifted back their veils and turned around to face the community. Singly, each then announced who she was, where she came from, and what she had to offer the community. A typical presentation was:

> I am Marilyn, daughter of Dorothy, granddaughter of Judith, great-granddaughter of Laura, who was a daughter of Hecate. If you would seek wisdom with a crone, seek me.

The crowd cheered each crone's declaration. Some of the "gifts" they offered were fairly traditional—wisdom, love, healing. But there were also crones who promised laughter, sexual love, and political power. The last offering evoked a loud, "Grandmothers in '92!"[9]

In claiming their cronehood, announcing their matrilineage, and declaring themselves valuable, these women shattered the stereotypes of aging females, both for themselves and those attending. A 22-year-old woman confided:

> It was really an exciting, emotional thing. Many of them went back three and four generations. That was amazing. And the power in their voices! In my family the women don't raise their voices and announce who they are. To see such strong women! One said, "If you would seek ecstasy with a crone, seek me." I've never seen older women in a sexual light before. It was really uniting and empowering.

And a 24-year-old said:

> I felt really connected with the joy and power in these women who were saying, "This is where I am. This is what I want to do, and this is where I'm going." They were like older sisters and what they gave me is what I have to look forward to.

What this ritual represented to her was that she could look forward to an old age in which she could be respected and valued by her community, an old age in which she could be serious, playful, sexual, wise, powerful, political, and humorous, should she so choose. In other words, the image is one of a woman who is old *and* whole. The crones rejected the limitations imposed by a culture in which female power, such as it is, is tied to youth, beauty, fertility, and male-directed sexuality. They were aging and aged post-menopausal women who symbolically redefined female beauty and worth and so reclaimed their autonomy and power. They clearly believed they had something of value to offer, and their community, in turn, rejoiced.

DISCUSSION

Clearly, each of these examples offers a celebratory vision of female power, female will, the female body, and of women's bonds. Rather than presenting role models for women that are defined and limited by their relationship to divine and secular male authority, as witches claim patriarchal religions do, each seeks to legitimate female power and authority. But instead of being based in dominance or hierarchy, the model of power and authority is rooted in strength and self-knowledge. The crones said: "This is where I am ... this is where I'm going." Mary "*had* a body" and apparently delighted in it. Diana "radiated power with her body" and provided a source of pride and identification. Each image presented a physical manifestation of the connection between the material and the spiritual and then went on to not only liberate female sexuality from concepts of sin, but actually celebrate the erotic. Taken together as images that contribute to the new mythos, they offer the possibility of what Spretnak calls "an embodied way of knowing and being in the world," which possibility she described as:

> ... the empowering realization that being is being-in-relation, that we come to know the larger reality of humanity, Earthbody, and cosmos through the body, not by escaping the personal to an abstract system, and that apprehending our dynamic embeddedness in the unitive unfolding brings wisdom and grace to our subjectivity—including our conceptualizing and theorizing. (Spretnak 1991:149)

This embodied epistemology provides a spiritual dimension to feminist critiques of epistemology explored in fields as diverse as psychology (Benjamin 1988), political science (Hartsock 1985), and biology (Keller 1985).

Of course, whether or not the women involved can sustain these feelings of power and celebration outside the ritual setting in a world that does not share their beliefs is problematic. But this difficulty is not limited to feminist witchcraft or the goddess movement, as many individuals experience conflict living up to their religious beliefs in a secular world. In addition, the power of mythopoeic imagery and religious symbolism in postmodern society may be open to debate. Yet regardless of intellectual debate, the women have felt the need to replace one set of mythic images with another, and have created religious images and symbols that have special significance and meaning for them. And as no two rituals are ever exactly alike, they continue to engage in this process of creation each and every time they do ritual.

This is a setting that offers rich material for further study. Do women who experience feelings of personal empowerment in goddess rituals feel empowered in their daily lives? If so, how are these feelings manifested and do the women attribute them to their religious beliefs and practice? Are they different for women who experience different kinds of oppression, such as women of colour or women with physical disabilities? In sum, specifically how do the spiritual beliefs and practices of these women help them to survive in a male-dominated world? What is the relationship between women in the goddess movement and those who choose to remain in traditional religions but work to incorporate into them the female experience of the divine?

Another area for study involves the differences in the goddess movement between essentialists, who believe there are universal and specific feminine and masculine qualities rooted in biology, and social constructionists, who argue that gender roles and distinctions are artificial, that they are socially constructed and imposed. How do these frameworks affect the understanding and analyses of patriarchal religious oppression experienced by women and how do they address the issues of race and class in the goddess movement? Do they affect the religious world view or how the new cultural vision is articulated? Are there demographic as well as ideological differences between the two groups?

It is clear that the goddess movement is successful in providing a new framework of meaning for some women who, in growing numbers, are alienated from patriarchal religions. Although it supports other feminist approaches to change, such as in the legal, educational, and political arenas, the goddess movement is radical in that it argues that the roots of gender oppression are deeper than these changes alone can reach. Religion defines the deepest values of a society, and, as Spretnak points out:

> Efforts to radically transform society must fall short if the deepest informing assumptions and core values are not challenged. (Spretnak 1991:149)

As these core values are challenged, new questions arise for sociologists. Not the least of these will deal with growing political tensions, which are already visible. Feminist witches claim that more and more women are "coming out of the broom closet" and making public demonstrations of their faith. Evidence to support this can be seen in a proliferation of recent mainstream media articles on witches as well as in the list of sponsors and participants for the 1993 Parliament of the World's Religions held in Chicago.[10] Evidence of the tension can be seen in the denouncements of feminist witchcraft and goddess worship by some leaders of traditional religions, and the tendency of these same leaders to link feminism and all its issues to witchcraft. This public challenge to core values and the resulting potential for conflict is another area in which research may be fruitful.

CONCLUSION

In creating mythopoeic images that are rooted in material manifestations, such as the seasons of the year and the female body, feminist witches and women in the goddess movement seek to shape a new cultural ethos. In presenting them in public rituals that are highly experiential, they attempt to share the world view that informs this ethos in the belief that eventually this will lead to social change. Whether or not this goal is likely to be realized is beyond the parameters of this paper. What is clear is that these women have rejected the ethos they believe is present in patriarchal religions and, through the conscious construction and enactment of myth, they seek a new cultural understanding and vision that will reconnect and, in the Weberian sense, "re-enchant" the world.

NOTES

1. Even less is known concerning numbers of practitioners as authority and records have never been centralized. Kelly (1987) extrapolated from subscriptions to pagan journals, attendance at pagan gatherings, registered coven membership, book sales, etc., to estimate fifty to one hundred thousand. Neitz (1990), however, believes that these figures leave out most feminist witches. In 1991, Budapest asserted to me that there were hundreds of thousands involved. Eller (1991) points out that for every woman who is actually initiated as a witch, many others read Budapest's books, participate in a study group, or attend a Goddess ritual. Typically, these individuals are not counted, as sociologists describe New Religious Movements "in terms of their most intense manifestations" (Eller 1991:280). What is clear is that the movement has grown dramatically since 1971.
2. This one Law is sometimes considered two, as it basically says do whatever you want to do as long as it doesn't hurt anyone. If you do hurt someone, be prepared to accept the consequences because whatever is "sent out" will return increased.
3. There is also a smaller, non-separatist Dianic Tradition based on the teachings of Morgan McFarland, which acknowledges both divine female and male principles. It is not represented in this paper.
4. Called "Cakes for the Queen of Heaven," this eight-week course, written and designed by Shirley Ann Ranck, makes heavy use of slides of representations of ancient goddesses, feminist consciousness raising, and experiential workshops.
5. The reactions of mainstream religious leaders to feminist witchcraft and the Goddess movement are a good example of this. See statements made by Pope John Paul, reported in the *New York Times*, 5 July 1993, and Pat Robertson's fund raising letter from August, 1992.
6. Each element also represents a cardinal direction and associated concepts and characteristics. For example, the East represents the mind, thought, air, hawks, speed, and beginnings. The South is fire, energy, action, heat, stars, passion, and childhood. The West includes water, dolphins, intuition, emotion, and friendship. And the North is earth,

harvest, body, stones, growth, and endings.

7. Dianic witches may choose to undergo specialized training of at least a year and a day after initiation into the coven in order to become priestesses. In Womancircle, however, women who believe they are "called" by a particular aspect of the Goddess may consider themselves her priestesses and use the title without further training.
8. Before being shot, the arrow had been passed around the circle so that we could touch it and focus our "will" or "do our own magic" on it. After the ritual, women praised Hypatia for her skill, and many of them told me they had seen the arrow hit the bull's eye and heard the thud as it hit. Some knew that Hypatia's hobby was archery. But as the target that night was lit only by the full moon and a distant torch, and because of the arrow's symbolic importance, I investigated. Hypatia admitted to me in private the next morning that she had thrust the arrow into the bulls' eye by hand before the group woke up. The arrow hadn't come anywhere near the target!
9. This was a clear reminder that it was only a few weeks before the elections, in the Year of the Woman, and Diane Feinstein was using her role as a grandmother in her California television campaign for the US Senate.
10. The Covenant of the Goddess, one of the national umbrella groups that provides legal recognition of witchcraft and neopaganism as a religion, was one of the Parliament's sponsors. Witches attending the meetings conducted a full moon Goddess ritual one night in the nearby public park. Among the leaders was Devi Moonsong, a witch from Redwood Moon.

REFERENCES

Adler, Patricia, and Peter Adler. 1987. *Membership Roles in Research.* Beverly Hills: Sage.

Baring, A., and J. Cashford. 1991. *The Myth of the Goddess: Evolution of an Image.* London: Viking Arkana.

Beckford, J.A., ed. 1986. *New Religious Movements and Rapid Social Change.* London: Sage.

Benjamin, J. 1988. *The Bonds of Love: Psychoanalysis, Feminism, and the Problem of Domination.* New York: Pantheon Books.

Bolen, J.S. 1984. *Goddesses in Everywoman: A New Psychology of Women.* New York: Harper & Row.

Budapest, Z.E. 1989. *The Grandmother of Time.* San Francisco: Harper & Row.

Campbell, J., with Bill Moyers. 1988. *The Power of Myth.* New York: Doubleday.

Chodorow, N. 1978. *The Reproduction of Mothering.* Berkeley: University of California Press.

Christ, C.P. 1982. "Why Women Need the Goddess: Phenomenological, Psychological, and Political Reflections." In *The Politics of Women's Spirituality,* edited by C. Spretnak, 71–87. Garden City: Anchor Books.

Daly, M. 1973. *Beyond God the Father: Toward a Philosophy of Women's Liberation.* Boston: Beacon Press.

———. 1992. *Outercourse: The Be-dazzling Voyage.* San Francisco: HarperSanFrancisco.

Eisler, R. 1988. *The Chalice & the Blade.* San Francisco: Harper & Row.

Eller, C. 1991. "Relativizing the Patriarchy: The Sacred History of the Feminist Spirituality Movement." *History of Religions* 30: 279–295.

Finley, N.J. 1991. "Political Activism and Feminist Spirituality." *Sociological Analysis* 52: 349–362.

Geertz, C. 1973. *The Interpretation of Cultures.* New York: Basic Books.

Gilligan, C. 1982. *In a Different Voice.* Cambridge: Cambridge University Press.

Goldenberg, N. 1979. *Changing of the Gods: Feminism and the End of Traditional Religions.* Boston: Beacon Press.

Hale, M.M., and R.M. Kelly. 1989. *Gender, Bureaucracy and Democracy.* Westport: Greenwood Press.

Hartsock, N. 1985. *Money, Sex, and Power.* Boston: Northeastern University Press.

Jacobs, J.L. 1990. "Women, Ritual and Power." *Frontiers* XI, no. 2/3: 39–44.

Keller, E.F. 1985. *Reflections on Gender and Science.* New Haven: Yale University Press.

Kelly, A.A. 1991. *Crafting the Art of Magic,* Book 1. St. Paul: Llewellyn Press.

Lozano, W.G., and T.G. Foltz. 1990. "Into the Darkness: An Ethnographic Study of Feminist Witchcraft and Death." *Qualitative Sociology* 13: 221–235.

Neitz, M.J. 1990. "In Goddess We Trust." In *Gods We Trust: New Patterns of Religious Pluralism in America*, 2nd ed., edited by T. Robbins and D. Anthony, 353–372. New Brunswick: Transaction Publishers.

Priest, J. 1970. "Myth and Dream in Hebrew Scripture." In *Myths, Dreams, and Religion*, edited by J. Campbell, 48–68. Dallas: Spring Publications.

Sanday, P. 1981. *Female Power and Male Dominance.* Cambridge: Cambridge University Press.

Spretnak, C. 1991. *States of Grace: The Recovery of Meaning in the Postmodern Age.* San Francisco: HarperSanFrancisco.

Stanton, E.C. 1895. *Women's Bible.* New York: European Publishing Company.

Starhawk. 1988. *Dreaming the Dark*, 2nd ed. Boston: Beacon Press.

Stone, M. 1976. *When God Was a Woman.* New York: Harcourt Brace Jovanovich.

Walker, B.G. 1985. *The Crone.* San Francisco: Harper & Row.

Wilder, A. 1970. "Myth and Dream in Christian Scripture." In *Myths, Dreams, and Religion*, edited by J. Campbell, 68–91. Dallas: Spring Publications.

CHAPTER 18
Finding a Goddess

Ronald Hutton

In the pagan ancient world goddesses were most commonly patronesses of cities, justice, war, handicrafts, and home fire, agriculture, love, and learning; they stood for aspects of civilization and human activity much more often than for those of the natural world. Furthermore, the overwhelming majority of ancient pagans genuinely believed that the different goddesses were separate personalities. In only one text from near the end of the pagan period, the *Metamorphoses* of Apuleius, was the writer's favourite female deity declared to be the embodiment of all other goddesses (or at least of the most important) and identified with the moon and with the whole of nature. It was, however, that highly atypical image from Apuleius that became the predominant concept of a goddess in the modern world. When did it come to do so, and how?

The short answer is, a couple of centuries ago. Throughout the Middle Ages and early modern period, the emphasis on pagan deities remained just where it had been in ancient times. A systematic survey of classical themes in English poetry between 1300 and 1800 reveals that the most popular goddess was Venus, patroness of love, followed by Diana, representing female chastity and (much more rarely) hunting, then Minerva, for wisdom, and Juno, symbol of queenliness.[1] A more impressionistic look at intellectual works shows Minerva, not surprisingly, to be apostrophized most often.[2] As a civic goddess, she also seems to appear most frequently in urban statuary, from the Renaissance to the nineteenth century.[3]

It is true that in the early modern hermetic tradition there was a concept, representing a blend of Apuleius and the Neoplatonic notion of a world-soul, of a female figure identified with the starry heaven, standing between God and the earth and functioning as a fount of life and inspiration.[4] This tradition was, however, by definition the preserve of a small minority of specialists.

It is more important that the ancient Greeks spoke of the earth as being feminine in gender and the sky as being masculine (in sharp contrast, say, to the Egyptians). As most Western science is ultimately based upon Greek thought, this language became embedded in it. It was reinforced by the mindset of the patriarchal societies that occupied medieval and early modern Europe, in which intellectuals in general, and those who dealt with the sciences in particular, were overwhelmingly male. Carolyn Merchant has led a number of writers in emphasizing the development of a scholarly language that identified the author and reader as male adventurers occupied in exploring and exploiting a female natural world.[5] A concomitant was that from the high Middle Ages scholastic writers sometimes used a female figure to personify that world, and occasionally this got into creative literature. Its most famous appearance is probably in Chaucer's *Parlement of Foules*, where he felt sufficiently self-conscious about the use of it to cite his source, the twelfth-century cleric Alanus de Insulis.[6]

This was the pattern that prevailed, with remarkable consistency, until the decades around 1800, when it was dramatically altered by that complex of cultural changes known loosely and conventionally as the Romantic movement. One aspect to this was the exaltation of the natural and irrational, qualities that had conventionally been both feared or disparaged and characterized as feminine. Cultural historians have devoted many works to tracing the course of this revolution in taste, which for the first time gave emphasis to the beauty and sublimity of wild nature and of the night.[7] None has hitherto made a study of its impact upon European images of the divine feminine.

The impact upon English letters is spectacularly clear, and once again the existence of a handy reference work provides an easy means of tracing it in the realm of poetry.[8] Between 1800 and 1940 Venus (or Aphrodite) retains her numerical superiority in appearances, with Diana (or Artemis) coming second. Juno, however, almost vanishes, and so does Minerva after 1830. The third place is now taken by Proserpine, as goddess of the changing seasons or of the dead, and the fourth by Ceres or Demeter, lady of the harvest. A reading of the texts listed discloses a much more striking alternative. Venus now appears not merely as patroness of love but related to the woodland or the sea. Diana is no longer primarily a symbol of chastity or of hunting, but of the moon, the greenwood, and wild animals. Furthermore, when a goddess is made the major figure in a poem, instead of the subject of an incidental reference, the supremacy of Venus is overturned. Diana now leads, or else a generalized female deity of moonlight or the natural world, most commonly called "Mother Earth" or "Mother Nature."

The pattern was clearly established by the 1810s, and shows prominently in the work of Keats and Shelley. From his earliest compositions, Keats felt himself to be enchanted by the moon, and identified it with a goddess, "Maker of sweet poets, dear delight of this fair world, and all its gentle livers."[9] [...]

*****

This shimmer of moonlight runs through the work of the Romantics, appearing in some of the least likely places. Traditionally, druids were regarded as sun-worshippers, but when Vincenzo Bellini wrote the nineteenth century's most famous drama about them, his opera *Norma* (1831), the libretto by Felice Romani made the heroine stand in a sacred grove and invoke the moon, in the most celebrated aria:

> Chaste goddess, who silvers these sacred trees,
> Show your face to us without a veil,
> Bring peace to earth as you have brought it to heaven.

The other favourite way of personifying a goddess at the period was represented by Shelley. When he came to write a wholly original ode to one (as opposed to a translation or imitation), he began:

Sacred goddess, Mother Earth,
Thou from whose immortal bosom Gods, and men, and beasts, have birth,
Leaf and blade, and bud and blossom.[10]

By 1820 the dominant image of a goddess in the English poetic imagination was already emerging as the beauty of the green earth and the white moon among the stars. It was thoroughly internalized by the next generation. When the devout Christian Robert Browning tried his hand at a classical subject in 1842, he chose Artemis, and this is how he made her speak:

Through heaven I roll my lucid moon along;
I shed in hell o'er my pale people peace;
On earth I, caring for the creatures, guard,
Each pregnant yellow wolf and fox-bitch sleek,
And every feathered mother's callow brood,
And all that love green haunts and loneliness.[11]

*****

The next stage of the process was to eliminate the creator god, leaving the composite goddess of nature as the single mighty source of all being, and this was taken by Swinburne in 1867, when he gave resounding voice to her under the name of the German earth-goddess Hertha:

I am that which began;
Out of me the years roll;
Out of me, god and man,
I am equal and whole;
God changes, and man, and the form of them bodily;
I am the soul....

First life on my sources
First drifted and swam;
Out of me are the forces
That save it or damn;
Out of me, man and woman, and wild beast and bird;
Before God was, I am.[12]

Simultaneously, in 1867 James Thomson was writing a poem entitled "The Naked Goddess," which he eventually published in 1880. Its heroine is nature, who comes to a town nude and attended by a train of adults. The adult humans offer her the choice between donning the habit of a nun or the robe of a philosopher. Only the children realize how beautiful she is, and go back with her to the wildwood. During the decades between its production and publication, George Meredith was evolving his own parallel poetic vision in work after work, by which all classical goddesses were different aspects of "great nature" or "earth," with whom humans needed to be reconciled in order to be complete once more. By 1880 the composite goddess was both a creatrix and a redeemer.

*****

To understand the hold that she achieved upon the Western imagination during the following 30 years, it is necessary to leave the world of poets for that of scholars, and to make a retreat once more into the eighteenth century. During its last quarter, a debate had developed over the nature of prehistoric religion. Crudely speaking, this was divided between those who suggested that primitive religious belief was a superstitious compound of ignorance and fear, and those who viewed it as an embodiment of sublime truths, which had degenerated and been forgotten among most modern tribal peoples. The first theory was especially popular among thinkers of the French and Scottish Enlightenments, the second among the German Romantics.[13] The Germans assumed that one of these eternal truths consisted of monotheism, and usually linked it to an instinctual understanding of the processes of nature and of human life.

In view of all the above, therefore, it makes sense that it was a German classicist, Eduard Gerhard, who in 1849 advanced the novel suggestion that behind the various goddesses of historic Greece stood a single great one, representing Mother Earth and venerated before history began.[14] As the century wore on, other German, and French, classicists, such as Ernst Kroker, Fr. Lenormant, and M.J. Menant, began to adopt this idea, drawing support for it from the assumption that the cultures of Anatolia and Mesopotamia were older than, and in some measure ancestral to, those of Greece.[15] Those cultures did contain some figures of powerful goddesses, identified with motherhood or with the earth (though never with both). The theory meshed with another, which had emerged from a debate between lawyers over the origins of society and of the human family. One of the contesting theories in this exchange, articulated first in 1862 by the Swiss judge J.J. Bachofen, was that the earliest human societies had been woman-centred, altering to a patriarchal form before the beginning of history; what was true in the secular sphere should also, logically, have been so in the religious one.

None the less, by the last decade of the century, the notion was still only tentative, and there was a reluctance to apply it to actual prehistoric data. When the female figurines of the Neolithic and Copper Age Cyclades were first described as a group, in the 1880s, there was no attempt to link them to a goddess.[16] The same is true of the Old Stone Age feminine statuettes recognized as a type in the 1890s: they were dubbed "Venuses" largely in mockery, by comparison with the famous Greco-Roman statues, rather than because of any religious connection.[17] The director of the British School at Athens in 1901 referred to Greece's Neolithic figurines simply as "idols" and avoided further speculation.[18] When Sir Arthur Evans first discussed the Cretan equivalents, in 1895, he explicitly dismissed the great goddess theory, suggesting that they and the similar Balkan figures were symbolic concubines placed in male graves.[19]

The breakthrough in belief occurred with the opening of the new century. In 1901 Evans, now excavating Knossos, underwent a conversion to the idea that prehistoric Crete had venerated a single mighty goddess. He henceforth interpreted all the images of apparent divine females at the site as aspects of this one deity, and male figures as portrayals of an equivalent single god, subordinate to her as her son and consort. This relationship was based on the classical legend of Rhea and Zeus, but his insistence that she had been viewed as both virgin and mother, with a divine child, owed an unmistakeable debt to the Christian tradition of the Virgin Mary.[20] By 1921 Evans had firmly associated the Neolithic figurines and the historic Near Eastern goddesses with her,[21] and his influence made this the orthodoxy of Minoan archaeology,[22] although there were always a few colleagues who pointed out that it placed a strain upon the evidence.[23]

In 1903 Sir Edmund Chambers, a civil servant who was also a respected scholar of the medieval stage, declared that prehistoric Europe had worshipped a great earth mother in two aspects, creatrix and destroyer, who was later known by a plurality of names.[24] Simultaneously, an influential Cambridge classicist, Jane Ellen Harrison, stated her belief in the same figure, but with a threefold division of aspect. Like Evans, she faced the problem of how to reconcile the apparently incompatible attributes of virginal and material historic goddesses. Instead of solving it with the appropriation of a Christian image, she pointed out that the pagan ancient world had sometimes believed in partnerships of three divine women, such as the Fates or the Graces. She argued that the original single one, representing the earth, had been likewise honoured in three roles. The most important of these were maiden, ruling the living, and mother, ruling the underworld; she did not name the third. Extending Evans's ideas, she declared that all male deities had originally been subordinate to the goddess as her lovers and her sons.[25]

One influence upon Harrison's thought in general had been her celebrated Cambridge colleague, Sir James Frazer. He had hitherto avoided the subject of ancient goddesses, but in 1907 he let himself be swept up by the burgeoning enthusiasm for the idea of a prehistoric great one. His acceptance of it was cautious, extending only to the conclusion that in western Asia, at least, the earliest civilizations had believed in a single goddess, "the personification of all the reproductive energies of nature," with a male son and consort representing the spirit of vegetation, who dies and returns. He got round the problem of how this deity could be both virgin and mother by arguing that primitive peoples had not understood the concept of paternity.[26] Seven years later, Frazer extended the Greek myth of Demeter and Persephone to suggest that all over prehistoric Europe people had venerated a double goddess, mother and daughter, who personified the corn.[27]

This sequence of works was further augmented in 1908, when a distinguished French archaeologist, Joseph Dechelette, proposed that the cult of the great goddess had been conceived in the Neolithic of Asia Minor and the Balkans and carried thence across the Mediterranean to the whole of New Stone Age western Europe. Like Chambers and Harrison, he conceived of her as having been visualized both as a giver of life and fertility and as a giver of death and rebirth; a light and a dark goddess.[28] The cumulative effect of this weight of opinion was decisive; by the 1910s it was a staple theme of textbooks upon ancient Greek religion that the worship of the Olympian deities had been preceded by a prehistoric age in which the great goddess or earth mother had ruled supreme.[29] Whether or not this was actually so is not a question necessary to the purposes of this book; it is sufficient to note that at the dawn of the twentieth century influential scholars had suddenly become very anxious to believe that it was. For the present it is only necessary to trace the development of the notion up to the 1940s.

Two important gains were made by it in 1929. The first was proposed by an Englishman, G.D. Hornblower, who linked for the first time the Paleolithic statuettes of women with the Neolithic figurines and the notion of the Near Eastern great goddess, to project the cult of the latter back to the earliest known human activity in Europe.[30] The second was the work of an American, E.B. Renaud, who made a much more ambitious parallel between apparently female figurines found in the Pueblo cultures of Arizona and those of prehistoric Europe, to suggest that the veneration of the one goddess, the life-giving mother, had existed all over the world before the coming of civilization. "The first god was a goddess!" proclaimed Renaud.[31]

Throughout this, however, specialists in the emerging field of northwest European prehistory, and especially of Britain, reserved judgment. This was because their Neolithic looked so different from that of the Levant and the Balkans. Its sites had failed to produce any of the female figurines, which were such an important prop of the great goddess construct in the southeast. Instead the western European neolithic was characterized by a very widespread monumental tradition, of megalithic tomb-shrines, the structures commonly called dolmens, passage graves, and long barrows. It was true that some of the French tombs contained a carved female figure, which gave some grounds for arguing in favour of a goddess cult; but the decisive evidence was lacking, and archaeologists did not feel able to pronounce upon the matter without it.

[...] The first scholars of European prehistory applied tribal models to its religions to produce an impression of savage beliefs and practices. Their successors in the early twentieth century were recoiling from these, as unverifiable given the state of the evidence. Between 1920 and 1940, three leaders of the emerging profession of British archaeology, Gordon Childe, Grahame Clark, and O.G.S. Crawford, all published surveys of prehistoric Britain that scrupulously avoided pronouncing upon the nature of its religious cultures. Childe and Crawford suggested that the megalithic tombs had been monuments of a single faith, and Childe even characterized it as spread by missionaries from the East (another comfortable fit with Christianity, and also with Dechelette's theory). Both, however, firmly declined to identify the being or beings upon which it had been focused.[32] No such caution restrained non-academic writers with an interest in archaeology. When Harold Massingham wrote a book about the Cotswolds in 1932, he took his information about their long barrows from Crawford's famous survey, but with the single difference that whereas Crawford had never discussed the religious beliefs of the builders, Massingham repeatedly declared, with perfect confidence, that they had been based on Mother Earth.[33]

For those scholars who wanted to think like Massingham, the barrier was apparently removed at last in 1939, when A.L. Armstrong claimed to have found the unequivocal proof of the worship of an earth goddess in the British Neolithic. At the bottom of a shaft at Grimes Graves, the big complex of New Stone Age flint mines in Norfolk, he allegedly uncovered a female figurine, seated upon a crude altar, with a vessel for offerings placed before her. From that moment onwards, the statuette appeared in books upon the Neolithic in general and Grimes Graves in particular, interpreted as a deity. The Ministry of Works, as custodians of the site, placed a picture of the "goddess" upon the cover of its official guidebook and reconstructed its "shrine" for visitors to see.

From the moment of its reported discovery, however, rumours also circulated quietly in some parts of the archaeological community to the effect that it was a fake, planted either by or upon Armstrong. Such was the discretion of that community that not until 1986 did one of its members, Stuart Piggott, raise the matter in print.[34] An investigation into it was carried out by Gillian Varndell, as part of a general reappraisal of the Grimes Graves material, and in 1991 she reported the following points: the excavation was never published; Armstrong's site notebook stopped abruptly on the day of the discovery, without recording it properly; on the day of the find, most unusually, he had directed all other experienced excavators to leave the area; the figurine and vessel look suspiciously freshly carved; and somebody on Armstrong's team was an expert carver because similar objects made from the same Chalk rock, like an Egyptian sphinx, were among his possessions from the dig.[35]

As no method exists for dating chalk objects, Varndell added, the authenticity of these cannot be objectively tested, but not surprisingly, she concluded that the circumstantial evidence makes their status extremely dubious. This doubt is increased by the fact that since 1939 not a single other figurine has been found in an unequivocally sacred context from the British Neolithic. It looks as if the Grimes Graves "goddess" was a fraud; like the Piltdown skull, it had success because it represented precisely what many were hoping to find at that moment. The way was now open for a general acceptance of the idea that the whole of Stone Age Europe and the Near East had venerated the great earth goddess.

The "conversion" of Sir Arthur Evans, which had commenced this landslide, had been propelled by a similar piece of apparent objective evidence, this time genuine, but misunderstood. It was the work of the American team, which had excavated Nippur in Iraq, then thought to be the world's oldest city, reported in 1898.[36] Evans interpreted the report as saying that the deity found in the earliest levels of its first temple was female, and represented by a clay figurine of the sort now familiar to him from Cretan Neolithic sites; he concluded that they all represented the same goddess, to whom the Nippur figure was ancestral.[37] Evans had got the chronology the wrong way round (the Cretan data is older), and the book on the Nippur excavations does not in fact decisively attribute the dedication of that temple to a goddess. What had in fact happened was that he and the scholars who preceded or followed him had projected backwards upon prehistory the goddess who had emerged as pre-eminent in the minds of poets and novelists during the nineteenth century. The actual, known, history of ancient Near Eastern religion had followed a precisely opposite course; the earliest records in each region show a wide plurality of deities, from whom more important figures gradually emerge, until eventually (by the time of Apuleius) some pagans were verging upon monotheism. The orthodoxy that had emerged by the 1940s (correct or not) required a chronological pattern resembling a diamond, whereby an original feminist monotheism had disintegrated into a rampant polytheism, which in turn simplified once more to culminate in a patriarchal monotheism. Or, to put things another way, between 1840 and 1940 historians and archaeologists had turned Neolithic spirituality into a mirror of Christianity, but one that emphasized opposite qualities: female instead of male, earth instead of sky, nature instead of civilization.

Significantly, in this respect amateur historians and prehistorians did not so much follow the emerging group of professionals as lead it. In 1898 a medical doctor, John Arthur Goodchild, published *The Light of the West*, a treatise that suggested that the great mother goddess had been the main divinity of the ancient Celtic peoples, and that Glastonbury had been one of her cult centres; he went on to propose that her worship be restored throughout Western civilization.[38] In his unhappy venture as editor of *The Pagan Review*, William Sharp had already shown interest in the same figure as "The Black Madonna"; in the 1990s, as Fiona Macleod, he also subscribed to the concept of a Celtic great goddess.[39] In 1927 another doctor, Robert Briffault, anticipated Renaud by two years, with the argument that most of the world's peoples had once venerated a mother goddess who was believed to have engendered all life, and who was commonly associated with a young god who was her son and consort. He made his own solution to the problem of the virgin mother by asserting that the original meaning of "virgin" was an essential independence of men.[40] Massingham, in the book in which he had confidently attributed the Cotswold long barrows to her cult, added a portrait of her as remaining the enduring spirit of the English countryside, like a Sleeping Beauty awaiting a recall to life: "she is so very fast asleep that, if you could win a way through the rose-maze to her, you would think her dead. But the faintest shadow of a smile is upon her divine face, and all these roses are the candid thoughts of her dreams."[41]

Such a deity remained instinctual to overtly creative writers, who after all had discovered her in the first place. In E.M. Forster's *The Longest Journey*, the main female deity of the ancient people of Wiltshire is suggested as having been "Erda," the German word for the earth, while human happiness is described as "Demeter the goddess rejoicing."[42] Algernon Blackwood's story *The Centaur* (1911) concerns the quest of a man for union with "his great Earth Mother," which culminates in the following ecstasy, in which the goddess meets the Book of Genesis:

> And the forms moved down slowly from their mountainous pedastels; the woods breathed out a sigh; the running water sang; the slopes all murmured through their grass and flowers. For a worshipper, strayed from the outer world of the dead stood within the precincts of their ancient temple. He had passed the Angel with the flaming sword those very dead had set there long ago. The Garden now enclosed him. He had found the heart of the Earth, his mother. Self-realization in the perfect union with Nature was fulfilled. He knew the Great Atonement.[43]

It remained a parallel literary cliche to identify the feminine, including the divine feminine, with the moon or with the night sky in general, and, as in the case of the Earth Mother, there were writers vivid enough to keep the image invested with real vigour. One was D.H. Lawrence, who explored it twice, in different moods. In *The Rainbow* (1915) the approach is sensuous and incorporative. At one point the heroine finds herself looking at the full moon and feeling as if she is literally drawing it into herself: "her body opened wide like a quivering anemone, a soft dilated invitation touched by the moon ... she wanted more, more communion with the moon, consummation." At another she lies on her back as her lover enters her, gazing at the sky above and "it was as if the stars were lying with her and entering the unfathomable darkness of her womb, fathoming her at last."[44]

Six years later, in *Women in Love*, Lawrence's feelings are much more bitter, and the image is one of alienation from the narrator. He makes his hero cry out against "the Great Mother of everything, out of whom proceedeth everything and to whom everything must be rendered up.... He had a horror of the Magna Mater, she was detestable." The man expresses this anger against womankind by making futile efforts to shatter the reflection of a full moon, upon a pond, with stones: he calls it the personification of two classical great goddesses, "Cybele" and "the accursed Syria Dea." Later still he refers to women as "the perfect Womb, the bath of birth, to which all men must come," and terms this "horrible."[45]

The image of goddess as moon was in fact the only part of this cluster of symbols that underwent any significant development during the first half of the twentieth century, and not until 1948, with the publication of the first edition of Robert Graves's *The White Goddess*. Using his full tremendous talents as a poet, his excellent knowledge of the Greek and Roman classics, and a rather slighter acquaintance with early Irish and Welsh literature, Graves developed the icon of the universal ancient European deity beyond the point at which it had been left in the 1900s. He took Harrison's imagery of three aspects, and related them to the waxing, full, and waning moon, to represent the one goddess most potently as a bringer of life and death, in her forms as maiden, mother, and crone. He divided her son and consort into two opposed aspects of his own, as god of the waxing and of the waning year, fated to be rivals and combatants for her love. An especially important function of the goddess, for Graves, was that she gave inspiration to poets; she was the muse who operated through myths and dreams, in contrast with rational modes of thought, which Graves identified with patriarchy, Christianity, and industrial modernity.

Two features of *The White Goddess* are especially relevant. The first is that Graves was determined that his readers should not treat it as a personal poetic reverie but as an authentic work of history, an accurate portrait of the old religion. The other is that, like most of the other writers discussed above, he treated his great goddess as a countercultural deity, who stood for values and associations opposed to those dominant in the European cultural world for most of recorded history and especially to those most closely bound up with modernity.

By the time that he wrote, the image of his goddess had been developing for about a 150 years. No temple had been built to her and no public worship accorded, yet she had become one of the principal cultural images of the nineteenth and twentieth centuries. She and the modern age had taken shape together, in polar opposition to each other, and truly she needed no tangible monuments as she existed so firmly in the hearts and minds of poets, novelists, polemicists, and scholars alike; the natural world itself had become her shrine.

NOTES

1. Eric Smith, *A Dictionary of Classical Reference in English Poetry* (Cambridge: Brewer, 1984), and sources cited there under goddess names.
2. For example, by writers as different as Pierre Abelard in the twelfth century, Christine de Pisan in the fifteenth, and Giordano Bruno in the sixteenth.
3. This was based on a personal survey of public architecture in the following sample of cities: Venice, Paris, and London.
4. Notable pictorial examples of it are in Robert Fludd, *Utriusque Cosmi Historia* (Oppenheim, 1617), and Athanasius Kircher, *Oedipus Aegyptiacus* (Rome, 1652).
5. Carolyn Merchant, *The Death of Nature* (San Francisco: Harper Row, 1980).
6. Geoffrey Chaucer, *The Parlement of Briddes*, or *The Assembly of Foules*, II. 295 ff. For the development of the concept, see George D. Economou, *The Goddess Natura in Medieval Literature* (Cambridge: Harvard University Press, 1972).
7. Most relevant for this study have been Keith Thomas, *Man and the Natural World: Changing Attitudes in England 1500–1800* (London: Allen Lane, 1983), 243–268; Sam Smiles, *The Image of Antiquity: Ancient Britain and the Romantic Imagination* (New Haven: Yale University Press, 1994), 21–22; Marjorie Hope Nicholson, *Mountain Gloom and Mountain Glory* (Ithaca: Cornell University Press, 1959), *passim*; C.A. Moore, "The

Return of Nature in English Poetry of the Eighteenth Century," *Studies in Philology* XIV (1917): 243–292.

8. Smith, *Dictionary of Classical Reference.*
9. "I Stood Tip-toe upon a Little Hill," 11.116–122.
10. "Song of Proserpine" (1820), 11.1–5.
11. "Artemis Prologizes," 11.1–6.
12. "Hertha," 11.1–15, in *Songs before Sunrise* (1867).
13. Especially in the *Werke* of Johann Herder, August and Friedrich von Schlegel, and Ludwig Tieck.

14. Eduard Gerhard, *Ober Metroen und Go'tter-Mutter* (Berlin, 1849), 103.
15. Peter J. Ucko, *Anthropomorphic Figurines of Predynastic Egypt and Neolithic Crete with Comparative Material from the Prehistoric Near East and Mainland Greece* (Royal Anthropological Institute Occasional Paper, 1968), 409–410, and sources listed there.
16. Theodore Dent, "Researches among the Cyclades," *Journal of Hellenic Studies* 5 (1884): 42–59.
17. Eduard Piette, "La Station de Brassempouy et les statuettes humaines de la periode glyptique," *L'Anthropologie* 6 (1895): 129–151.
18. R. Bosanquet, "Archaeology in Greece 1900–1901," *Journal of Hellenic Studies* 21 (1901): 334–354. See also M. Salomon Reinach, "La Sculpture en Europe avant les influences Greco-Romaines," *L'Anthropologie* 5 (1894): 15–34, 173–186, 288–305.
19. Arthur J. Evans, *Cretan Pictographs and Prae-Phoenician Script* (Oxford: Ashmolean, 1895), 124–131.
20. A.J. Evans, "The Palace of Knossos," *Annual of the British School at Athens* VIII (1901–1902): 1–124, and IX (1902–1903): 74–94.
21. Sir Arthur Evans, *The Palace of Minos* (London: Macmillan, 1921), vol. 1, 45–52.
22. Charles Henry Hawes and Harriet Boyd Hawes, *Crete: The Forerunner of Greece* (London: Ashmolean, 1909), 135–139; J.D.S. Pendlebury, *The Archaeology of Crete: An Introduction* (London: Methuen, 1939), 273; Charles Picard, *Les Religions prehelleniques* (Paris: Presses Universitaires de France, 1948), 74–80.
23. Especially Martin P. Nilsson, *A History of Greek Religion* (Oxford: Oxford University Press, 1925), 18–33, and *The Minoan-Mycenaean Religion and Its Survival in Greek Religion* (Lund: Gleerup, 1950), 290–394.

24. E.K. Chambers, *The Medieval Stage* (Oxford: Clarendon Press, 1903), vol. 1, 264.
25. Jane Ellen Harrison, *Prolegomena to the Study of Greek Religion* (Cambridge, 1903), 257–321. Republished 1991 (Princeton: Princeton University Press).
26. J.G. Frazer, *Adonis, Attis, Osiris: Studies in the History of Oriental Religion* (London: MacMillan, 1907), 34–36, 105–110, 219–35.
27. J.G. Frazer, *Spirits of the Corn and of the Wild* (London: MacMillan, 1914), vol. 1, 35–91, 129–170.
28. Joseph Dechelette, *Manual d'archeologie prehistorique Celtique et Gallo-Romaine*, vol. 1 (Paris, 1908), 594–596. Reprinted 1913 and 1927 (Paris: Éditions Auguste Picard).
29. E.G., Hawes and Hawes, *Crete*, 135–139; Arthur Bernard Cook, *Zeus: A Study in Ancient Religion* (Cambridge: The University Press, 1914), vol. 1, 776–780; Gilbert Murray, *Four Stages of Greek Religion* (New York: Columbia University Press, 1912), 45–46; Lewis Richard Farnell, *An Outline History of Greek Religion* (London: Duckworth, 1920), 24–36.
30. G.D. Hornblower, "Predynastic figures of Women and Their Successors," *Journal of Egyptian Archaeology* XV (1929): 29–47.
31. E.B. Renaud, "Prehistoric Female figurines from America and the Old World," *Scientific Monthly* 28 (1929): 507–513.
32. Gordon Childe, *The Dawn of European Civilization* (London: Routledge, 1925), 208–224; *The Prehistory of Scotland* (London: Kegan Paul, 1935), 22–105; and *Prehistoric Communities of the British Isles* (London: Chambers, 1940), 46–118; Grahame Clark, *Prehistoric England* (London: Batsford, 1940), 103; O.G.S. Crawford, *Long Barrows of the Cotswolds* (Gloucester: John Bellows, 1925), 23–24.
33. H.J. Massingham, *Wold without End* (London: Cobden-Sanderson, 1932), *passim.*
34. Stuart Piggott, "Ancient British Craftsmen," *Antiquity* 60 (1986): 190.
35. Gillian Varndell, "The Ritual Objects," in *Excavations at Grimes Graves, Norfolk 1972–1976: Fascicule* 3, edited by Ian Longworth et al. (London: British Museum, 1991), 103–106.
36. John Punnett Peters, *Nippur* (New York: G.P. Putnam's Sons, 1898), 141–171.

37. Arthur J. Evans, "The Neolithic Settlement at Knossos and Its Place in the History of Early Aegean Culture," *Man* 1 (1901): 185.
38. Patrick Benham, *The Avalonians* (Glastonbury: Gothic Image, 1993), 15–20.
39. Ibid., 21–43.
40. Robert Briffault, *The Mothers* (London: Allen and Unwin, 1927), Chapter 23.
41. Massingham, *Wold without End*, 171.
42. In chapters 13 and 34.
43. The brief quotation is on p. 345, the long one on p. 263.
44. Quotations are from the Penguin edition, pp. 365 and 516.
45. Quotations from the Penguin edition, pp. 244, 276–280, 348.

CHAPTER 19
The Roots of Feminist Spirituality[1]

Cynthia Eller

In only 30 years, mainly in the United States but increasingly in Europe and the broader English-speaking world, a vibrant religious subculture for women has been created virtually from scratch. Sharing ground with other alternative religions—especially neopaganism and New Age spiritualities—the feminist spirituality movement nevertheless breaks ground of its own, insistently privileging (rather than marginalizing or tokenizing) femaleness.

This feat of religious innovation can be credited to the intermingling of three social trends emerging in the late 1960s and early 1970s: radical (secular) feminism; Jewish and Christian feminism; and neopaganism. Radical feminism gave rise to concerns with religion and spirituality for some women whose experiences with feminism were particularly all encompassing. Jewish and Christian feminism went so far beyond the bounds of orthodoxy in some quarters that a new spirituality became necessary. These two social trends came from outside the domain of alternative religions where feminist spirituality would eventually make its home. But fortuitously, there was already an alternative religious presence in America that seemed nearly tailor-made for spiritual feminists' needs: neopaganism. Recently imported from Britain (though there were parallel, independent occult movements in the United States), neopaganism was not at the outset an explicitly feminist religion. But neopaganism quickly attracted women who later became feminists, and it eventually attracted feminists outright. Though feminist spirituality is nothing if not syncretistic—borrowing elements from religions and spiritualities worldwide—its earliest and still most important base is American neopaganism.

SECULAR FEMINISM

For some women in the late 1970s, the journey from secular feminism to feminist spirituality was direct and simple: Feminism precipitated such deep and comprehensive changes in consciousness that it already functioned as spirituality. A sufficient change in the quantity and scope of secular feminism became a qualitative change to religious feminism. This pattern of entry into spirituality through radical feminism was particularly marked in the lesbian community, where for many women religion came as an unexpected but natural outgrowth of their experiments in radical feminism. One of these experiments of the 1970s was *Womanspirit*, a magazine published by a small collective in Oregon from 1974 to 1984 that served as a weathervane for the early feminist spirituality movement. Though not limited to lesbian separatists, it was from the lesbian community that the greatest energy for *Womanspirit* came. That spirituality was for these women an acquired language rather than a mother tongue is perhaps evident in the fact that, according to Carol Christ, early contributors to *Womanspirit* hesitated to speak of goddess (1987:49).

For other women of the same era, feminism was not tantamount to a religious conversion experience, and did not naturally present itself as having spiritual depths. But a feminist perspective that began by asking why little girls had to wear pink and big girls had to wear high heels segued naturally into one that asked why God was a man and women's religious experiences went unnoticed. Jean Mountaingrove, one of the founders of *Womanspirit*, describes the process in this way:

> Feminism tells us to trust ourselves. So feminists began experiencing something. We began to believe that, yes indeed, we were discriminated against on the job; we began to see that motherhood was not all it was advertised to be. We began to trust our own feelings, we began to believe in our own orgasms. These were the first things. Now we are beginning to have spiritual experiences and, for the first time in thousands of years, we trust it. (Adler 1979:178)

This belief that feminist spirituality is the natural outcome of feminist questioning has been reified into what might be called the movement's "myth of origins." For when spiritual feminists turn to the topic of the movement's beginnings, they are inclined to talk about consciousness-raising as the seedbed from which feminist spirituality sprang. Consciousness-raising (CR) groups were active in the late 1960s and early 1970s, and were a place where many women first began to think through what being a woman in American culture entailed. The intention, captured in the phrase "consciousness-raising," was to wake women up to an appreciation of their oppression as women and to recruit them for the feminist movement. Early CR groups came together spontaneously, and were first called "rap sessions" or "bitch sessions," only later (around 1970) defining themselves as consciousness-raising groups. By 1972, the National Organization for Women (NOW) along with CR's pioneers, the New York Radical Feminists, took a hand in CR, helping groups to organize, providing a prepared list of discussion topics, and introducing new groups to the CR format. In 1973, probably the height of CR, an estimated 100,000 women in the United States belonged to CR groups (Shreve 1989:5–6, 9–14).

The basic format of CR was to select a discussion topic for the evening, and with the 5 to 15 women present sitting in a circle, each would take turns speaking about the topic. Each woman was to be allowed to talk without interruption, and without criticism or praise from the other women, in an effort to ensure that all felt free to say whatever was on their minds. Oftentimes women discovered that experiences they had believed to be unique to them were shared by many other women, and together they began to explore the reasons why. Some of the experiences women related were spiritual experiences, and one arena that came to be seen as male-defined was established religion.

It is surely true that some women began a process of questioning in CR whose end result was a denunciation of established religions and an attempt to create a religion for women. Yet the place of CR in feminist spirituality's self-understanding has become greater than the experiences of these few women (who do not make up the majority of women in the feminist spirituality movement). Now when spiritual feminists refer to CR, they see it not just as a type of discussion group, but as a ritual group, the natural predecessor of today's feminist spirituality groups. As Carol Christ puts it, "consciousness raising can be seen as a ritual in which stories are shared and sisterhood is affirmed" (1980:127). The tendency to enshrine CR as the birthplace of feminist spirituality reaches its apogee in a casual reference made by Jade, founder of the Reformed Congregation of the Goddess. In a discussion of women's exploration of the history of medieval witchcraft, she remarks, "Back in the consciousness-raising groups, which by now had turned into spirituality groups ..." (1991:11), seeming to indicate that the transition from CR to feminist spirituality was smooth, uncontested, and complete.

That spiritual feminists should hearken back to CR as their birthplace reveals much about how they perceive themselves and their movement. They could have seized upon a different homeland—for instance, feminist political demonstrations or the countercultural movements of the 1960s—but they did not, and their choice of CR is significant. CR was a place where women looked into themselves, into their personal lives, feelings, and reactions, to discover important truths about the status of women generally and the nature of a society that worked to exclude and belittle them. The move was inward, particularistic, but the discoveries were broad, even universal. In choosing CR to encapsulate a myth of their origins, spiritual feminists are seeing in CR a pattern that is essentially that of the religious quest: an inner journey, shared with other seekers, that reveals insights of cosmic importance reaching far beyond the bounds of any one individual's experience.

One final path secular feminists took into feminist religion was somewhat less direct, though it brought them to a similar place as those women who found feminism itself to be a religion, or at least a frame of reference that eventually led to matters of religious importance. This group of women took an excursion through political feminism that proved unsatisfying to them, and they turned to spiritual feminism in the hope of finding something better. Their primary disappointment with political feminism was that it did not seem to provide a position from which they could make broader criticisms of male-dominated society or from which they could create real alternatives. These women did not just want the freedom to do what men had always done (though they generally wanted that, too); they also wanted the freedom to do what women had always done, but to see it valued differently. Further, they wanted not just to use traditional political means for reaching these ends, but to utilize the full range of their capabilities to live in new, self-realized ways as women, and to offer other women the cultural space to do the same.

This branch of the women's movement is sometimes called "cultural feminism," and though the term has taken on pejorative meaning for many, it remains a useful term for distinguishing the quest for political equality and gender-blindness from the effort to incorporate traditionally female values into our common life (Kimball 1980:2–29). These two patterns of feminism are not mutually exclusive, but feminist spirituality encourages attention to the latter, and is frequently less interested in the former, even though it may share these goals as well.

JEWISH AND CHRISTIAN FEMINISM

Some women did not need to be led or driven to religious concerns by the strength of their feminism; their first language was religious, and they were already enmeshed in a religious world. These women were active in established religions when the feminist movement came along, and noticing and criticizing the male slant of these religions was an obvious focus for them. They were merely discovering the sexism in their own backyard—which is where secular feminism was encouraging them to look for it anyway. The first wave of feminism had provided important critiques of male-dominated religion, so religious feminists had foresisters to whom they could appeal. Elizabeth Cady Stanton and friends wrote a feminist exegesis of the Bible in the late 1890s under the title *The Woman's Bible*; in 1893, Matilda Joslyn Gage's *Woman, Church, and State* provided an analysis of how Judaism and Christianity worked to oppress women. Infused with the vitality of a growing women's movement, feminists in traditional religions updated and expanded on this work, and their attacks on sexism gradually gained force and momentum.

Initial feminist onslaughts against established religions demanded specific reforms: women should be admitted into the rabbinate, priesthood, or ministry; hymns and prayer books should use language that included women. But increasingly, larger targets emerged: biblical texts were found to be sexist, religious ethics were seen to fit men's experience and men's interests and not those of women. Eventually, feminists in established religions took on the Big Man himself, the God who was described and invoked in almost exclusively male terms, in spite of theological apologetics that insisted on his ultimate lack of gender. Many feminists felt a sufficiently deep attachment to established religions that they remained within them to work for change. But others came to believe that traditional religions were so laced with patriarchal ideology that the surgery necessary to remove it would end up killing the patient, and, as Mary Daly puts it, they "graduated" from Christianity and religious Judaism (King 1989).

Mary Daly, a brilliant Catholic theologian and an ardent feminist, led the way for many women to matriculate into feminist spirituality after long years as the perennial freshmen of the established religions. In 1971, Daly was invited to be the first woman preacher in Harvard Memorial Church. Her sermon topic was "The Women's Movement: An Exodus Community." She ended her sermon by walking out of the church in protest against it, and inviting the other women present to do likewise. She defended this exodus in her sermon, saying: "We cannot really belong to institutional religion as it exists. It isn't good enough to be token preachers.... Singing sexist hymns, praying to a male god breaks our spirit, makes us less than human. The crushing weight of this tradition, of this power structure, tells us that *we do not even exist*" (King 1989:70).

In an article published in *Commonweal* that same year, Daly advised: "The women's movement will present a growing threat to patriarchal religion less by attacking it than by simply leaving it behind. Few of the leaders in the [women's] movement evince an interest in institutional religion, having recognized it as an instrument of their betrayal" (Daly 1979:57).

This feminist rejection of established religions saw women's oppression in patriarchal religion occurring along many axes—theological, biblical, institutional, and so on—and all of these came in for feminist criticism. But the entire interlocking system of oppressions was finally summed up in a single metaphor: the maleness of God. Mary Daly explains: "If God in 'his' heaven is a father ruling 'his' people, then it is in the 'nature' of things and according to divine plan and the order of the universe that society be male-dominated" (1973:13). It was a matter of some consensus among religious feminists that exclusively male language for God was not in the best interests of women. But those feminists who came to believe that the maleness of God mandated the subordination of women took this one step further. In pointing the finger back at the god of established religions, these feminists said that he was not *a* cause of women's oppression, but *the* cause: the "ultimate prop," the "underlying rationale" (Starhawk 1982:72; Stone 1976:xi). This is in part a social analysis of how the patriarchy operates, but for most of these women, it was also a larger comment on how the world operates. It was not only that a male god happens to be the linchpin of this patriarchal social system, but that religion is always and inevitably the distilled essence of what a culture holds valuable.

This being the case, what is a feminist to do? Well, if male gods support male power, women must stop worshipping male gods. If the patriarchy is built on the foundation of patriarchal religion, male dominance will not be eroded until the foundation is razed. But more than this, a non-patriarchal society cannot exist until a foundation has been prepared for it, a foundation that must of necessity be religious. This is the true source of the surge of religious feminists into the feminist spirituality movement. Some feminists gave up on traditional religions when they decided they were too sexist to be tolerated or reformed, but were not inspired to sashay into the world of alternative religions. They were just tired of religion altogether. But for women who came to believe that religion is necessarily a culture's building blocks, the repertoire on which it can play variations but no new themes, religion could not be abandoned. It had to be transformed.

NEOPAGANISM AND FEMINISM

When feminists made their way toward an alternative religion for women, their initial point of contact was with neopaganism or witchcraft. Feminist spirituality's contact with neopaganism has left its mark on every aspect of feminist spirituality: its thealogy, ritual, and social organization. Indeed, many spiritual feminists happily call themselves neopagans or witches, though their particular feminist adaptations of neopaganism set them apart from the mainstream of that religion. Feminist spirituality and mainstream neopaganism coexist and overlap, usually (but not always) quite happily, but they are not the same thing.

Neopaganism in America is a movement organized (or not) in much the same way as feminist spirituality. Small groups of practitioners join together on a regular basis, though probably as many practise alone. There are large festivals and retreats, magazines and newsletters, bookstores and occult supply shops, and one effort at an umbrella organization (the Covenant of the Goddess), which serves as a clearinghouse of information and a badge of respectability (and tax-exempt status) for the neopagan community, particularly those who define themselves as witches. As with feminist spirituality, variety is the order of the day, and there are numerous schools of thought and types of practice available for the interested seeker, and plenty of interaction between neopaganism and other types of alternative spirituality. The number of people who are affiliated with neopaganism is difficult to estimate, since there is nothing remotely like an official membership roll. However, in the early 1990s, in an attempt to quantify the movement, Aidan Kelly extrapolated from book sales, mailing lists, and festival attendance to come up with a figure of somewhere between 50,000 to 100,000 "serious adherents" of neopaganism (Kelly 1993; Denfeld 1995:299).

Neopagans believe they are reviving (and sometimes creating anew) ancient nature religions. They usually trace their genealogy to Europe, and sometimes even more narrowly to Britain. Many call their religion "witchcraft" as well as paganism, since they believe that when paganism was forced underground by the Christian church, it was passed in secret from parent to child (or believer to believer) as witchcraft.[2] In spite of its insistence that it dates to ancient times, neopaganism also has a more recent history, dating to 1954, when Gerald Gardner published *Witchcraft Today*. Gardner was a British folklorist, nudist, and occultist, who after his retirement in 1936 joined an occult society with connections to the Rosicrucians and Theosophists. He says that he was initiated into Wicca (or witchcraft) by an old woman, Dorothy Clutterbuck, in 1939, she having herself been initiated by someone else in a line reaching back, presumably, to the Middle Ages if not further. Gardner wrote one book on witchcraft under a pen name, and after the last of the Witchcraft Acts were repealed in Britain in 1951, he wrote two more books in his own name, *Witchcraft Today* and *The Meaning of Witchcraft*. The witchcraft he described included the worship of a goddess and a god, the officiation of a priestess, and communal rituals involving dancing, nudity, chanting, and meditation that took place on the solstices, equinoxes, and the four cross-quarter days that fall between them (Adler 1979:60–66, 80–84; Purkiss 1996:37–58). All these forms are still common among neopagans today. Gardner himself initiated many individuals into a neopagan practice that came to be called "Gardnerian witchcraft" after him. Some of Gardner's apprentices split from him to create different witchcraft "traditions," and other sects of witchcraft sprang up with little connection to Gardner, giving rise to the tremendous variety found in modern neopaganism.

Gardner is what many neopagans would call "a hereditary witch," claiming to have fallen heir to a tradition of witchcraft that existed prior to the twentieth century. Those who say they are hereditary witches are rare; some practitioners note that their families passed along interesting bits of folklore, but nothing akin to the comprehensive religion that Gardnerian witchcraft purports to be. But especially in its early years, hereditary witchcraft was very important to neopagans as proof that the religion they practised had a real tradition behind it. Wiccan lineages and ancient practices are of less and less importance nowadays, as neopagans feel more secure in the religions they have created (or maybe only more certain that their hereditary claims will be disproved). Modern witches accept and sometimes even revel in the novelty of what they create. Still, the lure of the ancient calls to them. Gwydion Pendderwen does an excellent job of summing up how most neopagans feel about the newness of their religion:

> What has come down [from the Old Religion, or paganism] is so minimal, it could be thrown out without missing it. Many groups have received nothing through apostolic succession and do not miss it. Objectively, there's very little that has gone from ancient to modern in direct succession. But subjectively, an awful lot is ancient. It is drawn from ancient materials. It represents archetypal patterns. (Adler 1979:88)

Neopagans (who sometimes refer to themselves simply as pagans) agree on little, and count it as one of the advantages of their chosen religion that they do not have to *agree*. Still, many neopagans have tried to define just what holds them together, and the thing they mention most consistently is nature worship. Selena Fox, a priestess who heads up Circle Sanctuary, a pagan retreat centre in rural Wisconsin, offers this description of Wicca:

> The Wiccan religion is a nature religion with roots that go back to pre-Christian Europe. It's a religion that focuses on communing with the divine through nature.... Wiccans worship the "life force" in all people and animals, revere nature and harm no one. We believe that all of life is sacred and we see ourselves as part of a community of life forms on the planet. (Lux 1988)

What Fox doesn't mention is that most neopagans also worship a goddess. This is often coupled with worship of a god, and their gender polarity is frequently seen as expressing an important truth about the cosmos. But following Gardner, the goddess is usually given some kind of primacy,[3] and in some neopagan circles women's presence is required for rituals to occur.

The appeal of neopaganism to feminists searching for religious alternatives must have been tremendous: Here were people already worshipping a goddess, naming women as priestesses, and talking about "the feminine." There were no elaborate rites of entry, if one wished to avoid them; groups were small and intimate, leaving ample space for individual experience; and in a religion with no central headquarters, religious hierarchies were unlikely to get in the way. But well before feminists discovered neopaganism en masse, the word "witch" entered the feminist vocabulary in other, highly politicized terms. In New York on Halloween of 1968, a collective of women named themselves WITCH, an acronym standing for "Women's International Terrorist Conspiracy from Hell." This first group was followed by others across the United States, all of which used the same acronym, but different names to indicate the targets of their rage: "Women Infuriated at Taking Care of Hoodlums," "Women Incensed at Telephone Company Harassment," "Women Indentured to Traveler's [insurance company] Corporate Hell," and so on. These first feminist witches did not gather to worship nature, but to crush the patriarchy, and to do so in witty, flamboyant, and theatrical ways. They engineered various political actions, drawing on the witch theme. Though never pretending to be a spiritual group, and probably unaware of the neopagan revival in America, WITCH anticipated several of the motifs of the feminist spirituality movement that was to follow upon the meeting of feminism and neopaganism. In its manifesto, WITCH justified its existence by citing its political mission ("witches and gypsies were the original guerrillas and resistance fighters against oppression"); it posited a long-dead Golden Age ("the oldest culture of all ... a truly cooperative society"); named nature as one of the patriarchy's primary victims (along with human society); and rested its social analysis on the single cornerstone of male domination ("the Imperialist Phallic Society"). It advocated creativity and independence, and exulted in the innovative use of all manner of media to communicate personal and political views (Morgan 1970:538–539; 1977:77). But the most significant aspect of WITCH was its choice of central symbol: the witch. By choosing this symbol, feminists were identifying themselves with everything women were taught not to be: ugly, aggressive, independent, and malicious. Feminists took this symbol and moulded it—not into the fairy tale "good witch," but into a symbol of female power, knowledge, independence, and martyrdom.

This latter association with witchcraft, that of martyrdom, was particularly important to early feminists. Mary Daly in her 1973 book *Beyond God the Father*, and Andrea Dworkin in 1974 with *Woman Hating*, laid the groundwork for a feminist martyrology by researching the witch persecutions of the Middle Ages and labelling them "gynocide," the purposeful murder of women. This theme was further developed in Daly's 1978 work *Gyn/Ecology*, in which the witch burnings were portrayed as an instance of the patriarchal "Sado-Ritual Syndrome," a pattern of the abuse of women that Daly locates cross-culturally and trans-historically. This identification of women with witchcraft was not an explicitly religious one. Women were not named witches because they worshipped a goddess in circles in the woods or because they made herbal charms to encourage prophetic dreaming. Women were named witches because they refused to submit to demeaning and limiting roles, even knowing that this rebellion might literally cost them their lives.

Witchcraft was fast becoming a feminist symbol, even a religiously charged one, dealing as it did with ultimate commitment and ultimate value. But it was a symbol without a practice. It still remained for someone to lower the drawbridge and let religious neopaganism out and feminists in. The first to take on this task was Zsuzsanna Budapest, the closest thing feminist spirituality has to a founder. Budapest grew up in Hungary and took her city's name as her own when as a teenager she left for the West to escape the failing Hungarian revolution. Later, after immigrating to the United States and leaving her marriage, she moved to Los Angeles and became very active in the women's movement: organizing protests, attending meetings, helping to form an anti-rape squad. But, like others, she came to believe that the women's movement needed a women's religion, and she proposed to give it one. In this, Budapest did not come without resources: She claimed to be the heir of a witchcraft tradition at least 800 years old, inherited from her mother, Masika Szilagyi. According to Budapest, Masika was initiated into witchcraft by Victoria, a household servant, who in addition to teaching Masika psychic skills, took her into the woods at night to meet with groups of witches who invoked the goddess, sang of ancient shamans, and spat into the fire. Masika communed with the dead in her dreams, and could speak ancient Egyptian while in a trance, a talent Budapest attributes to Masika's previous incarnation as a priestess of Hathor in ancient Egypt (Kimball 1980:238; Adler 1979:76–77). In her *Holy Book of Women's Mysteries*, Budapest includes materials she received from her mother, including her "book of superstitions," "book of dreams," "book of cures," and "book of sorrows." They are a treasure trove of eastern European folk wisdom, including such gems as: "If a bird shits on you, you will have good luck all that day if you don't wipe it off until the following day"; "If you bang your elbow into a corner, an unexpected visitor will soon arrive"; and "If you are chased by wild animals in your dreams, it simply means you ate too much dinner" (1989:258–268).

If these provided the seeds for Budapest's women's religion, the sprouting and blossoming were strictly her doing, and that of her feminist sisters. Budapest's experiments in feminist witchcraft began in 1971, when she and a few friends celebrated the winter solstice together. They named themselves the Susan B. Anthony Coven No. 1 to stress their commitment to feminism—and, it would seem, to express their hope that others would follow in their footsteps, adding covens numbers 2, 3, 4, et seq. And others did follow, though with names of their own: the Amelia Earhart Coven in New York, the Elizabeth Gould Davis Coven in Florida, the Sojourner Truth Coven in the Catskills, the Jane Addams Coven in Chicago, and the Elizabeth Cady Stanton Coven in Orange County, California (Adler 1979:119). The Susan B. Anthony Coven itself grew rapidly, by its founders' reports, from the 6 women who met at the 1971 winter solstice to 700 initiated members just nine years later (Budapest 1979:82). Women came and went, and there were never 700 women meeting at one time, but it is reported that Budapest led rituals in the 1970s where attendance was well over 100 (Rhiannon 1983).

Though Zsuzsanna Budapest was a groundbreaking figure in the feminist move to neopaganism, she was not alone. In addition to the women working with her, there were other women across the country building bridges between feminism and paganism: some by reaching out to existing Wiccan groups in their areas, some by radicalizing the covens of which they were already members, some by creating new groups with new traditions. By the mid-1970s, resources were beginning to become available in the women's community, and feminists were able to invent their religion secure in the knowledge that there was a groundswell of feminist energy behind them. Interest in witchcraft as women's persecution history broadened into inquiry into ancient goddess worship. The publication of Merlin Stone's *When God Was a Woman* in 1976, a study of representations of prehistoric goddesses woven together with a story of their overthrow in historical times, gave the feminist Wicca movement credibility in new quarters, and inspired more women to search out the supposed surviving remnants of ancient goddess worship in neopaganism. Feminist imagery and politics was rapidly becoming feminist spirituality, as women went beyond talking about witches and goddesses as symbols of female power, and started to become them and worship them.

Yet the meeting of feminists and neopagans was not one big happy family reunion, with everyone rushing deliriously into each other's arms. The neopagan movement was small, and feminists entered in numbers large enough to make a real impact. Moreover, they did not usually enter humbly and meekly, asking if they might please be initiated into the wise ways of the Witches. Quite the contrary, they flung open the doors, squared their shoulders, and swaggered in, ready to rearrange the furniture. And in spite of substantial areas of shared interest, there were real differences between the newly anointed feminist witches and neopagans of older vintage.

The first point of conflict was that feminists by and large had no interest in sharing their circles with men, and precious little interest in worshipping a god of any sort. With their palate not yet conditioned to savour the new tastes of "traditional" neopaganism, they often had little patience for the measured pageantry and role-playing that characterized some neopagan rituals or for the encyclopedic lists of greater and lesser divinities and spirits. They wanted to worship a goddess—a big one, bigger than the God of patriarchy—and they wanted to worship themselves through her. For many neopagans, this was anathema. Polytheism and gender duality were considered essential parts of witchcraft: if true magic were to happen, both male and female deities had to be invoked and, according to some, both women and men had to be present, fulfilling their gender-prescribed tasks. A further conflict was that most neopagans valued secrecy, partly out of fear of persecution, but also out of a love of the concept of hidden lore, of mystical truths that could only be revealed to the initiated few. Feminist witches, in contrast, tended to be more evangelical, wanting to get the good word out to their sisters. Far from insisting on long periods of training and gradual initiation into higher mysteries, feminist witches hearkened back to a phrase from the WITCH manifesto: "You are a witch by being female ..." They encouraged one another to form covens of the utterly inexperienced, to make things up as they went along, and to publish accounts of what worked for them so that others could draw on their experience (Adler 1979:171–222).

The downside of the feminist/neopagan combination notwithstanding, overall the combination has proved to be a productive one. The success of the relationship owes much to Starhawk, a witch, feminist, and widely read pagan author. Starhawk found witchcraft and feminism around the same time, and though she saw them as having a real compatibility, she was not specifically drawn into one as the result of her interest in the other, as many women were. Having already been exposed to neopaganism, she was introduced to feminist witchcraft in the early 1970s by Zsuzsanna Budapest (Budapest 1989:xiv). Starhawk's covens are not all separatist (men are allowed to participate and be initiated), but her writings are insistently feminist, and it is clear that she regards witchcraft's attitude toward women and the female to be among its greatest strengths. In many ways, Starhawk has served as a translator and mediator between feminists and neopaganism: she has worked with gender polarity, but evolved away from it; she has developed convincing thealogical justifications for conceiving of goddess as both monotheistic and polytheistic; she has carved out a central, indisputable place for women without excluding men; and she has praised flexibility and creativity while upholding the value of things taken to be traditionally pagan.

Today there is considerably less friction in the United States between feminist witchcraft and the broader neopagan movement than there was initially. There are several reasons for this, one of which is that over the past 20 years of cohabitation, feminist witches have become acculturated to the neopagan world. Things that they initially found odd or off-putting—ceremonial tools and language, polytheism, male deities—have become familiar, even beloved to them, and in some cases have been incorporated into their practice. And for neopagans, feminists are no longer angry alien infiltrators in a settled world of happy, naked, dancing nature-worshippers; they have become a part of the scenery. Finally, controversy between the two parties has lessened in part because the feminists won their right to the goddess. By sheer force of numbers and enthusiasm, their success drowned out all but the most hardened opposition. Neopaganism flourishes today, perhaps more feminist and less hierarchical in flavour than it was before, and feminist witchcraft flourishes alongside and to some extent within it (Jade 1991:64).

In the feminist spirituality movement today, there is a subtle trend away from identifying oneself as a witch. Partly this is a transition into a more free-form type of spirituality precipitated by a growing conviction on the part of feminists that what they are doing counts as religion in its own right, without the added status conferred by an affiliation with neopaganism. As Anne Carson notes in the preface to her bibliography on feminist spirituality, "As the 1980s progress there seems to be less of an interest in Witchcraft per se among feminists, at least in terms of ritual practice, as we begin to leave behind one traditional structure in order to create our own visions and philosophies" (Carson 1986:9). Witchcraft has acted as a launching pad for a spiritual movement that is now far more diverse, reaching far beyond neopaganism, into Native American religions, other world religions, New Age practices, and even—sporadically—Jewish and Christian feminism.

NOTES

1. This chapter appeared in an earlier form in *Living in the Lap of the Goddess: The Feminist Spirituality Movement in America* by Cynthia Eller, published by Crossroads Press in 1993, and appears in this book with the permission of the publisher.
2. Most neopagans believe that the witchcraft persecuted by the Christian church in sixteenth- and seventeenth-century Europe was in fact this underground pre-Christian religion. Far from having the malicious intent associated with medieval witches, modern witches say that they—like their persecuted predecessors—are bending unseen forces

for the good of all. Time and again they stress that they are not Satanists. At a workshop on "Feminist Wicca Philosophy" (Feminist Spiritual Community retreat, Maine, June 1990), Delores Cole gave a fairly typical disclaimer, saying that one cannot have Satanism without Christianity, that "Satanism is the death side of Christianity," and thus bears no relation to paganism.

3. Some neopagans worship no deities or a goddess alone, but I have never encountered any who worship only a male god.

REFERENCES

Adler, Margot. 1979. *Drawing Down the Moon*. Boston: Beacon.

Budapest, Zsuzsanna. 1979. *The Holy Book of Women's Mysteries*, vol. 1. Oakland: Susan B. Anthony Coven No. 1.

———. 1989. *The Holy Book of Women's Mysteries*. Berkeley: Wingbow.

Carson, Anne. 1986. *Feminist Spirituality and the Feminine Divine*. Trumansburg: Crossing.

Christ, Carol P. 1980. *Diving Deep and Surfacing*. Boston: Beacon.

———. 1987. *Laughter of Aphrodite*. San Francisco: Harper & Row.

Daly, Mary. 1973. *Beyond God the Father*. Boston: Beacon.

———. 1979. "After the Death of God the Father: Women's Liberation and the Transformation of Christian Consciousness." In *Womanspirit Rising: A Feminist Reader in Religion*, edited by Carol P. Christ and Judith Plaskow, 53–62. San Francisco: Harper & Row.

Denfeld, Rene. 1995. *The New Victorians*. New York: Warner.

Jade. 1991. *To Know*. Oak Park: Delphi.

Kelly, Aidan. 1993. "An Update on Neopagan Witchcraft in America." In *Perspectives on the New Age*, edited by James Lewis, 136–151. Albany: State University of New York.

Kimball, Gayle, ed. 1980. *Women's Culture*. Metuchen: Scarecrow.

King, Ursula. 1989. *Women and Spirituality*. New York: New Amsterdam.

Lux, Anne Marie. 1988. "Witches Nothing to Be Scared of." *Sunday Gazette* (Janesville, WI, October 30).

Morgan, Robin. 1970. *Sisterhood Is Powerful*. New York: Random House.

———. 1977. *Going Too Far.* New York: Random House.

Purkiss, Diane. 1996. *The Witch in History.* New York: Routledge.

Rhiannon. 1983. Interview with author.

Shreve, Anita. 1989. *Women Together, Women Alone.* New York: Fawcett Columbine.

Starhawk. 1982. *Dreaming the Dark: Magic, Sex, and Politics.* Boston: Beacon.

Stone, Merlin. 1976. *When God Was a Woman.* New York: Harcourt, Brace, Jovanovich.

CHAPTER 20

The Colonial Mythology of Feminist Witchcraft

Chris Klassen

feminist witches construct (post)colonial identities for themselves through their interpretations of the history of Western societies. To make this statement may seem counterintuitive. How can feminist witches see themselves as a colonized people struggling to create a post-colonial world? They are, after all, predominantly White, middle-class women. What do I mean when I say their identities are (post)colonial? I mean, very simply, that feminist witches see themselves as the remnants of a society that was conquered and colonized by patriarchal forces, and persecuted when attempting to maintain its way of life. This article explores the construction of this (post)colonial identity within feminist witchcraft.

Feminist witchcraft, according to my use of the term, includes two major traditions, both of which first developed in the United States during the 1970s. The first of these is Dianic witchcraft, started by Zsuzsanna

Budapest. In an interview with Gayle Kimball, the Hungarian-born Budapest claims that "Dianic witches were in my family something like eight hundred years."[1] However, it was her encounter with both radical feminism and Wicca in the United States that Budapest used to shape that hereditary witchcraft into something more contemporary and relevant for today's women. She draws upon theories and practices of separatism and essential lesbianism, universal goddess imagery, and rage due to a long history of women's oppression best typified by the European witch hunts.

The second feminist witchcraft tradition is the Reclaiming Tradition, started by Starhawk and other San Francisco pagans as a combination of witchcraft, feminism, and environmental activism. Starhawk, feminist witch and political activist, first contributed to the development of feminist witchcraft with the publication of *The Spiral Dance* in 1979. This text has become, and remains to this day, one of the primary introductory books for those interested in witchcraft and goddess religion. As a highly popular and prolific writer, Starhawk has contributed a number of significant concepts to the pool of resources for feminist witches. Most notable are her understandings of power, the self, and gender, along with a clear articulation of a world view that incorporates immanence, interconnection, and community. Though I recognize that there are other practitioners of witchcraft who name themselves feminist witches and do not follow either of these traditions, for the sake of access to the written resources, these two traditions will be the focus of my study.

Throughout my article I will be referring to the technologies of identity formation that feminist witches utilize—opposition against patriarchal religion and culture and speculation in the sense of creating stories to stand in for missing or inadequately empowering history. Technologies of identity, as I am defining the term, involve strategies for crafting a sense of self and community. Technologies of opposition are strategies for reversing existing realities (for example, reversing binary values or opposing the very construction of binary categories), while technologies of speculation are strategies to invent new realities (for example, telling stories that have previously been unheard). These technologies can encompass both theoretical strategies (such as shaping discourse in such a way as to defy traditional norms) and practical strategies (such as participating in ritual practice that is written and performed by women). As technologies, they are human inventions that work to shape human cultures. Both technologies of opposition and technologies of speculation are essential aspects of feminist witches' identity formation. In this article, I focus on the (post)colonial identities constructed by these technologies of identity.

The most common version of the colonial stories that feminist witches tell about their place in the world is that long ago peaceful and egalitarian goddess-centred societies flourished in prehistoric Europe. These societies were conquered by patriarchal, warlike societies. The patriarchal nomads took over the European lands and infiltrated the local cultures. European cultures became more warlike and patriarchal as the goddess lost power. Eventually, with the Christianization of Europe, patriarchy and anti-goddess, anti-woman sentiments came to a climax. In order to maintain its position of authority over the people, Christianity (or the states associated with Christian societies) persecuted anyone it saw as threatening, including those still holding to the old religion. This old religion, now named witchcraft, went underground until the modern day when religious tolerance was more widespread. Today feminist witches are fighting for a return to the values of the "Utopian" peaceful past—the true heritage of European peoples. They are fighting the oppression that patriarchy has brought to women in particular but also to other disenfranchised groups.

This is not just a story about colonization and struggle. It is also a Utopian story: it suggests that there was once a Golden Age, and if we could only regain the value of that past, we will once again live in harmony and love. The Utopian elements of feminist witches' account of prehistory are so strong that it may seem more logical to focus on Utopian identity than (post)colonial identity. To do so, however, would be to ignore a crucial element of this construction. Feminist witches align themselves with other colonized peoples of the world; this alignment says something about how they see themselves as White women in a context of European colonial history and White privilege. The parallels are blatant. Budapest claims, "When they ran out of witches, the Christians looked to the 'savages' of Africa and became slave traffickers. Then onward to the New World, where they became Indian killers."[2] Though her conception of the causes and contexts of enslavement and

European and American colonialism is simplistic—and highly debatable—the association clarifies feminist witches' understanding of the witch hunts as colonial history. Starhawk suggests,

> To be a woman, to be a person of color, to be a tribal person in the dismembered world, to be among the dispossessed and disempowered, is to suffer continual loss. We suffer loss precisely because we have something to lose: a heritage, the rich gifts of a culture, a way of being.[3]

Hilary Valentine writes,

> From the burning of the Witches in Europe, to the murder of countless native people who would not "convert" to Christianity, to the outlawing of the drum voices of the kidnapped Africans under slavery, nature-based religions, along with their wisdom, their stories, their medicinal traditions, and their spiritual practices, have been repressed and, in some cases, driven underground.[4]

Feminist witches' account of prehistory and the early modern witch hunts is a Utopian, but (post)colonial, account of who they are as a group of people. How is the (post)colonial story constructed? Thanks to the work of Marija Gimbutas, a feminist archaeologist who worked on Old European civilizations (Neolithic Europe and Asia Minor, 7000 BCE to 3000 BCE), theories of patriarchal invasion of egalitarian civilizations percolate through various feminist circles. Through her archaeological research, Gimbutas has come to the conclusion that there was a society of goddess-worshippers who put more power in the hands of women than later patriarchal societies, particularly the Indo-European group(s) who eventually colonized Europe and Asia Minor. Gimbutas portrays these goddess-worshipping, Old European societies as peaceful and egalitarian: While they gave greater power to women than patriarchal societies, they did not deny men power. Gimbutas writes, in her influential book, *Goddesses and Gods of Old Europe*,

> In Old Europe the world of myth was not polarized into female and male as it was among the Indo-European and many other nomadic and pastoral peoples of the steppes. Both principles were manifest side by side. The male divinity in the shape of a young man or a male animal appears to affirm and strengthen the forces of the creative and active female. Neither is subordinate to the other; by complementing one another, their power is doubled.[5]

According to Gimbutas, the Old Europeans settled in fertile valleys and lacked military fortifications. As such they eventually became susceptible to invasion by patriarchal nomadic people—particularly the group Gimbutas names the Kurgans, after a particular type of burial mound found in the Russian steppes where these invaders are thought to have originated. The Kurgan people were Indo-European, and their invasion into Old Europe instigated an immense change in culture, social structuring, and language in European societies. Gimbutas argues,

> The Old European and the Kurgan cultures were completely opposite; Old Europe: sedentary-horticultural, dwelling in large agglomerations; Kurgan: mobile, living in small villages. The first—matrilinear, egalitarian, peaceful; the second—patriarchal, ranked, and warlike. The respective ideologies produced different sets of gods and symbols. The Old European ideology was focused on the eternal aspects of birth, death, and regeneration, symbolized by the feminine principle, a Mother Creatrix. The patriarchal Kurgan ideology (also known from comparative Indo-European mythology) was centered on the virile male, heroic warrior gods of the shining and thunderous sky. The Old Europeans put no emphasis on dangerous weapons, whereas the Kurgans (like all historically known Indo-Europeans) glorified the sharp blade.[6]

Gimbutas's theories of Old Europe and the Kurgan invasion set up a framework within which a technology of opposition can flourish. This technology of opposition is the construction of a dualistic structure of "us" (feminists, women, goddess-worshippers) versus "them" (patriarchs, men, God-worshippers). The goddess societies are peaceful, egalitarian, and focused on the "feminine" virtues of nurturance and compassion. The patriarchal conquerors are warlike, hierarchical, and focused on "masculine" virtues of aggression and competition. This construction allows for a clear delineation between the good and the bad, the victims and the victimizers. It provides a distinct enemy that can then be blamed for the destruction of peace and equality between the sexes.

Many feminist scholars criticize Gimbutas's construction of prehistoric goddess societies. Archaeologists Margaret Conkey and Ruth Tringham argue that the diverse figurines found in various European locales should not be bunched together to represent one great goddess. This critique is based on their concern for valid feminist archaeological practices that try to avoid placing modern interpretations of gender on prehistoric peoples, as well as a concern with the glorification of fertility, "perpetuating an equation of women with nature."[7] The problem, as Conkey and Tringham understand it, is that in Gimbutas's account

> "Gender asymmetry" is thus taken as an essentialized normative phenomenon, conceptualized only in terms of a male/female bipolarity that forecloses on the possibilities for any other possible genders or gender systems. The origins of this male/female sex/gender asymmetry and the origins of patriarchy become a "narrative of closure," which shuts down our imaginative powers about the many ways in which people could have lived, related to each other, or, in this particular case, responded to the Indo-European presence, itself a contested historical account.[8]

Using figurines found by archaeologists to maintain a male/female sex/gender asymmetry—either as evidence of a parthenogenetic goddess as the base of a woman-centred society or as evidence of patriarchal annihilation when these figurines disappear—denies the multiple possibilities that these figurines could represent. Conkey and Tringham point out the great diversity of images found in archaeological digs in what Gimbutas names Old Europe. Gimbutas's interpretation of ancient figurines as pointing to the worship of a Great Mother goddess denies the significance of male figurines or the evidence that, according to Conkey and Tringham, "by and large, most of the Paleolithic imagery of humans-humanoids cannot readily be identified as male *or* female."[9]

Gimbutas's construction of a dualism between patriarchal invaders and goddess societies is also problematized in well-known feminist witch Starhawk's account, whereby patriarchy is not blamed on an external force but is seen as due to social changes within the goddess societies. Starhawk does draw heavily on Marija Gimbutas in her conception of a "Utopian" prehistory. However, unlike Gimbutas who blames the Kurgan people for the conquest of goddess societies and the bringing of patriarchy to Europe, Starhawk tends to see the process as more gradual, with all people involved holding some responsibility. She suggests that "patriarchy" is less to be blamed on one group of people and more to be attributed to shifting social situations. She writes,

> The story of the transition to patriarchy is the history of the maximization of power. It came about through choices made by both men and women to preserve what they saw as their best interests. Although we can see with hindsight what each change led to, or imagine other choices, they could not.[10]

It is with the Christianization of Europe, though, that Starhawk is much more clear that the old religion was conquered by the new religion and "witches" were persecuted to maintain Christian religious and political dominance.

In portraying the early modern witch hunts as a "women's holocaust" and/or an attempt by the Christian churches and states to eradicate the old religion, feminist witches once again set up a dualism between the victims and victimizers, those who are oppressed and those who are oppressing. This again allows for a clear construction of "the enemy" whom one can fight against.

In *The Witch in History*, Diane Purkiss explores a variety of representations of "the witch" from contemporary feminist witches to historians and literary critics, to early modern women themselves. For feminists, says Purkiss, the myth of the witch, along with the myth of the "Burning Times," has become a foundation for opposing patriarchy. She writes:

> The myth has become important, not because of its historical truth, but because of its mythic significance. What is that significance? It is a story with clear oppositions. Everyone can tell who is innocent and who guilty, who is good and who bad, who is oppressed and who the oppressor. It offers to identify oppression, to make it noticeable. It legitimates identification of oppression with powerful institutions, and above all with Christianity. This is, above all, a narrative of the Fall, of paradise lost. It is a story about how perfect our lives would be—how perfect we women would be, patient, kind, self-sufficient—if it were not for patriarchy and its violence.[11]

Part of the problem with the myth of the Burning Times, according to Purkiss, is that the focus is on the body (woman's body which all women are to relate to) with little emphasis on the voice or mind (the early modern women's voice or mind, that is). Thus radical feminists tell stories about torture and killing—acts against the body—without telling us what those women said or without conceding that early modern women might not have thought about the issue of patriarchy or of witchcraft in quite the same way as twentieth-century women do. Purkiss writes, "History indeed becomes hystery when the unspeaking body is the only site which can be recollected, and when events become reduced to occasions for extended fantasies about other people's traumas."[12] In this sense radical feminists draw on the twentieth-century preoccupation with trauma, and attempt to paint the witch hunts in light of twentieth-century history, namely the Holocaust.

> Attempts to inflate the number of women who died in witch-persecutions into the millions may also reflect the Holocaust paradigm, since there is little actual evidence for such figures. Worryingly, this goes two million better than the Holocaust, as if a competition is afoot, and at times there does seem to be a race on to prove that women have suffered more than victims of racism or genocide (as though women have not been *among* the victims of racism and genocide). Finally, the very stress on *burning* itself seems to allude to the crematoria, although it may also point to Dresden and Hiroshima. Radical feminist witches *always* burn; they are never hanged.[13]

The construction of the Burning Times as a period of mass genocide analogous to the Holocaust is especially clear in the writings of Budapest. She personalizes the story by relating that "my family has painful records of how my ancestors were tortured and killed: how they had to dig their own graves and lie in them, buried alive, only their faces showing, which the Christians then bashed in with iron rods. My heart is filled with eternal distrust toward a religion that sanctioned that genocide."[14]

For Budapest, the horrors of the witch hunts have not fully ended. She suggests that "many of the archaic and repressive laws resulting from this period of mass hysteria are still on the books, and the persecution of the Goddess's children has not stopped to this day." Furthermore, unlike with the Jewish Holocaust, "no one has called for an accounting. No witches have been avenged through trials of accountability such as those for the Jews at Nuremberg. There has been no apparent opposition to the wave of hatred which caused the flesh of the mothers to be burned."[15]

The story of patriarchal conquest and oppression in feminist witches' construction of identity is shaped by colonial and post-colonial discourse. In feminist witchcraft this colonial and post-colonial discourse is wedded to Utopian notions of the ancient past and hope for the future. For many feminist witches, particularly those leaning toward radical feminism such as Budapest, pre-colonial times were idyllic, colonial times are oppressive, and post-colonial times will be idyllic once again. Patriarchy is seen as the universal colonizing agent. These feminist witches suggest, either implicitly or explicitly depending on the writer, that all colonizing forces are patriarchal and all colonized peoples, particularly indigenous peoples colonized by dominant European forces, were originally based on female or feminine values. Paganism/witchcraft/the old religion is the original innocent, preyed upon, victim of patriarchal colonization.

There is, of course, a need to question feminist witches' accounts of prehistoric Europe and the early modern witch hunts. Scholars in both areas are quite clear that neither historical era nor event can be delineated quite as simplistically as some feminist witches may wish to suggest. Cynthia Eller argues that the evidence to which Gimbutas and feminist witches point is not adequate to support a thesis of pre-patriarchal goddess societies. She argues:

> In theory, the golden era of prehistoric matriarchy may have happened just as feminist matriarchalists say. The scattered remains left to us from prehistoric times are open to a variety of interpretations, and there is simply no evidence that can *definitively* prove the matriarchal hypothesis wrong. But is the myth of matriarchal prehistory plausible to those not already ardently hoping that it is true? I will argue that it is not. It does not represent historical truth; it is not a story built or argued from solid evidence, and it presents a scenario for prehistory that, if not demonstrably false, is at least highly unlikely.[16]

Eller spends considerable effort in her book *The Myth of Matriarchal Prehistory* showing how implausible this "myth" really is. Feminist witches' accounts of the early modern witch hunts also simplify a complex situation. People at all levels of early modern European society (including women) were implicated in the witch hunts, not just church and state leaders.

In his comprehensive examination of the early modern European witch hunt, Brian Levack looks to a number of contributing causes—no one of which was sufficient in itself to cause the witch hunts. Simplistic theories do not adequately address this history, he says. There was no one reason, nor one model of what happened. He "adopts a multi-causal approach which sees the emergence of new ideas about witches and a series of fundamental changes in the criminal law as the necessary preconditions of the witch hunt, and both religious change and social tension as its more immediate causes."[17] Though Levack does not give as much consideration to a gender analysis of the witch hunts, much to the concern of scholars such as Carol Karlsen and Anne Barstow, his account does convincingly show the complexity of the situations in early modern Europe, including intellectual, legal, religious, and social aspects that led to witch accusations and executions.[18]

The concerns about the validity of feminist witches' interpretations of pre-patriarchal goddess societies and the early modern witch hunts lead to important academic questions. However, for many feminist witches, these questions are less important due to their utilization of a technology of speculation—that of storytelling or myth-making. Lesley A. Northup argues in *Ritualizing Women: Patterns of Spirituality* that storytelling constitutes "a new view of reality in the very act of being breathed into existence. Moreover, like any efficacious symbol set, it invites relationship and interpretation, promising to yield meaning. It is never 'only a story,' but comprises both the narrative content and the interpretive process incorporated into it each time it is retold."[19]

Feminist witches actively tell stories to make the histories of goddess civilization real for each other. They take aspects of the archaeological evidence and mould personal lives around these fragments. They give personality to the impersonal as a way to make these histories more accessible for other feminist witches today. For example, in the context of Barbara Walker's novel *Amazon* or Starhawk's novel *The Fifth Sacred Thing*, accurate representation of historic truth is less significant than imaginary trips through potentials and possibilities.[20] These texts are speculative; they involve fantasy. It is through this genre of fantasy that authors, according to Janice Crosby, "can escape the confines of rigid academic proof, and go straight to the project of re-creating history and legend."[21] But the fantasies of Walker and Starhawk are not merely escapist or entertainment. They are constructed within the ritual world view of feminist witchcraft and contribute further to religious and ritual identity. Crosby points out,

> Fantastic/speculative fiction not only depicts magic, it also works "magically." The female reader is taken into a past which has been hidden from her; she follows the journey of the protagonist to an understanding of the Goddess, and she may come away from the novel inspired to put the perspectives she has gained to work in her own life and world.[22]

A more significant issue that needs to be addressed when looking at colonialism as a theme in feminist witches' construction of history and their identity as post-colonial people is the merging of patriarchy with colonization and the related merging of sexism and racism. The statistics clearly show that the majority of feminist witches are middle-class (raised if not currently) White women.[23] What are the implications of these women claiming an identity as colonized people in the context of modern European imperial colonialism and White privilege?

The use of post-colonial imagery by feminist witches is ironic. As Leela Gandhi points out,

> Postcolonial studies follows feminism in its critique of seemingly foundational discourses. Unlike feminism, however, it directs its critique against the cultural hegemony of European knowledges in an attempt to reassert the epistemological value and agency of the non-European world.[24]

Using the language and imagery of colonialism and post-colonialism to reconstruct a European (pre)history that counters the patriarchal and imperial Europe of dominant Western society may seem to reinforce the Eurocentrism of colonial society. However, a significant aspect of the (post)colonial story told by feminist witches is about distancing themselves from European power structures. Feminist witches, who perceive themselves as members of an older European people who were conquered by migrating Indo-Europeans, are as victimized, according to their post-colonial constructions, as any other victim of European colonialism.

There are parallels between sexism and racism, as well as other oppressions of one group of people by another. However, to claim these "isms" as equivalent and/or essentially the same thing denies the historic contexts of each and, in a sense, allows White women to deny any culpability in their identities as White folk (i.e., White women cannot be racist because they are oppressed too). Unfortunately, many feminists have done so. Cynthia Eller claims the problem lies in trying to locate the origin of sexism as the origin of oppression. Because "origin stories tend to reduce historically specific facts and values to timeless archetypes," she says, "the solutions proposed by origins thinking are not tailored to specific cultural environments, but rather to a totalizing image of 'patriarchy.'"[25] The response to this merging of sexism and racism has been particularly critical by post-colonial theorists who point out the naïveté of such integrations. For example, in her book *Decolonizing Feminism*, Laura Donaldson criticizes the use of the "man = colonizer, woman = colonized" construction found in some feminist theories. Donaldson argues, "the woman = colonized, man = colonizer metaphor lacks any awareness of gender—or colonialism, for that matter—as a contested field, an overdetermined sociopolitical grid whose identity points are often contradictory."[26] The merging of patriarchy with colonialism simplifies very complex social structures and historical realities in such a way as to hinder useful analysis and limit understanding of women's (and men's) individual and group experiences. As a result, a universalizing of women's experience (all women experience sexism, therefore all women experience the same oppression) occurs, which, in essence, substitutes middle-class White women's experiences for the norm, denying any other social positioning a valid identity.

Women of colour increasingly critique the universalizing of White women's experiences found in some feminist theorizing. A poignant example of this comes from Himani Bannerji in her essay "But Who Speaks for Us? Experience and Agency in Conventional Feminist Paradigms." In this essay Bannerji talks about her own experiences as a student and as a teacher trying to see herself within the curriculum of the Western/European "classics." First she was in the discipline of English where she was unable to find a space for herself as a non-White immigrant woman. Then she became more involved in feminist studies, which she thought would be a prime location for anti-racism and anti-colonialism, but she found that gender was the only valid oppression to think about. She writes,

> Decontexting "patriarchy" or gender from history and social organization—which is structured by both cooperative and antagonistic social relations—obscures the real ways in which power works. Using this framework, we cannot conceptualize a reality in which women are complicit and "gender" is implicated in, both creating and maintaining class and racist domination.... This pre-interpretation of reality valorizes all women as woman and at the same time denies their actual lived relations.[27]

As Bannerji wrote in an earlier essay, "Feminist essentialism, in the end, becomes a cloak for smuggling in the interests of privileged women."[28]

Bannerji's concern is echoed in bell hooks's essay "Sisterhood: Political Solidarity between Women." Hooks argues that the idea of "common oppression" serves to maintain White supremacy and the ignoring of "the true nature of women's varied and complex social reality."[29] Hooks maintains that the construction of women as "victims" is one of the culprits of a White-supremacist universalized notion of women's experience. This is an idea shared by Jane Flax, who contends that constructing women as victims "prevents us from seeing the areas of life in which women have had an effect, are not totally determined by the will of the other, and the ways in which some women have and do exert power over others (e.g., the differential privileges of race, class, sexual preference, age, and location in the world system)."[30] Hooks points out that

> Sexist ideology teaches women that to be female is to be a victim. Rather than repudiate this equation (which mystifies female experience—in their daily lives most women are not continually passive, helpless, or powerless "victims"), women's liberationists embraced it, making shared victimization the basis for woman-bonding. This meant that women had to conceive of themselves as "victims" in order to feel that the feminist movement was relevant to their lives.... Ironically, the women who were most eager to be seen as "victims," who overwhelmingly stressed the role of victim, were more privileged and powerful than the vast majority of women in our society.[31]

Hooks and Flax argue that this focus on women as victims allows White women to deny their own positions as White women within White-supremacist societies.

Feminist theorists who argue for recognizing that sexism and racism are not the same thing are careful not to suggest that each woman look solely to her own experience and combat her own oppression individually. They are adamant about the need for social involvement, working together in coalition to combat all sorts of oppressions. Bannerji particularly is critical of the politics of "difference," which leave those differences isolated, that is, in an understanding that there is no connection between different situations and oppressions that implies that the "neutral" oppression (of gender) takes precedence over any "difference" oppressions (such as race or class) even though the "neutral" category is, in fact, one of White, middle-class women (whose "difference" gets subsumed under the neutrality of gender). Bannerji calls for a more holistic approach that looks at race, class, and gender as connected oppressions that are constructed within social contexts not individual situations. There are no suggestions here that sexism and racism are not *connected* or do not affect one another. However, this is very different from saying they are *the same thing*.

When feminist witches argue that their history (prehistoric goddess societies and early modern witch hunts) is colonial, they run the risk of claiming that sexism is the same thing as racism. For example, when Barbara Walker writes in her book *The Skeptical Feminist: Discovering the Virgin, Mother and Crone*, "The Judeo-Christian God has always been the world's greatest imperialist, because greedy men shaped him from the beginning in order to confirm and bless their own greed," she is making a direct connection between patriarchal Christianity (and Judaism, though less explicitly than Christianity) and European imperialism and colonialism (claiming either they are one and the same or patriarchal Christianity goes one further).[32] Because feminist witchcraft (or the old religion) is constructed as oppressed and victimized by patriarchal Christianity (and other patriarchal forces, but generally Christianity is associated with patriarchy *in toto*) it is the most victimized. This is, perhaps, an unconscious but convenient way to deny culpability of racial privilege and assuage White guilt. However, it does little to address actual situations of patriarchy and sexism, or colonialism and racism. This colonial identity runs the risk of creating such abstract and universalizing concepts of patriarchy and colonization that it does not fit with any historic reality and thus cannot be effectively analyzed or resisted.

I must point out that not all feminist witches tell the story of colonialism in such a way as to deny their own positioning as White or privileged people. Starhawk is quite clear that no one is solely a victim just as no one is solely a victimizer. In *Twelve Wild Swans*, a magical study guide written with Hilary Valentine, Starhawk writes:

> None of us alive today created our heritage of sexism, racism, poverty, social injustice, war, or environmental degradation. Sometimes these conditions may oppress us personally; at other times we may

> benefit from them directly or indirectly. We can respond with rage, with guilt, with grief or paralysis, but none of these will help matters much. Only ... the willing undertaking of responsibility, can lead to healing.[33]

For Starhawk and Valentine, falling into the identity of victim is problematic because it creates a simplistic identity that does not reflect the multiple positionings people have in society as well as reducing the effectiveness of any action. Victims are powerless. Power is necessary for change.

Therefore, if feminist witches continue to define themselves as victims of patriarchy, they will be unable to create change. However, in order to be able to move away from this victim identification, Starhawk argues that feminist witches must come to terms with their own heritage and ancestry (for most of them this means European heritage and ancestry). Thus they need to recognize when their ancestors have been oppressed and when they have been oppressors. This recognition can lead to feelings of guilt or shame. But no one, says Starhawk, has a purely oppressive heritage (just as no one has a purely oppressed heritage). Thus the search for a non-oppressive European heritage, for Starhawk, is not meant to deny European imperialism, but to add to it another heritage that can be drawn on in order to work for real change without wallowing in White guilt. Starhawk writes, "When we have acknowledged and integrated our own heritage and found those ancestors who can truly be our allies, we can begin to envision communities in which we are free to grow beyond the constraints of the past."[34] It is the pre-patriarchal Europeans and the early modern accused witches who become the ancestors who can be allies, who help feminist witches move beyond the constraints of the past.

In conclusion, I argue that in order to understand what is at stake for feminist witches in their construction of accounts of prehistoric goddess societies and the early modern witch hunts, scholars need to be aware of the colonial and post-colonial discourse that is underlying these stories. These stories are not just about internal patriarchy. They are about oppression of a "people" (women and men) by another "people." That these stories cannot be proven conclusively to be based on empirical fact is less significant for feminist witches' use of these stories. Rather they provide a personalized interpretation of prehistory that allows feminist witches to identify with other "oppressed" peoples today who are struggling for independence and agency. This association with post-colonial discourse does, however, lead to further questions about the desired identity of White women professing feminist witchcraft in a world in which White folk are typically deemed the oppressors rather than the victims.

NOTES

1. Gayle Kimball, "Goddess Worship in Wicce: Interview with Z. Budapest," in *Women's Culture: The Women's Renaissance of the Seventies*, edited by G. Kimball (Metuchen: The Scarecrow Press, 1981), 238.
2. Zsuzsanna Budapest, *The Holy Book of Women's Mysteries* (Oakland: Wingbow Press, 1989), 239.
3. Starhawk, *Truth or Dare: Encounters with Power, Authority, and Mystery* (San Francisco: HarperCollins, 1987), 33.
4. Starhawk and Hilary Valentine, *The Twelve Wild Swans: A Journey to the Realm of Magic, Healing, and Action* (San Francisco: HarperSanFrancisco, 2000), 283.
5. Marija Gimbutas, *Goddesses and Gods of Old Europe* (Berkeley: University of California Press, 1982), 237.
6. Marija Gimbutas, *The Kurgan Culture and the Indo-Europeanization of Europe* (Washington: Institute for the Study of Man, 1997), 241.
7. Margaret Conkey and Ruth Tringham, "Archaeology and the Goddess: Exploring the Contours of Feminist Archaeology," in *Feminisms in the Academy*, edited by Domna C. Stanton and Abigail J. Stewart (Ann Arbor: University of Michigan Press, 1995), 207.
8. Conkey and Tringham, "Archaeology and the Goddess," 211.
9. Ibid., 215.
10. Starhawk, *Truth or Dare*, 39–40.
11. Diane Purkiss, *The Witch in History: Early Modern and Twentieth-Century Representations* (London: Routledge, 1996), 8.
12. Ibid., 15.
13. Ibid., 17.

14. Budapest, *The Holy Book of Women's Mysteries*, 239.
15. Ibid., 271, 296.
16. Cynthia Eller, *The Myth of Matriarchal Prehistory: Why an Invented Past Won't Give Women a Future* (Boston: Beacon Press, 2000), 14.
17. Brian Levack, *The Witch Hunt in Early Modern Europe* (London: Longman, 1987), 3.
18. Carol Karlsen, *The Devil in the Shape of a Woman: Witchcraft in Colonial New England* (New York: Norton, 1987); Anne Barstow, *Witchcraze: A New History of the European Witch Hunts* (London: Pandora, 1994).
19. Lesley A. Northup, *Ritualizing Women: Patterns of Spirituality* (Cleveland: The Pilgrim Press, 1997), 75.
20. Barbara G. Walker, *Amazon: A Novel* (San Francisco: HarperSanFrancisco, 1992); Starhawk, *The Fifth Sacred Thing* (New York: Bantam Books, 1993).
21. Janice Crosby, *Cauldron of Changes: Feminist Spirituality in Fantastic Fiction* (Jefferson: McFarland & Company, 2000), 69.
22. Ibid., 34.
23. Cynthia Eller, *Living in the Lap of the Goddess: The Feminist Spirituality Movement in America* (New York: Crossroads, 1993), 18, 22; Tanya M. Luhrmann, *Persuasions of the Witch's Craft: Ritual Magic in Contemporary England* (Cambridge: Harvard University Press, 1989), 18.
24. Leela Gandhi, *Postcolonial Theory: A Critical Introduction* (New York: Columbia University Press, 1998), 44.
25. Eller, *The Myth*, 183.
26. Laura Donaldson, *Decolonizing Feminism: Race, Gender and Empire-Building* (Chapel Hill: University of North Carolina Press, 1992), 6.
27. Himani Bannerji, *Thinking Through: Essays on Feminism, Marxism and Anti-Racism* (Toronto: Women's Press, 1995), 69.
28. Ibid., 69–70.
29. bell hooks, "Sisterhood: Political Solidarity between Women," in *Dangerous Liaisons: Gender, Nation, and Postcolonial Perspectives*, edited by Anne McClintock, Aamir Mufti, and Ella Shohat (Minneapolis: University of Minnesota Press, 1997), 396.
30. Jane Flax, *Thinking Fragments: Psychoanalysis, Feminism, and Postmodernism in the Contemporary West* (Berkeley: University of California Press, 1990), 181–182.

31. hooks, "Sisterhood," 397.
32. Barbara G. Walker, *The Skeptical Feminist: Discovering the Virgin, Mother, and Crone* (San Francisco: Harper & Row, 1987), 14.
33. Starhawk and Valentine, *The Twelve Wild Swans*, 7.
34. Ibid., 56.

REFERENCES

Bannerji, Himani. 1995. *Thinking Through: Essays on Feminism, Marxism and Anti-Racism.* Toronto: Women's Press.

Barstow, Anne. 1994. *Witchcraze: A New History of the European Witch Hunts.* London: Pandora.

Budapest, Zsuzsanna. 1989. *The Holy Book of Women's Mysteries.* Oakland: Wingbow Press.

Conkey, Margaret, and Ruth Tringham. 1995. "Archaeology and the Goddess: Exploring the Contours of Feminist Archaeology." In *Feminisms in the Academy*, edited by Domna C. Stanton and Abigail J. Stewart, 199–247. Ann Arbor: University of Michigan Press.

Crosby, Janice C. 2000. *Cauldron of Changes: Feminist Spirituality in Fantastic Fiction.* Jefferson: McFarland & Company.

Donaldson, Laura. 1992. *Decolonizing Feminisms: Race, Gender and Empire-Building.* Chapel Hill: University of North Carolina Press.

Eller, Cynthia. 1993. *Living in the Lap of the Goddess: The Feminist Spirituality Movement in America.* New York: Crossroads.

———. 2000. *The Myth of Matriarchal Prehistory: Why an Invented Past Won't Give Women a Future.* Boston: Beacon Press.

Flax, Jane. 1990. *Thinking Fragments: Psychoanalysis, Feminism, and Postmodernism in the Contemporary West.* Berkeley: University of California Press.

Gandhi, Leela. 1998. *Postcolonial Theory: A Critical Introduction.* New York: Columbia University Press.

Gimbutas, Marija. 1982. *Goddesses and Gods of Old Europe.* Berkeley: University of California Press.

———. 1997. *The Kurgan Culture and the Indo-Europeanization of Europe.* Washington: Institute for the Study of Man.

hooks, bell. 1997. "Sisterhood: Political Solidarity between Women." In *Dangerous Liaisons: Gender, Nation, and Postcolonial Perspectives*, edited by Anne McClintock, Aamir Mufti, and Ella Shohat, 396–411. Minneapolis: University of Minnesota Press.

Karlsen, Carol. 1987. *The Devil in the Shape of a Woman: Witchcraft in Colonial New England*. New York: Norton.

Kimball, Gayle. 1981. "Goddess Worship in Wicce: Interview with Z. Budapest." In *Women's Culture: The Women's Renaissance of the Seventies*, edited by G. Kimball, 238–248. Metuchen: The Scarecrow Press.

Levack, Brian. 1987. *The Witch Hunt in Early Modern Europe*. London: Longman.

Luhrmann, Tanya M. 1989. *Persuasions of the Witch's Craft: Ritual Magic in Contemporary England*. Cambridge: Harvard University Press.

Northup, Leslie A. 1997. *Ritualizing Women: Patterns of Spirituality*. Cleveland: The Pilgrim Press.

Purkiss, Diane. 1996. *The Witch in History: Early Modern and Twentieth-Century Representations*. London: Routledge.

Starhawk. 1993. *The Fifth Sacred Thing*. New York: Bantam Books.

———. 1982. *Truth or Dare: Encounters with Power, Authority, and Mystery*. San Francisco: HarperCollins.

———, and Hilary Valentine. 2000. *The Twelve Wild Swans: A Journey to the Realm of Magic, Healing, and Action*. San Francisco: HarperSanFrancisco.

Walker, Barbara G. 1992. *Amazon: A Novel*. San Francisco: HarperSanFrancisco.

———. 1987. *The Skeptical Feminist: Discovering the Virgin, Mother, and Crone*. San Francisco: Harper & Row.

QUESTIONS FOR CRITICAL THOUGHT

Chapter 16: DuFresne

1. Does monotheistic goddess worship threaten men in the same way that monotheistic patriarchal worship threatens women?
2. Religiously and politically, do men belong in goddess worship?
3. What does DuFresne mean by "patriarchy in drag"?

Chapter 17: Griffin

1. What characteristics does Griffin use to distinguish between "feminist witchcraft" and "the goddess movement"? Are the two dichotomous, or do they exist along a continuum?
2. What differences does Griffin see between the mainstream world religions and feminist witchcraft/the goddess movement? Are these differences simply an inversion of patriarchal religions?
3. The goddess rituals described by Griffin are very different than the services we encounter in mainstream churches. Why might that be? Can you think of parallels to these rituals in mainstream religions?

Chapter 18: Hutton

1. How is the Romantically conceived goddess different from Judaism's creator God and Christianity's Creator and Redeemer? What does this imply about a possible shift in values through the nineteenth century?
2. Given Hutton's description of it, would the evidence used to support the great goddess hypothesis pass muster today? Why or why not? What cautions does this give to those who wish to study material culture?
3. What are the features of "industrial modernity" against which the great goddess of the Romantics stands opposed? In what ways can the goddess function as a liberating image from these conditions?

Chapter 19: Eller

1. According to Eller, what are the processes through which secular feminists come into feminist spirituality?

2. How might "feminist spirituality" differ from "spiritual feminism"? Or would the two be the same?
3. Should it be alarming to feminists that neopagan witches are using the word "witch" less and less as a term of self-identification, and instead are choosing less culturally loaded words such as Craft, pagan, or Wiccan to describe themselves and their religious beliefs?
4. Can feminist spirituality include men? If so, to what extent, and in what roles? If not, why not?

Chapter 20: Klassen

1. Drawing on Klassen's analysis of the "stories" (myths or sacred narratives) that feminist witches tell about themselves and the history of the world, does it matter if these stories are demonstrably true? Why or why not?
2. Klassen notes that in the merging of patriarchy and colonization, feminist witchcraft has also merged sexism and racism. Why is this problematic?
3. Klassen points out that it is possible to simultaneously be oppressed and an oppressor—that a victim status on one dimension does not release you from your responsibility for victimizing on other dimensions. Can feminist witchcraft effectively incorporate a narrative of White, European power and privilege?

SUGGESTED READING

Budapest, Zsusanna. 1976. *The Feminist Book of Light and Shadows.* Venice: Luna Publications.

This is the pioneering book of feminist witchcraft. Budapest gives a version of witchcraft as separatist religion—no men allowed—which is a major departure from the gender-balanced forms of witchcraft that came out of England. The book contains spells and rituals, along with its feminist commentary.

Daly, Mary. [1978] 1981. *Gyn/Ecology.* London: The Women's Press.

This is the first of Daly's "radical" books. In her two earlier works, *The*

Church and the Second Sex and *Beyond God the Father*, Daly retained some hope that the reforms of Vatican II would lead to a new role for women in the Christian Church. By *Gyn/Ecology*, this optimism has evaporated, and Daly is left with the task of finding a new language to discuss women as spiritual beings, trapped under the brutal rule of an oppressive patriarchy.

Eller, Cynthia. 2000. *The Myth of Matriarchal Prehistory: Why an Invented Past Won't Give Women a Future*. Boston: Beacon Press.

In this book, Eller reviews the evidence cited by feminists to support the idea that before their overthrow by patriarchal cultures, most of Europe had venerated a Great Mother goddess, and that women held the majority of leadership positions. This culture was supposed to have been egalitarian and peaceful, a state we could get back to if only women could achieve full equality with men. Eller concludes that the bulk of the evidence cited has long since been debunked, that most modern scholars do not support the great goddess hypothesis, and that women do not need to prove they once had power in order to demand it now.

Salmonsen, Jone. 2002. *Enchanted Feminism: The Reclaiming Witches of San Francisco*. London: Routledge.

This is an ethnographic, historical, and theological exploration of San Francisco's Reclaiming community. Reclaiming grew out of the collective efforts of Starhawk and several of her friends and colleagues in the Bay Area. Propelled by the success of *The Spiral Dance*, California Reclaiming now has sister communities throughout much of the English-speaking world. Salmonsen explores the meanings that Reclaiming has for its members.

Starhawk. 1982. *Dreaming the Dark: Magic, Sex and Politics*. Boston: Beacon Press.

This book expresses Starhawk's conviction that magic, sex, and politics are natural bedfellows. She combines her gender activism and environmental activism with magic's central premise that change is the outcome of a focused will. Starhawk includes chants, exercises, and questions to ponder in order to guide people toward their own fusion of magic and politics.

GLOSSARY

Immanent: Existing within, pervading all, inseparably present.

Matrilineage: Descent as reckoned through the female line. For example: Patricia, daughter of Jill, daughter of Margaret, daughter of Anne.

Mythopoesis: Storytelling, specifically, the creation of myth or sacred narrative through which human beings orient themselves to the universe and to other people.

Parthenogenesis: Physical reproduction by the female alone, without a male.

Patriarchy: The system whereby men exercise dominance over women through control of power and ideology; a society in which the male is identified as the norm or standard by which all are judged; a system in which women are subordinated to men on the basis of their gender.

Transcendent: Existing outside of, beyond, or above.

Copyright Acknowledgments

Chapter 1 by Doreen Valiente, "The Charge of the Goddess," from *Eight Sabbats for Witches* (London: Robert Hale Limited, 1981): 42–43. Copyright © John Belham-Payne. Reprinted by permission of John Belham-Payne.

Chapter 2 by Starhawk (Miriam Simos), "Creation," "The Wheel of the Year," and "The Goddess in the Kingdom of Death," from *The Spiral Dance* (San Francisco: Harper & Row, 1979): 17–18, 28–29, 159–60. Copyright © Harper & Row Publishers, Inc. 1979. Reprinted by permission of Harper & Row Publishers, Inc.

Chapter 3 by Selena Fox, "I Am Pagan," from http://www.circlesanctuary.org/aboutpagan/iampagan.htm. Copyright © Selena Fox, Circle Sanctuary. Reprinted by permission of Selena Fox.

Chapter 4 by Margot Adler, "A Religion without Converts," from *Drawing Down the Moon: Witches, Druids, Goddess-Worshippers, and Other Pagans in America Today* (Boston: Beacon Press, 1979): 14–23. Copyright © Margot Adler 1979. Reprinted by permission of Viking Penguin, a division of Penguin Group (USA) Inc.

Chapter 5 by Carol P. Christ, "Why Women Need the Goddess." Originally published in *Heresies 5* (*The Great Goddess Issue*, Spring 1978): 8–13 and in slightly revised form in *Womanspirit Rising* (San Francisco: Harper & Row, 1979): 273–287. Copyright © Carol Christ. Reprinted by permission of Carol Christ.

Chapter 6 by Sarah Pike, "We Cast Our Circles Where the Earth Mother Meets the Sky Father," from *Earthly Bodies, Magical Selves: Contemporary Pagans and the Search for Community* (Berkeley, Los Angeles and London: University of California Press, 2001): 1–9. Copyright © The Regents of the University of California 2001. Reprinted by permission of University of California Press.

Chapter 7 by Barbara Jane Davy, "Definitions and Expressions of Nature Religion in Shamanic Traditions and Contemporary Paganism," from *Journal of Religion and Culture* (2003): 27–37. Reprinted by permission of Concordia University.

Chapter 8 by Michael York, "Introduction," from *Pagan Theology: Paganism As a World Religion* (New York and London: New York University Press, 2003): 1–8. Reprinted by permission of New York University Press.

Chapter 9 by Graham Harvey, "Druidry," from *Contemporary Paganism* (New York: New York University Press, 1997): 1–8. Copyright © Graham Harvey 1997. Reprinted by permission of New York University Press.

Chapter 10 by Helen A. Berger, "To the Tribe Let There Be Children Born," (Prologue and Chapter 5) from *A Community of Witches* (University of South Carolina Press, 1999).

Chapter 12 by T.M. Luhrmann, "In Defense of Magic: The Philosophical and Theological Rationalization," from *Persuasions of the Witch's Craft: Ritual Magic in Contemporary England* (Cambridge: Harvard University Press, 1989): 283–303. Copyright © T.M. Luhrmann 1989. Reprinted by permission of Harvard University Press.